RESOURCE SHARING IN LIBRARIES

BOOKS IN
LIBRARY AND INFORMATION SCIENCE

A Series of Monographs and Textbooks

EDITOR
ALLEN KENT

Director, Office of Communications Programs
University of Pittsburgh
Pittsburgh, Pennsylvania

Additional volumes in preparation

RESOURCE SHARING IN LIBRARIES

Why • How • When • Next Action Steps

edited by

Allen Kent
University of Pittsburgh
Pittsburgh, Pennsylvania

Based on papers presented at the conference Resource Sharing in Libraries, held April 11-12, 1973 at Pittsburgh, Pennsylvania; cosponsored by the Pennsylvania Association of Colleges and Universities, the Pittsburgh Council on Higher Education, and the Pittsburgh Regional Library Center.

MARCEL DEKKER, INC., New York   1974

MARCEL DEKKER, INC.

305 East 45 Street, New York, New York   10017

LIBRARY OF CONGRESS CATALOG CARD NUMBER: 73-90724

ISBN: 0-8247-6130-8

Current printing (last digit):
10 9 8 7 6 5 4 3 2 1

PRINTED IN THE UNITED STATES OF AMERICA

PREFACE

On April 11-12, 1973, a group of some 175 people met in Pittsburgh, Pennsylvania to consider how to accelerate the process of resource sharing in libraries. It was recognized that the cost of self-sufficiency had long been prohibitive, and that there was considerable urgency to develop a plan of action which would counteract the pressures currently being faced.

The conference was designed for presidents and librarians of institutions of higher education. It was sponsored by the Pennsylvania Association of Colleges and Universities, the Pittsburgh Council on Higher Education, and the Pittsburgh Regional Library Center. The conference was coordinated by the University of Pittsburgh under a grant from the Buhl Foundation.

Allen Kent

CONTENTS

Part Three

WHEN TO PROCEED

Part Four

HOW TO PROCEED

INTRODUCTION

Allen Kent

The plan of this enterprise is to deal with an intractable problem — "the library problem" — one that may turn out to be unsolvable — but which nevertheless must be confronted.

Let me start with an observation that colleges and universities are not terribly successful in preparing their students for the future. This is simply because they do not know the future, and predict it only by extrapolating from trends. This approach is fraught with risks, and we are currently living with the consequences of this way of predicting the future. But perhaps higher education is faced with an unsolvable problem — in attempting to find a better way to predict futures.

The topic of the book "Resource Sharing in Libraries" is a derivative of the intractable, or unsolvable, problems of higher education. Libraries buy mostly for future needs. But the judgments of librarians as to future needs are no better than those of the presidents. Let us examine why librarians have such a difficult time guessing what future needs will be.

Their task is to select from the world's information store those materials that will be useful <u>and used</u>. These must be selected from great quantities of materials that are available. Thus

1. There have been 30 million unique titles published since Gutenberg — how many have anything more than 5% of these — I guess some have less than $\frac{1}{2}\%$.

2. There are 50-100 thousand journals published currently — how many subscribe to more than 10-15% — some subscribe to less than $\frac{1}{2}\%$.

3. About 500 thousand books will be published worldwide in 1974 — how many will buy more than 10-15% — some will buy less than $\frac{1}{2}\%$.

Given this situation it is like finding a needle in a haystack to pick the "right" materials that will be <u>both</u> useful <u>and used</u>. Since the needle is not frequently found, presidents, chancellors, provosts, deans, and librarians sometimes are confronted by students and faculty who demand a better acquisitions budget to try to relieve their frustrations.

The plan of the conference on which this book is based is to determine whether more money for materials alone can relieve these frustrations. It is the hypothesis of some of the organizers of the conference that there perhaps should be a resource sharing budget instead, devoted specifically to not buying materials but rather for developing the mechanisms for getting them from elsewhere.

One can seek some support for this hypothesis from many sources. One is the lead article, by Arthur McAnally and Robert Downs, of the March 1973 issue of "College & Research Libraries," which should be required reading for the presidents — librarians are already sensitive to the contents. It discusses "The Changing Role of Directors of University Libraries." I will quote a few sections and paraphrase some others that relate to the subject of this book.

The article starts with the observation that

> Traditionally the directorship of a major university library has been a lifetime post. Once a librarian achieved such a position of honor and leadership in the profession, he usually stayed until he reached retirement age. In the 1960's, however, an increasing number of incidents occurred which indicated that all was not well in the library directors' world.
>
> Exactly one half of the 78 directors of the Association of Research Libraries changed within the past three years, four of them twice.
>
> One reason advanced is that the problem reflects a highly critical attitude towards the library itself rather than just criticism of the directors.
>
> The criticism is derived from:
> — Changes in the world of learning and research
> — The information explosion
> — Hard times and inflation
> — Changing theories of management
> — Increasing control by state boards
> — But most important, the inability of libraries to react to these changes
>
> Escape from this criticism through increased budgets is not possible, as financial people are reluctant to make cuts elsewhere for the library, which is frequently regarded as a "bottomless pit."

It is becoming apparent that more money for materials held locally cannot be the total answer to the problem. The question to be examined is whether the thrust of resource sharing — making it really work — may not be the critical line of defense of the library in building a dam to withstand the information flood and inflation.

The book is organized into four parts, representing the four half-day sessions of the conference on "Why," "How," "When," and "Next Action Step," with position papers (Chapters 1, 6, 11, 15) distributed in advance to those who attended the conference.

As expected, it was possible to establish several points:

1. It is impossible for libraries to be self-sufficient — nor has it ever been possible in modern times.

2. Aside from library materials required in connection with specific courses, it is seldom possible to predict precisely which materials will be useful, and for how long. Despite this, some or much of the library budget, particularly in research libraries, is spent in stocking for future needs; accordingly, substantial portions of library collections are seldom used.

3. There is no reason why all library materials of potential usefulness on a campus must be physically stored on that campus — if materials can be made available at the point of need when the requirement arises.

4. The mechanisms for resource sharing are reasonably well understood.

5. There are no reasonable alternatives to effective resource sharing.

6. Based on the state of the art of resource sharing, the time for acceleration of effort is "Now."

In order to discover whether more effective resource sharing could indeed be stimulated, the conference participants were asked, and the readers of these proceedings are encouraged, to keep some questions in mind:

> Are you willing to participate aggressively in one or several resource-sharing consortia?
>
> What library resources are you willing to share?
>
> How much are you willing to invest, out of your library budget, even if tight, in attempting to realize these goals?
>
> Are there any other reasonable alternatives?

A process was set in motion following the conference to make these questions much more specific and to distribute a questionnaire based on the questions throughout the Commonwealth of Pennsylvania. The intent was to discover the criteria for resource sharing that would make sense in each library. Examples are

> geographic proximity
>
> type of institution
>
> size of institution
>
> source of funding
>
> size of budget
>
> level of available technology

The intent is to discover the natural allies who would pursue the developments to come.

It would be less than honest not to mention that certain tensions arose as plans for the conference were being developed. Perhaps some of these tensions can be glimpsed in Chapters 2 and 3 of these proceedings, which relate to differing interpretations of statistical information regarding library costs.

Part One

THE RATIONALE

Chapters 1-5 are aimed at exploring the "why" of resource sharing. The points of view of top administrators in higher education were solicited (Chapters 4 and 5) since it has been perceived that the gulf between the patron, the librarian, and the administrator, who must find money for the library, is becoming wider as the cost of self-sufficiency is becoming prohibitive.

Chapter 1

RESOURCE SHARING IN LIBRARIES — WHY?

John Fetterman

Assistant Director
Office of Communication Programs
University of Pittsburgh

THE RESOURCES THEMSELVES

The term "library resource" will be used to designate any and all of
the materials, functions, and services which constitute a modern library
system. I use the term "materials" to mean all of the imprinted material
which a library handles together with such nontraditional items as microforms, films, and machine-readable data bases. The term "functions"
describes the activities required to purchase, process, store, and retrieve
the material. By "services" I mean those activities and procedures used
to relate the users to the material. The resources of any library must
also include the expertise of the professional and nonprofessional staff.
It is this amalgamation of people, processes, ideas, materials, and
money which form the substance of a library and can be described as its
resources.

THE VIEWPOINT

As an organization a library can be compared to a person. Both
acquire, process, store, and retrieve information. Both possess "personalities" because of their substantive makeup and because of their adaptation
to their environment. Both develop their capabilities through interaction
with others.

In the historical development of libraries there can be observed an
ongoing adaptation to their environment until they have developed the
sophisticated personalities that they have today. The kind and amount of
material, and the kind and number of users have changed radically over the
centuries; the organism's adaptation has proceeded accordingly. Indications
are that we are now at a point where a major adaptation must take place.
The characteristics of information storage and retrieval in our times
together with the heavy, and often unpredictable, demands of users
indicate that resource sharing is the only way for libraries to survive.
Attempts at self-sufficiency will prove an impossible response to the
demands of the present environment. Resource sharing can provide the
best information to the most users at the most reasonable cost.

Although resource sharing has been a part of the librarians' armament,
the effectiveness of sharing resources has been inhibited. It is our purpose
to identify the inhibiting factors and seek ways to overcome them.

THE NEED TO CHANGE

There has been a growing recognition of the need for a major change
in the personalities of libraries. The history of this development will
show that the information environment has changed radically and that
libraries must adapt. This need for adaptation to a new environment has
been expressed in the recent publication of the National Academy of
Sciences on Libraries and Information Technology — A National System
Challenge [1].

It has been recognized for over a quarter century, however,
that the hoary ways of libraries are breaking down. The need for
better ways, by now proclaimed by many, was expressed by
Vannevar Bush:
"Professionally our methods of transmitting and reviewing
the results of research are generations old and by now are totally
inadequate for their purpose...

The difficulty seems to be not so much that we publish unduly in view of the extent and variety of present day interests, but rather that publication has been extended far beyond our present ability to make real use of the record. The summation of human experience is being expanded at a prodigious rate, and the means we use for threading through the consequent maze to the momentarily important item is the same as was used in the days of square-rigged ships. "

The need to share resources is probably almost as old as libraries themselves. Verner Clapp in his book The Future of the Research Library [2] leads our minds in this direction by acknowledging that "it would be interesting to explore whether the principle of sharing of resources was ever applied in those early days. Did Nineveh or Alexandria posses catalogs of books held elsewhere? Were books ever borrowed from distant places without the intention of either commandeering or copying them?" We do have some evidence to indicate that the library at Alexandria loaned books to the library at Pergamum around 200 B.C. Historical perspective is interesting, but our problem is very contemporary and very practical. Our own century began with an exhortation for cooperation by Ernest C. Richardson in the Library Journal of May, 1899 [3]; but that was in the days when Vannevar Bush's square-rigged ships could still do the job. The problem came to a state of critical proportions during the period of World War II. Science and technology played such an important part in that explosive event that the fallout threatened to overwhelm us. The legislative acts which created the Office of Naval Research (1946), the Atomic Energy Commission (1947), the National Science Foundation (1950), and the National Aeronautics and Space Administration (1957), all express a concern for the information storage and retrieval processes dictated by the very nature of these activities. The preamble to the act establishing the Office of Naval Research (1946) offers a good example of the growing concern. The act explicitly proposes "to provide within the Department of the Navy a single office, which by contract and otherwise, shall be able to obtain, coordinate, and make available to all bureaus ... worldwide scientific information." The National Science Foundation Act (1950) had as one of its eight specific responsibilities to "foster the interchange of scientific information among scientists in the United States and in foreign countries. "

In 1955 the Senate Committee on Government Operations chartered a special subcommittee, chaired by Senator John E. Moss, to study information operations at all levels of the federal government and to recommend to the Congress solutions to the growing problems. From 1957 to 1960 Senator Hubert H. Humphrey chaired the Subcommittee on Reorganization and International Organizations and produced the most comprehensive body of data on scientific and technical information problems ever compiled by a committee of the Congress." This latter committee studied: problems associated with documentation, indexing, and retrieval practices in government, industry, and discipline-oriented societies; management of information during the long chain of events prior to archival publication; coordination of information on current scientific research and development; and information handling in relation to federal budgeting for research and development.

During this same interval, 1958-1964, the House of Representatives was also concerned with information handling problems. The Baker Panel [4] (1958) considered two possibilities for coping more effectively with the mounting store of information: either establish a large, highly centralized, wholly or partially government-supported agency resembling that of the U.S.S.R. or develop a science information service of a coordinating type that would stimulate and improve upon the present system by taking full advantage of existing organizations and the specialized skills of those associated with them. The Baker Panel finally recommended the latter.

Deviating somewhat from the Baker Report, the Crawford Task Group [5] (1962) advocated centralizing the direction and review of federal information handling programs in a single agency. It also recommended that each government agency, where appropriate, establish in-house an agency for the control of scientific and technical information matters.

The Weinberg Report [6] (1963) constitutes a milestone for the development of scientific and technical communication. It stated that the entire information process must be made an integral part of research and development, and access and retrieval procedures are part of the responsibility of the organizations creating the information.

The Weinberg Report strongly asserted the importance of preserving the nongovernment communication systems so highly sensitive to user needs and offering a variety of approaches to communication problems. It was this report that led to the formation of the Committee on Scientific and Technical Information (COSATI).

In 1964 the Licklider panel [7] examined and assessed the situation and trends in scientific and technical communication. This panel reported the very limited success of the government in persuading the scientific community to cooperate in efforts to integrate public and private services into a unified system and stressed the need to develop guiding principles for the centralization of some functions.

The very act of involvement by the federal government indicates the dimensions and implications of the problems. The cultural development of the country had brought us to a critical dependence on science and technology and the success of science and technology was critically dependent on information.

Further indications that the information environment was changing can be seen in the statements of the professional library associations. In 1956 the Public Library Association published its "Public library service: a guide to evaluation, with minimum-standards" [8] in which it said: "Libraries working together, sharing their services and materials can meet the full needs of their users. The cooperative approach on the part of libraries is the most important single recommendation." PLA continued its commitment to library cooperation, and more than a decade later (1967) reaffirmed the same philosophy in its "Minimum Standards for Public Library Systems" [9]. Furthermore, the standards for college libraries adopted by the Association of College and Research Libraries in 1959 include a strong statement on cooperation with other college, university, school, and public library agencies in the community, region, state, and nation for the benefit of students and faculty.

In 1967 the boards of directors of four American Library Association (ALA) divisions — the Associations of Public, State, School, and College and Research Libraries — approved a joint statement on interlibrary cooperation [10]. The statement set forth "the imperative need for cooperation" within the assumption that "no one library can be self-sufficient" and that "libraries acting together can more effectively satisfy user needs." The statement outlines the prerequisites for fruitful inter-library cooperation:

1. That primary responsibility for each type of library to its special clientele must be defined before interlibrary cooperation can be established to augment service
2. That effective cooperation depends upon adequate resources, administrative capability, and efficient communications
3. That although the primary responsibility of each library must be respected, each library must realize its responsibilities to the network and assume its appropriate share of responsibility
4. That all libraries must maintain an attitude of flexibility and experimentation

It is the perception of responsibility which can make or break efforts at library cooperation. The situation is full of conflicts. A library may know that it cannot succeed by itself, yet it is afraid of losing its identity by becoming part of a larger resource sharing activity. There also arises the very human problem of the smaller institution not being able to identify its unique role in the larger scheme of things when it becomes part of a resource sharing activity. The smaller institution must be able to perceive that its needs and its efforts will receive due consideration in the resource sharing activity. The foregoing statement that effective cooperation depends in part on "administrative capability and efficient communications" points to many levels of activity. Information systems, like libraries, are not merely a conglomeration of books and the procedures for handling them, but a complex set of concepts and people dealing with the past and recorded aspirations of man and his present need to relate to that past. Such people-oriented activities as libraries easily develop "personalities" of their own and should be treated as such. Richard Dougherty sums up this line of thought when he writes that "in truth, cooperative programs succeed only as long as each participant perceives the arrangement as beneficial to his institution" [11]. It is axiomatic that people — individuals and institutions — choose to act only insofar as they perceive the action as beneficial to themselves. It is the awakening of just such a perception that challenges the communicating capacities of these involved with resource sharing activities.

The federal library legislation of the 1960's reflects the concern of the library profession and of Congress for the sharing of resources and services. For example, the Higher Education Act of 1965, PL89-329, under Title II A provides funds for "combinations of institutions of higher education which need special assistance in establishing and strengthening joint use of facilities." In the amendment to this act in 1968, Title VIII, Networks for Knowledge, was added "to encourage colleges and universities to share to an optimal extent, through cooperative arrangements, their technical and other educational and administrative facilties and resources in order to test and demonstrate the effectiveness and efficiency of a variety of such arrangements."

The most significant encouragement to interlibrary cooperation came with the addition of Title III to the Library Services and Construction Act in 1966 (LSCA). Under this act funds are provided to the states to "establish and maintain local, regional, state, or interstate networks of libraries for systematic and effective coordination of the resources of school, public, academic, and special libraries or special information centers." This act is particularly interesting in that the funds may be used for a great variety of library projects, but not for the purchase of library material. The practical consequence of this restriction is that it forces the linkage of existing resources and services, and a more creative approach to library problems than just more money for more books. The actual appropriations under this act have amounted to about $40,000 to each state, a sum which, if matched at the minimum level, as is common in most states, cannot fund the massive programs needed to make all the library resources of any state available to all its citizens. The funding under Title III has been minimal but it has resulted in serious planning efforts in forty-nine states and some actual linkages of resources in major libraries in each state have been accomplished.

SELF-SUFFICIENCY — AN ANTITHESIS

A certain intriguing and basically human tension has long existed between concepts of self-sufficiency and resource sharing. The whole of human experience demonstrates over and over again that no man is an island and neither is a library. Man is a sharing animal — at least at his best. It is through sharing that he finds self-realization, enlightenment and fulfillment. The development of man and his environment depends absolutely on how much and how effectively he shares.

What we have now is imperfect resource sharing because no information system has all the material on any significant segment of knowledge, nor is it possible for it ever to be gathered into one locally defined area. The true issue is not whether or not to share — there never has been a real choice in the matter — but how much to share. Since the great library at Alexandria shared its resources with the library at Pergamum in the second century B.C. libraries have known what has to be done to make the proper use of library materials.

Verner Clapp has defined the problem when he says that "from earliest times two principles have controlled the growth of libraries — the principle of local self-sufficiency and the principle of sharing the resources... Neither has ever won exclusive control and the likelihood is that neither ever will" [2, p. 4].

The increase in the volume of printed material has been occurring at an exponential rate since the beginning of this century. For example, between 1940 and 1960 the ten largest American libraries increased their acquisition rate by 71%. The growth in the number of scientific journals has been charted by D. J. deSola Price in his book Science Since Babylon [12]. He shows that there were about ten scientific journals being produced in the late 1600's. This number increased to about 100 at the beginning of the nineteenth century and then to 10,000 by 1900. His evaluation of the World List of Scientific Periodicals is that we are well on our way to the 100,000 mark. The data he presents show a remarkably constant doubling time of fifteen years, now maintained for nearly three centuries. The expenses involved in trying to cope with this flood are becoming intolerable. The logistics involved in providing space to house these growing collections is conjuring up its own administrative nightmares. For example, the Hillman Library at the University of Pittsburgh opened for business in 1967. The professional librarians estimate that the Hillman Library will be filled to capacity in about another seven years. The problem there is certainly not unique. Effective solutions to such problems must be planned well in advance. Hence, we are beginning to look for ways to solve the storage space problem creatively and cooperatively.

It would be a serious mistake to think that all forces in the library field are pushing in the direction of sharing of resources. There remains a great deal of pressure to maintain and even develop greater self-sufficiency. Sharing among libraries involves many formalities. There are delays, costs, and the problems associated with having one's own request subordinated to that of the home library. The siren call of mass photocopying of material in high demand makes self-sufficiency even more alluring.

We are faced with the dilemma of which direction to take. To make no explicit choice is to choose implicitly the status quo. I would like to appeal again to Verner Clapp's book The Future of the Research Library [2, p. 17].

> ...Unless we are prepared to support the local self-sufficiency principle by present methods through enormous expenditures for books, cataloging, and storage space — two lines of development are indicated: toward techniques for increased self-sufficiency at cost lower than those at present; or toward methods of sharing resources comparable with local availability.

If we make the choice to spend our library dollars in behalf of self-sufficiency we will demonstrably be spending more and more money for less and less goods and services. If the choice is for self-sufficiency then it must be based on a sounder reason than maintaining the status quo. To attempt to have both running in parallel is like trying to have a dialectic of thesis and antithesis without even attempting a synthesis. To assume that the status quo has its own rewards — as if it were a virtue — is to assume that the environment never changes.

One of the most beguiling perceptions men have pondered is the constancy of change. The rate of change in a consumer-oriented, capitalistic, technological society such as ours makes the status quo as flowing and as constant as a river. The needs of users are continually changing, the number and kind of books and periodicals is increasing, and the application of the computer to the processes and user-services makes the status quo fluid. The library is both the same and different and we need to deal with this dialectical situation more realistically than we have in the past.

The resolution of the tension between self-sufficiency and resource sharing is no easy task. Some of the advocates for library cooperation, like Richard Dougherty, make such apodictical statements as "Because the cost of self-sufficiency has become undeniably prohibitive, libraries can no longer afford to act as free agents" [11, p. 1767]. Ralph Blasingame

does not see the issue in these terms. He "takes issue" with the idea
"that tough financial times reinforce a need for cooperation" [13].
Mr. Blasingame invokes the greatness of the Widener Library at Harvard
and the New York Public Library as "two obvious examples" of success
without cooperation. That's like saying Social Security isn't necessary
because the Kennedy's don't need it. On the basis of recent reports about
its financial troubles, the New York Public Library may be a fallen saint
of self-sufficiency. At Harvard both the Widener Library and the Francis
A. Countway Library of Medicine have begun to make use of the MARC
tapes and MEDLARS, respectively [14].

In dealing with this question of self-sufficiency it seems that we must
rephrase the aphorism "where there's a will, there's a way." In the
light of even the present technology there are many ways to share resources.
The real problem is the will to share. The success of library cooperation
is at the mercy of people's intentions; not technological capabilities. If
we don't have enough of the right kind of material for those who need it,
then the fault is ours. There are ways even within the framework of
limited budgets, to make libraries succeed in the 1970's. The conditio
sine qua non is our willingness to do what is possible.

TO DO WHAT IS POSSIBLE — A SYNTHESIS

The sharing of resources can take place in any of the ways which
resourcefulness and technology provide. The Systems Development
Corporation under contract to the United States Office of Education has
identified four general types of consortia which may serve as a model.

1. Large consortia concerned primarily with computerized, large-
scale technical processing; e.g., The New England Library Information
Network (NELINET), and Ohio College Library Center (OCLC).

2. Small consortia concerned primarily with user services and every
day problems; e.g., Dayton Miami Valley Consortium (DMVC) in Ohio,
and Tri-State College Library Cooperative (TCLC) in Pennsylvania.

3. Limited purpose consortia cooperating with respect to limited
special subject area; e.g., The Consortium of Western Colleges, and
universities headquartered in California.

4. Limited purpose consortia concerned primarily with interlibrary
loan or reference network operations; e.g., Delaware Rapid Interlibrary
Loan (DRILL) in Delaware.

Both the content and the manner of the sharing are open to discussion and negotiation insofar as particular needs will indicate the type of response best suited to fill these needs. The point of view that leads to the best results is that real, objective, and mutual needs provide the solid ground on which to build resource sharing consortia. This is meant to exclude motivation from desires for self-aggrandisement and seemingly easy remedies for fiscal insecurity.

The Directory of Academic Library Consortia [15] proposes some very real and objective goals to orient the activities of resource sharing through consortia formation. Objectives like the following are suggested:

1. Assist member libraries in the selection of materials
2. Purchase, catalog, and process library materials
3. Coordinate cooperative acquisitions, interlibrary loans, and the reproduction of materials for the member libraries
4. Promote the development of programs for the expanded use of library resources
5. Stimulate the improvement of library facilities and services
6. Cooperate in the development of library personnel
7. Provide, through cooperative acquisition by voluntary agreement, materials beyond the reach of individual libraries
8. Achieve economies in the use of resources, both human and material
9. Facilitate sharing of materials among members of the group

The SATCOM Report adds to the concept of real and objective needs when it discusses "The Nature and Extent of Cooperative Efforts" [16]. The Report states:

One of the principal reasons generally advanced in favor of improving cooperation and coordination among secondary services, and between secondary and primary services as well, is to reduce wasteful duplication of intellectual effort and the expense incurred in providing duplicate coverage of the same material. Another major reason is to increase the opportunities for improving the performance of specific services through enhancing the speed or comprehensiveness of coverage or reducing costs. In addition, greater cooperation and coordination of services could reduce the number of sources that a user must check in a given field and would assist in deciding when new services are appropriate or feasible.

The goals and objectives of resource sharing have been specifically set forth in the foregoing statements. No unrealistic promises or panacea proposals have been invoked. The objectives and the motivating factors are the users' needs interacting with both the very large quantity of library material our culture is accumulating and producing and also the great expense of much of it. The objectives listed lead to the hypothesis that resource sharing is the lifestyle of the future for libraries.

The proliferation of journals in all disciplines and the emergence of more machine-readable data bases readily adapted to sharing through remote accessing suggest resource sharing as the best adaptation to the new environment. The SATCOM Report (1969) [16, p.1] said that the problem of how to communicate and use (information) has been a concern for at least the past two decades because of (a) expanding volume of scientific and technical information, (b) emergence of new disciplines and new links between existing ones, (c) increasing number and diversity of users' groups.

There have been a great many efforts across the country to share resources in areas not strictly defined by the science and technology information explosion. Some of the major ones are the following:

1. Central cataloging — Ohio College Library Center, Cooperative College Library Center (Atlanta, Georgia), Colorado Academic Libraries
2. Union cataloges — Union Library Catalogue (Philadelphia, Pennsylvania)
3. Bibliographic centers — Rocky Mountain Bibliographical Center
4. Storage centers — Center for Research Libraries
5. Acquisition plans — PL 480, Farmington Plan
6. Cooperative microfilm projects — University Microfilms
7. Consortia — Dayton-Miami Valley Consortium, Five Associated University Libraries (FAUL), New England Library Information Network (NELINET)

The presence of so much resource sharing activity in all areas, disciplines, and aspects of information systems indicates that the evolutionary process is well on its way. The goal is obviously to make the greatest amount of the best information available to the most users at the most reasonable cost possible. The SATCOM Report (1969) insists that "to avoid a crisis of major proportions...effort must rely on a proper blend of intellectual effort and complex machine processing. Shortcuts are not available" [16, p. 2]. The report of the National Academy of Sciences on Libraries and Information Technology — A National System Challenge (1972) takes us a step beyond the SATCOM Report (1969) by saying that "the new technology can be brought to bear gradually as various aspects of each process come into the range of practicality; there is no need to wait until an ultimate solution is available" [1, pp. 3-4]. It is critical at this point to face the issue head-on. The obstacles to resource sharing are no longer inherent in technology, but in people.

People have been working effectively at resource sharing. The Library of Congress report on automation points out that "cooperation among libraries exists in acquisition, cataloging, particular bibliographic projects, library lending, and in many other areas. This cooperation is an attemtp to make maximum use of limited resources" [17]. One of our most interesting challenges here will be to assess what the next steps must be.

Some significant patterns in networking already exist. Some networks appear to have a subject or discipline orientation such as the National Library of Medicine and Chemical Abstracts, but most are mission-oriented like the Atomic Energy Commission and the National Aeronautics and Space Administration. Standardization and coordination of responsibilities seems to point the way to some form of centralized administration. The communication links necessary to make such centralized administration possible while maintaining decentralized service to the user are available to us if we choose to use them. The SATCOM Report (1969) [16, p. 13] says that its foremost recommendation is one that calls for the creation of a broadly representative and high-prestige nongovernment body to stimulate greater coordination among private interests. The National Academy of Sciences report (1972) on Libraries and Information Technology — A National System Challenge [1, pp. 5-6] continues to emphasize the same point in the following recommendations:

1. The present collection of localized and fragmented efforts must be guided toward harmonious integration through experience with a comprehensive pilot system.
2. To develop information systems consistent with geographic dispersion of information users, increased stress must be placed on scientific design and modeling studies of broadly based information networks.

The art of the administrator must be applied to the science of the available technology to solve the information handling problems which now confront us. A system's design must be provided which will indicate enough advantages to warrant the initial inconveniences and uncertainties of resource sharing. From a purely human point of view one of the primary administrative tasks is to create an atmosphere of willingness on the part of the participants. The librarians affected by the projects should be involved in the planning phases as early as possible.

THE ARGUMENT

The argument proceeds from the definition and recognition of the need, through the phase of possible solutions, to a decision about the next action step. The need has been defined by the greatly increasing quantity and cost of library resources. Responsible people in both the library profession and the Federal Government have perceived this need and have proposed practical solutions. There has been a significant series of legislative acts and funding programs to indicate the viewpoint of the people with political power. Professional librarians and their associations have organized resource sharing activities across the country in practical commitments to resource sharing. All of this has demonstrated that resource sharing is possible and practical even within the limits of the technology now available to us. The motivation for deciding what the next step should be will come from our perception of the need, our confidence that solutions are possible, and our willingness to adapt. Gradual adaptation seems impractical because the rate of change is not gradual. The design of library systems to respond to this changing character of information must match the nature of the change itself.

OBJECTIONS

Even though the need is perceived and solutions are possible, objections remain. At this point I will discuss these objections in an attempt to separate the real problems from the supposed ones.

The American Library Association attempted to identify these barriers by holding a series of ten one-day meetings in 1968 in various parts of the country and invited a variety of people associated with libraries to speak to the question of barriers preventing cooperation. The participants identified forty-six major barriers to interlibrary cooperation. Orin Nolting has summarized these under the following five headings [18]:

1. Psychological barriers — fear of loss of local autonomy, clash of personalities, inertia and indifference, unwillingness to experiment, etc.
2. Lack of information and experience — lack of knowledge of the needs of users, unpredictability of demands on the library by its legitimate users, failure of small libraries to realize the value of resources of larger cooperative efforts in other states
3. Traditional and historical barriers — lack of adequate funds, fear of large libraries of being overused and undercompensated, inadequacy of

libraries to serve their own needs, limitations on access to academic and
special libraries, institutional competition between school and public
libraries

    4. Physical and geographical barriers — distance between libraries
and distance of users from libraries, difference in size of collections, lack
of space in public libraries to serve students, delays in satisfying needs
and requests of users

    5. Legal and administrative barriers — too many government units,
lack of communication across jurisdictional lines, lack of bibliographical
tools and controls, incompatibility of equipment and procedures and rules
between libraries, lack of properly trained staff, lack of appropriate state-
enabling legislation, lack of creative administrative leadership, etc.

    This summary of barriers to cooperation reinforces a previous asser-
tion that the problems to be faced and solved are not those associated with
technology but with people.

    It is simplistic, however, to speak of problems relating to interlibrary
cooperation as if there were only "people" problems and as if nothing else
stood in the way. There are, for example, legal problems of jurisdiction,
control, property titles, state library codes and channels for funding. Such
legal questions can only be acknowledged here and dealt with separately in
the proper context. It does seem advisable, however, to say a few words
now about the question of copyright laws.

    In addition to the expected statements about copyright laws being a
species of property right laws, something must be said about the change in
attitude concerning information. At the 1971 ASIS Conference, Robert
Jordan of Federal City College in Washington, D.C. summarized the attitudinal change when he said:

> People everywhere, and young people in particular are ignoring
> artificial institutional boundaries in fulfilling their informational
> needs. Increasingly they are acting on the assumption that all
> information resources should be available to all. [19]

    The attitude of viewing information almost as a "natural resource"
creates a polarity with the property right concept of information that is
difficult a conundrum as can be found in the modern world. No one would
deny that an author has a right to the fruits of his labor, but no one can
rightly claim exclusive control of information. Information in this context
is understood as being as vital to the welfare of the species as any other
"natural resource" more strictly conceived.

One of the more enticing temptations of contemporary academic life is to photocopy rather than buy. At present, there is no really effective means of control in the situation and authors are probably being cheated of their just rewards. Authors (and their publishers) have invested considerable amounts of time, talent and capital in producing their works and have a real claim to equitable compensation in terms of both recognition and money. This right of the author (and publisher) is not truly an absolute one but must be balanced against society's "right" to the free flow of information by every possible means.

As copyright laws have functioned to protect the author, so the concept of "fair use" has functioned to promote the welfare of society. There are those who claim that the use of photocopying procedures in libraries has done nothing to hinder just compensation due an author. In a study of the history, laws, and legislation relating to copyright, Dr. Charles Gosnell, Professor of Library Administration at New York University reports the following:

> Numerous studies have been made to determine what harm, if any, this easy availability of photocopies has done to the copyright proprietor. To date no evidence has been produced to show any substantial damage in loss of sales to the proprietor. Actually a large proportion of the copies comes from works in the public domain, not subject to copyright laws. [20]

In the same work on Copyright, the same writer goes on to explicate the difference between fair use and infringement as he sees it. The purpose, degree and the effect of the copying rather than the act of copying or publishing as such is the basic differential. The differentiation between the two is basically a matter of "balancing what the author must dedicate to society in return for his statutory copyright... against undue appropriation of what society has promised the author" [20, p. 61].

The use of photocopied material within an academic library system and between libraries through interlibrary loans is one of the basic propositions to be considered in discussing resource sharing. The Copyright Issue Committee of the American Library Association published the following guidelines in 1964:

1. The making of a single copy by a library is a direct extension of traditional library service.
2. Such service, employing modern copying methods, has become essential.
3. The present demand can be satisfied without inflicting measurable damage on publishers and copyright owners.

4. Improved copying processes will not materially affect the demand for single copy library duplication for research purposes.

The problems associated with the present copyright laws come largely from the slowness with which legal formularies respond to technological development. There are probably enough guidelines available for libraries to proceed without causing undue harm either to copyright holders or to library users. We would be hopelessly paralyzed in this and in many other endeavors if we delayed action until all legal doubts were resolved.

The obstacles to resource sharing are not basically technological, and the solution to the problems is not merely a matter of putting more money into the present systems. Richard Dougherty is so confident that money alone is not the solution that he asserts that "the millions of dollars spent on collection development since the enactment of the 1965 Higher Education Act have not significantly improved the bibliographical health of small college libraries" [11, p. 1768]. It is not at all clear that he need have used the word "small." No one, regardless of size, seems to be saying that they have enough of anything except debts and troubles.

The great danger is to think that the mere injection of much more money into the present library systems will cure all of the present maladies. It is equally as dangerous to think that bigger means better, if the implic- ation is that a consortium with networking ipso facto is better than an individual library. More money may do nothing more than compound existing evils in acquisitions, cataloguing, processing, etc. A bigger library environment may mean that the desired material is located in a more remote place and separated from the user by an horrendous jungle of red tape. More money and more materials will have no practical benefit to the user unless there is a correspondingly great effort at an unflinching analysis of the present, and creative planning and management in the future. It would be disastrous to take the present mode of library operations as a "given" in the equation and try to solve for better service to users by simply adding more money and more materials. Ellsworth Mason has taken issue with resource sharing concepts by attacking the proposition that bigger means better [21]. It is one thing to find fault with a misleading generality, and quite another thing to apply the generality in a misleading way. Resource sharing is not beneficial merely because it creates the "bigger" in this proposition, i.e., greater availability; its good lies in the greater potenti- ality it creates. To attack the "bigger means better" axiom in twentieth- century America, whose constituents have their own special identity problems because of the size and complexity of our environment, is to attack sin in church and imply inactivity as the only way to avoid evil.

In any efforts at resource sharing there should be a clear statement of priorities between the individual library and the group. A queuing program should be clearly stated; each participant must think in terms of the group, otherwise the resource sharing system will not work. The implementation of such a priority system can probably be accomplished best through some organizational system which is above any of the constituents. This is one of the recommendations of the SATCOM Report. It recommended the establishment of a broadly representative and highly prestigious nongovernment body to stimulate greater coordination among private interests. The establishment of an administrative unit chartered to provide for the welfare of the whole and enforce appropriate sanctions on those who break their contractual agreements is certainly an operational possibility. It will do more harm than good to enter into a resource sharing situation if it is done merely because this is becoming fashionable in the library world. Only conviction and commitment will make it work.

The commitment of any given library system is measurable in terms of its willingness to pay, or at least to allocate some of its financial resources for services derived from other libraries. Some federal and state funds may be available to inaugurate a resource sharing system, but these obviously cannot be counted on for long-range support. There will naturally be the temptation to view money paid as "dues" in any cooperative venture as money taken away from the home library budget — which is indeed true — but money is paid for the purpose of obtaining more library goods and services for the same budget dollar.

Systems incompatibilities may be invoked as an obstacle to resource sharing. Libraries, of course, do use different classification systems such as Library of Congress or the Dewey Decimal or some specialized arrangement of their own. There may also be significant differences in processing procedures. The problems with processing procedures can be minimized through intelligent planning and responsive administrative procedures. The business of changing from one classification system to another presents appreciable problems which should not be camouflaged in discussing the ideals of resource sharing. Some libraries may even withdraw from a cooperative venture because of the difficulty. The decision to stay with the cooperative activity or drop out is frequently made on the basis of the arranging of priorities, the paying of "dues," and the adjustment of system compatibilities.

In working through some of these difficulties it is possible to avoid some of the more aggravating problems by prudent planning and by attitudinal changes. The first changes to be inaugurated in a cooperative activity should be those which cause the least disruption of local policy and procedures and the highest degree of benefit to the local unit. High-benefit service activities, if handled well, can make users feel very pleased with their library's resource sharing activity. If the first activities to be attempted are those dealing with centralized processing or joint collection development, then the interest of the local library may be at a minimum. The disruption of the local environment will be perceived as great since there will be no

benefits coming to the local library immediately subsequent to the disruption.

The pursuit of perfection in cataloging may very well paralyze any
meaningful progress toward cooperation. A reasonably accurate catalog
which will be clear to the user and put him in contact with the material he
desires is the end to be achieved. Whether the catalog is the most perfect
one that can be devised is, at least, an irrelevant question if not an impert-
inent one. The satisfying of the users' information needs as expeditiously as
possible is the factor that determines the whole issue. The end product of
a shared cataloging system may not be the same as the local library has
been accustomed to, but if it is clear and precise, then it should be utilized.

Some have objected that resource sharing activities may bring about
a diminution in the number of jobs at the local library. In responding to
this we must say hard things. Some jobs may be lost because they become
superfluous, or are found to be that way already; however, that is not a
sufficient reason to avoid resource sharing.

Administrators can see to it that efforts to adapt to changing times are
not viewed as personal criticism. The world outside of the library organism
must adapt to that change if it is to survive. The only time adverse criticism
will be justifiable will be if adaptation is rejected and atrophy is the consequence. We can hopefully rely on Ellsworth Mason's assessment of
librarians when he says, "I still find more good will in the world of librarianship than in most areas of human activity, and despite all the accusations
about foot dragging, every librarian worth his salt is extending himself to
the utmost all the time" [21]. Mr. Mason has identified a basic issue
when he points out that a little cooperation will not do anybody much good.
Token gestures toward fashionable ideals won't help to solve the crucial
problems of money, space, and service which are facing us now. In an
article with the highly significant title of "A Trillion Dollar Bankruptcy,"
Mr. Mason advises us to recognize how greatly library demands have
expanded and "to move toward significant cooperation on a massive scale.
Anything else is merely gentle play" [21].

Finding solutions with enough magnitude to deal with the size of the
problem is the name of the game. The Pennsylvania Department of Education
through the Burea of Educational Statistics has published some illustrative
statistics in a study called Our Colleges and Universities Today. PLA
reports that collections grew from 16,353,678 volumes in 1966 to 25,862,009
in 1970. This is a growth rate of 50% in a five-year period. A little cooperation will do virtually nothing to harness the flood tide of such a rate of
expansion.

Some problems have been raised; some objections have been answered.
This process should be continued in the most thorough way possible. No
good will be achieved by assuming that implementation of cooperative ideas
will be as quick and easy as rhetoric is fashionable these days. Ronald

Miller, the former coordinator of the Five Associated University Libraries (FAUL) stated the guidelines as succinctly as possible when he said:

> Glossing over the struggles and rough edges would have been strategically wise perhaps, but the gut issues of network building must be raised... It should be clearly understood that FAUL and other consortia will be successful in the long run only if they face honestly the problems raised. [22]

FACE THE PROBLEMS

A study by Oliver Dunn plots library growth factors from 1951 through 1968-1969 and projects the growth curves to 1980:

> The average composite of the 58 university libraries included in this study indicates that the number of volumes held doubles every 17 years; the number of volumes added to the collections each year has doubled every 9 to 12 years; and library operating expenses double every 7 years. The report concludes: In short the records of growth since 1951, including the most recent years, and the unfaltering growth of even the largest libraries, indicate that this growth may not soon decelerate. [23]

The previously-mentioned report of the National Academy of Sciences using data from Knight and Nourse [24] and Price [25] computed the ratios of dollars per student and dollars per volume; a striking escalation of unit costs was found that significantly exceeds increases in the Consumer Price Index (Table 1).

TABLE 1

Unit Cost Escalation

Year	$/Student	$/Volume	Consumer Price Index
1962	47	.92	105.4
1966	54	1.21	113.1
1968	73	1.67	121.2

TABLE 2

Percentage Budget Increases 1965-1966, 1967-1968

General administration and general expense	38%
Instruction and departmental research	36%
Extension and public services	36%
Libraries	42%
Plant operation and maintenance	33%
Organized research	10%
Related activities	14%
Auxiliary enterprises	24%
Other current expenditures	13%
Gross additions in plant value	31%

The report noted that "the sparse numbers listed above must be used with great caution, but they suggest that costs are going out of control at an increasing rate."

An analysis of expenditure of institutions of higher education [26] tends to support the conclusions of the report in exhibiting that library budgets are increasing at a greater rate than many other line items (Table 2). Thus it can be seen that the percentage of budget for many line items is decreasing in relation to the larger increase for libraries. Only "student aid" (67%) and "sales and services" (144%) have increased to a greater degree than libraries.

Face the problem. The cost of library materials has risen at a rate of between 12% and 25%. This is obviously a considerably higher rate than the cost of living. The cost of labor is increasing beyond our control or capabilities to absorb. It has become almost axiomatic to postulate that 60%, or more, of a library's budget will be going into salaries and only a portion of the remaining percentage will go into acquisitions. Those proportions cannot be easily reversed within the present framework of library organization. Through resource sharing we can at least get more materials and service for the same dollar. We hope we may be able to construct a budgetary environment in which the gas will not cost more than the car. As automated circulation systems become more prevalent, librarians are becoming more aware of the level of usage of their collection. There are large areas of any collection with relatively low use which yet occupy very expensive space in the library. Such low-use items could more appropriately be stored in a common facility with other low-use regional library material.

Face the problem. The number and cost of journals is increasing each year. This increase is aggravated by the fact that abstracting services are alerting users in local libraries to much more journal material than their own libraries hold. It is absurd to ask a library patron to forego the use of valuable and relevant material, which could readily be obtained, merely because no one has applied the technology or developed the organizational patterns to deliver the goods.

Face the problem. In the name of self-sufficiency we are spending increasingly large portions of our library budgets on low-use items. A study of the use of currently published serials at the John Crerar Library found that 65% of the journals it currently receives are used less often than once a year. Another study of interlibrary loan use at the National Library of Medicine found that 88% of its serial titles were used less often than once a year. According to a recent study done by the Center for Research Libraries there is evidence that 25%, and probably more, of the journals received are used no oftener than once in every 25 to 100 years in any one library [27].

Face the problem. There is too much expensive material being produced for anyone to have it all. A recent study by the U.S. Office of Education (USOE) found that, of the 16,361 serials important to Chemistry and Chemical engineering, even collectively the 325 libraries surveyed held only 66.1% of the titles in complete files. The best single USOE region held 45.3% of the above number of titles, and the worst region held only 15.7%. Even though there are such incomplete holdings, high cost is forcing many libraries to cancel subscriptions. The Center for Research Libraries reports that of the fifty major universities in its membership, two thirds have already cancelled an average of 300 titles. Some members have had to cancel as many as 2,000 titles [27, p.4].

We have before us enough legislation, enough examples of past efforts, enough analysis of problems and suggested solutions to take some significant steps forward. The longer we talk, the more problems and expenses are developing. The longer we talk, the more uncoordinated program planning is taking place. Thousands of dollars are being myopically committed because College A, located very close to College B, does not know that the one is developing a curriculum in the same expensive support area as the other. The days when every college should work toward developing complete collections to support low-use courses, which a neighboring college is already supporting, should be as obsolete as one-room school houses.

CRITERIA

Now we can offer criteria and get on with the business of developing actual resource sharing systems. Ruth Patrick, in her work entitled

Guidelines for Library Cooperation [28], has suggested some elementary
criteria such as:

  1. Potential members feel they have common interests and would achieve
levels of service and/or efficiency by working in a cooperative mode that
they could not achieve by working alone.
  2. Potential members are willing to commit the required financial and
moral support on a continuing basis.

  We have already identified some of the areas and activities which would
easily fit under the first set of criteria. The remote accessing of centrally
stored tapes, collection development in low-use areas, common storage
facilities, are only a few of the examples in which cooperation is more
effective than self-sufficiency. We should be quick to include a more
thorough interlibrary loan policy. Let institutions really commit themselves
to each other and be willing to make available through interlibrary loan
everything they make available to their own patrons.

  The necessary moral and financial support mentioned in the second part
of the criteria statements tends to be as elusive as a piece of mercury on a
table top. It's there and you can feel it, but it's very difficult to pick up.
The moral support for resource sharing will continue to grow as the
impracticality and impossibility of self-sufficiency become more apparent.
The moral support must be unequivocal and coordinated as it comes from the
presidents and the librarians to the trustees or whoever controls the purse-
strings.

  Financial support can be developed in a number of ways. As an initial
step a case could be made for financing resource sharing activities out of
the same operating budgets as are being used at present for activities
designed to foster self-sufficiency. The great advantage to rechanneling
the funding is that, through resource sharing, it is realistically possible to
get more goods and services for the same dollar of operating expenses. The
problems involved in obtaining funds for capital expenses are obviously
greater and should be dealt with separately. It is appropriate to talk about
sharing operating expenses when analyzing the "why" of resource sharing,
because one of the more persuasive reasons for sharing now is precisely the
one just given. A good example of the principle is to be found in the recent
study made by Herman Henkle and Joseph Shipman on the feasibility of a
Metropolitan Pittsburgh Science and Technology Library (see Chapter 14).

  A Metropolitan Pittsburgh Science and Technology Library had been the
object of discussion for about twenty-five years. The basic concept was to
share the resources of the science and technology departments of Carnegie-
Mellon University, the Carnegie Library of Pittsburgh, and the University
of Pittsburgh. The moral support for such an activity had been fermenting
for a long time — too long, perhaps, in the sense that the idea could be

talked to death. In order to move the activity ahead within the framework of present operating budgets they recommended that the proposed cooperative activity take place within the management structure of the Carnegie Library of Pittsburgh, thus preserving the external funding channels which already existed. After two years of study the consultants felt confident enough to make the following statement as part of their formal proposal:

> It is our considered judgement that under the general terms of this proposal much better collections and library services would result than are now available with no increase in operating costs. By broadening the cooperative base to include other academic institutions and the very impressive complex of industrial organizations this improvement could be extended. [29]

With respect to the costs of resource sharing it will be informative to add the admonition which these consultants gave to the boards of trustees:

> With respect to operating costs, we might add one caveat. We did not see the primary objective of this assignment to be reduction of expenditures. We have been seeking for Pittsburgh what we sought for our respective libraries (John Crerar and Linda Hall) over more than two decades — to develop the strongest possible library resources in terms of collections, facilities and services that could be provided with the financial resources available. [29]

Let us take another statement of criteria and see if resource sharing among libraries is within the realm of feasibility according to these. Richard Dougherty has offered a suitable list in his article on The Paradoxes of Library Cooperation [11, p.1768]:

1. Has a more effective organizational pattern emerged?
2. Are professional and nonprofessional library staff functioning more effectively?
3. Has access to materials improved?
4. Have local collections and service policies been revised to reflect the new program?
5. Have library procedures been streamlined?
6. Has staff been retrained to take maximum advantage of the cooperative?
7. Have operational costs been stabilized, or better, reduced?
8. Have new services been introduced or existing services been expanded?

If these are the criteria, then the answer to the question "Why share resources?" must be that sharing is the solution for the 1970's. In point of fact, those criteria apply not merely to cooperative ventures but to optimum library service in any mode. If you say no to any of those criteria, you are saying no to good library service.

Dougherty's criteria suggest that successful resource sharing will have as much impact on the librarians and their attitudes as it will on the patrons and materials. A greater interaction between librarians will very probably bring about an expanded awareness of problems and solutions on the part of librarians. If librarians really share with each other we can look forward to new ideas for better service, better programs, and better budgeting.

In the same issue of Library Journal [30] in which Richard Dougherty proposed his criteria, there were other articles offering objections. Some of these objections have already been dealt with, such as the position that the Widener Library and the New York Public Library did not grow through cooperative activities, or that bigger necessarily means better. The basic objection to resource sharing must be postulated around an empirical evaluation of what has happened thus far and questioning whether it is worth continuing. The response can begin with pointing out that cataloging is more efficiently handled because of the MARC data base and because of OCLC, although neither system is the "perfect" answer to the problem. Even now, other activities are being proposed to handle cataloging activities, such as the new program suggested by EDUCOM and ETS. The betterment of service that has taken place in the area served by FAUL and NELINET, although not perfect solutions, indicates an increase in such activities rather than a lessening. Library operations have been improved through union catalogs as in Philadelphia and through acquisition information sharing such as exists among the members of PRLC, but these are only first steps. With all of these technical activities we need more cooperation, not less, so that there will be increasingly less duplication of effort in making the same product available to the same public in the same region.

The development of criteria for a resource sharing system can be helped by considering the work done at the INTREX Conference in 1965. The following was said about information transfer in the University of the Future:

> Three main streams of progress in the information transfer field were intensively discussed among us at the Conference:
>
> a. The modernization of current library procedures through the application of technical advances in data processing, textual storage, and reproduction;
>
> b. The growth, largely under federal sponsorship, of a national network of libraries and other information centers;

   c. The extension of the rapidly developing technology of on-line,
   interactive computer communities into the domains of the
   library and other information transfer centers. [31]

   The stated goal of Project INTREX was "to provide a design for evolution
of a large university library into a new information transfer system that
could become operational in the decade beginning in 1970." The ideal
proposed by that Conference can serve as a model for the future. The
INTREX Planning Conference will have more meaning now that some of the
proposals have been implemented to some degree. The whole thrust of the
Conference responds to our question of "Why share resources?" The
sharing is necessary because of the environment we live in; it is possible
because of the human and technical capabilities available for the task.

   The basic problem addressed by Project INTREX was that of access to
information, or more specifically to bibliographic material, documents,
and data banks. Many modern university libraries are selecting, acquiring,
and organizing such quantities of materials that the quantity itself tends to
make it inaccessible. The quantity and expense of this material imposes on
us the necessity of developing shared acquisition policies. The quantity
of it imposes the necessity of utilizing more modern means of access to it
than the card catalog. If we break the chains which currently bind us to the
traditional card catalog we can easily share and search our mutual holdings
through remote access points. In summarizing the needs of the future the
INTREX Planning Conference hypothesized problems which we are now
experiencing and proposed possible solutions. On the question of access the
Conference had this to say:

   It is evident that efficient access to information requires the development of a more flexible and sophisticated finding apparatus than the
   existing card catalogue. This apparatus, ideally, should lead one
   rather quickly through the universe of recorded knowledge to exactly
   those books, documents or bodies of information that are pertinent
   to the problem, and at the desired level. Such an instrument must
   be capable of readjusting to changing concepts of a subject, to
   changing terminologies, and to the handling of new forms of publications of many different types... There are likely to be many
   important advantages if access to this "catalogue index" can be gained
   through stations that are remote from the library, as well as in it.
   [31, p. 13]

   The best thinking about the information systems of the future emphasizes
resource sharing and not self-sufficiency. The implication is that we should

move in the direction of very large, even national, information networks.
The realities of the environment compel us to think in these terms. There
is now a doubling in the output of scientific information in some fields every
ten years; the quantity and quality of foreign-language materials is growing
and its impact on our information systems increases as our involvement with
previous political "untouchables" increases. The Center for Research
Libraries reports that even now 45% of the world's scientific journals are in
a language other than English. The proliferation of scientific disciplines
and forms of publication make cooperative activities our only practical hope
for survival. The so-called big academic libraries cannot adequately meet
users' demands for services and materials and the smaller ones are doomed
to intolerable feelings of inadequacy. The development of information networks through the application of even currently available technology offers
a realistic hope of providing quality service for the future.

The rhetoric in the literature is extensive on the subject of stating the
criteria for an information network. Becker and Olsen list four basic
elements in the concept. They say that there must be:

1. Formal organization: Many units sharing a common information
    purpose recognize the value of group affiliation and enter into a
    compact.
2. Communications: The network includes circuits that can rapidly
    interconnect dispersed points.
3. Bidirectional operation: Information may move in either direc-
    tion, and provision is made for each network participant to send
    as well as receive.
4. A directory and switching capability: A directory look-up system
    enables a participant to identify the unit most able to satisfy a
    particular request. A switching center then routes messages to
    this unit over the optimum communications path. [32]

Chapters 6 and 11 deal with the "how" and "when" aspects of networks
and resource sharing. It is necessary at this point only to say that the above
description is what is meant by a network and that it is as integral to resource
sharing as streets are to a city. Those who are experts in the technology
insist that the problems that we have to deal with now are people problems
and organizational problems and not technological ones.

One of the better examples of how a network actually operates is to be
found in the activities of the Five Associated University Libraries (FAUL)
in upstate New York. The Universities are SUNY at Binghamton, SUNY at
Buffalo, Cornell, Syracuse, and the University of Rochester. As a group,
these libraries have holdings of more than eight million volumes administered
by about 1135 staff members. Up to this point the financial support has been

provided by the member libraries. Each member pays base dues of $13,000 which provide central office staff salaries, travel, equipment, space rental, consultants, and the like.

The official objectives of the organization are typical of many consortia according to Ron Miller and can be summarized in the postulates (1) that five libraries can do some things in common at less than five times the cost of doing them separately; and (2) that a synergistic effect is possible whereby the whole can be greater than the sum of its parts. The purposes of the association are formally stated in Article II of its constitution as follows:

1. Improve and develop cooperation among the Five Associated University Libraries.
2. Work towards a coordinated policy for long-range library growth and development with coordinated acquisitions policies, shared resources, and development of compatible machine systems, provision of easy and rapid communications systems among the membership, the provision of shared storage facilities, and the exploration of other areas of cooperation. [22, p. 268]

FAUL is governed by a Board of Directors made up of the chief librarian and the academic vice-president from each member institution. The board has the responsibility of managing the affairs of the association and is empowered to hire employees, acquire property, and make contracts. The board frequently delegates much of its decision making to an Executive Council. This body is made up of the chairman and vice-chairman of the board, a third chief librarian on a monthly rotating basis, and the coordinator of library systems.

One of the most interesting facets of this resource sharing activity has been its definition of the word "resources." FAUL has defined it to include people's ideas and the work they do as well as the materials and the facilities which they use. FAUL has committed itself to maximizing the opportunities for mutual visits and meetings between the members of the various staffs. The concept has been formalized in the FAUL Staff Visitation Program. During a period of six months each library has invited staff members from the other member libraries to spend a day and one-half examining their facilities and procedures and talking with their counterparts about common problems. Reports made concerning these visits indicate that they were of great value to the participants. The participants have suggested that the activity be expanded into a continuing education program.

It would be comforting to be able to give a quantitative analysis of FAUL at this point and assert thereby that it is successful and imply that all

resource sharing activities will succeed. The current administration of
FAUL has confidence in its future and is critically evaluating its activities
against specific mission goals. Its principal project now is to hook up with
OCLC for shared cataloging. The success or failure of any particular
resource sharing activity must be evaluated on its own merits or demerits.
There is no special charisma about resource sharing that impels all such
activities to succeed. These activities have merit insofar as they are
meaningful responses to real needs. The proposal is not to imitate what is
currently fashionable in the library world, but to solve real problems in the
best way possible.

THE PENNSYLVANIA SCENE

Pennsylvania has begun to find some solutions to its problems through
resource sharing activities among its academic and research libraries.
The Pennsylvania Library Association Bulletin for September, 1972 [33]
lists the following examples of cooperative endeavors:

1. Lehigh Valley is interested in sharing data processing
2. Area College Library Cooperative Program, among other things,
    operates a delivery service headquartered at Lancaster County
    Library which has been funded with LSCA money
3. Pittsburgh Regional Library Center (PRLC) has linked with Ohio
    College Library Center (OCLC) for shared cataloging
4. Temple, Drexel, and Penn plan to go with OCLC
5. Tri-State College Library Cooperative has members in Southeastern
    Pennsylvania, Delaware, and New Jersey
6. Philadelphia Area Committee on Library Cooperation meets under
    the auspices of the Union Library Catalogue.

The State Library of Pennsylvania through its Bureau of Library
Development has issued the following statement of funds received for fiscal
1971-72 under Title III of the Library Services and Construction Act [33]:

1. Scranton Public Library, $30,500. The grant is being used to employ
a consultant team, headed by Charles Nelson, to do an extensive study of and
develop a model for interlibrary cooperation among libraries of all types in
Northeastern Pennsylvania.
2. Union Library Catalogue, $6,200. Three of the Catalogue's member
libraries are using these funds to experiment with cataloging information
from the Ohio College Library Center: Drexel University, Temple University, and the University of Pennsylvania. If the project is successful, other

libraries will be invited to join the system.

3. Gettysburg College and Susquehanna University, $950 each. The two college libraries will use grant funds for installation and operation of Tele-typewriter Exchange (TWX) equipment for interlibrary loan.

4. Lancaster County Library, $17,400. These funds are to be used for approximately 50% of the cost of the Southeastern Pennsylvania Library Delivery Service, involving 67 libraries.

5. Drexel University, $12,316. The University will do a study of the resources of different types of libraries and will conduct a workshop to explore the present systems of resource sharing among libraries and to consider possible improvements and extensions of those systems.

6. Allentown Public Library, $3,500. The grant will be used as partial funding of a self-survey of users and librarians to be done by members of the Greater Lehigh Valley Council on Inter-library Cooperation.

7. Pittsburgh Regional Library Center, $9,000. Center staff will revise and update the Union List of Periodicals which includes holdings of public, academic, and special libraries.

I have listed here some of the major and most recent resource sharing activities in Pennsylvania. A comprehensive survey of on-going activities has been prepared by Natalie Wiest, Lee Laurea, and Brigitt L. Kenney of Drexel University [34].

It is only within the past year that the state of Pennsylvania has been divided into eight planning regions for the purpose of developing interlibrary cooperation. The divisions seem to be functional even though they do not correspond to the ten divisions of the state used by the Department of Higher Education. The structure of the situation is not nearly so important as the functions which can and should be performed. From the list of grants of LSCA money already given it is possible to see the activity which is already underway, but it is only a beginning.

Statewide planning in interlibrary cooperation will have to be increasingly emphasized as programs like "Universities Without Walls" develop and the capabilities of CTV are developed. It will be inadequate for the administrators of information systems merely to respond to these program needs. Administrators of the appropriate information systems must seek active involvement and leadership now if they want to see quality programs which are within realistic parameters of budget, space, and technology.

CONCLUSION

The National Commission on Libraries and Information Science (NCLIS) was signed into law on July 20, 1970. Among its eight charges are the following ones relevant to our discussion:

2. To conduct studies, surveys, and analyses of the library and information needs of the nation.
3. To appraise the adequacies and deficiencies of current library and information resources and services and evaluate the effectiveness of current library and information science programs.
4. To develop overall plans for meeting national library and information needs and for the coordination of activities at the federal, state and local levels, taking into consideration all of the library and information resources of the nation to meet those needs.
6. To promote research and development activities which will extend and improve the nation's library and information-handling capability as essential links in the national communications networks. [35]

NCLIS held its first hearing in Chicago in the summer of 1972. The report of the hearing as given in the LJ/SLJ Hotline is that "(1) library revenues are more uncertain than ever and Revenue Sharing offers little hope, and (2) librarians need retraining, user-needs need studying, and librarians must decide what the future of the profession is" [36].

There is an information system challenge facing us. The flow of information from all sources will continue to increase at an even faster rate than in the present. Indications are that expenses associated with acquiring, processing, storing, and retrieving will continue to increase at a faster rate than library budgets. Our information systems are hardpressed now, if not overwhelmed, by the present rate of information production and that rate seems likely to increase. We cannot halt this evolutionary process, even for a time, even if we want to.

To a large extent our culture is producing information much like one amoeba produces another. The great amount is not the direct result of users making specific inquiries. It is the result of parent concepts generating offspring because there is an inevitability in the growth of knowledge. At this point in the history of man, that self-renewing community of parent concepts is so vast and is proliferating at such a rate that the user is presented with more information than he can assimilate. The impetus to produce more information is more a factor of what has already been produced than a user's demand for specific knowledge.

We have tried to indicate here the need to share resources by pointing out the great increases in the volume of information, the costs of acquiring and processing it, and the increasing demands from users. Attempts at self-sufficiency will not allow the library organism to survive in this changing environment. Adaptations as radical as the environmental changes are needed.

Adaptations through resource sharing activities are feasible now. Examples of major activities in this area show that the technology is available. The need to share can be satisfied in a variety of ways. We are not doomed to frustration. The fact that the need can be satisfied imposes on us the obligation of doing something and not just talking about it.

REFERENCES

1. "Libraries and Information Technology — A National System Challenge," A Report to the Council on Library Resources, Inc. The Information Systems Panel, Computer Science and Engineering Board of the National Academy of Sciences, Washington, D.C., 1972, p. 1.

2. Verner W. Clapp, The Future of the Research Library, University of Illinois Press, Urbana, 1964, p. 5.

3. Ernest C. Richardson, "Cooperation and Lending among College and Research Libraries," LJ, May 1899, pp. 32-36.

4. President's Science Advisory Committee, Improving the Availability of Scientific and Technical Information in the United States, Washington, D.C., 1958.

5. President's Science Advisory Committee, Scientific and Technological Communication in the Government, Washington, D.C., 1962.

6. President's Science Advisory Committee, Science, Government, and Information, U.S. Government Printing Office, Washington, D.C., 1963.

7. Office of Science and Technology, Report of the Office of Science and Technology Ad Hoc Panel on Scientific and Technical Communications, Washington, D.C., 1965.

8. "Public library service: a guide to evaluation, with minimum standards," American Library Association, Public Library Association, ALA, Chicago, 1956, p. 7.

9. "Minimum Standards for Public Library Systems," American Library Association, Public Library Association, 1966, ALA, Chicago, 1967, p. 66.

10. "Interlibrary Cooperation," American Library Association, ALA, Chicago, 1967.

11. Richard M. Dougherty, "The Paradoxes of Library Cooperation," LJ, May 1972, p. 1767.

12. D. J. Desola Price, Science Since Babylon, Yale University Press, New Haven, Conn., 1961.

13. Ralph Blasingame, "The Great Library in the Sky Prototype," LJ, May 1972, p. 1771.

14. Libraries and Information Technology — A National System Challenge, Annex B, 46–47.

15. Diana Delaney and Carlos Cuadra, Directory of Academic Library Consortia, System Development Corporation, Santa Monica, Calif., 1972.

16. Scientific and Technical Communication (SATCOM), A Pressing National Problem and Recommendations for Its Solution, A Report by the Committee on Scientific and Technical Communication of the National Academy of Sciences — National Academy of Engineers, National Academy of Sciences, Washington, D.C., 1969, p. 147.

17. "Automation and the Library of Congress," Library of Congress, Washington, D.C., 1963, p. 21.

18. Orin F. Nolting, "Mobilizing Total Library Resources for Effective Service," ALA, Chicago, 1969, p. 20.

19. Robert Jordan, "Info — U." ASIS Conference, 1971, Denver, Proceedings, Greenwood Press, 1971, pp. 327-329.

20. Charles F. Gosnell, "The Viewpoint of the Librarian and Library User," Copyright — Current Viewpoints on History, Laws, Legislation, R. W. Bowker Co., New York, 1972, p. 58.

21. Ellsworth Mason, "A Trillion Dollar Bankruptcy," LJ, May 1972, p. 1773.

22. Ronald Miller, "Network Organization — A Case Study of Five Associated University Libraries (FAUL)," in Interlibrary Communications and Information Networks, Proceedings of a conference sponsored by the American Library Association and the U.S. Office of Education, ALA, Chicago, 1971, p. 275.

23. Oliver Dunn, "The Past and Likely Future of 58 Research Libraries 1951-1980: A Statistical Study of Growth and Change," 6th Issue, Purdue University Library, Lafayette, Indiana, 1970.

24. Libraries at Large, Douglas M. Knight and Shipley Nourse, eds., B. W. Bowker, Co., New York, 1969.

25. Bronson Price, Library Statistics of College and Universities — Analytic Report, Fall 1968, Gov't. Printing Office, Washington, D.C., 1970.

26. Kenneth A. Simon and W. Vance Grant, Digest of Educational Statistics, OE-10024-70, Washington, D.C., 1970, Table 132, p. 99.

27. "Background and Proposal for a National Lending Library for Journals," Center for Research Libraries, Chicago, 1972, p. 2.

28. Ruth J. Patrick, Guidelines for Library Cooperation, System Development Corporation, Santa Monica, California, 1972, p. 47.

29. H. H. Henkle and J. C. Shipman, "A Metropolitan-Pittsburgh Science and Technology Library," Office of Communication Programs, unpublished report to the University of Pittsburgh, 1972.

30. "Cooperation — A Mini-Symposium with Richard Dougherty," LJ, May 1972.

31. INTREX — A Report of a Planning Conference on Information Transfer Experiments, ed., Carl F. J. Overhage and R. Joyce Harman, The M.I.T. Press, Cambridge, Mass., 1965, p. xv.

32. Joseph Becker and Wallace C. Olsen, "Information Networks," in C. A. Cuadra, ed., Annual Review of Information Science and Technology, Britannica, Chicago, 1969, p. 209.

33. Commonwealth of Pennsylvania, Workshop on Regional Planning for Interlibrary Cooperation, Oct. 30-31, unpublished report, 1972.

34. Natalie Wiest, Lee Laurea, and Brigitt L. Kenney (Drexel University, 1972). Inventory of Pennsylvania Interlibrary Cooperatives and Information Networks, Philadelphia, Pa.

35. "National Commission on Libraries and Information Science," in The Bowker Annual, R. W. Bowker, Co., New York, 1971, p. 267.

36. LJ/SLJ Hotline, 1 (41), December 1972.

Chapter 2

A COMMENTARY ON "RESOURCE SHARING IN LIBRARIES — WHY?"

Patricia Ann Sacks*
Director of Libraries
Muhlenberg and Cedar Crest Colleges

Libraries by the score are searching for the promised land — better services and more materials for the same dollar through resource sharing. Ideology flows into print by the pageful, and supports a basic quest for Melvil Dewey's practical efficiencies. The purpose of this commentary is not to doubt the faith, the promises it holds, or the systems it supports, but to examine John Fetterman's economic postulate — that library costs are consuming an increasing portion of higher education's budget — and respond to his analysis of causes.

In Chapter 1 Fetterman reviews the literature on library cooperation, and sets up the following case on page 11:

> The objectives and the motivating factors are the users' needs interacting with both the very large quantity of library material our culture is accumulating and producing and also the great expense of much of it. The objectives listed lead to the hypothesis that resource sharing is the lifestyle of the future for libraries.

Assigning the computer a major role in information management, Fetterman contends (page 12) that "the obstacles to resource sharing are no longer inherent in technology, but in people." The National Academy of Sciences report defines the complexity of the problem:

---

*Other members of the Pa. Library Assn. who assisted in the development of this report are: Joseph Falgione, Dan Graves, George Henks, Charles Ness and Lillian Smoke.

The primary bar to development of national computer-based library
and information systems is no longer basically a technology-feasibility
problem. Rather it is the combination of complex institutional and
organizational human-related problems and the inadequate economic
value system associated with these activities. National leadership to
solve these problems has not emerged. [1, p. 42]

The core of Fetterman's assessment of the need to share resources is
his analysis of the increasing number of dollars spent by libraries during
the 1960's. Citing data from The Digest of Educational Statistics, 1970,
Fetterman (p. 20) concludes that

the percentage of [the educational] budget for many line items is
decreasing in relation to the larger increase for libraries. Only
"student aid" (67%) and "sales and services" (144%) have increased
to a greater degree than libraries.
...The cost of library materials has risen at a rate of between 12%
and 25%. This is obviously a considerably higher rate than the cost
of living.

This statement of costs is reviewed here with specific reference to
Pennsylvania's academic libraries. * The data presented in the following
three tables describe the growth and cost of resources and services in
Pennsylvania's academic libraries. The percentage comparisons span a
four year period, from 1967 to 1970, when the Consumer Price Index climbed
16.3%, the prices of United States hardcover books and periodical subscriptions increased 20.2% and 32.9%, respectively, and the publication rate of
United States hardcover books rose 25% (Table 3). This examination of the
data indicates that Fetterman's economic analysis is incomplete.

The meaningful relationship between library and other educational and
general (E&G) expenditures is the comparison of library expenditures to the
E&G total, a relationship which Fetterman neglects. Library operating
expenditures as a percent of the total educational and general expenditures

---

*Pennsylvania data are the focus because the Pittsburgh Conference was
sponsored to stimulate the "Next Action Step" in Pennsylvania. Fetterman
uses aggregate figures for the United States, and although the validity of
the transition is not established (comparable United States figures are not
yet published), the variety and number of the State's academic libraries
qualify Pennsylvania as typical of the whole.

increased only 0.3% (3.9% to 4.2%) from 1967 to 1970* (Tables 1 and 2).
This 0.3% increase occurred while the following E&G line items also increased: physical plant maintenance, 2.7%; sponsored activities, 4.5%;
other, 7.1%. This 4.2% support falls below the ALA Standards for College
Libraries which recommend a minimum support of 5.0% of the E&G expenditures for the academic library [3].

The last columns of Table 2 extend Fetterman's part-to-part analysis of
the E&G expenditures to Pennsylvania's statistics. The current-funds
expenditures of Pennsylvania's colleges and universities indicate that the
costs of Pennsylvania's academic libraries rose 48% between 1967-1968 and
1970-1971 while the category which includes them, E&G expenditures, increased 35%. Library expenditures are increasing more rapidly than other
line items such as instruction (30%), but not as rapidly as plant maintenance
(76%) or other (329% and 98%) E&G categories. However, this analysis is
incomplete as it does not view library expenditures as a proportion of the
total E&G expenditures. When compared to the total E&G expenditures, the
48% increase amounts to the 0.3% increase previously stated. This 0.3%
increase is not substantial enough to motivate resource sharing activities
solely on the basis of rapidly rising costs atypical of other E&G expenditures.

The foregoing analysis is incomplete without our acknowledgment of the
following factors affecting library costs: technological innovations, inflation,
growth of new institutions such as the community college and external degree
programs, changes in users' needs and demands for library services, and
the unique product that is library services. The major increase in Pennsylvania's library expenditures is for salaries and wages, and covers a period
when some significant improvements were made in professional salaries
(although library faculty salary scales generally remain below those of the
classroom faculty) and wage increases were required to meet minimum wage
standards. Although new technologies promise some reduction in labor costs,
a study of library economics conducted by William Baumol concludes:

> One point emerges with special clarity: The nature of library costs is
> such that they will continue to rise overall, in spite of improved
> efficiency and cost-reduction efforts. This unavoidable phenomenon
> must be kept in mind in all future planning if the social value of the
> 'product' is to be realized.... Just as one cannot reduce without
> limit, year after year, the amount of faculty time in the educational
> process, the reduction of librarian time (the growth of the librarian
> productivity) is also circumscribed by the nature of the activity. [4]

---

*The average percentage of E&G expenditures of United States academic
libraries was 4.3% in 1969, as described in Ref. 2.

TABLE 1

Selected Categories of Data on Pennsylvania College and University Libraries,
with Percent Changes

1967–68 and 1970–71

Item	1967–1968	1970–1971	Percent change 1967 to 1971 (4 years)
Number of reporting libraries	144	143	—
Collections			
Total holdings[a]	20,510,820	29,630,470	+44%
Number of volumes	16,772,579	20,748,399	+24%
Number of microforms	3,508,029	7,083,687	+102%
Number of periodical titles	133,134	178,252	+34%
Library operating expenditures			
Total (excluding capital)[a]	$29,543,396	$41,398,725	+40%
Salaries and wages	$15,138,873	$22,969,241	+52%
Books and library materials	$11,781,438	$14,227,185	+21%
Binding	$1,068,106	$1,245,082	+17%
Other	$1,554,979	$2,957,217	+90%
Distribution of above expenditures			
Total	100%	100%	—
Salaries and wages	51.2%	55.5%	+4.3%
Books and library materials	39.9%	34.4%	−5.5%
Binding	3.6%	3.0%	−0.6%
Other	5.3%	7.1%	+1.8%
Library operating expenditures as percent of total institutional expenditures for educational and general purposes[b]	3.9%	4.2%	+0.3%
Students served			
Total students enrolled[c]	349,705	411,618	+18%
Number of holdings per student	58.7	72.0	+23%
Library operating expenditures per student	$84.48	$100.57	+19%

TABLE 1 — Continued

[a]Our Colleges and Universities Today, 6, 1, 32, April 1969.
Our Colleges and Universities Today, 9(4), 1, 25, 1972.

[b]Statistical Report of the Secretary of Education for the School Year Ending
June 30, 1968, Pennsylvania Dept. of Ed., Harrisburg, 1969, p. 136.
Statistical Report of the Secretary of Education for the School Year Ending
June 30, 1971, Pennsylvania Dept. of Ed., Harrisburg, 1972, p. 114.
Library expenditures reported here ($27,011,530 in 1967-68 and $39,912,932
in 1970-71) are lower than the totals in Our Colleges and Universities Today,
the only source reporting library expenditures for salaries, books, binding,
other as cited above.

[c]Statistical Report, June 30, 1968, p. 117.
Statistical Report, June 30, 1971, p. 95.

William Dix, Princeton's librarian, believes that the library's contribution to the educational process justifies increased expenditures for library
purposes.

> If it were possible to measure the source of each bit of education, it
> just might turn out that the library, even in its present imperfect
> state, is responsible for as much as half of the educational product.
> [5]

Dix proposes that a better balance between the library and teaching departments may increase the library's percentage of the E&G expenditures to 10%.

A problem common to both Baumol's study and Dix's observations is that
neither is the result of a cost-benefit analysis. Existing data on library
operations inadequately describes costs and activities. Many libraries cannot
define efficiencies for their users in terms of collection and distribution systems.
Consequently, firm answers to the basic question to be asked of any resource-
sharing proposal — Can it save money and improve operating efficiencies
without transferring a burden of inconveniences or costs to the user? — are
unavailable. Better methods of measuring and evaluating services and their
benefits must be derived if libraries are to engage in the most beneficial
resource sharing activities.

Both the resources to be shared and the mechanics for sharing them cost
money. Libraries' critical support needs should be acknowledged. The availability of library funds from colleges and universities depends not only on the
incomes and contributions received by these institutions, but is affected by

TABLE 2

Financial Statistics of Pennsylvania Colleges and Universities Current-Funds Expenditures by Function with Percent Changes 1967–1968 and 1970–1971

Items	1967–1968		1970–1971		Percent change 1967–1968 to 1970–1971 (4 years)
	Dollars	% of total current funds	Dollars	% of total current funds	
Number reporting	138		160		+16%
Total: current funds expenditures	$889,420,414	—	$1,295,749,619	—	+46%
Educational and general: total	698,482,467	78%	946,239,031	73%	+35%
		% of E & G		% of E & G	
Instructional and dept. research	291,603,130	41.7%	379,671,844	40.1%	+30%
Extension and public services	13,882,377	2.0%	11,830,478	1.3%	−15%
Libraries	27,011,530	3.9%	39,912,932	4.2%	+48%
Physical plant maintenance	64,884,453	9.3%	113,952,529	12.0%	+76%
Organized ed. dept. activities	63,303,036	9.1%	20,944,396	2.2%	−67%
Organized research	116,378,631	16.7%	106,520,805	11.3%	−8%
Other sponsored activities	14,265,782[a]	2.0%	61,264,533	6.5%	+329%
Other	107,153,528	15.3%	212,141,514	22.4%	+98%
Student aid grants	50,866,681	6%	74,752,208	6%	+47%
Auxiliary enterprises	121,427,830	14%	151,543,381	11%	+25%
Major service programs	—	—	106,855,999	8%	—
Physical plant assets	18,643,436	2%	32,613,015	2%	+75%

[a]Includes general administration category reported 1967–1968. Sources:
Statistical Report of the Secretary of Education for the School Year Ending June 30, 1968, Pennsylvania Dept. of Ed.,
Harrisburg, 1969, p. 136.
Statistical Report of the Secretary of Education for the School Year Ending June 30, 1971, Pennsylvania Dept. of Ed.,
Harrisburg, 1972, pp. 114–115.

TABLE 3

Price Indexes and Book Production

1967, 1970, 1971

	1967	1970	1971
Consumer price index[a]			
All items	100.0	116.3	121.3
Library materials index[b]			
U.S. hardcover books	100.0	120.2	134.6
Average price	$8.66	$10.41	$11.66
U.S. periodicals	100.0	132.9	151.0
Average price	$8.77	$11.66	$13.25
U.S. book title output[c]			
Output index	100.0	125.0	131.0
Number	28,762	36,071	37,692

[a]Statistical Abstract of the United States: 1972. U.S. Bureau of the Census, 1972, Washington, D.C., p. 348.

[b]The Bowker Annual: 1972, R. R. Bowker, New York, 1972, pp. 183, 185.

[c]The Bowker Annual: 1972, p. 176.

the competing demands of other college activities. The essential nature of a library's information services in an academic community must be recognized in assigning it a high priority in the budget allocation process. Funding sources must include federal aid because of libraries' importance for the nation's educational and research activity, and relatively modest need in comparison with other claimants upon government resources. Demonstrating this "essential nature" to academic administrators, governments, and foundations depends on the development and employment of adequate methods of evaluating the effectiveness of library services.

Fetterman directs us to "face the problem" — library costs and publication rates versus self-sufficiency. The answers are complex. There is a wide range of functions, sizes, sources of financing and operational environments for libraries and their interfacing information production and demand activities. The National Academy of Sciences Report acknowledges:

Acceptable costs in one situation are not tolerable in another. Nor does the appropriate operating mode for a small library provide the same unit cost and functional performance as for a huge library. Similarly, the method appropriate for serving a graduate student doing original research is not necessarily the same as quick-response support for a business executive [1, p. 16].

Or the instructional support needed for an undergraduate.

The demands of the curriculum for on-campus resources challenge the theory of resource sharing in the academic arena. A college curriculum is the domain of the faculty and their disciplines, and the faculty expect the library to provide the supporting books and journals on its shelves. Fetterman touches the problem briefly (page 21) when he states, "Thousands of dollars are being myopically committed because College A, located very close to College B, does not know that the one is developing a curriculum in the same expensive support area as the other." The catch here is to define, then to control "unnecessary duplication" in curricular offerings — a problem of considerable complexity, and one beyond the reach of the libraries. Enlisting the support of the academic community requires administrative leadership as well as some proof of resource sharing's benefits.

Pennsylvania's libraries — academic, public, school, and special — are already engaged in the resource sharing activities described by K. Leon Montgomery's paper in Chapter 15. Union catalogs, union lists, and delivery systems are operating successfully in various parts of the state, acquisitions agreements are beginning to emerge in some cooperative units, and CRT terminals to the Ohio College Library Center system are in use in a number of Pittsburgh and Philadelphia area libraries (although current costs of the OCLC system restrict its affordability). The problems faced by Pennsylvania's libraries are common to all libraries searching for the means to meet the information requirements of today's society. To practice the ideology of resource sharing, librarians must discover how to achieve reasonable standards, remain fiscally solvent, avoid unnecessary redundancy, maintain intellectual and other kinds of freedoms, provide for utility and convenience to the user, for rational diversity, for flexibility, for sound design — and at the same time avoid the creation of a monster.

REFERENCES

1. Libraries and Information Technology — A National System Challenge,
    The Information Systems Panel, Computer Science and Engineering
    Board or the National Academy of Sciences, Washington, D.C., 1972.
2. Library Statistics of Colleges and Universities — Analytic Report, Fall,
    1969, U.S. Office of Education, Washington, D.C., 1971, p. 4.

3. "Standards for College Libraries," in College and Research Libraries, July 1959, p. 275.
4. William J. Baumol, et. al., "The Costs of Library and Information Services," Libraries at Large, R. R. Bowker, New York, 1969, pp. 168, 195.
5. William S. Dix, "Reflections in Adversity; or, How Do You Cut a Library Budget?" in Library Lectures, Louisiana State University, Baton Rouge, 1972, p. 10.

Chapter 3

A RESPONSE TO PLA

John Fetterman

Assistant Director
Office of Communication Programs
University of Pittsburgh

This is a response to the critique of my paper in Chapter 2 prepared by Patricia Ann Sacks of the Cedar Crest College Library.

Mrs. Sacks writes (page 36) that "the core of Fetterman's assessment of the need to share resources is his analysis of the increasing number of dollars spent by libraries during the 1960's." In my own thinking, and I hope, in the writing in question, the core of the argument for resource sharing is much larger than the number of dollars spent by libraries during the 1960s. The rationale for resource sharing is also based on such factors as: amount of material available and needed, and the ability of information systems such as libraries to provide users with effective access to this material. I think that these factors of size and service are distinct, but not separate, from the factor of dollars spent.

Again, Mrs. Sacks reviews the "economic thesis" of my paper "with specific reference to statistics of Pennsylvania's academic libraries." The statistics used in the paper on the pages in question were aggregate figures for the United States. The logical transition from a general statement, like aggregate figures, to a particular instance, like Pennsylvania's library expenditures, is not always a valid transition in itself. However, in this case I do think that state of affairs which the aggregate figures reflect also exists in the Commonwealth of Pennsylvania.

Mrs. Sacks provides financial statistics (in Table 3) for Pennsylvania colleges and universities. Mrs. Sacks thereupon comments (page 36) that "the meaningful relationship between library and other educational and general (E&G) expenditures is the comparison of library expenditures to the E&G whole, a relationship which Fetterman neglects." I did not comment on this relationship because the discussion had been developing along other lines. I had been talking about the growth of one part of educational budgets in relation to other parts within the educational budget, and not the relationship of any part to the whole.

Mrs. Sacks points out (page 38) that the 0.3% increase in "library operating expenditures as a percent of the total educational and general expenditures is "meaningful" and I totally agree. Mrs. Sacks adds that this figure falls well below 5.0% minimum figure recommended by the Association of Colleges and Research Libraries' ALA Standards. I acknowledge that recommendation as being extremely important, but my argument had not been dealing with such a percentage relationship.

In effect, I think that Mrs. Sacks' observations about the relationship of the part to the whole greatly enhances my argument. The percentage relationships in the list of expenditures for Pennsylvania colleges and universities show that library expenditures in Pennsylvania have increased at a faster rate than other items in the budget. In fact, library expenditures have increased at a greater rate within the total budget than the total budget itself increased over previous years. By utilizing Mrs. Sacks' comments it is clear that even though library expenditures have increased at such a rate they nonetheless amount to only 0.3% of the total expenditures for educational and general purposes. I think that the statistical commentary provided by Mrs. Sacks adds greatly to the total argument in favor of resource sharing in libraries.

Chapter 4

REACTIONS AT THE PRESIDENTIAL LEVEL

(A summary of remarks made by: Dr. Henry J.
McAnulty, President, Duquesne University, Dr.
Edward R. Schatz, Provost, Carnegie-Mellon
University; Sister Jane Scully, President,
Carlow College; moderated by Dr. Rhoten A.
Smith, Provost, University of Pittsburgh)

Sr. J. Scully

Some of the problems libraries have to deal with now have little to do
with the information explosion or budgets, but rather with changes in the
attitudes of students. There seems to be a lessening of interest in the
humanities and a greater desire for career-related programs and information.
Students learn and faculty teach in ways which do not involve books, but
rather films and tapes, etc. Many of the students are older people who
come for evening classes or on a part-time basis and do not have the time
to give to intense library use.

It is not at all clear that faculty and librarians understand the learning
patterns of contemporary students. Better understanding and better collection development would surely be the result of more effective communication
within a college and among colleges. This inter- and intra-institutional
cooperation will be most effective if it is voluntary. This kind of planning
activity would certainly be made a lot easier if some foundation money were
made available. Even a small amount of seed money at this point could
result in large savings in the long run.

Dr. E. Schatz

I have some difficulty in seeing the need for this conference because the answers to two of the questions, "why", and "when", seem obvious to me; and the "how" seems to be up to the librarians.

I think that the most pressing problem for Carnegie-Mellon University is to find a way to continue to offer the good service that it offers at a cost the institution can afford. CMU does have some special problems because of the professional and advanced nature of many of its offerings. Yet the 1973-1974 library budget for CMU is scheduled to be less in absolute dollars than in the preceding year. The criteria to be satisfied can be summed up by saying that the material must be available to users within a reasonable turnaround time and at a reasonable cost.

The greatest factors favoring resource sharing for CMU are that there are some realistic possibilities for doing so with our neighbors. It seems to me that the factors of geography, collection compatibility, and management willingness all indicate a green light condition. The greatest factor inhibiting resource sharing is people, not technology. These inhibiting people, however, are not primarily librarians or administrators, but users of the collections. Users are generally very spoiled by the good service and availability of material which they have experienced in the past. In resource sharing activities, user habits will have to change and resistance to this change will probably be the major inhibiting factor. Many users have become accustomed to much free service and excessive multiple copies of books and journals. This kind of operation is not longer affordable. If there is to be resource sharing, then users must become cost conscious and even be asked to choose between tradeoffs.

I believe that resource sharing is inevitable but only a short-run solution because it too will not be able to keep up with user demand and the rising cost of materials. There is no better way available to us at the present to move along in the natural development of libraries. The ultimate solution must have some control of both the generation of information and the use of it. Unless this whole-system concept is applied, consortia will shortly have the same problems which "self-sufficient" libraries have had. Some serious study should be given to the limitations of resource sharing so that we will know when we have exhausted its possibilities, and know what to do next.

Rev. H. J. McAnulty

Duquesne is no different from anybody else in its library budget problems. The percentage has decreased from 4.18% to 3.8% of total expenditures for libraries. Like many others, we are engaged in a unit-cost study of the whole campus and probably within a year we will have a much clearer idea of what our costs really are. The statistics which we now have are good enough to indicate the decrease in money available for the library at Duquesne and I am sorry about that decrease.

I have been convinced for a long time that libraries cannot be self-sufficient. It is particularly important for those who are geographically close to each other to share their ideas about program and collection development.

We have made mistakes in the past by now considering what kind of library support would be necessary for new academic programs. This kind of lack of communication with the librarians within a college and between colleges has caused a great many problems in collection development.

I think that resource sharing can help institutions in many ways. It can benefit them individually and help them collectively when

1. It does not destroy their own particular character by making them conform excessively to the group
2. It is demonstrated that sharing resources is better than sole owner-ship particularly from the users' point of view
3. A more effective individual institutional operational pattern emerges
4. Operational costs have been stabilized or even perhaps reduced
5. New services can be introduced or existing services expanded
6. It results in a program of identifying what is not locally available and providing users access to such material
7. It meets the standards of the various accrediting agencies
8. It is clearly understood that the motivation is not to salvage one library at the expense of another

It has been my experience that one of the primary concerns of the funding agencies now is to know what efforts colleges are making to share.

Chapter 5

RESOURCE SHARING AND ACCREDITATION

Robert Kirkwood
Executive Director
Federation of Regional Accrediting
Commissions of Higher Education

As neither a librarian nor a current institutional administrator, I am probably freer to say some things than those who serve in those positions. However, the fact that I visited more than 350 college and university libraries over the past several years does give me some insight into the nature of the problems we are discussing here. Let me begin by observing that I believe that the quality of the papers presented above is outstanding, and I hope that some means will be sought to assure that every librarian and every chairman of the library committee on every campus in the country will read them. These papers should also be required reading matter for administrators and faculty members as well.

However, I must also point out that there are two notable omissions from the papers. One is any discussion of the role of the faculty in shaping library policies and about their attitudes toward resource sharing. The other is the lack of any mention about the relation of accreditation to resource sharing. Let me address these two points.

First, I must say that in the many visits I have made to campuses, one of the most vivid impressions I retain is that libraries are the most under-utilized resource. Nevertheless, almost every faculty member wants a self-sufficient library on his or her campus. The unreasonableness of faculty expectations (and often demands) is probably all too familiar to most.

But it is one of the realities of the situation, and you will miss an opportunity if you fail to educate faculty about the importance of resource sharing and enlist their support. You will note that I make no mention of students in my remarks chiefly because they usually reflect the attitudes of their professors. Occasionally students have valuable insights to add to our thinking about libraries, but they cannot begin to match the professional expertise of their teachers.

Faculty members, and occasionally students, sit on library committees in many institutions, and more than one librarian has found himself a minority of one in trying to introduce broader approaches to library planning and development against the implacable opposition of faculty self-interest. Perhaps one of the greatest problems with regard to faculty is the fetish so many make of back issues. Journals, periodicals, newspapers —whatever the item, they want their library to have every issue since volume 1, no. 1. As a historian by professional training I know whereof I speak, for often historians are among the worst offenders. Somehow, we must do a better job of educating our faculties, all faculties, about the wastefulness of stockpiling low-use materials and the futility of even the most affluent libraries trying to achieve anything like complete collections of all the important journals and periodicals.

In my experience, most faculty members are not sufficiently knowledgeable about libraries generally. Indeed, I have been appalled at the actual ignorance of some faculty members about the potential value of the library's resources to their teaching endeavors, and it is painful to have to say that some faculty members never cross the threshold of a library at all. These are exceptional cases, and by and large most faculty members take an active interest in their institutional libraries. So, unless we communicate the urgency of the message about resource sharing to our faculty colleagues, we will miss the opportunity to have vital allies in this essential undertaking.

Now let me turn to the subject of accreditation, which is of course my primary interest. Here we deal with some unfortunate myths. For years the ALA standards which specify that two-year colleges must have 20,000 volumes and four-year colleges 50,000 or more depending on enrollment, have been taken as gospel. The regional accrediting commissions do not specify numbers for libraries. However, many of the librarians who serve on evaluation teams have quoted the ALA standards, thus in effect making it appear that accreditation in fact depended on book count. This is simply not true. Not long ago Beverly Lynch and I had a chance to discuss plans for some regional workshops to review the current revisions being made in the ALA standards. I hope the regional accrediting commissions will be able to cooperate in some of these activities with the ALA. The number of books, while not entirely irrelevant, is far less important than the quality of the holdings and their direct relation to the academic programs. Moreover, in a day when audio and visual materials are so abundant, to define a library only in terms of numbers of books is like talking about automobiles as if they were all still Model T's.

There are also some who still seem to believe that unless a library has significant strength in its back collections the institution will not be accredited. Again, that is a myth which I hope participants at this conference will help to kill. Access to back collections by all means, but not every campus needs or should have long shelves of journals and periodicals whose only function is to collect dust and take up space.

In his list of objections to resource sharing, John Fetterman omitted the concern that many institutions have about jeopardizing their accreditation if they enter into cooperative arrangements. Either this reflects a misunderstanding about the nature of accreditation, or a misuse of it. Too often, when an institution wants to preserve the status quo, it uses accreditation as an excuse to camouflage its timidity. There is no danger to an institution's accreditation when it participates in a soundly conceived sharing program.

The major measure of a good academic library is the use it gets. Where a library is truly integrated into the teaching and learning activities on any campus, there will be little need to worry about accreditation. The concern of accreditation is excellence, and, rather than being an end in itself, accreditation is a means to the end of strengthening and improving the quality of education. When resource sharing can amplify the range and dimensions of learning materials available, what could be more consistent with the purposes of accreditation.

I am fully aware of the complexities of the problems involved in the subject under discussion at this meeting, but as one who tries to view the issues of higher education in the broadest possible perspective, it strikes me that resource sharing is an idea whose time has come. With imagination, initiative, and industry I believe the problems can be resolved. You can count on the positive support of the regional accrediting commissions in this important endeavor.

Part Two

THE MECHANICS

Chapters 6-10 explore the "how" of resource sharing. The assumption
has been that the obstacles to cooperation are not inherent in procedures or
technology, but in people. Nevertheless, the mechanics must be understood
before the "people" problems may be confronted.

Chapter 6

LIBRARY RESOURCE SHARING — HOW?
BASIC LIBRARY PROCEDURES

John P. Immroth

Graduate School of Library and Information Sciences
University of Pittsburgh

Within the framework of basic library operations we propose to discuss how a resource sharing consortium of academic libraries can be most effective. Theoretically, the development of a consortium with a central headquarters is advocated here. Resource sharing has been analyzed from four library operations — acquisitions, cataloging and processing, storage libraries, and the delivery of services. At the end of each section below a sequence of goals is stated. If these goals are taken separately they may be part of a cooperative resource sharing consortium; however, if these goals, as well as possible additional ones not mentioned, are developed concurrently a centralized resource sharing consortium could result. These goals are

1. Statement of the mission and objectives of the consortium
2. A common materials selection program
3. A specific statement of the optimum consortium collection
4. A union catalog of all materials
5. A union desiderata list
6. A common request and order form for all libraries in the system
7. A central order office (which could be a part of a centralized processing unit — see item 20)

8. A union on-order/in-process file
9. A consortium approval plan
10. Cooperative circulation of want lists of out-of-print material
11. Cooperative ordering of photographic or microform copies of material
12. A consortium exchange program
13. Use of the ISBD for all consortium cataloging
14. Consortium participation in or development of a MARC-based centralized cataloging center (which could be a part of item 20)
15. A centralized original cataloging unit (which could be a part of item 20)
16. Use of LC subject headings by all member libraries
17. Consistent use centrally of classification systems — possible use of only LC classification (another part of item 20)
18. A centralized original subject cataloging unit (including classification and subject headings) (another part of item 20)
19. A union shelf list
20. A centralized processing unit (possibly containing items 7, 14, 15, 17 and 18)
21. A consortium storage library
22. A union catalog of the storage library
23. A consortium agreement on the use priorities of stored material
24. A possible consortium exchange agreement for stored material
25. A clearly stated policy on the amount of time to retrieve material from storage
26. A consortium interlibrary loan system
27. A possible consortium SDI system
28. A consortium teletype network
29. A common circulation system
30. A consortium delivery system
31. A common library card (or reciprocal borrowing privileges)

A final and central concern is the difficulty of establishing within each institution, among faculty and students especially, an understanding of the dimensions of the fiscal crisis and the implications of steps to deal with it, both immediately and in the long term. The habits of students and faculty and their expectations for resources and services within their own institutions will have to be modified if constraints on collection growth are to be effectual in some libraries, if access to selected resources is to be extended to individuals from other institutions, and if special aspects of "custom-made" records and services are going to be sacrificed in favor of mass produced and, hence uniform products.

...no library, whether it be one sharply focused on limited institutional needs or one containing wide ranging research collections,

is self sufficient. The process of instruction has no distinct boundaries limiting absolutely the resources required, nor does research
preclude a need for certain basic and fundamental materials.

The foregoing statement was made by the Regents Advisory Council to
the New York State Board of Regents in 1972.

INTRODUCTION

Our purpose here is to examine simply and theoretically the basic
library operations: acquisitions, processing, storage, and delivery of
services. First, these operations will be examined in regard to their
execution within an individual or separate library; second, they will be
considered in regard to any differences in their execution that might occur
in resource sharing or library cooperation. For our purposes the phrase
"resource sharing" will be treated as a specific euphemism for "library
cooperation." Within the literature of this subject the words "cooperation,"
"centralization," "consortium," "network," and "resource sharing" are not
consistently or precisely employed. A group of libraries working together
in a cooperative manner may be called a consortium, a library network or
resource sharing system [1]. We will use these three terms interchangeably.
However, a clear distinction must be drawn between "cooperation" and
"centralization." A cooperative system or network can exist without central
headquarters. It may, in fact, be decentralized. A centralized system or
network implies the existence of central headquarters. Herman M. Weisman
cites the advantages of the two approaches: "Centralization offers the
advantages of greater efficiency, economy, and availability of full resources
of the system to many and every component of users. The advantages of
decentralization are quicker, direct, and personalized services." [2]. Further
discussions of the types of networks or system may be found in Ruth J.
Patrick's Guidelines for Library Cooperation [3]. Bibliographic sources on
library cooperation may be found in Refs. 4, 5, and 6.

We further propose to demonstrate that the technical processes for
resource sharing do exist and have in fact existed for some time. The basic
problem is willingness of libraries and their parent institutions to cooperate
even if local independence is weakened or lost. Can libraries and their
parent institutions continue to be independent and self-sufficient and not
rely on other libraries and instutitions in the locality or region? Can the
spirit of cooperation be coexistent with the stated mission and goals of the
parent institution? Must one's own community of users be served first and

best? Can libraries and their parent institutions afford the increasing costs of redundancy? What services can libraries afford to make available to noninstutional users? What is the priority or priorities of service among administration, faculty, graduate students, undergraduate students, non-institutional users? These are questions that must be asked, considered, and answered before a successful system of resource sharing can exist.

An all-important, overriding question is just how far are we willing to go to develop a resource sharing consortium. When the mission and objectives of such a consortium are written and accepted by its members, will these determine if the consortium is to be more important than any single member or will it be equal to a member library or will it be less important than any single member? Further, it must be asked if cooperation can succeed without centralization of some activities. For our purposes here it will be assumed that, at least theoretically, cooperation is one aspect of and may lead to centralization and/or federation — or even incorporation.

Another view of this problem may be found in Ritvars Bregzis' paper on library networks in the future.

> One of the reasons for reluctant engagement in network develop-
> ment should be concentrated in one or a few institutions. While such
> reasoning is perhaps true with respect to some overall aspects of
> the network development, it does not apply to the vast amount of
> procedural aspects that will always remain the prerogative and the
> responsibility of the individual institution. This largely applies also
> to the concept of sharing computer programmes, a concept frequently
> quoted but seldom materialized.
> The expanding information media, the mounting cost of acquisition
> of these materials, the magnitude of the acquisition and controlling
> effort associated with these materials and the progressively more
> universal orientation of information service force upon us the concept
> of network, and we have to be prepared to deal with it and to accept
> the challenge of closing the information circuit. [7]

A more concise statement may be the following single sentence from a paper written by Samuel Lazerow, chairman of the National Libraries Task Force on Automation at the Library of Congress, "The excellence of American Libraries over the years has rested in a large measure upon the extent to which cooperative enterprises have been successfully undertaken" [8]. One of Kilgour's justifications for the Ohio College Library Center seems to be particularly pertinent to the development of an academic Library consortium in Pennsylvania:

Early formulation of the problem that the Ohio College Library Center is to solve had occurred in a general way before the Center became a corporate entity. Put succinctly, the problem to be solved was one of increasing resources to Ohio colleges and universities. From the college administrative point of view, the problem was that of hiring new faculty and enrolling new students in the future. Presidents of Ohio academic institutions were particularly aware that new Ph. D. 's are research-oriented. If these younger men are not offered an opportunity to pursue research programs, they are reluctant to join a faculty. Moreover, changing educational objectives in colleges are requiring that undergraduates have an increasing opportunity to learn how to learn. Such opportunities can best be given to a student by providing him with resources for independent work. [9]

Although libraries handle a wide variety of types of materials of both a print and nonprint nature, this paper will deal specifically with examples of general print material with only occasional examples and uses of various special materials. Specifically monographic material (as librarians often call books) will be used in this paper as examples. A monograph may be defined as a work collection or other writing dealing with a particular subject or subjects. A monograph is usually self contained and not dependent upon other publications. Serial materials will also be considered as a primary type of general library materials. Serials are defined as publications issued in successive installments at regular or irregular intervals and intended to continue indefinately. Periodicals are one common type of serials. A work may be considered to be a periodical if it is not cataloged and classified and if it is simply arranged alphabetically with other periodicals or magazines. Nonperiodical serials are cataloged and classified and shelved with the monographic collection. Pamphlets are a special type of library material which is not cataloged or classified but rather filed alphabetically by subject.

There are many other types of materials which may be called special materials either because of their physical form (nonprint) or because of their special print nature (documents, manuscripts, maps, music, etc.). Nonprint materials include phonograph records, motion picture films, film strips, microforms, pictures, photographs, slides and all forms of machine readable data and records. An administrative decision within each library must be made in regard to cataloging and/or classifying each of these special materials. Very often libraries will catalog special materials but not classify them. As most special materials cannot be physically shelved with the corresponding book materials, a book classification system may not be applied to them. How a library handles these special materials is most important in relation to developing any resource sharing or library cooperation among a group of libraries. This is a particularly important point as this type of material is very often handled differently by different libraries.

Print materials include rare books, government documents, archival material, manuscripts, globes, maps, atlases, and music. These special materials are often processed in a different fashion from the general print material. The cataloging may be more extensive as in the case of rare books, or less extensive as in the case of government documents. Government documents collections often rely on published indexes to provide the basic cataloging. Both of these examples may use special classification approaches.

ACQUISITIONS

This unit will deal with the selection of materials, acquisition processes such as searching and ordering, and receipt and record keeping. The writer fully realizes that many specific functions will be defined in this section and the following sections and that although many of the readers of the paper are already quite aware of these functions their definitions and distinctions are included to provide the nonlibrary participants at the conference the basic information that they will need in order to contemplate the problems of resource sharing. The writer also fully realizes that this section and the following sections will have to generalize many of the basic library functions and not go into specifics or many specific examples. For the sake of this section acquisitions may be defined as all those processes involved in deciding, ordering, and receiving materials into a library's collection.

Selection involves the maintenance and development of the materials selection program, the handling of specific requests for material not in the collection, and the criteria for the decision to acquire such material. In addition the processes of searching the library catalog to determine whether or not the requested material is already in the collection and verification of the existence bibliographically of requested material are processes related to selection.

Materials Selection Program

A materials selection program consists of the following functions and may be considered as an organic substitute for a book selection policy. The first basic function of such a program is an analysis of the community to be served by the library. The mission and objectives of a parent institution must be used to determine the initial limits of the library. The user groups to be serviced by the library must be identified. Further, the priorities of the user groups and services to them must be established.

The influences of the budget, the curriculum, and past practices must be
taken into account and the nature of the service to be rendered by the collection must be clearly stated. This would also have a major effect on any
library involved in a resource sharing system. Resource sharing immediately expands the potential user group of an individual library and may
expand the nature of service to be rendered and certainly priorities for the
user groups must be taken into consideration.

At this point we must face the basic question of any possible consortium
or resource sharing system or network. Simplistically speaking is the
local library with its community of users to be given greater, equal or
lesser priority than the total community of users of the consortium? Further,
can the missions and objectives of the individual parent institutions be made
to articulate with the mission and objectives of the entire consortium? Every
effort should be made to allow the statement of mission and objectives of
the consortium to be in harmony with the missions and objectives of the
individual parent institutions. For example, cooperative use of library
resources may be compared with, but hopefully not equalled to, existing
cross registration systems of academic institutions. In all events, for a
cooperative materials selection program to be considered, the consortium
must have a clear statement of its mission and objectives. Further, the
totality of the user population must be identified and priorities among users
must be established.

The ideal priority may be to have all potential users on an equal basis,
but, realistic considerations, including budgetary commitments, may force
local priorities to have precedence.

Sarah Katherine Thompson in the preface to the <u>Interlibrary Loan</u>
<u>Procedure Manual</u> discusses possible priorities of interlibrary loan service
which may be applicable to an entire consortium operation:

> Every library has the right to specify conditions of loan and to
> decline to lend specific materials. Each lending library has an
> obligation to establish priorities of user demands upon its collections.
> In general, these priorities are:
> 1. Public library: a) its community; b) other libraries in its
>   system; c) other libraries in the same state; d) out of state
>   libraries.
> 2. College library: a) its faculty, students, research, staff;
>   b) local community, other libraries in its system; c) other
>   academic libraries; d) libraries in general.
> 3. University library: a) its faculty, students, research, staff;
>   b) other libraries in its system, academic and research personnel
>   in its area; c) other academic libraries; d) other libraries.
> 4. Special library: a) personnel of its organization; b) affiliated

organizations; c) other special libraries and university libraries
from which it borrows; d) other libraries. [10]

    The next phase of any materials selection program includes the influence
of the analysis of the community on the statement of the nature of the services, that is to say, the service policy. This must be considered in relation
to the optimum collection of materials. This ideal collection of materials
should be specified. First, subject areas of the collection must be indicated.
The type of material in each area should be determined; the quality and
quantity of material in each subject area should be given careful consideration. Second, the priorities of the service policy and the environmental
characteristics must be used as collection building criteria. Third, any
special collections should be designated and justified in a resource sharing
system. For instance, if one library assumes the responsibility for
building a particular subject area not only for its own users but for the
entire system, this must be taken into account. The fourth significant
point in a material selection program is the analysis of the existing collections in relation to the optimum or desired collection and the collection
specifications. This analysis will determine the current selection needs.
It must be remembered that such a materials selection program is a continuous one, recognizing and adapting to any changes in the priorities of
the library or the parent institution or the resource sharing consortium.

    The optimum collection of materials for a consortium should be
specified. At least the existing areas of specilization must be indicated.
Just as with the individual library, the subject areas should be indicated
first. For instance individual members can agree to concentrate for the
entire consortium on specific subject areas or the publications of specific
countries such as the Farmington Plan did. Patrick points out in relation
to fields of special responsibility:

        If this activity is selected by a consortium, the decision to be
    made is "What areas should each college or university specialize in?"
    One difficulty that arises is that this decision involves the faculty and
    presidents of the institutions, and affects - and is affected by - the
    curriculum of the institutions. An academic library cannot extensively
    delimit its collection, unless the college or university delimits its
    teaching program. A professor of African history and literature may
    be displeased to learn that the library will not collect beyond the
    minimal level in this subject area; however, his displeasure may be
    alleviated if he knows that another consortium member has been able
    to develop a comprehensive collection in African history and liter-
    ature, to which he has not only bibliographical access as the result
    of consortium exchange of bibliographies, but also physical access,
    in that a truck delivery system will bring him the book he requests
    within 24 hours. [3, p. 173]

J. Periam Danton develops this concept further and issues a basic
warning to academic research libraries:

> First, a library certainly need not buy the most specialized
> research materials if its clientele has ready access to them at
> another library in the locality; every library should, where possible,
> seek cooperative agreements of this kind which will increase its
> purchasing power, reduce the competition for scarce material, and
> further scholarship. Second, no library should expect another to
> bear the burden of its needs except for the rare, the unusual, and the
> relatively little used. A few university libraries, on both sides of the
> Atlantic, readily admit that they do not have, on the average, 40-80
> percent of the titles required for a dissertation. The justification
> for these universities offering work for the doctor's degree seems
> dubious. And third, the extent to which a library can afford not to
> acquire specialized research materials in fields of concern to its
> scholars, varies indirectly as the distance to a library which has
> those materials. No reasonable man will object to having to spend
> two hours in travel, or waiting a day or two (Princeton to Philadelphia
> or New York, Mainz to Frankfurt, Ann Arbor to Detroit, Stanford
> to Berkeley, Bonn to Cologne) once or twice a year. He will object
> mightily if he is asked to do so once or twice a week, and rightly so.
> And the greater and oftener his expenditure of time or the delay, the
> greater his objection. And rightly so. If his university cannot, most
> of the time, provide the materials which will enable him effectively
> to do his work as a scholar, it has no business pretending to be a
> research institution in the field. [11]

The existing materials selection policies of the individual libraries
should be collected and carefully analyzed and coordinated if possible.
Further, the existing collections must be evaluated in relation to the
proposed optimum consortium collection as well as the previously determined
collection specifications. In order to do this evaluation most effectively the
consortium may need to generate a union catalog of all the member libraries
in the consortium. Further, the results of this evaluation and analysis
should generate a union list of desired materials. As the suggestion for a
union catalog will recur in each of the following sections, it is appropriate
to discuss the meaning and potentials of a union catalog for a consortium.

A Union Catalog. Silvere Willemin defines a union catalog in his
Technique of Union Catalogues: A Practical Guide: "A union catalogue is
an inventory common to several libraries and containing all or some of their
publications listed in one or more orders of arrangement" [12]. He further
cites the following bibliographical functions for a union catalog.

The main function of the union catalogue is unquestionably to locate publications in order to facilitate access to books. It is a tool for the rationalization of interlibrary loans.

The second function derives from the foregoing and is to transform the union catalogue into the nucleus of a bibliographical research centre by reason of the identification work required for the sound operation of both inter-library and international loans.

Thirdly, the bibliographical centre which is essential to the sound operation of the union catalogue tends ultimately to become also a bibliographical information service carrying out a variety of tasks. [12]

Ruth Patrick in her Guidelines for Library Cooperation discerns five different types of union catalogs and lists: 1) complete union catalogs; 2) selective union catalogs and lists; 3) exchange of acquisition lists, catalog cards, or bibliographies; 4) lists of collection resources of the member libraries; 5) union list of serials [3, pp. 161-171]. A complete union catalog would contain all the monographic holdings of the member libraries. Patrick points out:

To produce a union catalog of the retrospective holdings of several large libraries would be an expensive undertaking. The advisable strategy on this activity seems to be to wait until the Library of Congress or the larger academic libraries have converted their retrospective holdings into machine-readable form, and to use their records instead of keyboarding the same bibliographic data in each individual library. [3, pp. 165-66]

Selective union catalogs and lists may be limited to special subject areas or collections of importance or may be limited to current material that has been processed centrally for the consortium. The possible exchanges of acquisition lists, catalog cards and bibliographies represent another form of a selective union catalog or list. The benefits and the cost of maintentance or exchanging the acquisition lists and catalog cards are open to serious question. The exchange of microfilm copies of individual library catalogs could be far more valuable. The exchange of locally produced bibliographies can have more potential merit. Patrick states:

Members of several consortia reported they felt it was useful to exchange bibliographies compiled by member libraries. A bibliography on a topic of current interest, such as ecology, may be of use to librarians as a selection tool, as well as to users seeking material on the topic. But in order to be of assistance to the users, bibliographic

access would ideally have to be accompanied by physical access to
the materials, such as could be made available through reciprocal
borrowing previleges or expanded interlibrary loan. [3. pp. 167-168]

Lists of collection resources of the member libraries may be seen as
another mechanism related to union catalogs and lists. Patrick defines this:

> as a partial substitute for a complete union catalog or list. One
> benefit of this activity is that it can facilitate interlibrary loans:
> instead of indicating a specific book that a library owns, it indicates
> the subject areas in which the libraries are strong. For example,
> if a library has a strong collection on the subject of education, other
> members will know, if they receive an interlibrary loan request for
> a book in this subject area, that there is a good chance of locating it
> at this particular library. [3, p. 168]

She continues:

> Another value of this activity is that a list of this kind does not take
> as long to produce as a union catalog, and this is a comparatively
> quick way of learning what is in the collections of the consortium
> libraries. Librarians reported that they learn of collection strengths
> in other member libraries of which they had been unaware previously.
> In one consortium that consisted of small college libraries only,
> librarians reported that they now consulted each other for inter-
> library loan requests, whereas before they had always consulted
> larger library on the assumption that the small libraries would not
> have the requested book. Although consortium activities have not
> made these libraries entirely self-sufficient, their interaction with
> consortium members has, to a certain degree, lessened their depen-
> dency on larger libraries. [3, p. 168]

A fifth type of union catalog is the union list of serials. This is one of the
most common developments for a resource sharing system. Patrick
discusses this in the following:

> The union list of serials can consist of serials or periodicals of
> all subject fields, or it can be limited to special subjects or to
> newspapers. It can be used for interlibrary loan by providing users
> with information about the resources of the consortium libraries. It
> can also guide librarians to plan more complete coverage of serials

and to help avoid unnecessary acquisition of low-use items already
owned by consortium members. Once a consortium has a union list
of serials, it can identify the strengths and weaknesses in the
members' collections. In this regard it may even be possible to
combine the partial holdings of several members for one serial in
order to get a complete run of that serial. [3, p. 169-70]

Furthermore, Patrick points out a basic advantage of developing some form
of union catalog.

Large libraries sometimes complain about smaller libraries over-
using their resources. One explanation may be that it is mainly the
large libraries that are listed in the national union lists. Once smaller
libraries have union lists of their own resources, they can be less of
a burden on the large libraries. Librarians of several smaller
libraries in our sample stated that once they learned of the library
holdings of other consortia members of about the same size, they
consulted them more often than before the union list had been
compiled. [3, p. 160]

As has been previously stated, a consortium should consider the potential uses of any existing union catalog before planning to develop their own
union catalogs. The major union catalogs in the United States include the
following in approximate order of size holdings: the National Union Catalog
at the Library of Congress; the Bibliographical Center for Research, Rocky
Mountain Region, Inc. at Denver; The Pacific Northwest Bibliographic Center
at the University of Washington; the Union Library Catalogue of Pennsylvania
in Philadelphia; the Cleveland Regional Union Catalog in the Case Western
Reserve University; the Union Catalog of the State Library of Ohio in
Columbus; the Nebraska Union Catalog in Lincoln; the Union Catalog at the
California State Library in Sacramento; the Union Catalog of the Atlanta-
Athens area in Atlanta; the North Carolina Interlibrary Center at the
University of North Carolina; the Vermont Free Public Library Service
at Montpelier; the Union List of New Hampshire Libraries in Concord;
and the Union Catalogue of Books in Nashville Libraries. Obviously in
Pennsylvania any consortium proposal must carefully consider the potentials
of the Union Library Catalogue of Pennsylvania.

Request

Normally, individual materials to be selected result from a request
for such material. Such a request for an individual monograph or serial
may be made by a faculty member, a student, a librarian, or other user of

a library. Basic bibliographic information concerning the requested material
should be received at this time; such information normally includes the title
of the material, the author if one exists, the publisher, the place of publication, the date of publication, and the sources of the material; that is to say
how the requester came upon this particular item. Libraries forming a
resource sharing system would also need to determine whether or not
requests could be accepted from other member libraries and from other users
from other member libraries. This, of course, can lead to the use of a
common request form for all libraries in the system. A common request
form is simply one example of the many forms of standardization which may
be necessary for a consortium to operate effectively. The standardization
of cataloging will be discussed in the next main section. The following
quotation from Leonard, Maier, and Dougherty is generally applicable to
any form of centralization within a consortium.

> Standardization of many of the participants' processing routine is
> a significant element in the design and successful implementation of
> centralized book processing. Exception procedures resulting from
> lists of local modifications may well render a center ineffective and
> uneconomical. Establishment of a set of well defined, workable
> specifications is the only realistic approach to the organization and
> operation of a processing center. [13]

Selection Decision

The next step in the process is a selection decision. The library
must decide if the requested material should fit into the collection according
to the material selection program and if the library can presently afford to
purchase the material. If the library wishes to purchase the material but
cannot at that time, the request may be filed for later consideration. If
the library can afford the material and wishes to purchase it, the next step
is searching. In a resource sharing system, libraries may wish to consider
whether or not other member libraries have the material available rather
than purchasing it themselves.

Searching

Searching is, simply, checking to see if the library already has a copy
of the requested book in its collection or if a copy of the requested book is
already on order from a publisher or dealer. Further, the library may wish
in a resource sharing system to determine if other member libraries have
acquired or are buying the requested material. Again we may see the
potential use of a union catalog for the consortium. If a copy of a requested

title is already held by a member library, the immediate request may be
fulfilled more quickly than by ordering and processing a copy for the individual library. This will also allow the requesting library to examine and
evaluate the further potential uses of requested material by examining the
copy in hand.

Verification

Verification is the next step in the process. Verification means checking
in some standard bibliographic source to see if the book or other requested
material really exists and if the information about the material is correct.
Is the author's name in correct form? Is the title correct? Who is the
publisher? When was the book published? How much does the book cost?
If there are any changes in the information about the book in this step the
request must be searched again. Again a union catalog would be helpful in
the verification process.

Acquisitions Processing

Acquisitions processing involves an analysis of the type of material to
be ordered or otherwise acquired. Material may be "in-print" or "out-of-
print" or may be available by exchange agreement or may be given to the
library as a gift. If material is currently available from a publisher it is
called "in-print" material. Such material may be ordered in the following
fashion.

Ordering

Each copy of a piece of material may be ordered separately. This is
often called "title-by-title" ordering. The individual titles may be ordered
direct from the individual publisher or other direct sources. In order to
avoid separate billing libraries may place a group or batch of orders through
a dealer or jobber who buys in bulk from many publishers. Such jobbers
may be national, regional, or local. There are in most cases two types of
local jobbers, commercial and institutional. Many academic libraries order
some or all of their material through the local campus book store. In a
potential resource sharing system libraries could go into bulk or batch
ordering by mutual agreement as such ordering might reduce the cost of
material.

A centralized order office for the consortium would facilitate this step.
This could also lead to a centralized order record file. The other uses of

such a file may be seen in the following discussions.

Even if a centralized order office is not initially established, consortium members can develop a system of prepurchase checking. Patrick discusses some possibilities in this.

> This activity consists of informing the other consortium members of purchases that exceed a certain amount of money, such as single titles costing $50 or more and multivolume sets costing $100 or more. The objective is to avoid unnecessary duplication. One consortium devised a special "intent-to-purchase" form for this activity. One problem several librarians encountered with this activity is that although the principle appeared sound, they sometimes forgot to initiate their own forms or to systematically take note of those they receive from other member institutions. [3, p. 177]

Materials may be ordered automatically if some form of standing order is used. The most common form of standing order is subscription to serial publications. Once such an order has been placed the order continues until it is cancelled. Such orders may be placed either with publishers directly or through serials jobbers. Further blanket order plans may be placed with some publishers for all of their publications or for all of their publications in a specific series. A blanket order plan provides an approach to monographic acquisitions that is similar to serial subscriptions. A third type of standing order plan is the approval plan. In an approval plan the profile of an individual library is analyzed and material within that profile is automatically sent to the library "on approval." As most approval plans require that libraries pay return costs, libraries try to select carefully their designated profile with the operator of an approval plan. The profile must carefully consider the collections specifications of the individual library. As a result there could be serious difficulties to be considered in applying a resource sharing concept directly to approval plans. Approval plans are available from publishers, jobbers, and dealers. There are approval plans for special subject areas as well as specific foreign material.

It is, of course possible to have an approval plan profile developed for the entire consortium. Such a plan would naturally evolve from the previously mentioned material selection program for the consortium. There could be central or regional locations for the display of approval material for all members of the consortium. Further, both the individual libraries and the consortium could possibly maintain separate approval plan systems for carefully specified areas and/or categories of material.

When material is no longer currently available from a publisher, it is called "out-of-print." Such material may be acquired in the following ways:

The most common sources for "out-of-print" material are dealers in used
or rare books. Although libraries in a resource sharing system may be in
competition for the same material, there could be cooperative circulation of
want lists to selected dealers as well as cooperative advertising in journals
dealing with book collecting. A second possible approach to this type of
material is having a photographic copy made. Often such a copy is done on
microfilm or some other microform. There could, of course, be cost
savings in this approach by the production of multiple copies for a resource
sharing network. In addition, if a book is in great demand it may be reprint-
ed by a publisher specializing in limited reprint editions. Often such an
edition is far more expensive than the original edition or the microform
edition. Finally, some libraries have acquired many "out-of-print" and
desired titles by purchasing an entire collection either from a dealer or
collector. Such purchases usually cover a specific subject and may cause
duplication with the current collection.

Exchanges and Gifts

Material may be acquired by trading or exchanging other material with
another institution or by receiving gifts. If an institution produces locally
a scholarly serial or series, such may be exchanged with other institutions.
In addition, many libraries offer unwanted duplicates for exchange. This
may be done by circulating lists of titles available for exchange or by
maintaining duplicate shelves. Such an approach means that one library may
choose the unwanted duplicates of another library. This would be a particularly appropriate relationship for a group of libraries in a resource sharing
system. Such relations cause exchange agreements to be developed.
Exchange agreements may be established on an item by item exchange, i.e.,
a one for one approach, or on a priced exchange in which service charges
for exchange privileges are developed. A third type of agreement is an open
exchange, i.e., one copy of everything published is exchanged [see Ref. 14].
Gifts provide another method of acquiring material in a library. Some
libraries may be the official depository library for a governmental or
professional type of material. This is often true of government documents
collections. Gifts may be solicited from local groups and local individuals.
If a local individual has an extensive private collection, he may give it to a
local library after he no longer needs or uses it. Local authors may be
encouraged to deposit their manuscripts. Further, many libraries annually
receive unsolicited gifts of varying value.

Centrally, a consortium could maintain exchange programs both with the
individual member libraries and with other libraries. In possible conjunction
with a central storage library for the consortium, there could be a common
housing for unwanted duplicates and other material from member libraries.
The consortium could then operate in a fashion similar to the United States
Book Exchange.

The United States Book Exchange (USBE), the successor to the American Book Center for Water-devastated Libraries, was established in 1948 and serves as a clearinghouse among libraries for duplicate materials. Duplicates received from its members are credited to their accounts; the member libraries may select items wanted from lists or directly from the USBE stock, paying a service charge for each piece selected. [14, p. 287]

Quite possibly the consortium book exchange could develop programs with the United States Book Exchange program as well as the existing exchange of duplicates programs of major American libraries, especially the program at the Library of Congress. Nathan R. Einhorn, Chief of the Exchange and Gift Division of the Library of Congress, points out that, "in addition to administering the official exchanges of sets of government publications with other nations, the Library also maintains more than 23,000 official exchange arrangements with educational institutions, learned societies, and government agencies in nearly all countries throughout the world" [14, p. 285].

Receipt and Records

The necessary acquisitions records and their maintenance in relation to the receipt of material complete the acquisitions process of a library. The records developed for "in-print" material must be related to and generated from the approach used to order the material. If a "title by title" approach is employed, the individual record may consist of an individual order letter, an individual order form, a multiple copy order form or even an automated order record. At all events these records must have different arrangements. For searching purposes order records must be arranged by author or title of the material already ordered. For claiming purposes some sort of publisher or source approach is necessary. Further, for invoicing purposes an arrangement by order number is useful. For this reason many libraries use multiple copy order forms. In addition, catalog card information may be ordered at the same time that the individual material is ordered. Cards may be ordered from the Library of Congress or from a regional system. This may change to some extent as publishers include more "Cataloging-in-Publication" information on the verso of the title page. Finally, such a system requires that the records are cleared upon the receipt of both the material and any catalog card information. Outstanding orders must be discerned and material claimed or the order cancelled. There may be possibilities for the use of union order files for a centralized system. Records for standing order material are simpler to maintain once a standing order has been placed. In this case the major problem is the receipt of the ordered material. Items must be checked in when they arrive. Approval

plan and blanket order plan material requires rejecting and returning some
titles. Cataloging information such as catalog cards must be ordered for all
monographic material acquired by standing order plans. Outstanding orders,
i. e. , material not acquired, must be claimed. Records for exchange
material and gifts often cause these two types of material to be more costly
than it might seem. Records of the individual exchange agreement must be
maintained and used. The conditions of the individual agreements must be
fulfilled and the agreed-upon material received. Records must be kept in
regard to what was sent and received whether a priced, piece for piece, or
open exchange is in effect. Outstanding exchange material must be claimed.
Gift and exchange agreements must continue to be negotiated or renegotiated.
Gift material must be acknowledged. Unsolicited gifts may need to be rejected,
exchanged or sold.

As already mentioned a union consortium on-order/in-process file would
be most useful for ordering materials. This would be a necessity if a
central ordering office were to be developed. This, of course, will naturally
lead into the next section dealing with cataloging and processing and the
possibilities of centralizing these activities.

Summary

In summary it may be said that the acquisitions processes are basically
the same for libraries whether they are buying solely for themselves or
whether they are in a resource sharing arrangement. There are, however,
some basic activities of a resource sharing consortium that must be implemented if the cooperative procedures are to be productive: first, the
services to be rendered by the collections to other member libraries must
be clearly defined. This would usually involve budgetary commitments.
Second, the cooperating instutitions would have to establish a basic materials
budget however high or low as a minimum on which the consortium could
count in order to assure that an adequate body of materials would be maintained
and augmented regularly be each of the member libraries. Further budgetary
commitments would need to be made on materials which might be bought
primarily for the use of the member libraries and not the local library.
Third, for resource sharing and acquisitions to be completely productive, a
form of clearinghouse would be needed. Union catalogs and union lists would
provide a record of the holdings of the member libraries; it may also be
necessary for some form of on-order/in-process file to be held in a union
fashion so that member libraries would know if someone else already had
ordered a book. Obviously, in a resource sharing system so far as acquisitions go individual steps could be taken before centralized acquisitions went
into effect.

In conclusion, a centralized acquisitions program should include the following if a resource sharing consortium is to be most effective:

1. Statement of the mission and objectives of the consortium
2. A common materials selection program
3. A specific statement of the optimum consortium collection
4. A union catalog of all materials including a union list of serials
5. A union desiderata list
6. A common request and order form for all libraries in the system
7. A central order office
8. A union or central on-order/in-process file
9. A consortium approval plan
10. Cooperative circulation of want lists of out-of-print material
11. Cooperative ordering of photographic or microform copies of material
12. A consortium exchange program

CATALOGING AND PROCESSING

This unit will include descriptive cataloging, subject cataloging and preparation of material for the shelves [see Ref. 15]. Just as we have seen in the previous section, these processes are basically the same whether one is dealing with a single library or a consortium. In the following discussion, however, it may be observed that certain local autonomies may have to be sacrificed if a consortium wishes to develop cooperation or centralized cataloging and processing. In this section just as in the preceeding section on acquisitions the writer fully realizes that many specific functions will be defined that readers of this paper are already quite aware of; however, these definitions are included to provide the non-library participants with basic library information.

Descriptive Cataloging

Descriptive cataloging consists of generating the necessary descriptive information about the material for the library's catalog. Such information includes the established form of the author's name, the title of the material, any necessary edition statement, the place, publisher and date of publication. This information may already exist on a printed catalog card, or as Cataloging-in-Publication information on the verso of the title page of the material, or may have to be originally generated by the cataloger.

Bibliographic Description

Any bibliographic description will contain certain common elements such as the author and the title of the material being described. Bibliographic descriptions or citations may be found in bibliographies, footnotes, indexes, publishers' catalogs, and on library catalog cards. In order to prepare the necessary descriptive information for catalog cards it is necessary to identify and describe certain prescribed parts of books and other material. The basic elements of a bibliographic description of a book, i. e. , a monograph, are the title, the edition, the place of publication, the publisher, the date of publication and/or the copyright date, the number of pages of the book, the type of illustrations, the height of the book, any necessary notes, and all possible entries in the catalog including the author, the editor, any joint authors, and any other desired access or index points in the catalog.

With development of ISBD (International Standard Bibliographic Description) we now have a common form for bibliographic citations. ISBD was developed by a working group of international catalog experts. Its purpose is described thus:

> By specifying the elements which should comprise a bibliographical description and by prescribing the order in which they should be presented and the punctuation by which they should be demarcated, it aims at three objectives; to make records from different sources interchangeable; to facilitate their interpretation across language barriers; and to facilitate the conversion of such records to machine-readable form. [16]

ISBD is being used in more and more national bibliographies, national catalogs and cataloging services. Hopefully, publishers will follow this form in describing material in their own catalogs. Certainly, a consortium should accept ISBD as its basic descriptive format for materials.

Library of Congress Cataloging

All the information necessary for a bibliographic description may have already been developed for the cataloger by the Library of Congress or some other bibliographic agency. The cataloger should check to discern if there is Library of Congress cataloging information available for the book being cataloged. This information may exist on Library of Congress printed cards, proofsheets, MARC tapes, or as CIP information on the back of the title page, or as an entry in the Library of Congress' printed National Union Catalog.

Many libraries order Library of Congress catalog cards at the same time they order a book. The cataloger must check to see if Library of Congress cards have been ordered and if these printed cards have already arrived. If the cards have been ordered but have not yet arrived the cataloger must decide if temporary cataloging should be done. In some cases libraries simply allow the book to wait for its printed LC cards. After the cards arrive they should be compared with the book to make sure they match the book in all the bibliographic characteristics.

Besides the possibility of ordering LC cards, many libraries receive paper copies of all the cards that are printed at the Library of Congress. These paper copies are called proofsheets. The filing of proofsheets is often quite time-consuming and hence expensive. If a library has the proofsheet for a book, there are various reproductive processes for making a set of catalog cards from the paper slip.

The bibliographic information may be available on MARC tapes, i. e. , Machine Readable Cataloging records on magnetic tapes; not all cataloging records at the Library of Congress are presently available on MARC tapes, but all current English language monographs are. In 1973, French language entries have been added to MARC records. Libraries may purchase or subscribe to the tapes or may participate in regional or commercial processing centers which have MARC tapes available. This is one of the most natural areas in cataloging for resource sharing. Henriette Avram, the principal developer of MARC, describes this computer-based system:

> The MARC Distribution Service grew out of a pilot project to test the feasibility of centrally producing and distributing machine-readable catalog records, The First Conference on Machine-Readable Catalog Copy in 1964, attended by representatives of the Library of Congress, universities, research agencies, government agencies, and private industry. Consensus was that early availability of machine-readable catalog copy as a by-product of LC's cataloging operations would be desirable. Since the record would be used for a variety of purposes in many libraries, agreement on data elements to be encoded was desirable, and the design of the machine-readable record by LC was probably the best means of standardization.
> The pilot project resulted in: (1) a standard interchange format (ANSI standard), (2) the definition of standard records for several forms of material, and (3) the inception of the MARC Distribution Service beginning with the provision of English-Language Catalog Records in 1969. Expansion to other languages and other forms of material is planned for the future. While the implementation of systems for the utilization of MARC has been slow no one has suggested that the MARC Distribution Service (or the card division

distribution service) be abandoned in favor of decentralized production
of catalog records by many institutions. [17]

In this region we have seen many libraries including both academic and
public make use of the Ohio College Library Center (OCLC) for the production of LC catalog cards from MARC tapes. Further, OCLC acts as a partial
union catalog for member libraries by indicating recent holdings of individual
libraries.

Susan K. Martin describes OCLC:

A significant step in the automation of cataloging is in development
of the Ohio College Library Center, mentioned above in the section
on networks. Under the direction of Kilgour, the system allows
member libraries to access, search, and add to a MARC-based on-
line bibliographic data base. When a search is successful, a
command to produce a set of catalog cards can be given, and the cards
are printed in batch mode and sent to the requesting library ready to
be filed. Changes may be made in the data that are displayed as the
master record; the library making those changes will receive a set
of cards altered to its specifications, while the master record itself
remains untouched. Original cataloging may be entered into the
data base by those libraries encountering unsuccessful searches, and
these records may be made available to other users of the system
and tagged as being locally input. The philosophy of OCLC is to
attempt, within reason, to accommodate unique library cataloging
features while continuing to maintain a generalized system. The
network may encounter conflicting standards when many libraries
begin to input original records; the resolution of this problem will
be of importance for cooperative bibliographical system. [18, see
also Ref. 19]

The director of OCLC, Frederick J. Kilgour, points out in describing
the inception of OCLC:

Incorporation of the Ohio College Library Center (OCLC) as a
not-for-profit corporation occurred on July 6, 1967. As expressed
in the Article of Incorporation, the purpose of the corporation is
"to establish, maintain and operate a computerized, regional library
center to serve the academic libraries of Ohio (both state and private)
and designed so as to become a part of any national electronic network
for bibliographical communication." The director of the Center took

up his duties in Columbus in early September and spent most of the next two months consummating legal organization. System design was initiated, however, during this period, and following OCLC formal organization meetings at the end of October, system design became the main order of business. This article narrates the development of the design of a computerized regional library system in the early months of the Center's existence. As a case history, the paper contains early efforts and diagnosis; at this writing it is too early for prognosis.

The history of events leading up to the establishment of OCLC helps shed light on the Center. The Ohio College Association (OCA) was responsible for founding OCLC. The Ohio College Association is a venerable organization that came into being in 1867 as the Association of Ohio Colleges; it changed its name to the present form in 1890. In 1867 there were a dozen charter members, including both state and private institutions; a century later, there are over sixty full and associate members. For a hundred years these Ohio institutions have been working together with effectiveness that has long since spawned mutual confidence and allowed for the stability of OCA. Perhaps the major factor behind the establishment of OCLC is this long and quiet tradition of effective cooperation among Ohio academic institutions. [9, p. 79]

Other regional centers such as MARC-Oklahoma and the New England Library Information Network (NELINET) are already in operation while many more are in the planning or development stage.

MARC-Oklahoma (MARC-O) is based in the Oklahoma Department of Libraries and provides MARC tape services to users [see Ref. 20]. The New England Library Information Network is a computer-assisted center for centralized technical processing. It included initially the universities of Connecticut, Maine, Massachusetts, New Hampshire, Rhode Island and Vermont. Writing in 1970, Alan D. Ferguson states about NELINET:

Now a system has been created on an experimental but solid basis. It can produce library cataloging products on demand from local libraries addressing a central computer. These products can be in the hands of the requesting library within 48 hours, and can be produced at a cost which, while relatively high because of the experimental production system, gives reasonable promise of soon being reducible to a competitive level with existing charges.

NELINET does not yet have its own facilities, staff, or machinery. It must be subsidized extensively even though some cataloging services can be sold to participating libraries. It is the conviction of the project's administrators that a point has been conclusively made: automated technical processing services for large networks of college, university, and research libraries can be rendered efficiently by a centralized, regional, computer-assisted center.

These services can go far beyond cataloging and can probably include acquisitions control, the production of book-type library catalogs and serials holding lists, circulation control, and library management information systems.

The payoff in case terms will be long term. But more important, the library's capacity for service to users will be immeasurably increased and the campus library undoubtedly remain the dynamic informational core of higher educational institutions. [21]

Definitely, a consortium should participate in or develop its own MARC-based centralized cataloging center.

On the back of the title-page of some current American books partial bibliographic description is being given as the result of the program called Cataloging-in-Publication (CIP). William J. Welsh, Director of the Processing Department at the Library of Congress, describes this newly developed LC service:

> Briefly expressed, the CIP entry will contain everything now on an LC printed card except for the information between the end of the title proper and the beginning of the series statement. Spelled out, the following information will be supplied: author, title, series statement, notes, subject and added entries, LC classification number, DC classification number, and LC card mumber. The entry will normally appear on the verso of the title page, printed in a format similar to the LC catalog card format. Entries for children's books will add annotations of the type now carried on our catalog cards for juvenile literature. Typography of the cataloging entry will probably match that of the book. [22]

CIP information is supplied chiefly on American trade books for major publishers. It is planned to be expanded to include additional publishers in the future. There are presently similar national systems in the Soviet Union, Colombia, Brazil and Peru. Canada is also in the process of developing such a program [23].

Another source for bibliographic description are the printed catalogs of the Library of Congress, especially the <u>National Union Catalog</u>. These catalogs consist of photographically reduced copies of Library of Congress Cards. The purpose of the printed National Union Catalog (NUC) is stated below:

The National Union Catalog is designed as a current and cumulative
continuation of A Catalog of Books Represented by Library of Congress
Printed Cards and its supplements. It represents the works cataloged
by the Library of Congress and by the libraries contributing to its
cooperative cataloging program during the period of its coverage.
In addition, it includes entries for monographic publications issued
in 1956 and thereafter reported by about 950 North American
Libraries and not represented by LC printed cards. It constitutes a
reference and research tool for a large part of the world's production
of significant books as acquired and cataloged by the Library of
Congress and a number of other North American libraries. For
monographic works published since 1956 it indicates at least one
library where the publication is held and serves thereby, at least for
these imprints, as a National Union Catalog. It serves also, by
indicating the LC card number, as a tool for the ordering of LC
printed cards. It is supplemented by the other parts of the Library
of Congress Catalogs. [24]

Original Cataloging

If there is no Library of Congress cataloging information available for
the book, then the cataloger must do original cataloging indicating the author,
the title, the edition, the number of pages in the book, and any other pertinent descriptive information. All of this information is included on the
catalog card as well as the call number and the subject headings. The call
number consists of the classification number and the author number. The
subject headings are descriptive words or phrases indicating the subject
content of the book.

The first element on a catalog card is the heading or the main entry.
This is usually the verified form of the author's name. The main entry may
occur in four possible forms. It may be a personal author, a corporate
author, a uniform title, or even a title entry. Personal authors are the most
common form of main entry. A corporate entry is the entry under some
corporate body such as a society, association, government, or institution
which is chiefly responsible for the existence of the work. The third
possibility is entry under a uniform title, as for example "Mother Goose."
Finally, if none of the above may be chosen for main entry, then a work may
be entered under its own title. In this last case the heading and the body are
combined and hanging idention is used.

There are two ways used by catalogers to determine or establish the
correct form of a main entry - whether it is a personal author, a corporate
author, or a uniform title. The first method may be called verification.
In this case a cataloger must determine the correct form by consulting one
or more bibliographical authorities. The two most common authorities are

the Library of Congress Printed Catalogs and the H. W. Wilson company's
Cumulative Book Index. The verifier must take care not to be confused by
these two sources. Occasionally there will be variations as to how an
individual name is entered. In cases of doubt it is usually better to follow
the Library of Congress practice. In addition, there are many other possible biographical dictionaries and directories which may be used for
verification purposes. The other method of establishing the proper form for
main entries is to use the rules given in the standard cataloging codes, of
which the Anglo-American Cataloging Rules is our present one. By using
rules and principles the cataloger will also have to consult bibliographical
sources.

The second element on a catalog card is called the body of the card.
The body consists of the title-page elements of the description. The first
part of the body is the title of the book. This is followed by any necessary
repetition of the author statement as it appears on the title page. The third
element of the body includes the edition, the editor, the illustrator, the
translator, etc. The last element of the body of the card is the imprint,
consisting of the place of publication, the name of the publisher, and the
date of publication, in that order. If the latest copyright date differs from
the date of publication both are given. The four sections of the body of the
card are consistent in that order. If any information necessary for one of
the four sections does not appear on the title page but, let us say, on the
page following the title page, that information will be incorporated in the
body of the card.

The third part of the card is the collation, which is the cataloger's
physical description of the material. It consists of three parts: the pagination, the type of illustrations, and the size. The pagination is recorded
from the last numbered page of each numbering section for single volume
works and the total number of volumes for multivolume works. The type of
illustrations may be simply cited as "illus." with only maps receiving
special indication. The size of the book is measured in regard to the height
of the book in centimeters. The order of the collation is also consistent.

The fourth section of the unit card is for notes about the material. If a
book is part of a series it may well have a series note at the end of the
collation line. All other notes will appear as separate paragraphs below the
collation. The fifth section on a catalog card is the tracing. This is a
record of the necessary supplementary entries that should be produced to
complete the card set. The subject headings are listed in arabic numbers
and the other added entries are listed in Roman numerals.

From this description it may be observed that original cataloging is a
time-consuming and hence expensive operation. Individual libraries should
always avoid original catalogings if at all possible. Although the use of
ISBD will simplify this to some extent, individual libraries still face the

possibility of each library doing original cataloging for the same material. Centralized cataloging for a consortium can resolve this problem if a centralized office were to do all original cataloging for the members of the consortium. Just as a MARC-based center can provide existing descriptions for material on catalog cards, it could provide a common original descript- ion for material. Individual libraries might have to give up special local cataloging customs or custom cataloging but the problem of each library cataloging the same book would be solved. The problem of local or custom cataloging practices had to be resolved before NELINET could be fully operational. Ferguson says of this problem:

> As everyone expected, the problems were numerous. Since every library has pet practices it uses in its local cataloging system, the first job to achieve a wide area of acceptance of the data which would be incorporated on catalog cards produced by a regional center. (Rumor has it that it took three months for the six librarians to agree on a single symbol for an oversized book.) [21, pp. 23-24]

Avram also cites this problem:

> The non-uniformity clearly is evident in comparing the biblio- graphic records of large research libraries in information centers. Without engaging in an evaluation of the merits of one system or the effects of following one set of convention, it is sufficient to say that the cumulative consequences of these disparities is costly duplication of producing records for the same item and minimization of the users facilitated tap all the services of an integrated system. [17, p. 93]

Further, individual libraries could agree to catalog originally material from specific subject or national areas and then submit such to the regional center for the use of all member libraries. Such original cataloging could include not only the descriptive cataloging but also the subject cataloging as mentioned in the following section.

Subject Cataloging

Subject cataloging deals with the assignment of classification numbers and subject headings to the individual books being cataloged. Library of Congress cataloging services include a complete Library of Congress class- ification call number, and Library of Congress subject headings. The

Library of Congress classification and the Dewey Decimal classification are
the two most common general library classification systems in this country.
The subject cataloger must determine if the classification and subject headings assigned by the Library of Congress for an individual book are
appropriate to the local library. In resource sharing the cataloger may also
consider the demands of other libraries. Further, he must determine if
the subject headings will require any cross references to be added to the
library's catalog.

As the L. C. classification call number, the Dewey Decimal classification
class number, and the L. C. subject headings are all on MARC tapes, a
regional MARC-type center can provide any of these to a member library.
A consortium may decide to use either classification system or even allow
member libraries to choose whichever they prefer. All libraries in the
consortium should use L. C. subject headings as other systems of subject
headings, even those developed by local libraries, are not compatible with
L. C. subject headings. Often L. C. classification is preferred to Dewey
Decimal classification because an entire L. C. call number is given on the
L. C. catalog card. Only the class number is given for D. C. users. For
D. C. users, the remainder of the call number must be generated originally
- this often includes the author and/or book number for the material.

Classification

If there is no Library of Congress cataloging information available for
a book being cataloged, the cataloger must assign original call numbers and
subject headings to the book. Classification brings like or similar academic
disciplines and their subordinates together, separating them from unlike or
different disciplines. Philosophical classification attempts to create a
library classification which is really a complete classification of knowledge
- not knowledge as it is represented in books. The Dewey Decimal
classification is an example of philosophical classification. Book classification attempts to be a system based on the books themselves, not simply
the knowledge represented by them. The Library of Congress classification
is an example of book classification.

The codification of a classification system into numbers, letters and/or
symbols is the notation. The notation is simply a process or method of
representing by symbols a specific subject or subjects in a classification
system. The notation is naturally a function of the classification and not the
classification a function of the notation. The call number consists of the
entire notation or coding device given to each particular book. This
particular notation is used to locate relatively the position of a book on the
shelves. The class number consists of the part of the notation resulting
solely from the classification system. The book number or author number

consists of the remainder of the entire notation or call number. It is
normally used to create an alphabetical order within a specific subdivision
of the classification on the shelf. From the latter part of the nineteenth
century until the present, many general and specialized library classification
schemes have been developed. The two most important schemes in English
are the Dewey Decimal classification and the Library of Congress classification. Melvil Dewey published the first edition of his system in 1876 and
it has undergone many revisions and new editions. The latest edition of D. C.
is the eighteenth, published in 1971. L. C. classification was developed by
subject specialists at the Library of Congress to class the largest collection
of material in this country. Its individual classes have been published from
1901 to the present time. L. C. uses a mixed notation consisting of letters
and numbers.

Original classification using either L. C. or D. C. can create problems
for individual libraries. If a library is using L. C. classification the
classifier must attempt to classify originally material in a fashion like the
material would have been classified at the Library of Congress. This means
that the classifier must not only be familiar with the L. C. classification
schedules and tables, but also with the actual application of these schedules
and tables. He must compare his original class numbers with the library's
shelf list of previously classified material. If a library is using the Dewey
Decimal classification, the classifier may be following the D. C. numbers on
L. C. cards for existing cataloged material or he may be following local
autonomies within his library. In either case he must carefully consult the
shelf list to determine the proper call number.

In a consortium it must be first decided if the classification is to be done
locally or by a centralized cataloging unit. If classification is done locally,
there may be no changes in the present practices; however, if for the sake
of efficiency and economy subject cataloging as well as descriptive cataloging
is to be done centrally, the local library must give up any local classification
autonomies. All of the copies of an individual title would receive the same
L. C. call number or D. C. call number. Although both systems could exist
in a consortium, a single system would be more efficient. If both systems
are in use, material would have to be classified twice - once by L. C. and
once by D. C. In order to have subject cataloging performed by a central
agency for the entire consortium, a union shelf list must be maintained. A
shelf list is a card catalog arranged by classification numbers. To classify
originally a shelf list is a necessity. However, it is possible that a union
shelf list could be stored in a machine readable record; in fact, the same
machine readable record could also be the union catalog. This then suggests
the possibility of a centralized cataloging and classification agency for a
consortium.

Subject Headings

Subject headings are descriptive words or phrases designed to convey
subject content of books. In 1914 the Library of Congress issued the first
edition of Subject Headings Used in the Dictionary Catalogues of the Library
of Congress. The present edition is the seventh and was published in 1966.
L. C. subject headings, just as is the case with L. C. classification, are
developed from the actual holdings of the Library of Congress. L. C. subject
headings appear on L. C. printed cards. L. C. subject headings may be used
either with L. C. classification or any other classification system, especially
D. C. Subject headings may be simple nouns, qualified nouns, phrases,
proper names, or geographic names

A centralized cataloging and classification unit for the consortium would,
of course, provide subject headings for any original cataloging. In order to
do this, a union catalog would be necessary. Also records on the subject
headings used in individual library catalogs may need to be maintained to
determine what cross reference cards should be added to the individual card
catalogs.

Marking and Binding

The final step in processing the book consists of marking the call number
on the spine of the book and including any necessary circulation materials in
the books, such as book cards, pockets, etc. All such materials may be
produced centrally. The cataloger must also determine if the book's binding
is acceptable for circulation. If the binding is not acceptable the book must
be sent to the bindery or given a special binding at the library. The final
step in the processing of the catalog cards is to reproduce as many copies
of the basic or unit card as is necessary. In a resource sharing system
cards may be made for a union catalog. The copies will have separate index
entries typed at the top of each card for the subject headings and the title
and any other basic index or access points. Then, the card set for the book
is filed in the public catalog and the shelf list.

If a centralized acquisitions unit is established for a consortium and if
a centralized cataloging and classification unit is established for a consortium,
then it naturally follows that a centralized processing unit could easily evolve.

Centralized processing may be defined as "those steps whereby library
materials for several independent libraries, either by contract or informal
agreement, are ordered, cataloged, and physically prepared for use by

library patrons, these operations being performed in one location with
billing, packing, and distribution to these same libraries" [25].

All marking and any necessary binding could also be accomplished
centrally; thus material could arrive at member libraries ready to be
shelved. If such a system is to be effective, efficient, and economical,
member librarians must accept material as it comes from central agency
and not change the cataloging or classification. In the processing step, all
materials for a common circulation system for the consortium should be
added to the book.

Summary

In summary: the cataloging activities are analogous or nearly identical
whether libraries perform these for themselves or in a consortium.
However, there are some points that must be reemphasized. First,
cataloging and classification is often done by many libraries for the same
book. Second, libraries that follow special cataloging formats or custom
cataloging may introduce differences that are time-consuming to perform
and expensive to pay for, often without a cost benefit rationale. Internal
consistency does not necessarily mean that the catalog will be easier for the
user: it may only be easier for the librarian to use. In a resource sharing
system standardization of cataloging and the catalog card would be essential.
In most cases this can easily be done by following Library of Congress
cataloging exactly. Third, cooperating institutions may wish to agree on the
use of a common classification such as the Library of Congress classification
provided on Library of Congress cards. However, autonomous classification
can create serious if not impossible problems for resource sharing. Users
of one institution within the system should be able to access effectively the
holdings of another institution with a common classification. Fourth, for all
materials needing original cataloging a temporary author title file may be
necessary to permit access to that material. This can relate directly to the
previously suggested union file for on-order and in-process material.

In conclusion, a centralized cataloging and processing program should
include the following if a resource sharing consortium is to be most
effective:

1. Use of the ISBD for all consortium cataloging
2. Consortium participation in or development of a MARC-based
   centralized cataloging center
3. A centralized original cataloging unit
4. Use of L. C. subject headings by all member libraries

5. Consistent use of centrally of classification systems – possibly, use of only L. C. classification
6. A centralized original subject cataloging unit (including classification and subject headings)
7. A union shelf list
8. A union catalog
9. A centralized processing unit

STORAGE

As the existing shelf space in libraries becomes crowded, many libraries have developed special or separate storage libraries to warehouse little used material [see Refs. 25, 27, 28, and 29]. The criteria for storage decisions are concerned with whether to discard a book, to microfilm it, or to store it. These decisions need to be made in regard to minimum use of the material, the cost to store it, the available space in both the library and the storage area, and the accessibility of the storage area. The minimum use of desirable books for a research library will be different than for an undergraduate library. Also the minimum use will often be different between the sciences – social and physical – and the humanities. The cost of storing individual material must be carefully considered. Is it worth the storage cost or should the book be discarded? Further, is there adequate space in the storage library for the material? Finally, how accessible is the storage library? Will the need for the material be reduced if the user is delayed in receiving the book? All of these factors will affect the development of criteria for storage decisions.

The problems and processes of a storage collection include the actual selection of materials for storage, the changing of existing library records, the physical moving of the materials into storage, the arranging and storage marking of the materials, the processes of retrieving materials, and the building costs of storage libraries. After criteria have been developed, the material to be stored must be selected from the library's collection. All of the records in the library's catalogs must be changed to indicate that the material is in storage. Further, the material may be given new markings for special storage shelf arrangements. Often books are stored by size to allow more compact shelving. If a large number of books are to be moved into storage at one time, the plan for the physical move must be carefully made, including the arranging of the material in the storage library. The amount of time to receive a book from storage as well as the actual retrieval system must be readily known to library users. The distance between a storage library and the main library can often be a factor, as storage libraries are often built in areas where land is not as valuable as is the land

where the main library is located. Besides the cost of the land, there are
other different building costs to be considered. Although a storage library
will allow greater square footage to be used, it will need to have stronger
floors than a normal library building. Also, a storage library should have
a lower lighting bill as the lights only need to be in use when material is
being retrieved from a particular area.

The actual shelving for a storage library may make use of conventional
library shelving or restricted access. Conventional library shelving and
shelf placement is not necessary in a storage library. Narrow aisles may
allow installation of more shelves per square foot. Further, there are
various systems of mechanical or compact movable shelving as well as
automated shelving systems [see Ref. 30].

The possibilities of regional storage libraries for a consortium of
libraries may provide the most immediate and dramatic effects in a
resource sharing system. A regional storage library used by several
members of a library resource sharing network could easily relieve the
high costs of building separate storage libraries. In addition, a common
storage library could also act as a potential agent for exchanging material
from a library that is not using it to a library that may have use of it. Such
a system of storage and exchange would have to be set up very carefully,
but under specific contractual arrangements could easily be done. Further,
a common storage library may allow individual members to see material
that may be discarded from the collection if enough copies are already in
storage.

A consortium of libraries may need more than one storage library.
Perhaps there should be separate storage libraries for each center of
library concentration within the consortium. This could lead to storage
libraries similar to the New England Deposit Library. This cooperative or
joint storage library opened in 1942 in the Boston area. Each participating
library rents individual storage space. Materials and records are not
integrated. F. S. Doherty states: "However, beyond the storing books,
the Deposit Library has accomplished little. It has made no inroads towards
the elimination of duplication or toward increasing library specilization"
[31]. Furthermore, as Jerrold Orne points out:

        There is, in fact, no gain for cooperation here. Each library
    rents its space, holds ownership and responsibility for its own
    materials. Cooperative use, extremely infrequent, offers no more
    than is now commonly obtained elsewhere by Interlibrary Loan.
    [29, p. 24]

On the other hand, a more integrated single storage library, such as the Midwestern Center for Research Libraries, may be desirable. This storage center, completed in 1951, is located on the University of Chicago campus. James D. Lee describes its development and differences from the New England Deposit Library:

> As joint storage became more attractive and expedient, the spectrum of participation grew broader. In 1949, ten universities cooperated to organize the Mid-west Inter-Library Center (MILC) with the primary purpose of increasing library research resources for member institutions. Participating libraries, representing universities located in eight states of the Midwest, provided supporting funds. The building, with a capacity of three million volumes, was completed in 1951; the first years were confined to the pooling and cooperative purchasing of materials, with emphasis on the deposit program. Communication with the Center by member was by teletype for some years, but was discontinued for lack of use. By 1965 deposits had reached the two million mark; the deposit program was reduced and more emphasis was placed on acquisitions. From the outset there were some functions on a national basis at the Center, such as service to all libraries irregardless of membership. Another was a serials program funded by the National Science Foundation. By 1960 the membership comprised twenty-one institutions over a vast geographical area, including university and research libraries throughout the United States and Canada. The logical conclusion reached by the Directors of the Center was that participants should not be limited to the Midwest, and consequently, in 1965, after a review of its purposes and programs, it was reorganized as the Center for Research Libraries with a national scope of operations. The Center had evolved from a storage warehouse serving a limited clientele to a national center for research. [28, pp. 162-63]

In either case all the previously cited criteria for a storage library must be considered.

For a consortium storage library to be effective, its program of operation should include the following:

1. A union catalog of storage library
2. A consortium agreement on the use of priorities of stored material
3. A clearly stated policy on the amount of time to retrieve material from storage
4. A possible consortium exchange agreement for stored material

DELIVERY OF SERVICES

The informational services of libraries include direct searches, researching questions and topics, interlibrary loans, and referrals to other libraries. First, direct searches involve the immediate delivery of library informational services to a patron. This includes such searches as supplying simple factual answers to questions, or providing the desired document to a patron. Second, researching questions or topics includes providing a patron with a list of citations which refer to a stated question or topic; also, some libraries have developed SDI system (Selective Dissemination of Information) based on individualized patron profiles to keep the patron aware of developments in the areas of his interest. Third, a library may supply desired documents for research purposes on the National Interlibrary Loan system developed by the American Library Association. Journal articles may be copied and sent to the library requesting the loan of the material. The patron can then receive a photocopy of the article he wishes and only has to pay the copying fee of the lending library. Monographic material can be loaned from one library to another and the patron requesting the material may use if for a stated period of time - usually two to three weeks. It is the responsibility of the patron's home library to return the material to the lending library. A full statement of the National Interlibrary Loan Code may be found in Sarah Katherine Thompson's Interlibrary Loan Procedure Manual [10; see also 32]. Finally, one library may directly refer a user to another library or other information source. In this case, the home library should act as a professional referral agency. The user should be sent with specific instructions as well as potential named contacts in much the same manner that one physician might refer a patient to another physician or a lawyer might refer a client to another lawyer. The home or original librarian should follow up with both the user and the outside contact to determine if the user receive the desired information or material. If there is any potential service charge for the information or material, the home librarian should carefully alert the user of this. Patrick's study finds forty percent of her consortia sample providing this type of referral reference service.

Based on the literature and case study, it would appear that this service consists of members consulting each other by telephone or teletype for reference questions they cannot answer. One librarian described this service as an "interlibrary loan of ideas and answers." One procedure being considered by one of the case study consortia was to employ a reference librarian, who would be assigned to the largest library, to handle reference questions of the consortium members. One librarian's reasoning was that if he could have access

in this manner to the reference collection of the larger library, he
would not have to build as extensive a reference collection for his own
library. [3, p. 182]

Obviously a consortium may develop a more sophisticated system of
interlibrary loan among members. One possible expansion would be the
adoption of ALA's "Model Interlibrary Loan Code for Regional, State, Local,
or Other Special Groups of Libraries" [33]. The basic difference between
this model code and the previously cited National Interlibrary Loan Code
may be observed in the following statements of purpose and scope. The
purpose of the National Code is: "to make available, for research,
materials not owned by a given library, in the belief that the furtherance of
knowledge is in the general interest. Interlibrary loan service supplements
a library's resources by making available, for the use of an individual,
materials from other libraries not owned by the borrowing library [10,
p. 2]. The purpose and scope of the Model Code obviously broadens interlibrary loan to include non-research materials. The Model Code states:

Purpose
    Since it is increasingly evident that it is impossible for any one
    library to be self-sufficient, and in the belief that the furtherance of
    knowledge is in the general interest, interlibrary borrowing and
    lending is regarded by the libraries subscribing to this agreement as
    essential to library service.
Scope
    Any type of library material needed for the purposes of study,
    instruction, information, or research may be requested on loan or
    in photocopy from another library. The lending library has the
    privilege of deciding in each case whether a particular item should
    or should not be provided, and whether the original or a copy should
    be sent. [33, p. 514]

An immediate advantage of expanded interlibrary loan services is cited
by Patrick:

Judging from the case studies, the new interlibrary loan services
means that services have been expanded beyond the limits set in the
ALA code to include undergraduate as well as graduate (or serious)
students and faculty. Another way in which interlibrary loan has
been expanded is to arrange for the loaning of materials in bulk, to
support seminars, tutorials or research projects in areas outside a
college's regular curriculum. This imaginative use of resources

may have existed before, but it has been facilitated by the consortium framework. [3, p. 178]

Within a region there can be a common delivery truck system. Other forms of delivery services have been discussed and investigated by Patrick:

Once bibliographic access has been provided so that the locations of books are known and after interlibrary loan services have been expanded to include more categories of users, if the user does not borrow the book in person, then arrangements are needed to provide physical access to the book. Of the 125 consortia, 35% provided delivery service. Various methods of providing transportation were encountered in the case studies. One consortium instituted a study to examine alternatives of moving library materials between libraries. Alternatives ranged from helicopter service to United Parcel Service. One of the observations was that the major delay is within the libraries, not between them.

As with all the possible cooperative activities, a solution suitable for one consortium may be unsatisfactory to another. One consortium concluded that the U. S. Mail was the most economical method for them because of the low volume of materials moving between libraries; another felt that the rapidity of delivery service more than compensated for the slightly higher expense. In one consortium, one of the reasons for having a truck delivery system was that several of the members who were not on a direct mailing route found the mailing service too slow. One somewhat unique solution was to rotate the responsibility for providing transportation among the members, once every 5 weeks. The type of transportation was decided by each member and ranged from a student's car to a university-owned panel truck to a taxicab. The director reported that for 1 year, for 4,000 transactions (which he felt was a relatively small number), the unit cost was 50¢ per volume transferred. [3, p. 180]

Further consortium SDI systems may be developed for members of the consortium in a fashion similar to MARC-Oklahoma's SDI system. Kenneth Bierman, data processing coordinator of the Oklahoma Department of Libraries, explains this particular SDI:

The Selective Dissemination of Information (SDI) service provides for subscribing state agencies and libraries a quick, personalized alerting service to new books in the specific subject areas of their

direct interest and responsibility. Subject profiles of Dewey and/or
L. C. classification numbers are first developed by a reference
librarian. These profiles are "fed" to the computer. The computer
then searches each weekly MARC tape and selects MARC records
which fall within the profiles and prints out a notice of bibliographic
information on that new book. Each participating state agency or
library receives a weekly printout of complete bibliographic information on new books in their subject fields of interest. [20, p. 5]

By use of a consortium teletype direct referrals for materials and
services may be done among the member libraries.

In order to use any library, the patron must be aware of the potential
documental citations within the library. The user must be aware of and
able to use or receive assistance in use of the library's public records.
The library's public records include the individual library's card catalog.
This record should demonstrate to the user the actual monographic holdings
of other libraries; the user should be aware of these. Further, the user
should consider using the standard bibliographies and indexes of monographic
and periodical literature. After a user has discerned the existence of
potential desired bibliographic sources, he must determine the availability
of these sources. The items listed in the card catalog should be available
as part of the library's holdings; so should any items in the library's
periodical or serial holdings. Union catalogs, bibliographies, and indexes
all will provide potential sources which may be included in the individual
library's holdings or may need to be ordered on Interlibrary Loan.

Further, libraries should assist their users in using other libraries.
It must be explained what other libraries' circulation rules are, and where
and how far the other libraries are.

Perhaps the ideal delivery of library services would allow a user to be
advised whether a library in the area has the desired material or not. This
would allow the user to determine whether to order the material on Interlibrary Loan, use some sort of regional cooperative delivery service, or
go to the other library himself. This would further and perhaps more
importantly imply that there need be a common library card and borrowing
provisions for all area, or regional, or even national libraries. This sense
of delivery of services would imply basic concepts of the resource sharing
of libraries. Reciprocal borrowing privileges are certainly an inducement
for the organization of a library consortium. Patrick lists three advantages
to the user of libraries in a consortium:

Reciprocity was of special benefit to commuting students, who
are now permitted to use libraries closer to their homes. Another

benefit is that it enables junior college students to become acquainted with the facilities of colleges or universities they may be considering for further study. Also, in some cases a user can obtain a book he needs more quickly if he goes directly to the lending library than if he were to wait for the material to be conveyed via interlibrary loan. [3, p. 179]

She also cites three problems which would require consideration and resolution for reciprocal borrowing privileges to be successful:

Possible incompatibility of loan periods (e. g. , the loan period may be 1 month for some libraries, 2 weeks for others)
Possible incompatability of circulation systems (especially if the systems are automated)
Possible overuse of libraries in central convenient locations
[3, p. 179]

In a summary, the delivery of services by resource sharing has been one of the oldest cooperative activities of American libraries. This may be seen through the practice of interlibrary loans. With the development of a union catalog for a consortium, some of the costs of interlibrary loans may be reduced and limited to the libraries within the consortium. It is also possible to use common delivery methods such as trucks going from one library to another in an area. Furthermore, the potential of telecopying can provide another mechanism of transferring material from one library to another. Finally, cooperative activities in delivery of services should stimulate and encourage the development of common circulation systems, in short, the emergence of the common library card.

The delivery of services for a consortium can be most effective if its program of operation includes the following:

1. A consortium interlibrary loan system
2. A possible consortium SDI system
3. A consortium teletype network
4. A union catalog
5. A consortium delivery system
6. A common circulation system
7. A common library card

REFERENCES

1. Joseph Becker and Wallace C. Olsen, "Information Networks," in
   Annual Review of Information Science and Technology, Vol. 3, (Carlos
   A. Cuadra, ed.), Encyclopedia Britannica, 1968, p. 304.
2. Herman M. Weisman, Information Systems, Services, and Centers.
   Becker and Hayes, New York, 1972, p. 44.
3. Ruth Patrick, Guidelines for Library Cooperation: Development of
   Academic Library Consortia, Systems Development Corporation, Santa
   Monica, Calif., 1972.
4. Judith Babcock, "Cooperation between Types of Libraries, 1968-July,
   1971: An Annotated Bibliography," Drexel University, Philadelphia,
   1971.
5. David K. Carrington, "Bibliography of Library Cooperation," Special
   Libraries 57, 395-399, (July-August 1966).
6. Ralph H. Stenstrom, Cooperation between Types of Libraries, 1940-
   1968: An Annotated Bibliography, American Library Association,
   Chicago, 1970.
7. Ritvars Bregzis, "Library Networks of the Future," Drexel Library
   Quarterly, 4, 270.
8. Samuel Lazerow, "National Collaboration and the National Libraries
   Task Force: A Course toward Compatibility," in Stanford Conference
   on Collaborative Library Systems Development: Proceedings of a
   Conference held at Sanford University Libraries, October 4-5, 1968
   (Allen B. Veaner & Paul Fasana, eds.) Stanford University Libraries,
   Stanford, 1969, p. 69.
9. Frederick G. Kilgour, "Initial System for the Ohio College Library
   Center: A Case History," in Proceedings of the 1968 Clinic on Library
   Application of Data Processing (Dewey E. Carroll, ed.), University of
   Illinois, Graduate School of Library Science, Urbana, 1969, pp. 81-82.
10. Sarah Katherine Thompson, Interlibrary Loan Procedure Manual,
    American Library Association, Chicago, 1970, p. x.
11. J. Periam Danton, Book Selection and Collections: A Comparison of
    German and American University Libraries. Columbia University
    Studies in Library Service, No. 12, Columbia University Press, New
    York, 1963, pp. 128-129.
12. Silvere Willemin, Technique of Union Catalogues: A Practical Guide,
    Unesco, Paris, 1966, p. 6.
13. Lawrence E. Leonard, Joan M. Maier, and Richard M. Dougherty,
    Centralized Book Processing: A Feasibility Study Based on Colorado
    Academic Libraries. The Scarecrow Press, Metuchen, N.J., 1969,
    p. 143.
14. Nathan R. Einhorn, "Exchange of Publications," Encyclopedia of
    Library and Information Science, Vol. 8 (Allen Kent, Harold Lancour,

and William Z. Nasri, eds.), Marcel Dekker, Inc., New York, 1972, pp. 282-289.

15. John Phillip Immroth and Jay E. Daily, Library Cataloging: A Guide for a Basic Course. The Scarecrow Press, Metuchen, N.J., 1971.

16. International Standard Bibliographic Description: for Single Volume and Multi-volume Monographic Publications recommended by the Working Group on the International Standard Bibliographic Description set up at the International Meeting of Cataloging Experts, Copenhagen, 1969, IFLA Committee on Cataloguing, London, 1971, p. iii.

17. Henriette D. Avram and Josephine Pulsifer, "Bibliogrpahic Services for a National Network," Proceedings of the Conference on Interlibrary Communications and Information Networks, sponsored by the American Library Association and U.S. Office of Education, Bureau of Libraries and Educational Technology held at Airlie House, Warrenton, Virginia, September 28, 1970-October 2, 1970 (Joseph Becker, ed.), American Library Association, Chicago, 1971, p. 95.

18. Susan K. Martin, "Library Automation," in Annual Review of Information Science and Technology, Vol. VII, (Carlos A. Cuadra, ed.), American Society for Information Science, Washington, D.C., 1972, p. 263.

19. Frederick G. Kilgour, "A Regional Network - Ohio College Library Center," Datamation, 16, 87-89, (February 1970).

20. Kenneth Bierman, "MARC-Oklahoma," Oklahoma Librarian, 21 (4), October 1971.

21. Alan D. Ferguson, "Six Cooperative Libraries," College Management, February 1970, p. 22.

22. William J. Welsh, "Report on Library of Congress Plans for Cataloging in Publication," Library Resources & Technical Services, 15, 23-27, (Winter 1971), pp. 25-26.

23. S. Elspeth Pope, "The Immediacy of Cataloging Information for Newly Acquired Books," unpublished Ph.D. dissertation, University of Pittsburgh, 1971, pp. 117-123.

24. United States Library of Congress, The National Union Catalog; a Cumulative Author List Representing Library of Congress Printed Cards and Titles Reported by Other American Libraries, Compiled by the Library of Congress with the cooperation of the Resources Committee of the Resources and Technical Services Division, American Library Association, December, 1972, Library of Congress, Washington, D.C., 1972, p. v.

25. James R. Hunt, "The Historical Development of Processing Centers in the United States, "Library Resources & Technical Services, 8, 54, (Winter 1964).

26. Ralph E. Ellsworth, The Economics of Book Storage in College and University Libraries. The Association of Research Libraries and the Scarecrow Press, Metuchen, N.J., 1969.

27. Helan J. Harrar, "Cooperative Storage Warehouses," unpublished Ph.D. dissertation, Rutgers University, New Brunswick, N.J., 1962.

28. James D. Lee, "Book Storage as One Aspect of Cooperation," South-
    eastern Librarian, 21, 161-68, (Fall 1971).
29. Jerrold Orne, "Storage Warehouse," in The State of the Library Art,
    (Ralph R. Shaw, ed.), Vol. 3, part 3, Rutgers, The State University,
    Graduate School of Library Service, New Brunswick, N.J., 1960.
30. Stanley Humenuk, "Automatic Shelving and Book Retrieval: A Contribu-
    tion toward a Progressive Philosophy of Library Service for a Research
    Library," University of Illinois Graduate School of Library Science
    Occasional Papers, No. 78, January 1966.
31. F. S. Doherty, "The New England Deposit Library: Part 2," Library
    Quarterly, 19, 18, (January 1949).
32. Sarah Katherine Thompson, Interlibrary Loan Involving Academic
    Libraries, ACRL Monograph no. 32, American Library Association,
    Chicago, 1970.
33. "Model Interlibrary Loan Code for Regional, State, Local, or Other
    Special Groups of Libraries," ALA Bulletin, 63, 513-516, (April, 1969).

Chapter 7

ACQUISITION

Joseph C. Shipman
Director
Linda Hall Library
Kansas City, Missouri

Though I plan to address myself to the "How?" of resource sharing in libraries, I would like first to quote a few comments on the "Why?" question made by Keyes Metcalf speaking at Hamilton College in September 1972 at the dedication of a new building. He made a strong plea for struggling to "cooperate with each other in spite of our belonging to the human race, which, alas, is not inclined to be cooperative." He pointed out that Hamilton and Kirkland Colleges, with their new Burke Building and their collections of library materials, cannot and should not expect to house within their own walls all the material that the faculty and students will want and should use. "The same situation," he goes on to say, "applies to all other libraries in this country and the world. It applies even to Harvard with its over 8 1/2 million volumes. There is a limit to the funds available to us." He suggests that the new library set an example for other libraries in the area and that each institution in the group make readily available to all the others the expensive and little used materials which it now possesses or which it will acquire later by gift or purchase. He hopes that we can avoid, wherever and whenever possible, the acquisition of unnecessary and undesirable duplicates of infrequently-used material. This means cooperative acquisition programs are needed, especially for periodical sets, and expensive retro-spective and new publications of all kinds which, obviously, will seldom be in demand." It seems to me that there could be no more economical statement of the overall problem facing all libraries, large, medium, and small, public, academic, and special, in a day of continuing proliferation of available literature and the inflationary pressures working on it.

This is not a new approach for Mr. Metcalf. Many years ago, talking about the essentials of an acquisition program he stated his conviction that "the administration of the book selection is in the long run the most important single task for which a librarian is responsible." While he felt that the public library had done well on its book selection program, because public libraries as a whole knew where they were going, and that much the same held true for college libraries. Metcalf had, even then, no great confidence in the book selection programs of our large university libraries.

Robert Downs has pointed out that:

> Pioneer American university and research librarians were strongly addicted to rugged individualism in the methods of book procurement. Funds were limited and the collections grew at a snail's pace... nevertheless, each American library was regarded as a completely independent entity, its development proceeding with little or no consideration of its neighbors. It should be remembered that growth of most library collections in the early 19th century was largely the fruit of individual munificence, and therefore, probably could not have taken any other course. The Harvard collection in 1830 numbered about 30,000 items including books from the great presses of Europe, manuscripts in Greek, Latin, Oriental and other languages; mathematical works; and the "most esteemed counts of recent travel in Asia and in other parts of the world, celebrated works in Belles Lettres, History and Theology." Harvard had also by 1830 accepted responsibility for state papers; political, religious and other tracts; reports and proceedings of ecclesiastical bodies, and of societies and institutes for various purposes; for local publications; occasional pamphlets and public documents of every description, where they will not only have the best chance of being preserved, but will accessible to all **persons** who may at times wish to consult them.

These were ambitious goals adhered to on an individualistic basis by most of the great research libraries which succeeded Harvard about a century later.

By 1969, the 30,000 volumes Harvard possessed in 1830 had grown to more than **eight million,** but the goals of the collection building for the great research library had not altered radically in the intervening one and one-half centuries. The collections are still added to by gifts, purchases, exchanges, and in the case of the Library of Congress, by copyright deposit. The emphasis has shifted to original selection by the library rather than by the donor, and to a principal reliance upon purchase rather than upon the other devices of acquisition. The chief and most remarkable difference is a quantitative one, in which Harvard today adds about 1/4 million volumes annually and expends over seven million dollars yearly to support its library operation; this is quite a contrast with its earlier dependence upon individual munificence.

The Purdue studies of fifty-eight reserach libraries reveal comparable startling growth in holdings, in annual additions to the collection, and in total expenditures since 1951. The average composite research library, derived from a review of these selected 58 institutions, has increased its total collections from 900,000 volumes in 1950-1951 to about 1,900,000 volumes in 1969-1970, has added on an annual basis 115,000 volumes in 1969 compared to about 35,000 volumes in 1950-1951, and has expended for books, periodicals, and binding about $950,000 in 1969 compared to $150,000 in 1950-1951. Holdings have therefore roughly doubled, while costs involved have increased by a factor of 6.

The fitted curves, extended some years beyond 1980, indicate inconceivably high levels in collections, and acquisitions expenditures — ten, twenty, or fifty times present levels. Some deceleration is inevitable, and though growth has been continuous since 1951, there is now evidence that among the largest libraries growth is currently faltering; current data indicate a definite deceleration in volumes acquired for large and medium-large ARL Libraries. Since there is no evidence that I know of that would indicate a deceleration in publication rate, there is no conclusion that can be drawn, other than that these large research libraries must decline in the effectiveness of their coverage of current output.

I believe we could already seriously challenge the effectiveness of current coverage, even under the optimum conditions which have existed at ever increasing cost, over the past twenty-five years. Chemical Abstracts in 1966 surveyed chemical documentation resources in three metropolitan areas, New York, San Franicsco, and Detroit, including such egregious institutions as Columbia University, the New York Public Library, the University of California at Berkeley, and the University of Michigan, representing a fairly wide range of population, geographic location, and library holdings. The assumption was that data on these areas should be indicative of local document resources in other United States metropolitan areas. In metropolitan New York 5450 titles (56%) out of the 9734 titles abstracted by Chemical Abstracts were available in the combined holdings of 16 cooperating libraries. In San Francisco the combined resources of seven libraries could produce 5051 titles or 51.9% of the whole list. In Detroit five combined library resources held only 3343 or 34.3%.

The study also demonstrated that most library collections are deficient not only in the rarer journals but also in many of the more popular journals in which new chemical and chemical engineering information is reported. Picking 250 chemical titles out of more than 9000 titles abstracted as the top journals in the field, the surveyors found that the New York Public Library had only 179 of these top journals and Columbia had only 144. In San Francisco, the University of California had 225 and Stanford, the next best, 138 of these important titles. In the Detroit area, the University of Michigan held 182, and the Kresge Library 152. Rugged individualism in selection and acquisition at least in the field of chemistry has resulted in a situation in which a user or group of users interested in the full range of chemistry and chemical engineering could expect to find one third to one half of the necessary documents through his total local resources.

Forty years ago, there were only four or five libraries with holdings of more than one million volumes. In 1970-1971 there were at least 53 research libraries with more than one million volumes, 20 with more than two million, 12 with more than three million, and 6 with more than four million. These are formidable figures when you consider that most of this growth has been largely uncoordinated, at least on a national and regional basis. In a few instances there have been arrangements between local institutions of large size, such as between the University of North Carolina and Duke University, but very often the divisions of responsibility have been too flimsy, too erratic, too narrow, and too evasive of the big issues.

Arthur McAnally in a recent article investigating the question as to why so many directors of large and distinguished research libraries have retired, resigned, or transferred to teaching during 1970-1971, comes to the conclusion that (in spite of unparalleled library growth and prosperity in the last two decades) "the university library is becoming increasingly less able to meet legitimate needs of its university community." He gave as the causes: the information explosion, inflation, more students and continued fragmentation of the traditional disciplines coupled with hard times. A recent study at Harvard concluded that with eight million volumes the library was less able to cope with the demands of scholars than it was when it had only four million volumes. Ralph Ellsworth in his 1971-1972 annual report at Colorado came to the same conclusion. David Kaser states the lugubrious fact that our ability to supply the books and journals needed by Cornell teaching and research programs is rapidly diminishing, and no one seems to know what to do about it. Computerization of information, cooperation, and microminiaturization have not provided solutions. The somber conclusion fast being arrived at by the library staff is that the only solutions likely to be effective are more money, or a substantially reduced academic program for the library to serve, Neither of these solutions appears imminent. Like the university itself, the library has rarely done a good job of planning, either long-range or short-range. The traditional library objectives summarized cynically in such phrases as "more of the same" and "bottomless pit" are probably unrealistic and yet little is offered in their place. "Now that higher education in all its aspects is under critical review, the lack of realistic, practicable, and acceptable goals, and of long-range planning, is a major handicap". In his suggested solutions to the problem, McAnally gives high priority to the promotion of a national acquisitions program and to the development of plans for more effective sharing of resources for research. Once again, he sees only the federal government as the source for the sizeable funds needed for a proper national plan.

Perhaps the ideal of encyclopedic comprehensiveness stemming from Enlightment, as Lawrence Thompson has suggested, is a will-of-the-wisp in the midst of a period characterized by geometric growth of literature. A coordinated comprehensive scheme of subject specialization has for nearly a century permitted special libraries in various parts of the world to approach the ideal of completeness far more closely than general libraries. The National Lending Library (NLL) is achieving such a goal with scientific serials. In Germany in the last century efforts were made to encourage university libraries to collect intensively in fields in which they already possessed considerable strengths. Toward the end of the nineteenth century, collecting in specialized areas was accepted by the three principal libraries in Frankfurt: the subjects selected were natural science and medicine, art and technology, and modern languages and music. Königsberg, Breslau, and Munich followed the example, and existing specialization among German libraries was later formalized by the government in 1909. From that time on, interrupted by two world wars, the collecting of special fields has been specifically assigned to various German libraries.

Thompson summarizes the distinctive characteristics of the German plan of fields of specialization in the following way:

"1. It is an emergency program, born of poverty, not a program of research libraries in a comparatively rich country, which are striving for completeness.

2. It is selective. All material acquired is assumed to be of primary value to scholars. Selection is done by scholars trained both in the field concerned and in librarianship.

3. The national regulating body, the Forschungsgemeinschaft is only a fiscal and regulatory agency. Selection of books and selection of dealers is an individual matter.

4. The plan assumes the presence of more subject specialists than we find in all but a half dozen major American libraries. The last ten years have seen a shift among many American research libraries. It also assumes a far greater volume of interlibrary loan than we have."

Acquisition on a specialized basis has more recently been attempted in another area of Europe. First in Sweden, then in all of Scandinavia, the illusion of self-sufficiency has been abandoned. In 1955, the four great general libraries in Sweden (the Royal Library in Stockholm and the University libraries of Uppsala, Lund, and Gothenburg) reached an agreement, dividing the responsibility for subject coverage of certain literature from foreign countries. The plan came into operation in the same year, and, with various modifications, is still functioning within the wider framework of the Scandia Plan. The cooperation had to be restricted to what, from the Swedish point-of-view, might be called peripheral subjects. (We might label them rarely used materials.) Where the particular university is involved in intense research, it is still necessary for each library to attempt to procure all the essential books and periodicals. Each library was left to decide by itself what materials it should acquire to do its job, but beyond this, each library undertook the responsibility for certain peripheral fields of research (most of them in the humanities) assuming the obligation of systematically acquiring material, both old and new, on the subject in question.

The plan was extended to all of Scandinavia in 1959. The accepted basis of division of responsibility was subject, geographic, or logistic. A feature of the broadened scheme was the decision to include Scandinavian special libraries in this cooperative effort, building on already existing special library strengths in (1) engineering and technology, (2) agriculture, veterinary medicine, and forestry, (3) commerce and business administration, and (4) statistics. In fields such as the natural sciences, medicine, art, and music, special libraries had not developed in Scandinavian countries and these subjects therefore were to be the responsibility of the national libraries. At a later date, based upon information requested earlier, the first assignments made were to the little-used, esoteric areas and languages — papyrus research, runic scholarship, Himalayan languages, Iranian, and Arabic). In accepting primary responsibility for collecting in these fields, each library committed itself to making the materials available to scholars throughout Scandinavia, and committed itself to function as a bibliographic center for the designated subject. Temporary changes of scholarly interest or emphasis in these subjects were not to alter the established division of responsibility.

Thomas Buckman, looking at these efforts of Scandinavian libraries to create an international plan for cooperative acquisition of library materials, felt that the results could not yet be fairly assessed, and that their problems must be solved from the point of view of Scandinavian conditions. Nevertheless, he concluded "the general type of library cooperation toward which they are moving in Scandinavia is certainly one which will have significant applications in other parts of the world as book and journal production continues to rise and as future developments are made in electronic communication and air transportation."

The story of cooperative acquisition in the United States is as old as the Prussian and German scheme, and specialization by fields perhaps even older, though usually quite local, rather than regional or national, and much more sporadic. There was a time in the middle of the nineteenth century when the American Academy of Arts and Sciences had more notable holdings than Harvard across the broad areas of the sciences. Its collection was acquired largely by exchange with the many flourishing academies throughout the world as well as by gifts and deposits by the United States government agencies, state agencies, and foreign government agencies involved in the publication of scientific and technical material. After the establishment of the New England Museum of Natural History in Boston, an agreement was reached by the Academy and the Museum which divided primary responsibility between them for the physical and natural sciences. The collection of the American Academy of the Arts and Sciences approached 50,000 volumes and a library building was constructed to house it. Gradually, other libraries in the Boston area duplicated most of its holdings, the cost of maintaining it continued to increase while use decreased, and, in 1947, the Academy decided to sell the bulk of the collection to the incipient Linda Hall Library in Kansas City, in an area where the book resources were much less rich, and where the new library was designed to make materials available to all comers. The nearly 200-year-old exchange arrangements were continued in the new quarters, so that the Academy, though no longer housing, servicing, and maintaining a collection still maintained its historic function at least as an intermediary in collection building in a limited subject area.

In the 1890's, early for the United States, Chicago's two privately endowed libraries, the Newberry and the John Crerar, divided subject responsibility, with Crerar specializing in physical and biological sciences and medicine and Newberry in the humanities and related disciplines. At the time, some transfers and sales of materials between the two institutions were involved. The arrangement prospered for about fifty years, but beginning in the period after World War II, the demands upon John Crerar's available support by ever burgeoning costs of acquisition in the sciences and medicine have limited the library's ability to keep abreast of current output in many divisions of its special subject responsibility. While designed as a local, rational division of subject responsibility, both Crerar and Newberry's collections have long served as regional and national resources and should play important roles in any future cooperative development which will take place regionally and nationally. The problem is one of adequate support and some way must be found to support these established strengths on a cooperative basis. Perhaps in terms of critical mass, involving collections and costs there are some lessons, for Linda Hall Library as well as for John Crerar Library.

Robert Downs and others have cataloged the many developments, be beginning with the establishment of the National Union Catalog in 1900, and

the publication of the "Union List of Serials" in 1927, which marked the
change in direction in this country from widespread self-sufficiency among
libraries to a larger frame of reference in which sharing of resources
would be seen as a matter of immense mutual benefit. The Depression
seems to have been influential in the creation of the early regional cooperative
bibliographic centers in Denver. Philadelphia, and Seattle as well as
numerous local and state union catalogs. After World War II, the Library
of Congress sponsored the Cooperative Acquisitions Project for Wartime
Publications which demonstrated that our national library could provide
leadership in large cooperative activities, and that the American libraries
could work together in an acquisition program involving research materials.
Other national efforts that followed included L. C.'s project for Wartime
Publications, and of course, the Farmington Plan, which recently, after 25
years' activity, has come to an end. After 1961, Public Law 480 made
possible the acquisition of millions of items which were distributed to several
hundred American libraries. The most ambitious and promising program of
all is the National Program for Acquisitions and Cataloging, with the goal of
eventually bringing to the United States, promptly after publication, the
world's publishing output, cataloged and ready for use.

Most of these plans are primarily concerned with comprehensive or
elusively complete coverage of the total output, distributed, in many instances,
among hundreds of existing research libraries. The other side of the coin,
however, is illustrated by the creation of the Center for Research Libraries
and the Hampshire Inter-Library Center, designed to acquire and to store
highly specialized, little used materials. The Hampshire Center's primary
collecting interests are current and retrospective serial files, and monu-
mental sets, and increasingly the Center for Research Libraries is also
concerned with hundreds and perhaps thousands of serial titles in the
chemical sciences and biological sciences which are not found in the collections of the constituent member libraries. Also under consideration is the
possibility of establishing a National Lending Service for serial and periodical
titles on the model of the British National Lending Library for Science.
These are very significant moves, which show every sign of materializing
and growing, with the likelihood that they will find national and regional
financial support. In a country of this size, not one, but perhaps ten or
twenty such efforts might do a great deal to relieve the pressures on the
large and beleaguered research libraries. In the case of the little used
materials it would be obviously less expensive to provide direct support
rather than to acquire, house, and service such titles in every institution
concerned, or even in any considerable number of them.

The acquisition process in its simplest expression is concerned with
selection of materials, searching, and ordering, and receipt and record
keeping. In the context of resource sharing, these activities are carried on
at a series of levels for a number of institutions in a local, regional, state,
or national framework.

At each level, as the working paper indicates, goals must have been defined, responsibilities established, priorities arranged, and sanctions agreed upon. Strengths and weaknesses must be appraised.

Before the starter can be pushed, university administrators must agree on which institution is to develop which academic programs, especially in areas requiring high-cost, little used materials — a broad prescription covering much that goes into a research library acquisition program. Libraries are often caught in a squeeze, and often receive the blame for that which they cannot control. There are presidents and deans, often well endowed with the competitive spirit, and faculties basing their prestige and attractiveness on special collections in their own fields. Metcalf has pointed out that the one unfortunate factor in interlibrary rivalry is that it is commonly only on a numerical basis:

> This may be absurd; but measurement of library quality is a very different matter, while it is easy to compare the number of volumes on the shelves. Some of the volumes may be worthless and some may be almost impossible to locate through the catalog, but all can be counted. It is easy also to boast of rarities and special collections, regardless of whether or not they are used. Manuscript collections are impressive even if the library does not know how to care for them. The universities, on their part, may be duplicating professorships in fields where there are not enough students to go around; some institutions have boasted that they have more departments than any other in the state or region. Any competitive absurdities of which libraries may be guilty can be matched in other parts of the institution... enough has been said, perhaps, to indicate why the general atmosphere has not encouraged cooperation.

Changes are beginning to show, often after pressure from above. California, after a special audit by the State Finance Officer, has come up with a proposal that the 8 campuses of the University of California and 16 of the 19 campuses of the California State University and College System form "two regional intersegmental consortia for library cooperation" with the Northern Consortium at UC Berkeley and the Southern Network at UCLA.

Under this plan UC Berkeley and UCLA would continue to maintain huge research libraries, but each of the other 25 libraries "would purchase low-use materials only in the areas in which it is specializing (if any). Specialties would be arranged by subject area, so that the total range of subjects receives coverage, but not duplication, within each region. A complex system of buses and trucks carrying books and book-users from campus to campus would be employed."

Much was made of the fact that these California libraries had purchased 37 sets of the British Parliamentary Papers, costing between $40,000 and $60,000 per set. "The report emphasizes that it is not suggesting that the acquisitions policy be governed solely on the basis of a popularity contest. Within the realm of scholarly works, though, it does seem possible to differentiate between high utility and low utility items, and to make purchasing definitions accordingly."

In Missouri, at least for the state-supported universities, another state-wide plan is now under extensive study with some decisions made and some objections under consideration. Doctoral programs in particular areas are to be limited generally to one of the institutions — largely where existing strengths are established and evident and where they fit into related favorable circumstances outside the university community. It will not be easy, but the future development of the libraries involved will inevitably be better clarified, their acquisition programs more readily defined and delimited, and perhaps their faculties and students more reconciled to the impossibility of self-sufficiency and more inclined to accept the techniques and communication devices which will be required to meet their needs.

Chapter 8

PROCESSING

John Charles Finzi
Library of Congress
Washington, D.C.

The topic on which I have been asked to write is "Processing" within the broader context of "How to Share Resources." I am not an expert in computerized library techniques and networking, nor am I a "processing librarian" in my professional career, if one speaks strictly in terms of cataloging and other processing techniques. My professional library career has, in fact, been devoted almost exclusively to acquisition and to the development and management of scholarly library resources. But, when I started looking closely at what was involved, at least two redeeming features about the request that I write on this topic occurred to me. First, the position which I have occupied at the Library of Congress for the past eight years is, in one of its major aspects, one of liaison between the Reference Department, which is the custodian and the exploiter of the collections, and those other departments of the Library of Congress which are engaged in the acquisition and processing of the materials destined for the Library's collections. This has meant a constant awareness of the impact of these processing activities on our library resources and of the impact of these same activities on the complex bibliographic apparatus maintained by our Library. The second redeeming feature that occurred to me was that, not being primarily a processing librarian, I might be able to look at the complex interface between processing and the utilization of library resources in a more detached and perhaps cooler way. And this is exactly what I have tried to do. I shall try in fact to stay away from technical problems and details, to which I could not contribute anything new, and shall instead try to look at the total picture of shared processing activities from a more general and philosophical angle, drawing from time to time conclusions that to me seem valid.

At this point, however, before proceeding any further, I must introduce one final caveat. I must make it clear at the outset that I come from an institution which, while engaged in the processing of vast quantities of library materials and in the creation of a large percentage of the national bibliographic data, does not, in a highly technical sense, share processing activities, outside of certain exceptions, with any other institution. The exceptions to this statement will be discussed later, but the point must be made that from our point of view the most important elements we can contribute to a conference on the subject of "resource sharing" are those that deal with the many ramifications of the use of the original data created by the Library of Congress and of the vast possibilities for its exploitation within a national network or a system of networks.

And here I should make my position clear. Not only do I think that the sharing of resources has today become an inescapable necessity, but I should also stress the fact that the sharing of resources is already taking place at an increased tempo and in wider and wider circles. In thinking and reading about this matter, two fundamental facts immediately became apparent to me. First, the literature on the subject is already enormous from both the theoretical and technical sides, and, second, the term "resource sharing" as applied to processing activities can and should be looked at on many different levels. What do we mean by sharing resources for processing activities? Cooperative efforts in this area can include all of the various library functions normally performed between the time the material is selected for the collections to the time when it is made available to the user. Such traditional functions as ordering, accessioning, cataloging, classification and subject analysis, pasting book and spine labels, and so on, can all be considered proper activities of cooperative processing centers. The variety of arrangements throughout the country today is very great and ultimately each cooperative system will have to decide which activities it wishes to centralize for maximum benefit.

The benefits that are generally cited in the literature, and the various technical processes involved, are indicative of the fact that we are confronted with a complex of operations which are amenable to many different solutions and could not and should not be approached with the hope of finding a single answer. Centralized procurement and cataloging of multiple copies of books for a number of libraries is certainly a form of "resource sharing," but so is the tapping by several libraries of cataloging bibliographic data from a central computerized system. Yet the two approaches are essentially different and are designed to meet different needs. Configurations of "resource sharing" seem in fact to have developed in many different patterns, of individual libraries or consortia or cooperative groups; the arrangements are generally based on the specific local situation and local needs. Centralized procurement and processing, on the one hand, and the use of cataloging data prepared elsewhere, on the other, are different aspects of "resource sharing," but they are neither contradictory nor exclusive and could, in many cases, overlap advantageously. It also seems clear, however, that centralized activities such as procurement, cataloging, and the preparation of books for the shelves are generally restricted for maximum benefit to geographic proximity, and by the willingness and ability of a certain number of libraries thus to pool their resources, while the use in the cataloging process of bibliographic data already available through national or regional channels is less limited by geographic factors and not as bound by the many constraints that, especially in the use of academic libraries, seem to make such arrangements as centralized procurement and processing exceedingly difficult.

Between these two types of "resource sharing" there is, however, a whole gamut of variations and discrete arrangements. It is here, it seems to me, that each proposed cooperative project should engage in a severe examination of needs and in a cost analysis of the current individual library's operations and those of the proposed centralized system. But aside from this, the most important considerations for each library in joining a cooperative system would be the viability of the project, and the benefits to be gained by the ultimate users of the library's resources. As important as cost analysis of operations are surveys and other relevant data concerning the needs of a member institution and its public.

I feel, however, that when we talk today about "resource sharing," especially in the area of cataloging, we must face up to the fact that our horizons have considerably expanded in recent years. The sharing of cataloging data across the country and across the world is no longer something projected for the future, but a reality that is developing before our own eyes. No consortium of libraries being planned today can ignore the fact that a vast percentage of the bibliographic data needed for the control of current materials is being created centrally by the Library of Congress and other institutions and made available either directly or through subsidiary channels to other institutions across the country. While the procurement of library materials and their physical preparation for use will, in most cases, remain the function of well delimited consortia sharing a commonality of interests and geographic proximity, the bibliographic data needed for their control will, I assume, be shared nationally through a network of services and will know no geographic barrier.

The experience of the Centralized Processing Center run by the University of Massachusetts Library at Amherst for the public institutions of higher education in the State of Massachusetts may serve at this point as

a very good example of what I am talking about. In a speech delivered at
the National Program for Acquisitions and Cataloging meeting at the 1973
Midwinter Conference of the American Library Association in Washington,
Richard Talbot, acting director of libraries, reported the following information which, I think, is highly relevant to this discussion. For the last
three years the Centralized Processing Center has processed $6,000,000
worth of library materials or 610,000 physical volumes and 78,000 microforms and produced 3,200,000 catalog cards. The costs for the first year
were 82.5 cents per volume for an average of 12 copies per title, and for
the second year they rose to 93 cents per volume for an average of four
copies per title. These costs covered the development and programming
costs as well as the entire processing cycle: the production of selection
cards produced from MARC tapes which were sent the participating schools;
the processing of orders; the receipt of materials; production of catalog
cards and labels; and finally the dispatch of the books to the participating
institutions. It is evident that even the cost of $1 per volume would seem
to be a remarkably low cost for such services. This low cost was achieved
only because the Center was able to use MARC data in a kind of closed loop
system. From a single MARC record already edited and in machine form,
the Center manipulated the data to produce selection cards, order forms,
an on-line accounting system, and catalog cards. Mr. Talbot thinks further
reductions in the total costs are possible. At the present time, MARC can
be used by the Massachusetts Centralized Processing Center for about 25%
of its total acquisitions. It is clear that in future years, when foreign
languages will be added to the MARC tapes, this percentage will considerably
increase.

The pattern of what is happening here is quite clear and can be stated
very simply. Here we have a centralized processing operation for a group
of academic libraries which engages in procurement, processing, and book
preparation, but, superimposed on this, we also have for at least 25 percent
of its acquisition, the use of cataloging data which is created elsewhere
and which is made available to the Center not through the work of local
professional catalogers but through a steady flow of magnetic tapes received
from a central source. This pattern is spreading, albeit with many local
variations and adaptations, but exhibiting a consistent thread which seems
very promising for the future. The activities of an increasing number of
consortia throughout the country and of such regional or state operations as
those of the Ohio College Library Center and the New England Library
Information Network, are too well known for me to mention. I shall come
back later, however, to the operation of the Ohio Library Center in order to
illustrate more complex elaborations and certain problems which also should
be faced.

At this point, however, I should like to devote some time to a review of
those activities of the Library of Congress that have and will increasingly
have an impact in this area. Having said at the beginning of this talk that the

Library of Congress does not, in a highly technical sense, share processing activities with other institutions, I must set the record straight by pointing out and underlining some very important exceptions. These exceptions fall in two main areas. First, the area of true technical processes. In one library activity at least the term "shared" is purposely used: the shared cataloging aspect of the National Program for Acquisitions and Cataloging. Under this program the Library of Congress uses in its cataloging of current foreign materials from countries that produce up-to-date and current national bibliographies the descriptive data prepared overseas for those bibliographies. This is a form of sharing, one that has appreciably accelerated the cataloging operation for these materials. Moreover, this form of sharing cannot but become more meaningful in years to come when, it is hoped, it will be possible to have direct access to the machine-readable data, produced in standard MARC format and using the International Standard Bibliographic Description or ISBD, from foreign bibliographic centers. At the present moment several foreign countries have already adopted or are planning to adopt a MARC format in their operations. While we are discussing the area of shared technical processes, it is worth noting that the Library of Congress is presently very active in studying, in cooperation with the other two National Libraries, the National Library of Medicine and the National Agricultural Library, possible areas of fruitful cooperation. Through the activities of the United States National Libraries Task Force on Cooperative Activities, several working groups have been active during the past few years in analyzing problems such as acquisition, descriptive cataloging, subject headings, serials data, authority files, etc., with the aim of introducing both standardization and cooperative undertakings wherever possible. This work has been very productive and the evolutionary approach taken in all these areas is very promising. The second area of exceptions, and the one more pertinent to this discussion, is the one where sharing is performed not at the primary level of actual processing activities, but in a secondary stage where the actual products of these activities are made available in a variety of forms to all other libraries throughout the country. It is safe to say, in fact, that all the bibliographic activities of the Library of Congress have been addressed historically to this goal. Beginning with the distribution of printed cards at the beginning of the century and moving on from the preparation and distribution of a variety of printed catalogs to the rapid distribution of increasing quantities of machine-readable catalog records for current publications this trend has remained unmistakably clear. Several generations of librarians have devoted much thought and work to the idea that library materials should be cataloged not repetitively by each individual library but once at one single place and that the cataloging data be made available to other libraries. This idea is closer to realization today than at any other time in the past. Such large undertakings as the Public Law 480 Program, the National Program for Acquisitions and Cataloging, the Cataloging-in-Publication Program, and the distribution of MARC tapes have been addressed to this national need. Coverage is not by any means complete and there is still a long stretch of road ahead, but the percentage of current publications which are now centrally cataloged is steadily increasing.

Leaving aside for the moment the traditional LC printed cards which supply cataloging data for a large percentage of the world scholarly output in languages other than English, let us look, for example, at what now is included in the MARC tapes and rapidly available in machine-readable format to libraries and secondary distributing centers throughout the country: first, a large percentage of the current United States publishing output, including at quite an early prepublication time the materials which are now cataloged in the Cataloging-in-Publication Program; second, all other monographic materials in the English language received and cataloged at the Library, be they from Great Britain, Canada, Australia, New Zealand, South Africa, India, Pakistan, or any other source, for a total annual output of approximately 80,000 records.   It is currently planned that materials in the French language will have been added by the summer of 1973, and that later, by progressive stages, other foreign languages will steadily be added to the MARC output. Other series of MARC tapes already contain films and audio-visual materials, serials, and single maps both American and foreign.

As the Library of Congress expands its MARC program to other languages and forms of materials, the MARC service will have to be augmented to allow for selective distribution: by language, data, media, etc. In addition, to insure timeliness, the current weekly tape service could be replaced, where applicable, by daily distribution via data transmission equipment and on-line access should be made available to developing regional networks. The concept of a national network, based on actual operational experience, is emerging and just as the manual system is able to provide selective information, so must a machine system ultimately have this capability. These matters are still in the study and planning stage and no time schedule can be assigned to these developments, but it is clear that the potential for the future is very great.

I mentioned earlier the inclusion in the MARC tapes of cataloging data being produced by the Cataloging-in-Publication operation and I should like to return to this because of its implications for processing activities in individual libraries and cooperative projects. Under the Cataloging-in-Publication program, books issued by a number of participating publishers are cataloged at the Library of Congress several months prior to publication so that the cataloging may appear in the printed volume, when published, on the verso of the title page. Currently approximately 385 publishers are participating in this program and it is safe to say that between 60-70% of the American monographic trade output is presently included in the CIP program. Between 225 and 325 titles are input to MARC from the CIP program weekly, and from the beginning of the program on July 1, 1971, approximately 16,000 titles have been cataloged in this manner. Currently, the average annual figure is between 15,000 and 16,000 titles. The presence of the cataloging records in the MARC tapes means that libraries using these tapes will be able to select American materials needed for their collections long before publication and to have at their disposal nearly complete cataloging data. On the other hand, the presence in the published volume of the same information will make possible for libraries acquiring them to have at their disposal an immediate form of control.

Well known as they are, it could not be possible to end this brief review without mentioning, even in passing, the various printed catalogs issued by the Library of Congress and their key function as national tools. The National Union Catalog of Pre-1956 Imprints, nearly one half of which has already been published and which, when completed, will comprise approximately 600 volumes, is particularly worth mentioning for the role it is already playing and will increasingly play in the interlibrary loan activities of American libraries.

I have spent some time on some of the current activities of the Library of Congress in the area of bibliographic control and in the preparation of current cataloging data, because these activities are today basic not only to the processing activities of individual libraries, but, and even more so, to any cooperative undertaking addressed to the transmission and sharing of such information. Carol Ishimoto, senior cataloger in the Harvard College Library, puts across this point very neatly in her recent article in College and Research Libraries concerning the impact on university libraries of the National Program for Acquisitions and Cataloging, when she states that without this program "virtually no major academic research library, in view of the tight budgetary situation in recent years, could have continued to maintain present levels of bibliographic control" [see Reading 13, p. 134].

Basic, however, to any exchange or sharing of bibliographic data in processing activities are the standardization and compatibility of the formats and of the entries and subjects assigned to the individual items. This requirement is today becoming crucial to any expansion of dissemination of bibliographic information in machine-readable form through networks and distributing services. Some current well known problems affecting the Ohio College Library Center, where the data bank now receives cataloging data from various sources which are often not compatible from the point of view of entry or subject, is indicative of the imperative work that remains to be done in this area before a totally satisfactory sharing of bibliographic information can be achieved on a national scale. In this connection, it is the hope of the Library of Congress that the authority file for authors and the one for subjects may some day be issued in machine-readable form. If this were done, an enormously useful tool for file control, permitting all kinds of cross-reference systems, would be made available to other libraries, distributing centers, and networks.

I have mentioned some of the tools and some of the problems, but in conclusion I should like to stress that "sharing resources," despite all the organizational and technical problems that still remain to be solved, is here to stay and that it is incumbent upon us all to see that an orderly and well planned national system emerges from all this for the benefit of all libraries

COLLATERAL READINGS

1. "Academic libraries in Utah form cooperative council," LJ, <u>97</u>, 1658-1659 (May 1, 1972).
2. H. D. Avram, <u>Transferability and the NELINET project</u>, New England Board of Higher Education, Wellesley, Mass., 1970.
3. L. R. Baker, "United we stand, divided we...the case for cooperation among CAE libraries," <u>Australian Library Journal</u>, 15-22 (Sept. 1971).
4. (C. K. Balmforth and N. S. M. Cox, eds.) Interface; library automation with special reference to computing activity. M.I.T. Press, Cambridge, Mass., 1971.
5. (Barry E. Booth, ed.) "Intertype library cooperation," <u>Illinois Libraries</u> <u>54</u>, (May 5, 1972).
6. "Cooperation in action," <u>LJ</u> <u>98</u> 1074-1076 (April 1, 1973).
7. "Cooperative programs, problems and progress" <u>Proceedings of American Society for Information Science, communication for decision-makers; 34th annual meeting, Denver, November 7-11, 1971</u>, Vol. 8, Greenwood, Westport, Conn., (1971) pp. 217-237.
8. Carlos A. Cuadra and Ruth J. Patrick "Survey of academic library consortia in the U.S." <u>College & Research Libraries</u>, <u>33</u>, 271-283 (July 1972).
9. Diana Delaney and Carlos A. Cuadra. <u>Directory of Academic Library Consortia</u>, System Development Corporation, Santa Monica, Calif.,1972.
10. (Henry J. Dubester, ed.) "Issues and problems in designing a national program of library automation," <u>Library Trends</u>, <u>18</u>, (April 1970).
11. Paul J. Fasana, "The collaborative library systems development project; a mechansim for interuniversity cooperation. <u>Bookmark</u> <u>29</u>, 365-368 (July 1970).
12. Paul J. Fasana and Allen Veaner, eds. <u>Collaborative library systems development</u>. M.I.T. Press, Cambridge, Mass., (1971).
13. Carol F. Ishimoto, "The National Program for Acquisitions and Cataloging; its impact on university libraries," <u>College & Research Libraries</u>, <u>34</u>, 126-136, March, 1973.
14. Joe W. Kraus, "Cooperation among academic libraries in Illinois, <u>Illinois Libraries</u>, 54, 468-472, (June 1972).

15. James O. Lehman, "Cooperation among small academic libraries," College & Research Libraries, 30, 491-497 (Nov. 1969).
16. Lawrence E. Leonard, Joan M. Maier, and Richard M. Dougherty, Centralized book processing; a feasibility study based on Colorado academic libraries. N.J., Scarecrow Press, Metuchen 1969.
17. Ronald F. Miller, "Network Organization- A Case Study of the Five Associated University Libraries (FAUL)" in Conference on Interlibrary Communications and Information Networks, Airlie House, 1970, Proceedings, American Library Association, Chicago, 1971, pp. 266-276.
18. Thomas Minder, "The Regional Library Center in the mid 1970's; a concept paper," University of Pittsburgh, Graduate School of Library and Information Sciences, Pittsburgh, 1968.
19. National library services," in Council on Library Resources, 16th Annual report, 1971/72. Washington, D.C., 1973, pp. 17-22.
20. Edwin E. Olson, Russell Shank, and Harold A. Olsen "Library and information networks," in Annual Review of Information Science and Technology, Vol. 8, American Society for Information Science, Washington, D.C., 1972, pp. 279-321.
21. Ruth J. Patrick, Guidelines for library cooperation; development of academic library consortia. System Development Corp., Santa Monica, Calif., 1972.
22. "Two library consortia to go online with OCLC," LJ 97, 3528, (Nov. 1, 1972).

Chapter 9

TOWARD A NATIONAL PLAN FOR COOPERATIVE STORAGE
AND RETENTION OF LITTLE-USED LIBRARY MATERIALS

Robert H. Muller

Queens College, City University of New York
Flushing, New York

There is no special virtue in cooperative storage as such. It is a
means to an end. We should resort to it only if it can save us money without causing too much inconvenience. In theory, it may appear advantageous
and logical to store little-used materials in a common facility built at low
cost, located on cheap land, and less costly to maintain than storage
facilities operated separately for each institution. Those advocating cooperative storage would argue that it will also reduce duplication of materials
and free space in existing buildings, which will then not have to be expanded
until much later.

There are some who question whether any of these objectives can
actually be attained. One student of the subject in particular, H. Joanne
Harrar, wrote a doctoral dissertation [1] on cooperative storage, and
concluded that it has been "limited in realization" despite the fact that in
theory it would seem to make good sense. She analyzed the three most
prominent examples of cooperative storage, the Midwest Interlibrary Center
in Chicago (now called Center for Research Libraries), the New England
Depository Library in the Boston area, and the Hampshire Inter-Library
Center at Amherst, Massachusetts, and concluded that processing costs had
increased instead of having been reduced, due to the added steps required
to transfer the books from the main collections and to reprocess them for
storage. She discovered that cooperative storage had eliminated duplication

to only a limited extent and that the originally anticipated economies had not
been demonstrated in operation. On the positive side, however, she pointed
out that storage centers had stimulated the development of certain other
programs not originally envisaged, and these programs may, indeed, have
proved to be beneficial, notably, the joint acquisitions programs and
cooperative specialization in subject collecting. However, she points out
that in order to achieve these objectives, one does not really need a physical
facility for the joint storage of materials. She further concluded that the
three storage facilities she studied should not "be looked upon as successful
models upon which future storage facilities should be patterned" [2].

Not everyone would necessarily agree with Miss Harrar. It would
depend upon how you measure success of an enterprise. When Keyes
Metcalf was recently asked what he now thought of the New England Depository Library, which he was instrumental in getting started beginning in 1937
and which commenced operations in 1942, he thought it was successful
because it had saved money in the cooperating institutions and the 30-year
mortgage had been paid off in 15 years. However, F. X. Doherty, who
reported on this storage venture, had said earlier that it had not done much
toward reducing duplication or increasing library specialization [3]. This
library storage center is controlled by 12 member libraries, including
Harvard, M.I.T., Boston Public Library, Massachusetts Historical Library,
etc.; it was constructed in an accessible location on land donated by Harvard.
The total cost of the building was about $215,000, and the building is still
in operation; it has a capacity for 1.5 million volumes. The Director of
the Center for Research Libraries in Chicago, with its 3 million volumes in
compact storage, probably also regards his cooperative as a success.
However, if one were to measure success in terms of original objectives,
one may have to conclude, as Miss Harrar did, that most of these objectives
had not been achieved. Yet if one considers the conversion of the midwest
storage center into a major national bibliographic resource, its enlargement
from its ten charter members in 1951 to a membership of over 90 institutions,
one may assume that the original investment of $750,000 from the Carnegie
Corporation, plus $250,000 from the Rockefeller Foundation, has paid off.
As at the New England Depository Library, the land for the Midwest Inter-
Library Center was donated, in this case by the University of Chicago. The
Center has enabled member libraries to weed their collections, to reduce
standing orders, to keep subscriptions to foreign newspapers and little-used
scientific journals at a lower level than would otherwise have been possible,
and to curtail collecting activities in such categories as foreign dissertations,
college catalogs, state government documents, telephone directories, etc.
Recently (March 19, 1973), a $40,000 agreement was signed between the New
York State Library and the Center for Research Libraries, providing interlibrary loan access to the materials in the Center to any library in the state
of New York which is not already a member of the Center. This program is
an experimental one, to last for six months. Undoubtedly such far-reaching
innovative cooperation would not have taken place without the existence of
this Center.

The Hampshire Inter-Library Center, for which a special facility was not constructed, was first housed in the library of Mount Holyoke College and later transferred to the library of the University of Massachusetts. Because overhead costs were supported by the institutions in which the Center was housed, it is difficult to determine the exact magnitude of the benefits achieved. However, construction of new space was probably postponed at some of the cooperating institutions.

If we examine the basic motivation and logic supporting the development of storage libraries, there seem to be essentially two conditions involved: (1) Libraries run out of space, and relief must be obtained in some fashion. If construction funds for new storage facilities on a given campus are not available, the existence of a storage center will naturally seem to be appealing because construction can then be postponed even though storage will cause a considerable amount of inconvenience and extra expense. (2) A perhaps more important condition is that all large libraries contain a great deal of material that is not being used very much. For instance, Ralph Ellsworth reported for the University of Colorado that at peak times only somewhat less than 15 percent of the collection was in active use. In his comprehensive treatise on the economics of book storage in college and university libraries, he mentions that this condition may not be true of all libraries at all times and may differ from field to field, but he says that "stories are legion about the books and journals that remain on shelves year after year with their pages uncut" [4]. It is the characteristic of a research library that a great many of its books are very infrequently used. Fussler and Simon showed that if the least used 50% of a collection is removed, 93% of the books called for will still be available. If 80% is removed from the collection, 80% of the demands will still be satisfied. If you remove 25% of a large research library, you can expect that the average book in the storage facility to which the books have been moved, will not be called for more often than once every 35 years [5]. This use pattern is the basic fact which leads many to conclude that something should be done to remove the less active part of the collection to a facility that costs less to build than a typical library building on a main campus and where books can be shelved more densely, e.g., by size, and which costs a great deal less to maintain. However, Miss Harrar concluded that there is no evidence that such a facility, built on land owned by a given institution for its own storage needs alone (as was done at Michigan, Princeton, Yale, and Berkeley), is more costly than banding together with a number of institutions for the purpose of cooperative storage [6]. Granted that the Fussler and Simon conclusions concerning the use of a large research library are correct, the problem still remains as to how we can determine which part of such a large collection is not likely to be used, and this is the problem to which Fussler and Simon addressed themselves in considerable detail. They attempted to identify the factors that should govern us in selecting books for storage, the primary factors being the publication date and the use of the book. (The publication date would, of course, vary from field to field.)

Those who have studied cooperative storage in actual operation, do not seem to agree that it is advantageous. Nevertheless new proposals have continued to crop up. For instance, at my own college, Queens College, it was proposed in 1967 that a very large storage facility for the libraries of New York City be constructed underground. This idea was not acted upon after it was subjected to scrutiny by a special projects committee of METRO. In A Study of Seven Academic Libraries in Brooklyn and Their Cooperative Potential [7], it was proposed by Rice Estes in 1963 that for these institutions, which included Long Island University, Pratt Institute, and the Polytechnic Institute of Brooklyn, a large central research library be constructed and, failing that, the idea of a storage center be explored; it was to be modeled after the Hampshire Inter-Library Center. As in the case of Queens College, nothing came of it. More recently, in 1970, the five associated university libraries of New York (the New York State Universities of Binghamton and Buffalo, plus Cornell, Rochester, and Syracuse) issued a report entitled An Analysis of Book Storage and Transportation Requirements, written by Tesfaya Dinka and Davut Okutev, both associated with the Industrial and Engineering Department of Syracuse University [8]. In this report it was stated that "data clearly show that it is advantageous to construct a high density storage library at a central location [8, p. 32] (Ithaca or Syracuse), to be operated with vehicles owned by the corporation. It is a detailed and penetrating study of the various factors involved in a central cooperative storage facility, covering such matters as land, construction costs, transportation of materials, compact storage options, and selection of storage equipment. This proposal has not yet been acted upon.

Another proposal which did not materialize was for a Northeast Regional Cooperative Library Center. It was discussed between 1948 and 1952 and might have included the Library of Congress, University of Pennsylvania, Princeton, Columbia, New York Public, Yale and Harvard. The idea died after it was proposed that $150,000 first be sought to finance a feasibility study.

The possibility of a storage program has also been considered by METRO (the New York Metropolitan Reference and Research Library Agency, one of the nine such agencies in the State of New York). Hendrik Edelman wrote a report in 1969, entitled Shared Acquisitions and Retention System [9]. Edelman did not recommend that a storage building be constructed but that METRO contract with one or more libraries in its geographical area to take responsibility for the retention of last copies of certain types of material. Such a "retention center" would be financially supported by a fixed fee for each title handled for a requesting member library. This proposal, in the absence of any possibility of construction money, assumed that there would be enough empty space in existing libraries that could be used for the storage of last copies. Thus the stored materials would be distributed or scattered rather than centralized [9, p. 14]. METRO has since embarked upon a modest joint acquisitions program supported by contributions from its member libraries. Expensive materials, which need not be acquired by any one of the libraries independently, are bought from this cooperative fund; and the acquired materials are accessible to any member library upon request to the library which agreed to store the material. The retention-center proposal, however, has currently a low priority on the METRO agenda.

Thus the idea of cooperative storage has not vanished despite the reservations that have been expressed about it. If we accept Miss Harrar's contention that the three major existing storage centers are questionable because they failed to fulfill the original objectives, we may now ask if there is not a model that is worth emulating. One viable enterprise that comes to mind is the Medical Library Center, located in New York City at 102nd Street near 5th Avenue, which was chartered in 1959 and which began operating in 1964. It was sponsored by the Academy of Medicine and other medical libraries to house a collection for shared use. Those cooperating now number 30 medical libraries, with those designated as sponsoring paying $10,000 a year, and those who are merely participating (that is, hospitals and smaller research institutions) $3,000 a year. This center now houses nearly 40,000 volumes of 6,000 titles of medical and scientific periodicals and about 97,000 unbound pieces of periodicals; in addition, it has 27,000 textbooks and monographs. These materials were transferred from member libraries. The opinion was expressed that if it had not been for Dr. Howard Reid Craig, then Executive Director of the New York Academy of Medicine, which was desperately in need of space, the project would not have gotten off the ground. As in the case of the Midwest Inter-library Center and the Hampshire Inter-Library Center, it required foundation grants, which in this case amounted to half a million dollars and a loan of $450,000 to enable the Center to purchase an existing garage and loft building erected in 1920. The building has 8 stories, and the Center occupies only one and a half stories of this space at present and rents the rest of it, mostly on short term leases. It derives a substantial amount of its income from the rental of these spaces. It is a viable institution with an operating budget of $200,000 a year and is probably saving the member institutions substantial amounts of acquisitions money, even though there is at least one institution (Columbia) which is known to have been reluctant to transfer much of its little-used materials despite overcrowding, and there seems to be a reluctance of some of the other member libraries to give up their books unless forced to do so in view of excessive overcrowding. The present Director of the Center, Mrs. Jacqueline W. Felter, expressed the view that one does not have to have a physical depository facility in order to make a cooperative program possible. However, a program of distributed joint storage among existing libraries is obviously a much more fragile entity because there is no guarantee that it will be feasible to continue to make stored materials readily available to member institutions indefinitely.

At present a crucial part of the operating program is the daily messenger service, by means of two trucks rented from the Hertz Corporation, with a driver employed by the Center [10]. Without such assured delivery service, the program is likely to be much less acceptable, and it is noteworthy that in the study of the Five Associated University Libraries, major attention was, indeed, paid to the transportation problem including insurance; and the conclusion was reached that the fastest service of all could be obtained if the proposed center operated its own delivery system with leased or bought vehicles, equipped with special racks, which were claimed to reduce dramatically the packaging costs and time.

It would seem that the Medical Center Library may well serve as a prototype and has much to recommend it, particularly because of one feature which is not characteristic of the libraries that joined together in the other centers. This feature is a common subject matter. I suspect that if more libraries of a similar type, such as law libraries, theology libraries, engineering libraries, music libraries, tried to join together for the purpose of cooperative storage or distributive storage, greater benefits could be achieved than if we confined our thinking to inter-institutional arrangements among diverse neighboring institutions*.

We should not be too optimistic, however, about the attractiveness of the central storage idea to all concerned since there are some basic forces that work against it. Among these impediments are the following:

1. In most libraries book storage costs are not considered part of the operating budget. If libraries had to pay out of their annual budgets for the amortization of the capital that created the space used for the storage of books, their directors would probably evince a great deal more interest in cooperative storage centers. In business and industry, one pays for space as part of the operating budget, but most libraries are not held budgetarily accountable for the cost of space. Whenever the library runs out of space, it tries to solve its problem first by creating its own storage library or resorting to some kind of compact storage, to postpone the day on which they have to ask for new construction funds.

2. In recent years, many libraries have, indeed, been able to build new space without too much difficulty, especially with the help of Federal loans and grants; and as long as such funds are obtainable, there is no great incentive for seeking cooperative storage as a possible solution.

3. There has always been, and still is, a reluctance on the part of libraries, especially when faculties are involved, to have some of their books located at some distance. The inconvenience of having a delay-time

---

*Edelman states, "We should like to urge the further development of group-ings of special libraries with comparable subject interest." He notes that this is already in existence among theology libraries [9, p. 7].

for delivery and the handicap of having to do one's work at some distance
are considered serious.

4. As has been shown in the examples, a considerable capital-plus-
land donation has been required to convert a storage idea into reality and to
get it started. In addition, there seems to be needed a sustained effort on
the part of one individual or several who are connected with an institution
which has a self-interest in creating space not readily obtainable otherwise.

5. There is concern over the high cost of selecting material for storage
and the cost of record-changing; it has also been claimed that the cataloging
cost is higher since a scholar needs a more detailed and accurate description of material if it is stored in inaccessible locations. In other words, it
is not clear that in all situations there is likely to be a cost-reduction in the
processing of library materials unless materials are immediately funneled
into a storage facility, as was done at Harvard in the early stages of the
New England Depository, so that decataloging or changing of records is not
required.

6. One cannot overlook the element of local pride in the size of the
collection. Many librarians and presidents are quite reluctant to see their
own libraries shrink in size; they may fear that such reduction may also
mean a loss in stature and reputation.

7. There is also the question of library property and the legal restraints
that prevent some libraries from transferring materials from its own
campus to a centrally operated facility. This problem has been neatly taken
care of by the Center for Research Libraries through the establishment of
a category of books stored in that Center to which the institution does not
lose title. However, it is often assumed that there are legal obstacles to
the transfer of materials that stand in the way.

8. There is also a point overlooked which may be called the inability or
unwillingness of administrators, politicians, and bureaucrats to make long-
range plans and work toward long-range benefits. It is so much more
normal to look for immediate tangible solutions to problems and leave the
crises that are likely to arise twenty or thirty years hence to our successors
to solve. Short-term solutions are often more readily applauded and
rewarded by one's immediate and present constituency, and many of us tend
to operate on the assumption that the future will somehow take care of itself.

For the United States as a whole, there really seems to be no adequate
program to cope with the continuing accelerating growth of research library
collections on each and every campus of the major universities of this
country. It seems that we need a program that goes beyond local, state or
regional boundaries; and the only hint found in the literature on the subject
was in a 1960 monograph on storage warehouses by Orne, who envisaged
possibly five major libraries in the United States to entertain a new concept
of national responsibility, with a nationwide plan calculated to utilize every
major, minor, private, and public institution, to the extent that it should
participate in the national responsibility [11]. Such a plan, Orne said,

could be directed by the Library of Congress or even by some supranational library authority. Basic to Orne's concept is the principle of nation-ownership of library materials. Orne admits that his ideas may seem visionary.

We are likely to continue to build on the base of existing structures instead of creating a setup based on a broader concept commensurate with the total task. What we may need is one national center (or several centers) to which every low-usage book is routed for deposit and where at least two copies will be preserved and stored. One of these copies would be non-circulating; the other one could be readily and quickly borrowed upon request. If such a library existed today, our acquisition and retention policies throughout the library community would be fundamentally altered. Such a concept could probably only be brought into existence if one were to start from scratch at a given date. We could make available everything from, say, 1976 on, and would include photocopying and royalty payments to copyright owners as well as access to computer-based bibliographic records of the titles stored, rapid interlibrary lending and teletype links and facsimile transmission for urgent requirements. There is nothing "blue-sky" about such a model. The only forces that would keep us from developing such a nationwide system are our separate institutional strivings toward local comprehensiveness.

It is doubtful if such a plan can materialize before the year 2000; we are more likely to continue to use expediencies and temporize until enough institutions have reached the breaking-point beyond which they can no longer afford to maintain collecting and retention programs as presently conceived and operated. The sooner we realize that narrowly based storage centers can merely postpone the evil day, and the sooner we begin to work toward the establishment of a comprehensive, centrally directed national program for preservation and ready dissemination of predictably little-used books, the better off we will be. We must begin to plan more rationally for the future and not limit ourselves merely to what is feasible locally or regionally.

The three major existing storage libraries should not be looked upon as prototypes. They came about as a result of a combination of felt need, seed money, land grants, strong leadership, and strong direction. They constitute what happened to be practicable and attainable to gain short term benefits. The ultimate solution requires a national plan for the storage of readily lendable little-used materials, plus a computer-based catalog of such materials and speedy transportation. However, researchers and scholars must lower their expectations and not insist on immediate delivery of little-used materials. If users continue to be unreasonable, cooperative storage will not be realized.

The optimal requirements of a national retention center would be a location on inexpensive land in a nonpolluted location near air transportation. If speed of delivery is regarded as important, the center might include in its budget the operation of aircraft or helicopters, plus contracts with existing airlines, plus speedy local delivery. The storage and use of the non-circulating second copy of each retained title should involve proper security measures to guard against natural disasters and acts of war, theft, and vandalism. Special preservation measures are also required to guard against deterioration of paper; and transfer of text to microform may be indicated in some cases. For security reasons it may be necessary to provide for two such centers, with the second one in a secret location serving as a backstop. With a sufficient number of library members, the envisaged retention and service system could probably be supported by institutional membership fees, which might be lower than present burdens carried for comparable purposes by each institution separately. However, if support by membership fees should prove insufficient, seed money and continued partial support by the federal government would be justifiable since the system would constitute a major national resource.

The idea of a central agency for the preservation of little-used materials is not entirely original. It has previously been proposed, but in a different context, where the emphasis was on preservation for posterity rather than on achieving current cost savings. The proposal was made in 1964 and published in 1966 by Gordon Williams, on behalf of a Committee of the Association of Research Libraries concerned about the preservation of deteriorating books. The summary report stated that "the most practical solution requires the establishment of a federally supported central agency that will physically preserve, for use when required, at least one example of every written record of significance, and that will insure the ready availability of adequate copies of these books and other records to all libraries" [12]. Part of the proposal involved deacidification of the paper and storage at deep-freeze temperature of minus 2 degrees to prolong life expectancy of books to a span of over 4000 years. The proposal also considered a duplicate location, but did not actually come out in favor of such extra protection. Nor did it endorse the idea of a separate catalog, but recommended instead appropriate number designation within the National Union Catalog.

A final question might be asked: why can the present Center for Research Libraries not assume the task of preserving little-used materials on the comprehensive scale proposed in this paper? The answer is that, theoretically speaking, there is no fundamental obstacle. In practice, the Center has currently insufficient space, is located in an urban atmosphere, and is inadequately subsidized. A branch of the Center is conceivable that would overcome present restraints and place its operation on a base commensurate with its total task to serve all the research libraries in a more systematic and consistent way than has hitherto been attempted.

REFERENCES

1. Helen Joanne Harrar, Cooperative Storage Warehouses, unpublished Ph.D. dissertation, Rutgers, the State University, New Brunswick, N.J., 1962.
2. Helen Joanne Harrar, "Cooperative Storage," Library Trends 19, 328, (Jan. 1971). See also "Cooperative Storage Warehouses," College and Research Libraries 25, 37–42, (Jan. 1964).
3. Francis X. Doherty, "The New England Deposit Library: Organization and Administration," Library Quarterly 14, 18, (Jan. 1949).
4. Ralph E. Ellsworth, The Economics of Book Storage in College and University Libraries. The Association of Research Libraries and the Scarecrow Press, Metuchen, N.J., 1969, p. 28.
5. Herman H. Fussler and L. Simon, Patterns in the Use of Books in Large University Libraries, University of Chicago Libraries, Chicago, 1961, p. 143.
6. Rutherford D. Rogers and David C. Weber, University Library Administration. H. W. Wilson, New York, 1971, p. 238. See also Lucinda Conger, "The Annex Library of Princeton University: The Development of a Compact Storage Library," College and Research Libraries 31, 160-167, (May 1970).
7. Rice Estes, A Study of Seven Academic Libraries in Brooklyn and Their Cooperative Potential, Council of Higher Educational Institutions, New York, 1963, p. 70.
8. Tesfaya Dinka and Davut Okutev, An Analysis of Book Storage and Transportation Requirements, Office of the Coordinator of Library Systems, Five Associated University Libraries, Syracuse, N.Y., August 1970.
9. Hendrik Edelman, Shared Acquisitions and Retention Systems (Shares) for the New York Metropolitan Area, New York Metropolitan Reference and Research Library Agency (METRO), 1969.
10. Jacqueline W. Felter, "The Medical Library Center of New York: A Progress report," Medical Library Association Bulletin 56, 13-20, (Jan. 1968). See also Eugene T. Boice, Richard G. Noble, and Faye Simkin. The Medical Library Center of New York, METRO Miscellaneous Publication No. 6, New York, New York Metropolitan Reference and Research Library Agency, August 1970.
11. Jerrold Orne, "Storage Warehouses", in the State of the Library Art, vol. 3, part 3. Rutgers, The State University, Graduate School of Library Science, New Brunswick, N.J., 1960, p. 32.
12. Gordon Williams, "The Preservation of Deteriorating Books," LJ, 91, 51 (January 1, 1966).

Chapter 10

DELIVERY OF SERVICES

Glyn T. Evans

Director of Library Services
State University of New York
Central Administration

In this discussion of delivery of service I am assuming as a starting point that resource sharing is essential both because of the growth in the volume and variety of materials, and because of the state of siege in which higher education finds itself; and that academic programs will consolidate, but that library collections must acquire maximum flexibility and mobility. I propose a view of delivery of service which includes the librarian in the dual role of both deliverer and recipient.

DEFINITION

Effective delivery of service requires that we increase access to records and materials to two groups of people: librarians and users. In some cases the transaction will be complete in itself; in others the operation is an intermediate step.

TABLE 1

Pattern of Demand for Service

	Item	
Recipient	Records	Materials
Librarian	Complete transaction	Partial transaction
User	Partial transaction	Complete transaction

This table is clearly an oversimplification. On some occasions, a citation without an item will itself satisfy a user, for example, but the table will help as we consider the development of mechanisms for the delivery of service.

Records to Librarians

Librarians need records which will locate items. These records need not be full bibliographic citations, but rather only comprise sufficient data uniquely to identify an item and its location. The location may be at local, regional, state or area level. Each location is assumed to have, or have access to, a full bibliographic description of the piece held. The location list may include circulation and in-process records.

Librarians also need full authoritative bibliographic records which they can use — copy, or (worse) adapt — to describe their own collections. They need a greatly expanded subject approach to the literature via abstract and indexing services. And, of course, finally, they need the essential linkage between these three levels of record, which are not as discrete as this section suggests, but are totally interdependent. For example, presenting a list of citations from a retrieval system to a user has not solved his problem; it has merely changed it. We should flag such citations from the outer ring of records with location and availability information from the inner records the further to assist the enquirer.

Records to Users

The user will rarely require a full authoritative bibliographic citation other than as a confirmatory mechanism. The user generally wants to know what and where the item is.

Items to Librarians

The receipt and handling of an item which is intended for addition to a collection is out of the scope of our discussion here. Rather, we are concerned with the librarian's role as intermediary in the interlibrary loan transaction or the movement of material to and from a central store.

Item to Users

Three mechanisms are possible for the delivery of an item to a user. The user can rely on his own library to seek and obtain; or he can go to another library and borrow directly; or he can rely on the item being delivered directly to him, from any source.

*   *   *

In addition to records and materials, two other factors, or rather, resources which have to be shared, must be considered.

The first of these is professional library expertise. Very good librarians are rare, and they are expensive. A good librarian supported by a good reference collection can deliver an astonishing amount and variety of service to a wide range of users and other librarians. How much utilization of such a service would be made by smaller libraries in a consortium if one were initiated?

The second factor is space. I am not so much concerned here with storage space (Dr. Muller (see Chapter 9) has already excellently analyzed that problem) but rather the provision of reading space for users of libraries. A particularly expensive aspect of this resource is the provision of access to the wide variety of hardware needed to access audio-visual and computer-aided-instruction software.

G. T. EVANS

MECHANISM FOR DELIVERY OF SERVICE

Records

It has now been amply demonstrated that on-line computer technology
is the method of choice for the delivery of bibliographic records among
libraries.

It is possible to point to systems which work at the three levels of
record defined above. The Ohio State University Library control system
provides a short bibliographic record sufficient to identify an item and its
location. We are replicating this system in State University, initially for
the Albany campus, but also hope to expand the system in order that it
become the basis of a University-wide location list. Syracuse University
has developed a similar system.

The relationship between the location record and an interlibrary loan
system has to be considered. The instantaneous knowledge of available
locations changes the emphasis from finding a location to assigning the
most appropriate location from which an item should be requested, probably
on the basis of geographic proximity, traffic and communications patterns,
and equal distribution of load.

The success of the Ohio College Library Center in providing authoritative bibliographic records which libraries can use for cataloging is well
known. This system also provides a Union List of holdings as libraries
take records from, or contribute to, the data base. As the system gets
older this Union List will clearly increase in utility. The Center will
expand its services to include serials cataloging and control, and an acquisition or technical processing system.

On-line access to indexed citations for medical information is at present
available to libraries through two networks. Based on the Medlars tapes
from the National Library of Medicine, State University of New York's
Biomedical Communication System and NLM's own Medline system between
them serve some 120 biomedical libraries, including a link to Europe.
State University will expand the services offered through the Biomedical
Communication Network in the near future to include data bases in a wider
range of subjects which the user or librarian may search for information.

We are presently considering ERIC, CBAC, BA Previews, and Excerpta
Medica.

A number of factors have contributed to these development, including
the advance in computer and communications technology with a comparative
reduction in digital data storage costs, the development and acceptance of
standard formats for data description, the general readiness of libraries to

accept technological change and, not least, the remarkable people involved in the system design. That such success has been achieved will help us.

One of the reasons that resource sharing among libraries has been so unsuccessful is that, unless information can be exchanged almost instantaneously, the overheads, delays and general demoralization resulting from interminable paper pushing is just too time consuming, and too inefficient. When a conscientious and diligent interlibrary loan librarian remarks that sending out a request for an item is like throwing a bottle containing a message from a raft, one has a measure of the level of service — and the level of frustration entailed in attempting to provide service.

This is as true of cooperative acquisitions as interlibrary loan. It is also true that on-line control of collections and, in particular, location lists, makes ready and easy change of records a very cheap operation, in contrast to Dr. Muller's reference to nine separate operations to change records prior to cooperative storage of material.

I have been asked to pay some attention to the critical mass of users, and the costs of providing service. Obviously, different systems and services will be different and I therefore propose the following as a reasonable administrative goal: The size of the system must be large enough to be able to service all users on a total cost recovery basis on terms which will be cost-beneficial to the user library.

At first glance this seems like an obvious statement, but implicit in the statement are the assumptions that size produces economy of scale, and that libraries will have to support the service from their own budgets.

The major problem which has to be faced is the generation of linkages between the different levels of records, on the one hand, and interfaces between different systems providing similar services in different regions of the country, on the other.

I submit that with the above exception, however, we are almost out of the research phase in on-line library technology. The systems cited above are not perfect, by any means, but they work, and are cost-beneficial to the participants. I believe that we are now at the stage of synthesis as we combine the known building blocks into a total system of service. We know how to deliver service in the form of bibliographic records.

Material

We do not know how to deliver service in the form of material, which is a much more difficult task. Even given that an efficient on-line record system is available, we still have to move pieces, either as originals or copies. There is a certain bitter irony that, at precisely the time when on-line transmission of records is at last available, the United States Mail service, the method of choice for interlibrary loan service, should undergo such a monstrous and dramatic deterioration. We are, I think, forced to look at alternative methods.

It is necessary first to establish criteria for service. What period of time should elapse between request and delivery? Should we aim for 95% of all items in 24 hours? Is two days a tolerable delay? Is a week? The pattern of traffic also has to be ascertained. A study done by the Five Associated University Libraries in Upstate New York reported that over an 18 month period 47% of the interlibrary loan traffic among the group was between one pair of libraries, and only six links each contributed greater than 5% of the total traffic, or 95% of all traffic. Indeed, some pairs of libraries were not connected during that period. What effect does a traffic pattern like this have on planning a delivery service? To what extent can a commercial carrier, United Parcel Service for example, be used to move materials? What other delivery services with regular schedules to link campuses are available? Food, drink, and laundry services, perhaps?

Whichever technique is adopted, and whatever standards of service are accepted for the system, there always must be a system override for the urgent case. We do have to be prepared to send items off by car or motor-bike, or even to have secretaries dictate sections of papers over telephone lines if the need warrants it. Finally, what fiscal support mechanisms must be devised to underwrite interlibrary loan transactions?

Thus far I have assumed that the piece or a photocopy will be moved physically and mechanically. It may well be that electronic communication systems will be the best technique for item transmission, as they are for record transmission. Telefacsimile is an established technology with a growing number of users. An experiment conducted in New York State some years ago concluded that this technique was too expensive, and further, no user apparently needed that degree of urgency. But as costs come down it may be worth looking again.

Is video transmission the system of choice? If it is, to what extent is it necessary to support it with hard copy follow up? Are there other techniques in development which are likely candidates? To what extent should the user be forced to attend a center where there is hardware available for this type of transmission, or rather, is it possible to provide service in the user's own home or office?

There is one other mode for the delivery of service as material to users. It is conceptually the simplest technique of all and yet it seems to be the hardest to realize in practice. I refer to a system of open access or borrow-ing privileges among institutional libraries. Under this system a student or faculty member from one institution is allowed to borrow items from

another, reciprocating, library. Here the difficulties stem from libraries
and their administrations fearing systematic plunder and pillage of their
collections, and lack of control over borrowing. And yet, systems can be,
and have been, developed which assign responsibility for borrowing and
protect the lending libraries. Such a system is available to graduate
students and faculty in the Five Associated University Libraries. It is well
used and there have been very few cases of abuse since its introduction some
years ago. Southern Illinois University has such a system on its own
campuses and the Council of Head Librarians in Illinois has recently embarked on a system of a universal borrowers card as a statewide experiment;
this is presently a subject of active discussion within the State University of
New York.

The tacit assumption that the large libraries will bear most of the
traffic may not be borne out by experience. As we work in SUNY it will be
interesting to observe the movement of undergraduate students from
University Centers to four-year and two-year institutions to access those
library collections.

The planning mechanism has to account both for use during sessions
and intersession use. The home location and enrollment of students by
geographic area is a valuable planning tool. This kind of report is available
to State University from its office of Institutional Research.

There are clear advantages to a system of open access. The potential
borrower has a chance to see the piece, and others on the same topic,
before it is borrowed, and at least part of the load on interlibrary loan
systems is relieved. The final question which I want to raise in this section
is, to what extent should we be prepared to move users to books rather than
books to users? Perhaps there is some Archimedean principle at work
here that states, "If the user is going to displace a weight of paper greater
than his own weight..." although I fear that such a statement is discriminatory
against the larger of us.

ORGANIZATION OF SERVICE

The essential precursors to resource sharing and delivery of service
are a suitable administrative superstructure and an appropriate fiscal
foundation. A permanent organization to ensure delivery of service, indeed
all resource sharing, is essential. It should have responsibility for stimulating,
coordinating, implementing, and maintaining cooperative efforts. A form of
governance in which both librarians and administrators are represented is

needed. Administrative participation is important in order to support and represent the librarians within their own institutions; the librarians should not be making their decisions in a vacuum. The permanent staff need to respond to their internal environment, and the changes which will take place in their external environment, while attempting to balance the two to get the best for their own membership. In particular, they will have to judge when it is necessary to perform "research"; and when it is possible to "develop" or adopt existing mechanisms. The member institution must clearly be able to justify participation and usage on a cost-benefit basis.

I have already indicated that on-line systems of bibliographic information, which are showing cost benefits to participating libraries, are available. What is necessary now is the seed money to make the systems available to more libraries.

Money is needed to train computer personnel and librarians in the use of the new systems. Computer hardware and software have to be acquired and installed. Communications networks have to be designed and terminals placed in the libraries. After some time the systems must be self-supporting with the libraries totally carrying the cost of system maintenance; however, I doubt that many can easily raise the implementation money from their own budgets.

It is perhaps worth noting here that any work undertaken along these lines would not be performed as a pioneer endeavor. I meet regularly with representatives from library consortia which totally encompass the Eastern seaboard from Canada to Mexico. All are working along the lines I have indicated above, and all are working together on an inter-regional basis.

Library cooperation is a difficult undertaking. It requires a certain type of leadership, which can get results by persuasion and example, rather than by demand or fiat. It requires careful participatory planning by those it will affect. It requires patience, understanding, and faith on the part of administrators and legislators. It requires the careful assignment of priorities as libraries' needs differ. It may set standards which will be difficult for some to attain.

I believe that we can arrange our affairs so that we can deliver service to a larger constituency and from a larger total collection if we are prepared to cooperate and share our resources. In doing so, we will both be fulfilling our obligations to our users, and helping in our own survival.

NOTE ADDED IN PROOF

The State University of New York university-wide open-access system began operation in January, 1974.

Part Three

WHEN TO PROCEED?

   Cooperative programs succeed only as long as each participant
perceives them as beneficial to the institution.

   The question of whether now is the time to move ahead in resource
sharing depends, in the minds of some, on the technological state of the art.
For others, it is the state of the art of cooperatives at the local, regional
and national levels.

   Chapters 11 through 14 explore this question from the several viewpoints.

Chapter 11

NETWORK TECHNOLOGY FOR LIBRARY RESOURCE SHARING — WHY?

Isaac L. Auerbach and Herbert B. Landau

Auerbach Associates, Inc.
Philadelphia, Pennsylvania

INTRODUCTION

In the past 20 years, information systems technology has made significant progress. The current state of information handling art is indeed sufficient to support and encourage the sharing of resources among academic libraries. The pace of technological improvement shows no signs of abatement and librarians will find it rewarding to explore the realm of networking possibilities that this new technology makes feasible.

When will the technology be capable of supporting effective library resource sharing? The answer is now; and network resource sharing is already an accomplished fact of life. To paraphrase one of the key findings of the recent National Academy of Sciences' sponsored study into libraries and information technology [1], the primary bar to development of automated library networks is no longer a technology feasibility problem. Rather it is the combination of institutional, organizational, human related and economic value system problems. Therefore it is our aim here to demonstrate that readily available information storage, information processing, and information transfer technology can facilitate the sharing of library resources.

A BASIC NETWORK MODEL

  Before moving into information technology, it may be worthwhile to take a brief look at how information flows in a network (Fig. 1). While bibliographic to networks may assume a variety of sizes and configurations, they usually exhibit three basic classes of functions:

1. Information storage
2. Information processing and control
3. Information transfer

  The general relationship among these functions is as in Fig. 1.

  Information may be stored in various forms. It may be extracted from the stores and processed in various ways. It may then be transferred back to the original store or to various other stores. Information users can extract information directly from an information store or indirectly via the information processor and controller node. There is no theoretical limit to the number of stores or processors. In a library network, the basic

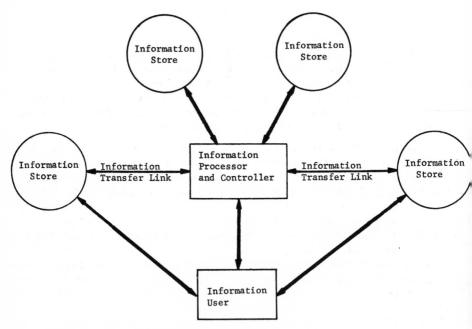

FIG. 1. Simplified information network model.

form of storage (or at least the original input form to the system) is the printed document, and the primary storage facility is the library. The user may be considered an information network himself, as he is both an information processor and an information store. He can create information, extract information, intellectually process it, and store it for later use. He may even return his stored and processed information to the library in the form of a new document. Therefore, to serve its users effectively, a library network should have the means for information storage, information transfer, and information processing and control.

Modern technology can now provide us with many ways in which library networks can store, process, and transfer information to facilitate resource sharing economically, effectively, and on a scale that would be near impossible with traditional manual operations. Some current examples of the state of the art in these three functional areas are discussed below.

INFORMATION STORAGE TECHNOLOGY

Most living things possess the ability to store and retrieve information. Man, however, has expanded significantly his ability to store and retrieve information through the development and application of various forms of technology. This ability to artificially store information resources for future retrieval and utilization is the raison d'etre of the library. Without the capacity for relatively large scale information storage and retrieval, the library network cannot function effectively.

There is a wide range of media which can be used to store information. Camras [2] in his review of the subject identified over 20 potential information storage media with different storage densities, storage capacities, and access speeds. Among these are:

1. Graphic Storage Techniques (Paper)
    Typed page
    Book page
    Halftone picture
    Snapshot photo

2. Graphic Storage Techniques (Non-Paper)
    35mm color slide
    Microfilm
    Videotape

3. Sound Storage Techniques
   Phonodisks
   Sound Tape

4. Digital Storage Techniques
   Computer data register and logic
   Magnetic core memory
   Magnetic drum
   Punched cards
   Thin film memory
   Magnetic disk file
   Computer tape

5. Biological Storage Techniques
   Human brain and nervous system
   Genetic

Figure 2 presents Camras' ranking of a number of these storage systems according to a figure of merit (known as "CDS Rating") which considers storage Capacity, storage Density and Speed of access. Although several years old now, Camras' comparison is still valid and interesting.

In the discussion below, we would like to review some developments in the two areas of storage technology that most lend themselves to the library network environment, digital storage technology and graphic storage technology.

The distinctions between digital and graphic storage are essentially the form in which the information is stored. Graphic information may be stored in the form of books, catalog cards, photographs, microfilm, and videotape. Digital information generally includes any coded representation which can be processed by machines without first requiring transformation to machine language.

Digital Storage Technology

Digital storage normally refers to a form of machine readable information storage which will allow the information to be processed by computer. Libraries have begun to store more and more of their information (particularly cataloging data) in digital form to allow for rapid and efficient processing by computer. As Mathews and Brown [3] point out, a digitally stored catalog has many advantages over the common card catalog, the book catalog and the microform catalog. These major advantages include:

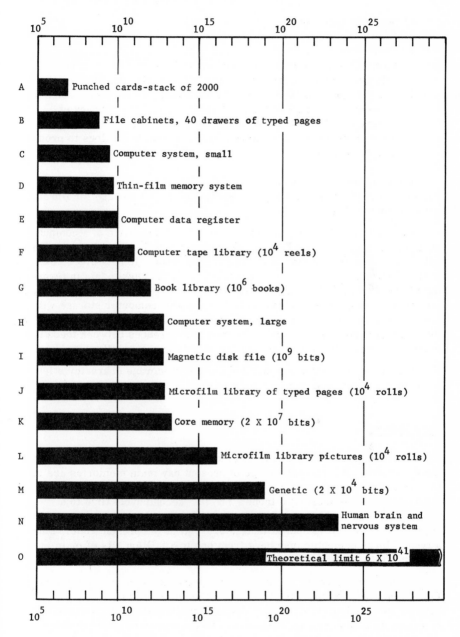

FIG. 2. CDS rating, total bits x bits/cm³ x bits/sec. Taken from Ref. 2.

1. Speed in searching
2. Ease of updating
3. Ease of restructuring to facilitate different search strategies
4. Ease of conversion to other media, such as microform (via computer output microfilm) or paper (via a high speed printer)
5. Ease of rapid duplication of additional machine readable copies for dissemination to other libraries (such as with the Library of Congress MARC [Machine Readable Catalog] magnetic tapes)
6. Ease of merging two or more machine readable catalogs to produce a union catalog

These advantages (despite the attendant disadvantage of high input cost) definitely justify serious consideration of digital storage for library network applications.

When we talk about digital storage we mean those parts of a computer system that hold both data and the programs that determine what processing will be performed upon that data. In a digital automatic data processing system, storage contains a representation of alphanumeric data in terms of digits (see Price, [4] for a fuller discussion of digital character representation in a bibliographic environment). Generally, computer storage will consist of two types of storage (or memories as they are sometimes called): main storage and mass storage. The major differences between these two classes of computer storage are access speed (or accessibility) and cost.

Figure 3 [5] gives a comparative picture of storage characteristics for both main and mass memory technology.

Main Memory

The most quickly accessible and most expensive form of storage is the main memory. A large percentage of present day main memories are in the form of arrays of magnetic cores. Within the past 15 years core memory speed has increased from a 1×10^{-6} second cycle time to a 3×10^{-7} second cycle time. During the same period, cost has dropped from over \$1 per bit to approximately \$.01/bit at the present time. Since a typical large computer may have from one to 8 million bits of main memory, this can be an appreciable cost savings.

While some increase in core access speed can be expected in the near future, this will not be on the level of another order of magnitude. New devices such as integrated circuit devices and laminated ferrites are emerging and these new techniques may increase access speed to some degree. However, current levels of internal storage speed have been found generally adequate for handling library problems [6].

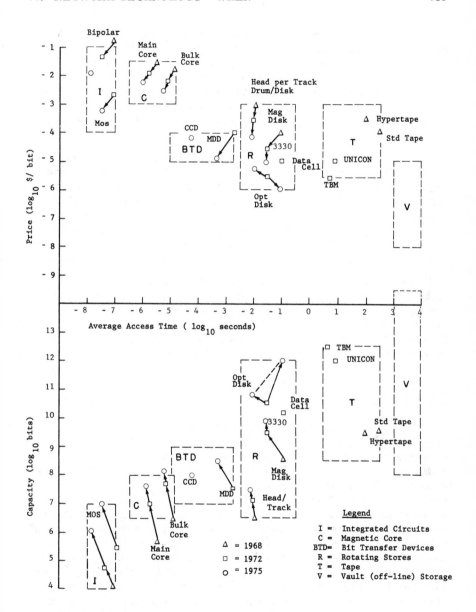

FIG. 3. Digital storage characteristics.

With regard to core size, however, a primary limitation to the development of truly large scale cooperative bibliographic data bases has been the
need for large quantities of core storage of its equivalent. This is due to
the need to store both data files being processed and also the extensive
software needed for multiprogramming and for on-line interactive retrieval
systems. Sophisticated data management systems may require in excess
of one million characters (or bytes), equivalent to 8 million bits of relatively
fast memory.

As can be noted on Fig. 3, until recently this requirement came close
to exceeding the limits of the memory core capacity state of the art and
required distribution of software between main memory and secondary mass
storage devices. However, with the expansion of core capacity and the
advent of bulk core or extended core storage (ECS) modules, which can
extend core capacity by another 7-8 million bits, it is now possible to
accommodate virtually all library system software requirements in main
memory with reasonable access times and at reasonable cost.

Another technique for dealing with limited core capacity is known as
virtual memory. Essentially, virtual memory amounts to using high speed
disks and drums to provide relatively inexpensive (but slower) expansions
to main memory. This approach gives the programmer the illusion (hence
the name virtual) that he has a very large main memory at his disposal
even though the computer may have a relatively small main memory.

Mass Memory

Mass Memory (or bulk storage devices as they are sometimes known),
provide large stores of accessible digital data as a supplement to the main
memory. Generally, mass storage may be considered to be either random
acess (e.g., magnetic disk) or serial acess (e.g., magnetic tape). Data
on these devices must be transferred to the main core memory before it
can be processed. Of particular significance to the library community, the
mass random acess storage device technology has advanced to the stage
where large capacity and relatively low storage cost now make it practical
to store large volumes of bibliographic data on-line, where any given record
can be rapidly accessed regardless of file location. Recent technological
progress now makes the central, multiple input and multiple access on-line
data base a reality. This type of capability is necessary to accomplish
effectively such network activities as cooperative cataloging, centralized
acquisitions, centralized circulation control and cooperative index file
building and searching.

Low cost mass storage is a prerequisite for large-scale library networking because of very large file size associated with cooperative bibliographic data bases, as opposed to typical business data processing

applications. For example, it has been estimated [1] that when the Ohio College Library Center expands to full operation in several years, it will have to provide access to six million unique items, located at multiple locations among 50-60 different libraries. At approximately 600 bytes (at 8 bits/byte) of bibliographic cataloging information for each item, a storage capacity of 3.6×10^9 bytes (or about 3×10^{10} bits) is needed just to store the catalog records alone.

As an extreme example, it has been estimated that the information content of the Library of Congress is in the range of 10^{14} - 10^{15} bits, requiring 10^{11} - 10^{12} bits for the catalog files.

Random Access Mass Memories. The most common random access mass memory devices in use today are the rotating magnetic disk and the data cell or magnetic card. These devices utilize magnetic oxide coatings which are rapidly passed before stationary magnetic heads to record, erase, and read data. Conventional devices of this type, as shown in Fig. 3, represent a current storage capacity upper limit of 10^{10} bits with average access times of from 10 to 600 milliseconds for disk to about one second for magnetic cards.

A drum storage device may store as much as four hundred million (4×10^8) characters of data with an average access time of from 10 to 35 milliseconds, at a cost of about a tenth of a cent per bit. This access time is faster than magnetic tape but slower than main memory core. However, the cost is far less than that of core, although greater than tape.

Magnetic disks are a further development in random access mass memories representing a compromise between drums and tapes in terms of capacity and speed. The disk pack (a small group of attached disks), unlike the drum, can be removed from the computer and stored in an off-line vault like a magnetic tape. A modern 10 disk (20 surface) disk pack typically stores up to one billion (10^9) bits employing current technology. Access time is in the order of tens to hundreds of milliseconds with costs of about a tenth of a cent per bit or less.

Magnetic cards (such as the IBM Data Cell system), though still in use in some bibliographic operations, are losing popularity because of their relatively slow access speeds. Their major advantage is their ability to store large quantities of data at a relatively small cost per storage bit. A typical magnetic card system can store 4×10^8 characters or bytes of data (equivalent to 3.2 billion bits) at a cost of roughly 1/1000 of a cent per bit. However, access time is rather poor, approaching one second, which is normally not acceptable for most on-line applications.

Advanced Random Access Mass Memory Technology. It has been predicted that several significant advances in mass memory technology can be anticipated. Dr. William Shockley (as quoted in the New York Times of January 7, 1973), inventor of the transistor, recently stated: "It is in the

area of computer memory that man's greatest inventions will likely come.
Machine memory will be increased a billion-fold, not a million-fold over
its present level."

Several emerging areas of mass storage technology, now in the experimental or developmental stages, hold the promise of improving access time
and of extending storage capacity at least two orders of magnitude to 10^{12}
or 10^{13} bits without appreciable increase in cost [7]. These developments
may encourage library resource sharing by enabling larger numbers of
libraries to pool data economically while ensuring rapid retrieval access.

The magnetic bubble memory, a major technique being developed by
Bell Telephone Laboratories and others, bears close watching. This
experimental memory, also known as the Bit Transfer Device (BTD) and
the Magnetic Domain Device (MDD), may provide random access devices
in the billion bit range with a reduction in access time of at least two orders
of magnitude [8]. This feat is accomplished by eliminating mechanical
rotational and read head movement. Another experimental form of BTD is
the Charge Coupled Device (CCD) which uses Metal Oxide Semiconductors
(MDS).

Laser optical recording on magnetic and amorphous semiconductor
media can increase storage density to the point where the trillion bit random
access disk store may be commercially available within the next two years.
As evidence of the advancing pace of mass memory technology, a potentially
significant breakthrough was announced recently [9]. This is the 10 trillion
(10^{13}) bit optical laser memory. The performance characteristics and
price of this new development were reported as "staggering" and they
represent significant potential for library system applications. This random access optical mass memory provides access rates of only 20 nanosec-
onds (20 $\times$ 10^{-9}) at a cost of about 2 $\times$ 10^{-5}c per bit. That means that
this memory is capable of storing a library of 2.5 million books a cost of
about $8 per book. With a device such as this it now becomes possible to
store the equivalent of all available Library of Congress catalog card data
on a single random access device. The company that has announced this
new memory (Laser Computer Corporation) is also planning to develop an
atomic lattice memory with the mind-boggling storage capacity of 10^{40}
bits!

A little further on the horizon is the holographic, as opposed to bit by
bit, recording technique. A device using this principle should be able to
achieve storage capacity of 10^{10} bits or more.

Serial Access (Magnetic Tape) Mass Memories. Although it was the
first form of digital computer storage, magnetic tape is rapidly losing
favor as a mass storage medium. As random access drums and disks
become larger and cheaper, the relatively slow access speed of the tape,
engendered by its serial search mode, becomes more of a problem.

(Magnetic tape, however, is gaining in popularity as a bibliographic information dissemination device to be discussed later in this paper). The advantage of magnetic tape is that it is the least expensive form of mass storage (about 5/100 of a cent per bit, or .015c per 30 bit word). Magnetic tapes, because of their compact size, are as easy to store as books. It has been estimated [10] that the storage cost of a book on magnetic tape is about $30 as compared with $25 for the bound volume (not considering hardware and software costs).

A standard magnetic tape is capable of storing over one million English language words. However, to pass the entire tape from beginning to end in order to access a particular piece of information, may require as much as five minutes. This delay may be intolerable under certain circumstances despite the relatively low storage cost of magnetic tape.

Despite the drop in popularity of conventional magnetic tape storage, it is interesting to note that several new mass storage devices using magnetic tape media have recently been developed. Two separate trillion bit storage systems using magnetic tape, the Ampex Terabit Memory (TBM), and the Gruman Masstape, are now operational. A third magnetic tape trillion bit system, the CDC Scroll, is in a developmental phase.

Another operational trillion bit system, the UNICON 690, employs a laser to encode binary data on polyester film strips which are then handled in a manner similar to magnetic cards.

Associative Memories

Content addressable or associative memory systems have been under; investigation since 1955. Of interest to the library community is the capability of the associative memory to identify and correlate information items on the basis of their content, not only by their name or position.

Although relatively small scale associative memories have been constructed and are operational [(11, 12)], there is no evidence today that indicates that associative memory arrays with a capacity of a billion bits will be available within the next five to ten years.

Graphic Storage Technology

Graphic Storage Technology (Paper)

The most common form of graphic storage device, and, in fact, the most common information storage device, in current use is the one most common to libraries: the print on paper (or hard copy) medium exemplified by the book. Although the thrust of this paper is directed at nonbook media, there are several technological comments which can be made about the book, as contrasted with other technology based information storage systems. This contrast was made by Bruno W. Augenstern, vice president of the RAND Corporation [13]. The major advantages of the book as a information storage and dissemination medium are:

1. The match to the human scale (the hand and eye particularly)
2. Portability — no artificial power needs or requirement for power outlets (who will ever use an electronic visual information device in places like the bathroom and the beach?)
3. Indefinite storage life without degradation
4. Relative permanence of information, compared to risks inherent in electronic devices where sheer inadvertence can destroy the information
5. Ability to function as an informative transmission and storage device over an extremely wide range of environments
6. Excellent file, random access, and search features
7. Ability to be marked up, annotated, or make corrected manually
8. High information density capability
9. Immediate usability (no need for warm up, programming or reprogramming, reformatting, etc., as use requirements shift)

We feel that it is important for the librarian investigating the various applications of modern technology to information storage and retrieval to keep these points in mind. The book is a very well engineered storage medium and one should very carefully weigh the cost benefit tradeoffs involved in replacing it with other forms of information storage.

Microform Storage Technology

At this point in time, the digital storage of full text documents is still not economically feasible. Therefore, as an alternative to paper hard copy document storage, increasing attention has been directed at microforms as both an information storage and transfer medium. In fact there is a distinct trend towards hybrid systems which couple the information manipulation capabilities of the computer with the full text storage qualities of microforms. Two examples are the computer driven microform information retrieval systems [14] and computer output microfilm [15] better known by its initials, COM.

Microform as a storage and transfer medium offers a number of distinct advantages which could be exploited in library network applications:

1. Compact storage of information (with a storage density of about 10^8 bits/CM^3 compared to 10^3 bits/CM^3 for a magnetic disk and 10^4 bits/CM^3 for a book page [2]

2. High fidelity recording of both text and images in black and white and color

3. Economical and facile replication (1/10c per page or less for microform to microform replication)

4. Ease of dissemination and transport (an entire microfiche document can be mailed in a single letter-size envelope for 8c first class postage)

Microforms come in several types. The principal types are:

1. Roll microfilm — The medium first used in modern microfilming applications. The microimages lie on a roll of film, either in cine orientation (arranged like the frames on a roll of motion picture film, with the horizontal lines of the microimages perpendicular to the edge of the film) or in comic strip orientation (arranged like the frames of a comic strip, with the horizontal lines of the microimages parallel to the edge of the film). Both perforated and unperforated film is used; the most common film widths are 16mm and 35mm, but 70mm and 105mm film are desirable in certain situations. In some systems, the microimages are paired so that two frames lie across the width of the film. Up to 35,000 catalog cards, tab cards, or similar documents can be microfilmed onto a 100-foot roll of film in this manner, if a 45:1 reduction is used.

2. Cartridges — A convenient way of handling roll microfilm. Film is packed in a cartridge, in much the same way as film is packed for cartridge-type amateur cameras. The cartridge is easily placed on the reader; film advance and rewind are usually motorized.

3. Aperture cards — Single microfilm frames mounted in 3-1/4 x 7-3/8" cards. The film fits into a window cut in the card. Cards can carry printed legends identifying the frames and can also be coded with Hollerith punches for machine sorting, since they have the same overall size as standard EDP cards. After selecting the correct card, the operator places it on the reader and adjusts it manually until the image is properly positioned on the viewing screen.

4. Film cards — Cards containing one or more pockets to hold strips of microfilm. The strips are removed from the pockets and placed in the reader for viewing.

5. Microfiche — A group of microfilm frames arranged in a rectangular pattern on a piece of film. The fiche are manually inserted into the reader and moved until the desired microimage is projected onto the screen. Horizontal and vertical coordinates of the projected item are often indicated by a pointer moving across a grid card or by built in scales.

A number of different fiche sizes and configurations are possible. The most common size is 4" x 6", the most common configuration is the

COSATI (President's Committee on Scientific and Technical Information) and NMA (National Microfilm Association) with a 98-page format filmed at 24:1 reduction; and DoD (Department of Defense) with a maximum of 60 pages at 20:1 reduction or 98 pages at 24:1 reduction.

Even greater reductions are possible if the microfiche are made by a newer high-resolution photochromic process that permits a ratio of about 150:1. A standard 4 by 6-inch fiche can thus hold up to 3,200 $8\frac{1}{2} \times 11$-inch pages at 150 reduction or up to 2,100 pages at 120 : 1 reduction. Such fiche are often called "ultrafiche".

6. Microprint — Rows of microimages on an opaque paper card. Except for its opacity, it resembles microfiche. The opacity, however, prevents use with standard microfiche readers. Special readers are available.

What has traditionally been a drawback in the use of microforms, the lack of low cost high quality viewing equipment, may be eliminated as the result of a recently announced breakthrough [16]. A completely new technique, under development by Dr. Adnan Waly, employs a "fly's eye" system of 3500 minute spherical lenses which break down a page into a matrix pattern, requiring a projecting distance of less than an inch.

This development has tremendous potential impact on the library community. Dr. Waly has estimated that with this system, a 625-page book can be reproduced on microfilm for less than $25. Equally interesting, pocket-sized readers, employing multiple lenses, may be mass produced for about $5 each.

Should this system become operational, libraries could readily reproduce their collection for dissemination to users and other cooperating libraries. Each student in a particular course could be given a low cost reader, and a full set of reference books, which are now commonly held in reserve in the library. A library could reproduce its entire catalog cheaply (and perhaps even major segments of its collections) on film and distribute film copies to other cooperating libraries. It should be recognized, however, that some problems may be encountered in trying to focus on individual characters, due to proportional spacing of the print.

Network Applications of Microforms. In an information exchange network context, perhaps the greatest sponsor of microform has been the Federal Government. In fact, much of the recent popularity of microforms (particularly microfiche) is the result of a new approach to libraries by the Government, that of converting the library from an information circulation to an information distribution agency with microfiche serving as the storage and disseminator medium. Federal agencies such as the Office of Education's ERIC, the Defense Documentation Center, the National Technical Information Service, NASA, and the AEC have all fostered the network concept by making widespread distribution (at no charge or at a low fee) of no-return technical documents on microfiche through the United States.

This widespread distribution of entire microfiche document collections, with access facilitated through abstracting and indexing journals sponsored by the distribution agency, has fostered a national network of satellite libraries which provide users in all parts of the country with rapid access to technical reports which would have been impossible without low cost microforms. As a spokesman of the AEC stated [17], "This medium (microfiche) fills a critical need in that it makes possible circulation of information which should be disseminated but which has no other practical means of issuance."

An interesting commentary on the relative costs of the paper hardcopy form of storage vs. the microform is the fact that the Defense Documentation Center will provide a microfiche copy of a technical report at no charge, but imposes a $3 service charge on the hard copy version of the same document.

Videotape Technology

A graphics storage medium of increasing interest to the library community is the videotape [18]. Videotape stores high resolution tele-vision images on magnetic tape instead of optical images on film as with microforms. As with microfilms, videotape can be used in conjunction with a computer to provide an automated retrieval system.

Videotape systems can store $8\frac{1}{2}$" × 11" pages at a density of about 36 frames per foot of 2" wide tape and $5\frac{1}{2}$" to $8\frac{1}{2}$" pages at a density of 72 frames per foot, including the digitally encoded address for each page. Viewing stations are television monitors which can be linked to computer terminals on-line search and retrieval.

As a full text storage medium, videotape is still beyond the budget range of most libraries. However, as libraries begin to consider on-line storage of full text, videotape should be considered as an alternative to digital storage. Comparative studies [19] have shown that for large volume on-line storage of up to 40 million pages of text, videotape systems are cost-competitive with digital disk storage.

INFORMATION PROCESSING AND CONTROL TECHNOLOGY

As our simplified information network model in Fig. 1 shows, a net-work requires a node which both processes and manipulates information stored within the network and also provides both the operators and users of the network with a means of controlling and accessing that information.

In the context of the modern information network, this processing and control function quite often entails the use of a computer. Because of its ability to keep track of and manipulate large volumes of data at extremely high speed, the computer is ideally suited to this task.

In a library network environment, we find that the data processing demands placed upon the computer may be somewhat different than those normally encountered in business or scientific applications.

The common nonlibrary data processing environment tends to have many sets of applications programs not related to each other and further tends to involve the processing of many smaller files, some of which have complicated structures. However, in the bibliographic network environment we normally find that we need a relatively small set of applications programs all relating to the processing of one huge relatively simply structured file whose indexes alone are considerably larger than the complete files encountered at other types of installations. Therefore, both the hardware and computer software requirements of the library network are somewhat different than those of other applications.

Computer Hardware

With the advent of larger and faster main and mass memory devices (as discussed above), providing on-line access to huge bibliographic data bases is now within the realm of economic feasibility. Similarly, advances in computer construction, such as large scale integration and advances in computer control such as multiprogramming, multiprocessing, and virtual memory have significantly reduced the cost of computer power to the point where computer processing costs are less of a problem in information processing. It has been predicted that this trend will continue [1].

Such features as timesharing capability which facilitates multiple use of a data base, and the so called intelligent terminal — a terminal equipped with certain logical and processing capabilities — all contribute to dramatic reductions in processing costs. As a result, we have been able to achieve an improved price-performance ratio which brings the computer within the grasp of the many in the library community. For example, in 1959 on second generation equipment, it cost approximately $5 to process a million instructions. The third generation of computer hardware has reduced this cost to only $.15. Figure 4 illustrates this decrease in operating costs for a representative type of computer, from $.10 per second of operation in 1960 to approximately $.005 in 1970.

The National Academy of Sciences study on libraries and information technology [1] has identified the trend toward minicomputers as having

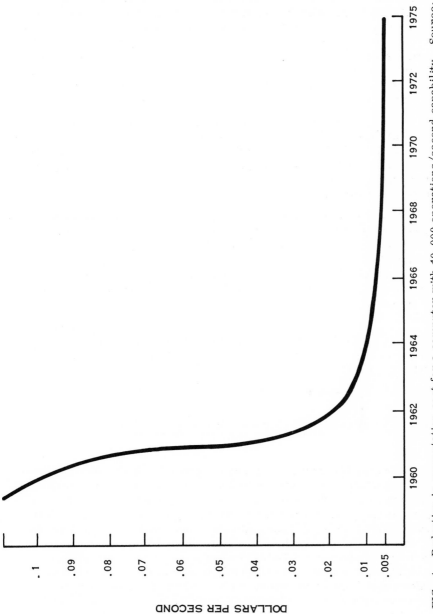

FIG. 4. Reduction in computation cost for a computer with 10,000 operations/second capability. Source: Auerbach Computer Technology Reports, Auerbach Publishers Inc., Philadelphia, Pennsylvania, 1971.

great significance to libraries. Coupled with intelligent terminals, the minicomputer may foster networks built upon the concept of "distributed intelligence" [20] whereby low cost small local files may be effectively interfaced with larger central data bases and computers. The decreasing cost and increasing power of minicomputers is impressive. Their price-performance index has been improving at a rate of about 50% per year since their introduction in 1963. This trend is expected to continue through 1975 at least, as semiconductor logic and memory technology continues to evolve.

It is expected that in the near future one will be able to obtain a 4000-word minicomputer with respectable performance for a cost between $1000-$2000. This decreasing cost should improve the minicomputer's price-performance index to the point where a distributed intelligence network represent a viable economic alternative to the large centralized data processing network.

It is interesting to note that when one begins to distribute information processing functions throughout a network, such as in the case of a mini-computer network, the computers are required to perform many communications functions such as polling and switching. It therefore becomes difficult to separate information processing functions from information transfer functions, which is perhaps a sign of a true network relationship [21].

With hardware related processing costs decreasing, increasing attention has been directed towards the development of information storage and retrieval of software capable of supporting bibliographic data base applications.

Information Storage and Retrieval Software

The area of computer programs or software is where some of both the greatest information technology problems and the most fertile areas for real progress can be found. For the computer hardware to perform its function properly, the software systems must fully exploit its technical capabilities. However, in an evaluation of current software technology [22] Auerbach's analysts found that a definite gap exists between hardware and software developments. To fill this gap in the area of document storage and retrieval, a whole new class of applications programs, known as Information Storage and Retrieval Software, has developed over the past seven or eight years. This is true despite the fact that the National Academy of Sciences' (NAS) report on Libraries and Information Technology [1] found this area of software technology still in an "embryonic state."

Information storage and retrieval or data management software systems as they are also called can be characterized as performing several basic functions on the large files (or data bases) normally found in the library environment.

1. File creation
2. File maintenance (or management)
3. File manipulation
4. File searching and retrieval

These systems may operate in either batch or on-line mode, may be full text of fixed vocabulary and normally exhibit a wide range of capabilities, file structures, retrieval characteristics, and search strategies. However, there are still (and always will be) particular cases where a software package is unsatisfactory and only a custom made set of programs will do the job. As in this area of software technology develops, librarians are finding that they can select from an ever increasing variety of "off the shelf" software systems with a variety of capabilities, characteristics, and price tags.

Appendix A presents a recent Auerbach review of information retrieval software packages. There are also a number of published papers which review current available information storage and retrieval software packages [23, 24, 25, 26, 27].

Similarly, original software created for such networks as OCLC or SUNY may also be applicable to the needs of newly emerging library cooperatives. The administrators of any planned library cooperatives might do well to look into the possibility of obtaining software from a successful network such as OCLC. Aside from the potential savings of obtaining a proven product specifically designed for network applications, use of the same software by two or more networks will provide for a greater degree of compatibility should it ever be decided to link the systems together.

An example of an attempt to accomplish this software transferability is the project of the New England Library Information Network (NELINET) to test the transferability of the OCLC's system to its operations [28].

INFORMATION TRANSFER TECHNOLOGY

A critical and necessary function of a library network is the transfer of bibliographic information between information stores or component

libraries and between libraries and system users. When one begins to
consider computer based network activity, one must also determine whether
the data communications technology is capable of supporting the required
information transfer functions at the various levels, ranging from transferring bulk information between central information storage nodes to
providing information users with individual access to specialized data bases.
As the NAS study of library technology stated,

> . . .it is necessary to explore the specific conditions under which
> electrical transmission becomes economically competitive with
> local facilities and physical transport and/or enables sufficient
> savings to be realized in development and operations to cover its
> cost. [1]

This question of the economic feasibility of applying telecommunications
technology to library networks was also addressed by the Conference on
Interlibrary Communications and Information Networks which was jointly
sponsored by the American Library Association and the United States
Office of Education [29]. This group found that existing commercial
telecommunications services were already available to accommodate most
of the spectrum of communications requirements of a library network at
reasonable cost.

The finding that the existing communications networks are technologically able to satisfy library network needs is not new. Ten years ago, at a
conference on library automation it was stated that communications technology was not a limiting factor in interlibrary communication, but instead,
the degree of telecommunication was a function of balancing benefits of
geographical extension against costs [30]. Communications networks have
for some time now been capable of effectively transmitting digitally encoded
messages and facsimile images over long distance. The real problem has
been that of libraries finding the means to use this available capability
effectively and economically. The increasing costs of bibliographic materials, and the labor to catalog and process these materials, along with the
decreasing costs of machine readable bibliographic data and other economies
of scale, are now tipping the cost benefit balance of telecommunication
towards the benefits side of the scale.

The discussion below examines the current capability of commercially
available telecommunications services.

Telecommunications Cost Parameters

As a critical consideration in determining the feasibility of a tele-communications based library network is usually cost, a general introduction of telecommunications cost parameters should be of some value before discussing the technological question.

As Dittberner [31] points out, telecommunications costs are a function of three basic parameters

1. Distance
2. Amount of usage
3. Channel capacity (or bandwidth)

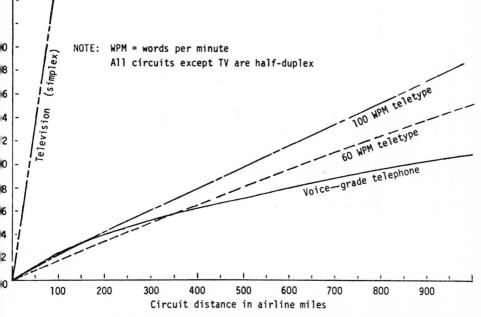

FIG. 5. Comparison of wide band and narrow band transmission costs. Source: W. J. Kessler and M. J. Wilhelm, "Narrow Bandwidth Communications in Proceedings Conference on Interlibrary Communications and Information Networks (J. Becker, ed.), American Library Association, Chicago, 1971, pp. 170-182.

Transmission distance is a basic rate parameter used in calculating telecommunications costs. Existing rate structures are such that total cost increases with distance while cost per transmission unit either increases or remains constant with increasing distance.

Amount of usage has a direct effect on cost. Generally, charges for telecommunications services are directly related to the length of time the service is in use. This is particularly true for message rate usage (such as with the switched dialup telephone network) where many users employ the same telephone plant. There are also flat rate programs whereby a user pays a flat fee for a certain level of telecommunications service using either dedicated or shared facilities. This type of service is also really dependent on amount of usage as the decision to employ the flat rate

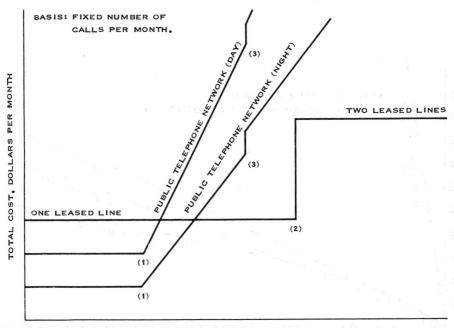

NOTES:

(1)   COST PER CALL REMAINS CONSTANT FOR SHORT CALLS UP TO THE 3-MINUTE MINIMUM.

(2)   AT THIS POINT THE REQUIRED CAPACITY EXCEEDS THE CAPACITY OF ONE LEASED LINE.

(3)   AT THIS POINT THE REQUIRED CAPACITY EXCEEDS THE CAPACITY OF ONE LINE; ADDITIONAL LINES TO THE EXCHANGE AND DATA SETS ARE REQUIRED.

FIG. 6. Cost relationships between message-rate and flat-rate facilities. Source: "Data Communications," in Auerbach, Technology Evaluation Service Report EDP Series 9, Auerbach Publishers Inc., Philadelphia, Pennsylvania, 1971.

structure is economic, based on an estimated minimum use rate. If you fall far below the minimum rate, your cost per unit of time utilized will increase.

Channel capacity refers to the information transfer capabilities of the telecommunication facilities employed. Capacity is generally expressed in terms of bandwidth, measured as hertz/second or data rate (bits/second). The costs for communication facilities generally go up as bandwidth increases. There is generally a tradeoff between channel capacity and transmission time.

Figures 5 and 6 demonstrate the relationship of these parameters to telecommunications costs.

Common Carriers

In the United States, communications facilities can only be provided under federal authorization or by state governments. Those companies authorized to provide communications facilities are referred to as communications common carriers. The authorizations by which they are permitted to function are called tariffs; they define the acceptable operating environment such as accounting procedures, the specific geographical area of operation, and the types and costs of the offered communication facilities and services.

The major U.S. communication common carriers can be divided into five main categories:

1. Bell System companies
2. Independent telephone companies
3. Western Union Telegraph
4. Specialized common carriers
5. Communications Satellite Corporation

Of these, the first two groups, Bell System and independent telephone companies, generally provide dial telephone service for voice transmission — the stereotype of a telephone company. These organizations also offer private line facilities and certain types of terminal equipment. Western Union Telegraph and specialized common carriers provide a form of communication facilities and services primarily for data transmission. They represent communication common carriers that emphasize data or information communications; they do offer alternate voice communications facilities and services.

162   I. L. AUERBACH AND H. B. LANDAU

Specialized Common Carriers

In 1971, the FCC issued a ruling on the definition of a communications common carrier. This statement permits the formation and operation of specialized communications common carriers and allows an organization that meets basic technical and financial qualifications to request and obtain communications common carrier status. These organizations can then market communications facilities and services that are competitive with the traditional communications common carriers. Like the traditional common carriers, these new carriers must operate under tariffs.

Although a number of organizations have filed applications with the Federal Communications Commission requesting communications common carrier status, only two have been authorized to proceed with building their communications network: Microwave Communications Incorporated and Data Transmission Company.

At this time the new communications common carriers are in a formative stage. Rather than providing a broad spectrum of communications facilities and services, they have elected to market only certain types of communications facilities and services. This characteristic of specialization led to the nomenclature "specialized common carriers."

As data communications (see below) appears a prime area of interest for the specialized common carriers, library networks should definitely evaluate these organizations as potential telecommunications vehicles. It is possible that the increased competition generated by these new carriers may result in decreased library network communication costs.

Communications Satellite (COMSAT) is a publicly held corporation, which has the charter to develop and maintain communications satellite facilities. COMSAT is actually a communications common carrier's common carrier. The only legitimate customers are other authorized communications common carriers; COMSAT is not permitted to market communications satellite facilities to the general public.

Classes and Types of Facilities

Communications facilities offered by the common carriers can be broken into two classes: switched and fixed. While both categories are part of the same general communication network, the distinction is based on the manner of implementation.

1. Switched facility: a temporary communications connection that is available on a demand basis to one of a number of locations. It is charged on a distance/time-available basis.

2. Fixed facility: a permanent communications connection that is provided on a scheduled, preordered basis to one or more selected locations. It is charged on a distance basis.

A switched facility generally has the system advantages associated with flexibility of time, duration, and location of connection but typically has the system disadvantage of unknown transmission characteristics. Switched facilities have virtually infinite backup capability.

A fixed facility generally has the system advantage of known transmission characteristics but the system disadvantage associated with a rigid configuration of connection. It is directly dependent on the maintenance responsiveness of personnel from one or more communications common carriers for backup capability.

The communications facilities offered by the common carriers are of three types: narrowband, voiceband, and wideband. These types are provided in both switched and fixed categories. FCC Tariff 260 defines the fixed category of facilities.

Data Communications Facilities and Services

The term data communications, as commonly defined [32], refers to the transmission and receipt of alphanumeric characters over common carrier or privately owned transmission facilities. Data originates or terminates at terminal devices such as teletypewriters, cathode-ray tube (CRT) alphanumeric display consoles, digital plotters, line and page printers, punched paper tape terminals, magnetic tape units, and punched card terminals. Data transmission facilities link such terminals to remote computers or to switching centers and also link computers to each other. Record communications between terminals, as provided by the TWX and Telex teletypewriter exchanges, are also included within our definition of data communications.

The transmission and reception of data is accomplished through the following media. These facilities may operate alone or may be used together.

1. The public switched telephone network transmits digital data. It is operated by Bell System companies and the independent telephone companies.
2. The public switched telegraph network provides two-way connections between low-speed terminals. It is operated by Western Union Telegraph Company.

3. Leased private wire service provides the user with exclusive use of a communications line.

4. Privately owned microwave radio systems provide high-capacity transmission capability to users with high traffic rate.

The need for data communications results mainly from the development of computer systems in which computer terminals are placed at considerable distances from the computer itself or in which data interchange between two or more remotely located computers is desired. As data communications is a key to effective library resource sharing, the discussion below will present a number of considerations in this area.

Channel Capacity

Each of the three classes of data communications facilities, narrowband, voiceband, and wideband, has different channel capacities. The bandwidth of each type of facility is a measure of its signal carrying capacity in hertz (one hertz = one cycle per second). Therefore, in general, the broader the band, the greater the signal transmission rate (usually expressed in bits per second). Examples of typical data rate requirements [33] are:

1. Data rate of user presenting a query to a search system — 100 bits/second
3. Data rate of system reply to query — 1000 bits/second
3. Instant cathode ray tube display of data — 1 million bits/second

Narrowband Facilities

The narrowband facilities generally offer a transmission spectrum of less than 1 kilohertz. Transmission rates of up to 300 bits per second can be achieved. Switched facilities of this type include Western Union's TWX and Telex.

Fixed or leased narrowband facilities offered by the major communications common carriers are summarized in Table 1. The cost data is for illustrative purposes only and is subject to change. Rates shown are exclusive of any terminal equipment.

In general, the basic charges for a fixed or leased narrowband facility include these items:

1. Interexchange mileage charge — a monthly charge for the narrowband channel itself. (This charge is based on the distance between the common carrier's exchange offices.)

TABLE 1

Narrowband Series 1000: Interchange Mileage Charges

Channel	Transmission	Type	Rate per mile per month ($)[a]				
			First 100 (0–100)	Next 150 (101–250)	Next 250 (251–500)	Next 500 (501–1000)	Over 1000 (1001 up)
Type 1001	Half-duplex	DC[b]	1.00	0.70	0.40	0.30	0.20
	Full-duplex	DC	1.10	0.77	0.44	0.33	0.22
Type 1002	Half-duplex	DC/CXR	1.40	0.98	0.56	0.42	0.28
	Full-duplex	DC/CXR	1.54	1.078	0.616	0.462	0.308
Type 1003	Half-duplex	DC/CXR }	Same as Type 1002				
	Full-duplex	DC/CXR }					
Type 1005	Half-duplex	DC/CXR }	Same as Type 1002 plus 10%				
	Full-duplex	DC/CXR }					
Type 1006	Half-duplex	CXR }	Same as Type 1002 plus 15%				
	Full-duplex	CXR }					

[a]These rates are subject to tariff changes and are representative of FCC Tariff 260; they are based on usage 24 hr/day, 7 days/week. If the narrowband facility is between common carrier exchanges in the same state, the state tariff rates apply for both the interexchange mileage and the service terminals.

[b]DC refers to a telegraph grade line. A carrier line (CXR) requires data sets.

2. Service terminal — a monthly charge applied for each city in which one or more terminal is located. This charge provides for the circuit from the local common carrier exchange office to each of the customer's locations.

3. Installation — a one-time charge used to compensate the labor of installation or setup. It is usually equivalent to one month's termination charge.

Narrowband facilities are available as either half-duplex or full-duplex channels. A half-duplex channel only permits transmission in one direction at a time. Two-way communication is possible, but not simultaneously, due to the fact that some circuits or components of the narrowband facilities are used for both transmission directions, thereby creating a common transmission path.

A full-duplex channel is capable of supporting simultaneous two-way communications because each transmission path has its own circuits or components totally isolated from the other transmission path.

If an additional service terminal is required from the same common carrier exchange office on the same interexchange channel, the monthly rate is reduced for each service terminal added [Table 2].

Narrowband facilities, such as Telex and TWX have limited applications to library resource sharing [34]. These can include telefacsimile

TABLE 2

Narrowband Communications: Service Terminal and Installation Rates

Channel	Installation ($) [a]	1st service terminal in an exchange ($/ml)		Additional service terminals ($/ml)	
		Half-Duplex	Full-Duplex	Half-Duplex	Full-Duplex
Type 1001	10.00	25.00	27.50	7.50	8.25
Type 1002	10.00	25.00	27.50	7.50	8.25
Type 1003	10.00	25.00	27.50	7.50	8.25
Type 1005	10.00	27.50	30.25	8.25	9.08
Type 1006	10.00	31.25	34.37	9.38	10.32

[a] 1-time charge.

[b] On same exchange as 1st terminal.

transmission, off-line transfer of machine readable data and data base query operations (e.g., acquisitions, circulation records update, etc.) where speed is not a critical factor.

Voiceband Facilities

Generally voiceband facilities provide a transmission spectrum of three kilohertz. Depending on the type of data set utilized, a transmission rate of more than 9600 bits per second is possible; however, 2400 to 4800 bits per second is more common. The switched facilities of this type are the public voice switched network.

This bandwidth represents a compromise between intelligibility and cost. While the human voice has a considerably greater spectrum than 3000 Hertz, the ability of a human receiver (i.e., the human ear) to receive and understand the information content (intelligibility) is not appreciably enhanced by an increase in bandwidth.

In general, the communications common carriers make no distinction between the physical facilities used for voice transmission and those for data transmission. The same transmission facility can be used in a voice, data, or alternate voice/data arrangement, with the common carriers providing a separate series of fixed voiceband facilities for data transmission.

Fixed Voiceband Facilities. A fixed or leased voiceband facility is a communications channel permanently connected between two or more customer locations. This channel is normally provided on a full-time availability basis and is subject to a monthly charge based on direct airline distance between the points connected. (See Table 4.) In general, the basic charges for a fixed or leased voiceband facility include:

1. Interexchange mileage charge — a monthly charge for the voiceband channel itself, based on the distance between the common carrier's exchange offices.
2. Service terminal — a monthly charge that applies for each exchange in which one or more terminations are located. This charge covers the circuit from the common carrier's local exchange office to each customer location. It applies only to interstate services.
3. Installation — a one-time charge to compensate the labor of installation of setup.

Voiceband facilities are available as either half-duplex or full-duplex channels.

The communications common carriers provide a number of flexible switching arrangements, which can be used with fixed or leased voiceband facilities to configure a particular voice or data communication system.

TABLE 3

Voiceband Series 3000: Interstate Conditioning Rates

Conditioning level	Monthly charge ($) [a]
Type C1	
2-Point, no switching (per exchange)	5.00
2-Point, switching (per exchange)	10.00
Multipoint (per exchange)	10.00
Type C2	
2-Point, no switching (per exchange)	19.00
2-Point, switching (per exchange)	28.00
Multipoint (per exchange)	28.00
Type C3 (e.g. CCSA[b] systems)	
Local access line (each)	3.50
Interexchange access line (per exchange)	13.75
Trunk line (per exchange)	12.00
Type C4	
2-Point channel (1st station in exchange)	30.00
2-Point channel (each additional station in exchange)	9.75
3-Point channel (1st station in exchange)	36.00
3-Point channel (each additional station in same exchange)	9.75
Type C5	
2-Point channel (no switching per exchange)	37.00

[a] No installation charges apply to circuit conditioning services provided under FCC Tariff 260.

[b] CCSA (Common Control Switching Arrangement) is a leased/switched network whose use is usually limited to very large (widespread) organizations.

Tables 3 and 4 illustrate typical costs for Series 3000 and 4000 voice-band channels which are intended for transmission of data signals. Due to the flexibility and variety of voiceband facilities, a wide range of system configurations with varying prices, too numerous to mention here, are available.

Voiceband facilities are applicable to almost all library network needs except where large data rates require wideband facilities. Because many long-distance interlibrary services can be provided over voiceband lines, it should be possible to rely upon the commercially available dial-up network for low-volume applications. The advantage of this approach is that it allows any library or user to connect directly with any other library using the commercial network's switching capability. However, when heavy traffic develops, cost savings can be achieved by using dedicated private facilities with computers at the nodes performing the switching functions. Figure 6 illustrates the cost ratio between public and leased lines.

Wideband Facilities

Wideband (or broadband) facilities have an extremely wide transmission spectrum that is capable of being used as a continuous spectrum or of being subdivided into channels equivalent to voiceband or narrowband facilities. The switched facilities include Western Union Broadband Exchange Service and AT&T Data-Phone 50.

TABLE 4

Voiceband Series 4000: Interexchange Mileage Rates

Miles	Rate per airline mile per month ($)	
	Half-Duplex	Full-Duplex
First 25 (1-25)	4.00	4.40
Next 75 (26-100)	2.80	3.08
Next 150 (101-250)	2.00	2.20
Next 250 (251-500)	1.40	1.54
Each additional mile (501 and over)	1.00	1.10

Source: Auerbach Computer Technology Reports, Auerbach Publishers, Inc. Philadelphia, Pennsylvania, August 1972.

In the Auerbach Data Communications Reports, all communications facilities that have a frequency spectrum of 48 kilohertz and greater are classified as wideband. Wideband facilities are utilized for ultra-high data transmission or are channeled into a number of channels of lesser band-width, (i.e., derived channels). The practice of channeling is primarily to achieve a lower cost per derived channel mileage figure. The continuous spectrum wideband facilities are occasionally identified in terms of a transmission rate throughput in bits per second. This is not a totally incorrect method of definition, but it does assume that the terminating data sets are an integral part of the facility.

Fixed Wideband Facilities. A fixed or leased wideband facility is a communication channel permanently connected between two or more customer locations. These channels are normally provided with full-time availability and are subject to a monthly charge, although some types of video channels (Series 7000) may be installed on an hourly availability basis. The monthly charge is based on the airline mileage between the points connected. In general, basic charges for a fixed or leased voice-band facility include the following:

1. Interexchange mileage charge — monthly charge for the wideband channel itself. This charge is based on the distance between the common carrier's exchange offices that are associated with the originating and terminating customer locations.
2. Service terminal — a monthly charge applied for each exchange termination. This charge provides for the circuit from the local common carrier's exchange office to each of the customer's locations. Wideband service terminals are categorized — and priced — by the type of channel, wideband or derived, at the customer's locations.
3. Installation — a one-time labor charge for installation.

Wideband facilities are available as either half-duplex or full-duplex channels. Identical charges exist for either type of operation.

TABLE 5

Wideband Series 5000: Interexchange Mileage Rates

Type	Cost per airline mile per month ($)
5700	30.00
5800	85.00

TABLE 6

Wideband Series 5000: Service Terminals and Installation Rates
(Wideband channels)

Terminal	1st station		Each additional station
	Installation ($)	Monthly rate ($)	Monthly rate ($)
TYPE 5701			
10-20,000 Hz	200.00	425.00	300.00
40,800 bps	200.00	425.00	300.00
50,000 bps	200.00	425.00	300.00
TYPE 5703			
29-44 kHz	200.00	425.00	375.00
19,200 bps	200.00	425.00	375.00
TYPE 5706			
50,000 bps	200.00	425.00	—
TYPE 5751			
200-100,000 Hz	200.00	650.00	—
230,000 bps	200.00	650.00	—

Source: Auerbach Computer Technology Reports, Auerbach Publishers, Inc.,
Philadelphia, Pennsylvania, August 1972.

Tables 5 and 6 give illustrative costs for Series 5000 (formerly
Telpak) wideband channels with bandwidths ranging from 240 to 1000 kilohertz and data rates of 40 to 230 kilobits per second, depending upon the
type of terminal equipment used.

Very large wideband facilities are necessary for certain applications.
For example, the conventional television system uses a bandwidth of four
megahertz, enough to accommodate 1000 simultaneous telephone conversations or 20,000 teleprinter channels. The cost is, of course, quite high.
However, in a library application, such as using a cathode ray tube (CRT)
terminal to search a data base, slow scan television requiring a bandwidth
of only two kilohertz should be quite adequate.

It has been predicted, however, that "all major national and regional
(interlibrary) nodes undoubtedly will be inter-connected initially by

broadband channels since heavy traffic can be expected between these nodes as soon as connections are established" [29].

One can see the value of using wideband lines when one looks at Becker's [35] estimate that an 8" x 10" page transmitted over telephone voiceband lines takes about six minutes as compared to 30 seconds over a wideband channel.

Facsimile

Facsimile communications are secondary today to digital communications although a number of library networks have employed this technique [36, 37]. Facsimile allows for the transmission from one point to another of a full page image, including printed text, drawings, and photographs. Although considered by some as the sleeping giant of telecommunications, facsimile has several drawbacks in a library network environment. One is expense. Jackson reported [37] facsimile transmission costs of from $7 to $31 per page at Penn State. Another drawback is the relatively slow speed of transmission over voice lines (about six minutes per page). Finally, a major facsimile roadblock is that most currently available facsimile devices lack the ability to scan directly from pages of a bound volume.

However, because of the ability of facsimile to transmit full text, microforms and both color and black and white photographs, it represents a potentially useful information transfer tool if its major drawbacks can be overcome.

Distribution of Bibliographic Data on Magnetic Tapes

While it may yet be some time before library networks exchange full text data in digital form, the dissemination of digitally encoded document surrogates among libraries and information centers is now becoming common. This technique represents a relatively low cost means by which libraries can share cataloging and other bibliographic data. With libraries having greater access to computing equipment, these low cost bibliographic records are gaining in popularity.

The potential products and services to be derived from the use of these readily available machine records are manifold, such as master data base building, computer search services, automatic preparation of catalog cards, and elimination of redundancy, cost, and effort in processing bibliographic records. Indeed, certain academic network operations [38] such as those at the University of Pittsburgh, University of Georgia, Illinois Institute of Technology, and others have built their services around these machine readable data bases. One of the oldest cooperatives of this sort is the State University of New York (SUNY) regional biomedical communication network which went into service in 1968. This network provides typewriter terminal search access to over one million medical journal citations from the National Library of Medicine's MEDLARS tapes to 16 medical centers [39].

These collections of bibliographic data in machine readable form represent a tremendously valuable resource of already prepared indexing and cataloging information in a variety of subject areas. A resource such as this cannot be overlooked in view of the tremendous costs and staffing problems encountered in the large scale indexing, abstracting, and cataloging of the literature and should serve as an incentive to networking so that libraries may band together to exploit these resources.

While investigating the nodes by which a library might utilize available machine readable data, Landau [40] identified 34 private and government organizations regularly supplying bibliographic records in digital form. These are listed in Table 7. A soon to be released publication [41] lists 81 commercially available machine readable bibliographic data bases. This growth is significant when one considers that Medlars introduced the first bibliographic tape service only ten years ago in 1963.

However, to exploit these data bases fully, the librarian should be armed with the necessary hardware, software and, above all, a conceptual understanding of how to use these resources, in the area of how to handle the variations among machine formats found on these magnetic tapes supplied by different organizations. The only logical long-range solution to this machine format problem requires the promulgation of bibliographic standards for machine readable records. Fortunately, progress is now being made in this area.

STANDARDIZATION AND COMPATIBILITY

A growing number of observers have expressed concern over the need to address compatibility problems both within, and, even more importantly, between bibliographic and computer networks [29, 42, 43]. If effective and economical resource sharing is to be accomplished, there must be a means to ensure compatibility of information between the various network nodes. The only logical means to accomplish this is via standard, as Stevens [42] points out.

It is to be noted, first, that system implementation will involve a great variety of decisions and choices to which standardization, compatibility, or convertibility requirements will apply. Such choices include, but are not limited to, questions of hardware, software, data elements, data-content-representation conventions, formats, communication link requirements, routing requirements, file structuring, search structuring, machine and programming languages, documentation requirements, system accounting and performance measurement, error detection and error correction, and information control more generally, protection requirements, and the like.

TABLE 7

Roster of Organizations Regularly Distributing Bibliographic
Records in Machine Readable Form (Magnetic Tape)*

Organization	Records
American Geological Institute/ Geological Society of America	Bibliography and Index of Geology
American Institute of Aeronautics and Astronautics	International Aerospace Abstracts
American Petroleum Institute	Abstracts of Refining Literature Abstracts of Refining Patents
American Psychological Association	Psychological Abstracts
American Society of Mechanical Engineers	Applied Mechanics Reviews
American Society for Metals	Metals Abstracts
Armed Forces Pest Control Board	Military Entomology Information Service Bibliographic Information
Atomic Energy Commission	Nuclear Science Abstracts
Automation Instrument Data Service	Product Specifications for Electronics, Instrumentation and Automation
BioSciences Information Service	BA Previews

*Taken from Ref. 40.

TABLE 7

Roster of Organizations Regularly Distributing Bibliographic
Records in Machine Readable Form (Magnetic Tape) (continued)

Organization	Records
R. R. Bowker Company	Publisher's Weekly Forthcoming Books Paperhound Books in Print Subject Guide to Books in Print Children's Books for Schools and Libraries
CCM Information Sciences, Inc.	Pandex Weekly Tape Service
Chemical Abstracts Service	Chemical Abstracts Condensates Basic Journal Abstracts Chemical — Biological Activities Chemical Titles Polymer Science and Technology — P(atents) or J(ournals) Patent Concordance
Clearinghouse for Federal Scientific and Technical Information	U. S. Government Research and Development Reports and Index
Defense Documentation Center	Technical Abstract Bulletin
Derwent Publications, Ltd.	Farmdoc Plasdoc Ringdoc
Educational Resources Information Center (ERIC)	Research in Education

Engineering Index, Inc.	Current Information Tapes for
	    Engineers
	    (CITE) Electrical/Electronics
	    Plastics
	    COMPENDEX

Paul De Haen, Inc.	De Haen Drug Information Services
IFI/Plenum Data Corporation	Uniterm Index to U.S. Chemical Patents

*Taken from Ref. 40.

TABLE 7

Roster of Organizations Regularly Distributing Bibliographic
Records in Machine Readable Form (Magnetic Tape) (continued)*

Organization	Records
Institute for Scientific Information	ISI Source Data Tapes ISI Citation Tapes Index Chemicus Registry System Automatic Subject Citations Alert (ASCA)
Institute of Textile Technology	Keyterm Index to Abstracts in the Textile Technology Digest
Library of Congress	MARC Tapes
M.I.T. Libraries (Project TIP)	The Current Journal Literature of Physics
National Aeronautics and Space Administration	Scientific and Technical Aerospace Reports
National Agricultural Library	Bibliography of Agriculture Subject and Corporate Author Indexes Pesticides Documentation Bulletin Citations International Tree Disease Register Herbicides Data File
National Library of Medicine	Index Medicus NLM Current Catalog
Preston Technical Abstracts Co.	Computer Tape for Searching the Gas Chromatographic Literature Nuclear Magnetic Resonance Liter- ature Retrieval System
Project URBANDOC, Library, City University of New York	Bibliographic Records Related to Urban Planning and Renewal
Share Research Corporation	Abstracts of U.S. Government Report Literature (NASA, AEC, DOD, etc.) Citation to Journal Literature

*Taken from Ref. 40

TABLE 7

Roster of Organizations Regularly Distributing Bibliographic
Records in Machine Readable Form (Magnetic Tape) (continued)*

Organization	Records
State University of New York at Buffalo, Technical Information Dissemination Bureau	Bibliographic information on U.S. Government Reports
U.S. Geological Survey	Abstracts of North American Geology
University of Michigan	VELA Seismic Information Analysis Center Citations
University of Tulsa	Petroleum Abstracts (Exploration/Development/Production Literature and Patents)

*Taken from Ref. 40

Several groups, most notably American National Standards Institute
(ANSI) Committee Z39 on Library Work, Documentation and Related
Publishing Practices, are directing their efforts towards the development
of standards applicable to library networks. Of particular interest is the
recently published American National Standard for Bibliographic Information Interchange on Magnetic Tapes (No. Z39.2). This standard defines a
generalized format structure which can be used to transmit, between
systems, records describing all forms of material capable of bibliographic
description as well as related information such as authority records for
authors and subject headings. Other standards of interest to library networks available or now being developed by ANSI Committee Z39 include
those related to identification of numbers for serial publications (No.
Z39.9), abbreviation of periodical titles (No. Z39.5), library statistics
(No. Z39.7), literature abstracts (Z39.14), bibliographic references,
bibliographic terminology, indexing, standard book numbers, thesaurus
rules and conventions, technical reports format and numbering, and
microfiche and roll microfilm formats. In addition, there are many more
ANSI standards which address specific requirements for telecommunications
and data processing quality and character representation.

The recognition of the importance of standards by the United States
Government can be seen in the publication of the Federal Information

Processing Standards Index [44], which should be studied by those involved in networking.

CONCLUSION

Libraries represent valuable collections of knowledge. Technology can provide a means to store, manipulate, and exchange this knowledge between libraries and between libraries and users in ways heretofore considered impractical if not impossible. Technology can foster the creation of resource sharing networks which can achieve economy by eliminating redundancy while offering network users an expanded scope of services through their local library node.

However, not all libraries, nor library networks, have yet availed themselves of the fruits of modern technology, some of which have been summarized in the preceding pages. This appears to be particularly true in Pennsylvania (see Appendix B) where there has been surprisingly little automated network development for such a large state.

The gap between conventional, and often outmoded, libraries and modern information systems must be bridged quickly, for the challenge to libraries to keep pace with the growing volume of information has already been clearly stated. Academic library collections expanded by 50% from 1966 to 1970 [45]. Many libraries have not met this challenge and many more will also fail unless we can give each library, no matter how limited its scope, the opportunity to exploit the information processing potential of the computer and its concomitant technology.

Yet a paradox exists with respect to library automation activities. While librarians of every nature are exhibiting an intense and increasing interest in the application of information technology library operations, relatively few are actually participating in "hands on" mechanization activity. It appears that the imposing economic, administrative, educational, and staffing problems encountered in mechanizing library operations have led many librarians to adopt a "wait and see" attitude with respect to automation. This dilemma is not in the best interests of the American library community.

Rather than wait, librarians should immediately begin to study and evaluate the state of the art of information technology to determine how their needs can be met and their services improved. They should be aware of the new developments in the area of memory technology that are forcing information storage costs down. They should investigate the capabilities of available software which they may be able to plug into their own systems without extensive modifications, particularly software which has proven itself in a library network environment such as OCLC's. The capabilities of computers and their peripheral devices should be evaluated on a cost benefit basis. The now emerging specialized common carriers, such as Datran and MCI, should be monitored to determine if their rates will make remote telecommunications more attractive.

This evaluation should be conducted in the context of a realistic statement of the library's service needs and economic and administrative contraints. Only in this way will a library or a group of libraries be able to accurately determine when and how information technology can be employed.

Many librarians have indeed conducted such analyses on their own and have found that while the technology is now available to satisfy their needs, they do not have the resources to fully exploit it. Byrn [46] brings this out when he cites as the three most prevailing reasons for the relative lack of progress in university library automation:

1. Critical lack of properly skilled personnel
2. A shortage of funds available
3. Lack of facilities to properly carry out a meaningful automation program (including problems in dealing with outside support)

The strength in numbers effect of the cooperative library network can assist in mitigating these problems as shown by the successes exhibited by several existing networks in achieving highly automated and yet cost effective networking.

The sharing of information, information processing, information storage, and information transmission facilities among a number of libraries via a network is technically feasible. In addition it will distribute cost and, in turn, diminish the burden on the individual library center. Cooperative information processing activities also put the participants in a better position to impose their demands on the huge and occasionally unsympathetic hardware, software, and communication suppliers.

The technology to facilitate cooperative resource sharing is now available. There are many economic, administrative and service incentives for a cooperative approach to exploiting this technology. However, because technology utilization doesn't come cheaply, in terms of both investment of dollar and intellectual resources, the successful utilization of technology on a cooperative basis requires much detailed planning and analysis, plus a firm commitment from the participants.

The technology to allow implementation of automated library networks is here and is available at prices that are becoming more and more attractive. However, to exploit this technology effectively the librarian should be aware of the relevant state of the art in information storage, information processing and information transfer. As existing networks have demonstrated, this investment can yield significant returns.

However, it appears that librarians may have to rely on their own resources for this investment as government supplied R&D funds are becoming quite scarce. Libraries will have to band together voluntarily to share resources, staff, and know-how. An effective means of accomplishing this can be the establishment of relatively small regional cooperatives which could serve as pilot test beds for both the applications of information technology and the administrative efficacy of multilibrary resource sharing. Those pilot cooperatives that prove feasible can serve as models which can be expanded and replicated elsewhere with appropriate regional modifications. This activity will, of necessity, require a concerted cooperative effort on the part of librarians, information systems architects, and the administration of the involved libraries' patent organization if it is to succeed. Each of these groups must contribute not only its know-how, but its support, both moral and financial, and must effectively employ the collective experience of others who have addressed these problems in the past.

In this way, the hierarchy of a resource sharing network will begin to form: first local, then regional, then statewide, and eventually, national. This evolving network will have to begin at the grassroots level with local libraries providing initiative and funding on their own with little or no help from outside sources.

To paraphrase two United States Presidents, ask not what the government can do to provide library network technology, but ask what you can do yourself, and when. The answer is clearly now.

REFERENCES

1. Libraries and Information Technology: A National System Challenge National Academy of Sciences, Washington, D.C., 1972.
2. M. Camras, "Information Storage Density," IEEE Spectrum, $\underline{2}$(7), 98-105 (July 1965).
3. M. V. Mathews and W. S. Brown, "Research Libraries and the New Technology," in Libraries at Large, Bowker, New York, 1969, pp. 265-81.
4. C. E. Price, "Representing Characters to Computers," American Documentation, $\underline{20}$(1), 50-60 (January 1969).

5. Recent Auerbach Associates, Inc. work for the United States Government under the direction of Dr. J. D. Sable.
6. "Library Technology," in Libraries at Large, Bowker, New York, 1969, pp. 600-643, Appendix F-3.
7. J. W. Weil, "An Introduction to Massive Stores," Honeywell Computer Journal, 5(2), 89-92 (1971).
8. A. H. Bobeck and H. E. D. Scobil, "Magnetic Bubbles," Scientific American, pp. 78-90, June 1971.
9. "It's the Real Thing: 10 Trillion Bit Optical Memory," Electro-Optical Systems Design, 4(11), 5-6, 8 (Oct. 1972).
10. "Document vs. Digital Storage of Textual Materials for Network Operations," EDUCOM 2, 1-5 (December 1967).
11. Application of Associative Array Processor to Data Base Management, Goodyear Aerospace Corporation, GER-15260, June 9, 1971.
12. M. H. Cannell, et al., Concepts and Applications of Computerized Associated Processing, Including Bibliography, MITRE Corp., ESD-TR-70-379, December 1970 (AD 879-281).
13. UCLA Librarian, 23(2),11 (Feb. 1970).
14. J. A. Murphy, "Microfilm Retrieval Systems," Modern Data 5(12), 46-51 (Dec. 1972).
15. Computer Output Microfilm, (Auerbach Technology Evaluation Service EDP Series 2), Auerbach Publishers, Inc., Philadelphia, Pennsylvania, 1970.
16. Walter Sullivan, "625 Page Book Reduced to Sheet of Microfilm," The Sunday Bulletin (Phila.) Section 1, p. 8, Nov. 26, 1972.
17. R. L. Shannon, "Atom Agency's Information Falls Out Via Microfiche," Data System News 9(7), 8-10, (April 1968).
18. "Coming through Your Front Door: Prerecorded Video Cassettes," American Libraries, 1(11), 1069-1073, (December 1970).
19. R. A. Miner, "Digital/Graphic Record Access," Modern Data 3 (1), 66-70, (January 1970).
20. I. L. Auerbach, "Computer Technology Forecast — 1971," presented to IFIP Congress 1971, Ljublgana, Yugoslavia, August 1971.
21. D. D. Cowan and L. Waverman, "The Interdependence of Communications and Data Processing: Issues in Economies of Integration and Public Policy," Bell Journal of Economics and Management Science 2(2), 657-77 (Autumn 1971).
22. "Computer Software," (Auerbach Technology Evaluation Service EDP Series No. 7), Philadelphia, Pennsylvania, Auerbach Publishing, Inc., 1971.
23. L. H. Berul, "Document Retrieval," in Annual Review of Information Science and Technology, (C. Cuadra, ed.), Vol. 4, Britannica, Chicago, 1969.
24. G. G. Dodd, "Elements of Data Management Systems," Computing Surveys 1(2), 117-133, (June 1969).

25. E. Fong, A Survey of Selected Document Processing Systems, National
     Bureau of Standards Technical Note 599, Government Printing Office,
     Washington, D. C. , October 1971.
26. J. P. Fry, et al, Data Management Systems Survey, AD 684707,
     MITRE Corporation, Washington, D. C. , January 1969.
27. A Survey of Generalized Data Management Systems, CODASYL Systems
     Committee Technical Report, Association for Computing Machinery,
     New York, May 1969.
28. W. T. Brandhorst and P. F. Eckert, "Document Retrieval and Dissem-
     ination Systems," in Annual Review of Information Science and
     Technology, (C. Cuadra, ed.), Vol. 7, 1972, pp. 379-437.
29. "Working Group Summary on Network Technology," in Proceedings of
     the Conference on Interlibrary Communications and Information
     Networks, (J. Becker, ed.), American Library Association, Chicago,
     1971, pp. 149-152.
30. J. W. Emling, J. R. Harris, and H. J. McMains, "Library Communi-
     cations" in Libraries and Automation, Library of Congress, Washington,
     D. C. , 1964, pp. 203-219.
31. D. L. Dittberner, "Telecommunications Costs" in Proceedings of the
     Conference on Interlibrary Communications and Information Networks,
     (J. Becker, ed.), pp. 160-162.
32. "Data Communications," Auerbach Technology Evaluation Service
     Report EDP Series 9, Philadelphia, Pennsylvania, Auerbach Publishers,
     Inc. , 1971.
33. D. A. Dunn, "Principles of Telecommunications Planning," in
     Proceedings of the Conference on Interlibrary Communications and
     Information Networks, (J. Becker, ed.), Chicago, American Library
     Association, 1971, p. 163-169.
34. W. J. Kessler and Wilhelm, "Narrow Bandwidth Telecommunications,"
     in Proceedings of the Conference on Interlibrary Communication and
     Information Networks, (J. Becker, ed.), Chicago, American Library
     Association, 1971, pp. 170-181.
35. J. Becker, "Telecommunications Primer," Journal of Library Auto-
     mation 2(3), 148-156, (September 1967).
36. W. C. Jackson, "Telefacsimile at Penn State University: A Report
     on Operations 1968-69," Library Resources and Technical Services,
     15(2), 223-228 (Spring 1971).
37. S. Schatz, "Facsimile Transmission in Libraries: A State of the Art
     Survey," Library Resources and Technical Services 12(1), 5-15
     (Winter 1968).
38. M. C. Gechman, "Machine-Readable Bibliographic Data Bases," in
     Annual Review of Information Science and Technology, (C. Cuadra, ed.),
     Vol. 7, 1972, pp. 323-378.
39. J. Egeland, "User Interaction in the State University of New York (SUNY)
     Biomedical Communication Network," in Interactive Bibliographic
     Search: The User/Computer Interface, (P. Walker, ed.), AFIPS
     Press, Montvale, N.J. , 1971, pp. 105-20.

40. H. B. Landau, Research Study into the Effective Utilization of Machine-Readable Bibliographic Data Bases, Auerbach Corporation, Philadelphia, Pennsylvania, 1969 (PE 184616).
41. J. H. Schneider, M. Gechman, and S. Furth, Survey of Commercially Available Computer-Readable Bibliographic Data Bases, American Society for Information Science, Washington, D.C., (to be issued in early 1973).
42. M. E. Stevens, Standardization, Compatibility, and/or Convertibility Requirements in Network Planning, National Bureau of Standards, Washington, D.C., May 1970 (PB 194179).
43. T. H. Bonn, "Standards for Computer Networks," Computer 4(3), 10-14, (May/June 1971).
44. U.S. National Bureau of Standards, Federal Information Processing Standards Index, U.S. Government Printing Office, Washington, D.C., January 1971.
45. Our Colleges and Universities Today 8(4), (1970-1971).
46. J. H. Byrn, "Automation in University Libraries — The State of the Art" Library Resources and Technical Services 13(4), 520-28, (Fall 1969).

APPENDIX A
SOFTWARE: Information Storage and Retrieval*

INTRODUCTION

The explosion of information accompanying the massive technical
advances of recent years has placed great emphasis upon controlling the
flow of information from originator to user. This involves maintaining
cognizance of what is available as well as storing and retrieving information for specific users. Information storage and retrieval (IS&R), which
connotes all variations of the problem of storing, locating, and selecting
information of any kind, is the function that serves as the interface between
the originator and user of information. Such an interface is necessary in
today's technological society since an originator of information cannot
disseminate it directly to all appropriate users, and conversely, a user
cannot be aware of all information that exists in his areas of interest.

It is natural to look toward the computer for assistance in performing
IS&R functions. The great amounts of material that must be stored and
maintained as well as the repetitive nature of the searching process used
to retrieve this data inherently lend themselves to computerization.

Background

Normally, the objective of IS&R systems is to facilitate the retrieval
of documents or text extracted from documents. Document retrieval
includes helping the user locate the document, putting out textual document
summaries (e. g. , abstracts, extracts), and amplifying information (e. g. ,
bibliographic citations containing title, author, publisher), and providing

---

* © 1972 Auerbach Publishers Inc. The material contained in this appendix
was extracted from Auerbach Software Reports, an analytic reference
service that provides comprehensive coverage of the software industry. It
has been obtained from reliable sources and has been evaluated by experienced technical personnel. However, due to the rapidly changing nature of
the technology and equipment, the information cannot be guaranteed.

entire documents. Some types of IS&R systems retrieve formatted data that is not part of documents or text.

Documents, text, and data can be handled by various types of IS&R systems. The fundamental types are:

1. Document oriented: In systems of this type, the basic storage and output elements is an intact document, or condensation thereof, along with the necessary descriptive data (e.g., location in storage, bibliographic citation). This basic element is entered and stored as an entity with no significant rearrangement of text.

2. Text oriented: These systems accept textual information and convert it into a form that is more appropriate for various intrasystem functions (e.g., storing, searching). Such conversions utilize the programmed analytical capabilities of the computer. The basic storage and output element is this text, which is converted, stored in its revised form, but retrieved in original form after restructuring.

3. Data oriented: In these systems the stored elements are individual data items. These items are stored accordingly to predetermined formats and are retrieved as separate entities, not as part of a document or prestored text.

4. Combinations of the above types: Within the spectrum of IS&R applications, various combinations of these system types exist.

In the remainder of this report, unless otherwise noted, assume that the IS&R system under consideration performs document retrieval.

Elements

The typical sequence of tasks performed upon information as it passes from originator to user is as follows:

1. Originate: Information is generated and packaged into a document.

2. Acquire: The document is acquired by persons, groups, or organizations.

3. Analyze: The information is analyzed and, when appropriate, a surrogate is created. The surrogate is a substitute for the document. It normally contains a bibliographic citation (document number, title, author, journal, volume, date), abstract (brief summary of document contents), and extract (direct quotations from the document). It allows the user to survey the material quickly without actually retrieving the document.

4. Index: A set of index terms that characterize the document is usually assigned and associated with the surrogate.

5. Store: The material is then stored for future use in a manner that facilitates retrieval.   Creation of the index is completed by associating the location of the surrogate or document with each index term assigned to the document.

6. Announce: Potential users must be notified that the document is available at a apsecified location.

7. Browse: The availability of the information can also be determined by using the index or surrogates to perform preliminary interrogations.

8. Search: A search is conducted based upon a question posed by the user.   The terms of the query are usually compared with the index terms to locate information.   The query is often formulated using the results of the preceding browse.

9. Select: In response to the search, specific information is physically correlated with the query and fetched from storage.

10. Extract: The appropriate selected information is gathered and integrated into reports.

11. Disseminate: The information is then provided to the user.

Computers can be used to accomplish various combinations of the tasks described above.   However, since the core of IS&R involves the analysis, index, storage, browse, search, and selection functions, this report concentrates upon the computer techniques used to accomplish these tasks. Entire documents can be stored either interior or exterior to the computer system.   A document may be accessed using the surrogates that are often created during the analysis phase.   A surrogate (or the document itself) can, in turn, be located using the index.   The surrogates and index are stored within the computer.   Queries are processed during the browse and search phases to determine the availability and location of information. Specific information that satisfies the query is then selected.

DISCUSSION

The central role assumed by computer systems in IS&R can be seen by considering the following topics:

1. Indexes
2. Queries
3. Data extracting and reporting
4. Data base characteristics
5. Data processing concepts that relate to IS&R

Indexes

An index is a table that enables information to be retrieved more rapidly. In the index, sets of terms that describe a document are associated with the storage location of the document or its surrogate. The creation of index term sets is called indexing.

Indexing Concepts

In formulating a document surrogate and, in particular, its set of index terms, text is examined for the single purpose of representing it in a systematic form. The basic problem of indexing is to predetermine precisely how to represent this material to unknown users. Among the possibilities are to represent the document by its subject)s), author(s), or some numerical code (e. g. , contract number).

The following considerations are pertinent when creating the index term set:

1. Point of view: This aspect of indexing refers to considering the viewpoints of the author and the various types of users to determine the significance of words and phrases in the document and, hence, their suitability for inclusion in the index term set.

2. Generics: The indexing method should allow for the possibility that the user will request information in terms that are either more general or more specific than those appearing in the document. For example, an article indexed only by "airline," "railroad," and "bus" could be sought using the query term "transportation."

3. Semantics: The author and user of the document may associate different meanings with the same word (homographs), associate with same meaning with different words (synonyms), and use different forms of the same word (lexical differences).

4. Syntactics: If possible, the indexing method should capture the positional relationship between words in the document. Otherwise, for example, a document on fish food could be accessed in response to a query for fish as food.

Both manual and automatic methods are used in creating document surrogates. Automatic techniques exist to accomplish abstracting, extracting, and indexing. Their capabilities include rearranging material to facilitate index searches and using statistical methods to determine word and phrase significance within text.

Other manual and automatic techniques are used to control the vocabulary with which the index is formulated. Foremost of these is the thesaurus, which

1. Lists vocabulary terms authorized for use in the system
2. Exhibits relationships among these terms, such as generic (i. e., hierarchy) and semantic (e. g., synonym) associations
3. Defines the vocabulary

This permits creation of an index that describes the information in documents more fully, at different levels of generality, and from various points of view. The thesaurus may be generated, stored, and maintained either internally or externally to the computer system.

Indexing Languages

After the best way to represent a document has been conceived, the actual structure of index term sets can be described relative to indexing languages. This essentially refers to the vocabulary and syntax used to write each indexed ite. The vocabulary consists of the total set of alpha-numeric index language terms (i. e., natural language words and phrases that must be considered as entities in the index language), and the syntax is the set of predetermined rules for combining these terms. The most prominent indexing languages are:

1. Hierarchical: The index is arranged in generic-specific array where a given class is associated with its subclasses and, in turn, is itself a subclass of higher level entries. Numbers are often assigned to topical categories and to all subdivisions down to the lowest appropriate level. Such a hierarchical structure is shown in Fig. 1. Typically, this structure would appear in the index as follows:

Code	Subject
2	Transportation
2.1	Airline
.	.
.	.
.	.
2.2	Railroad
2.2.1	Passenger
2.2.1.1	Long Distance
2.2.1.2	Medium Distance
2.2.1.3	Short Distance
2.2.2	Freight
.	.
.	.
.	.
2.3	Bus
.	.
.	.
.	.

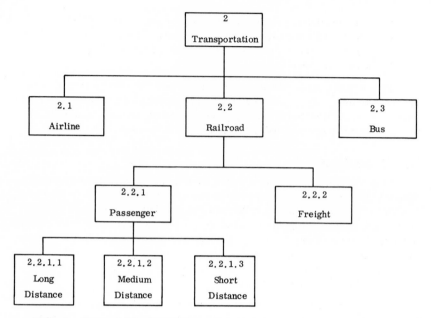

FIG. 1. Hierarchical structure.

In the hierarchical language, the vocabulary usually consists of the subjects and their associated (numeric or alphanumeric) codes. The document is assigned the subjects that are indicative of its relationship to the hierarchical structure.

2. Subject heading: The document is assigned a subject heading based upon a list of generic terms having no relationship (e.g., hierarchy) to each other. The index is arranged alphabetically according to the subject headings of the documents contained in storage. For example, a subject heading index could include:

Banks
Cashiers
Checking Accounts
Data Processing Services
Savings Accounts
Security
Tellers

3. Key word: Words are selected from the text or title of the document. These key words are placed in the index to represent the document. Key-word indexes provide more depth than subject indexes. Also, whereas the subject indexing vocabulary frequently includes natural language phrases, the key-word index terminology is more apt to consist of single natural language words. Key-word language includes no syntax. For example, the underlined words in the following passage could be selected as its key words.

A Chicago rock-music festival erupted into rock-throwing and gun-fire, and one report said two youths were shot and wounded. Witnesses said the trouble began when a group of youths seized the bandshell and rampaged through Grant Park on the downtown lake-front last night, throwing stones and setting two cars afire. More than forty arrests were made. Police fired volleys of tear gas into the crowd, and a police helicopter ordered the group to disperse. The source of the gunfire wasn't immediately known.

4. Syntax: Unlike the preceding languages, the indexing methods that involve syntax combine terms to form phrases in the index language according to a predetermined syntactic relationship. Among these methods are faceted, phrase, and permuted indexing.

In faceted indexing, each position in a string of terms has a specific attribute (or facet). For example, consider:

computer, programmer, Fortran IV
computer, operator, IBM System/360

Analogous terms in these strings modify their predecessors in essentially the same way.

When the syntactic rules permit the terms to be grouped as they are in natural language, a phrase index is obtained. The strings of the preceding example can become:

computer programmers in Fortran IV
computer operators on the IBM System/360

In other cases, each of the possible key-word permutations of a phrase can be presented in the index. Hence, in permuted indexing, the key-word-in-context (KWIC) approach is used to produce the following index entries in which the key words are underlined:

	computer operators on the IBM System/360
	computer programmers in Fortran IV
computer programmers in	Fortran IV
computer operators on the	IBM System/360
computer	operators on the IBM System/360
computer	programmers in Fortran IV

This method enables the key words of a phrase to be emphasized and examined within their context.

Queries

A query is a command that initiates a search of the computer data base to obtain desired information. Retrieval yields either an actual document, its surrogate, or information that will assist the user in locating the document. The query is entered into the IS&R system, which, in turn, interprets the query, performs the requested search, and selects specific information.

Query Formulation

The first step in formulating a query is deciding what information is to be extracted from the data base. Subsequently, the actual query can be considered. Like document index term sets, queries are written in a particular language. When an index exists, the vocabulary and syntax of the indexing language form a basis for the query language. However, the query language is usually much more complex in the sense that terms using the basic grammatical elements can be combined by such connectives as logical operators, logical comparators, and arithmetic operators as well as by the formulation of various complex expressions. The effects of performing the logical operations upon two sets, A and B (i.e., sets that satisfy parts of a query), are shown in Fig. 2 where C, the resultant set (i.e., the set that satisfies the entire query), is depicted by the shaded area.

Logical comparators involve the inequalities such as equal/not equal to, greater/less than, greater/less than or equal to, and between. The arithmetic operators (add, subtract, multiply, divide) are well known, while expression complexity includes such characteristics as nested expressions (i.e., one expression contained in another).

Among other characteristics sometimes included in a query language are the following:

1. Hit level: Although all terms of the query need not be satisfied, a minimum number of correlations (hits) may be required. For example, if some combination of A, B, C is sought, it can be stipulated that at least two hits be achieved in order to satisfy the query.
2. Weighting: Each word or phrase of the query can be associated with a numerical value (weight) that, upon correlation with stored information, is added to a running sum of weights derived from all such correlations. Then, when the entire query has been processed, this sum

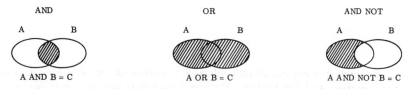

FIG. 2. Logical operations.

is used to determine the degree to which the stored information is responsive to the query. For example, the query A AND (B OR C) can be
processed as follows:

Query	A AND (B OR C)		
Individual Weights	2	1	1
Group Weights	2	1	
Minimum Sum	3		

3. Relative word position: The positions of specified query words
can be required to relate to one another in a particular manner within the
document. Some of these relationships are word proximity (e.g., query
words "theory" and "number," required to be within two words of one
another in the document or its surrogate, would retrieve all mathematical
references to theory of numbers and number theory but not all references
to the relatively common word "theory"), word order (e.g., "abstract"
could be required to precede "algebra" in the source material so that only
references to "abstract algebra" would be retrieved), and words in the
same sentence or paragraph.

Retrieval

Retrieval connotes responding to a query by searching the data base
for pertinent information and physically selecting specific portions of this
material. The characteristics of the retrieval operation depend upon
whether it involves the index, the source material (i.e., documents or
surrogates), or both.

1. Index only: When only the index is involved, the retrieval produces
   a listing of documents locations.
2. Index and source material: When both the index and source
   material are involved, the index is searched to obtain the locations
   of documents or surrogates that satisfy the query. Then specific
   documents or surrogates in these locations are selected.
3. Source material only: In some systems, the text of documents or
   surrogates is searched directly without the use of an index. The
   direct search may call for special construction of the data base to
   facilitate the accessing of this information.

In some systems several of these searches can be performed in succession,
with the information retrieved in any given step automatically applied to
subsequent searches.

Evaluation of Retrieved Information

After searching the data base and selecting the information that satisfies a query, the user must evaluate these responses. The relevance of the response to the query indicates the degree to which the query is satisfied. Attempts have been made to accomplish the difficult task of quantitatively determining relevance. For example, the weighting process described above in the section on Query Formulation can be used to associate each query with a numerical value that is indicative of relevance. A preset value can serve as a threshold and only the responses having values higher than the threshold are retained. Or, using these weights in another way, only the responses associated with the highest values (e.g., top five values, top 25% of the values) are retained. These weights and the method of eliminating the lower values can be either built into the computer program or supplied by the user.

Other facets of evaluation involve the completeness and validity of the responses. Since errors are primarily a function of bias built into the retrieval system, they are not easily determined quantitatively. However, these errors essentially involve cases in which not all information that satisfies the query is chosen, and those in which material is retrieved that does not actually satisfy the query.

Query Aids

Many systems assist the user in formulating a query by utilizing one or more of the following techniques.

1. Thesaurus: The thesaurus-like aids described in the section on Indexing Languages queries. This permits users to formulate queries that are appropriate to the scope and degree of their interests.
2. Guidelines: The rules applicable to query formulation must be available to the user either by written instructions, by well-defined forms on which the user writes his query, or by a human specialist who actually writes the query for insertion into the system.
3. Intermediate output: The computer system may provide the user with information prior to supplying the source material that he ultimately desires. This information is indicative of the progress of the search to help the user refine the query. For example, the user may enter successively more precise queries using the information obtained from prior interrogations. This information can be extracted from the index or the source material. Valuable intermediate output is also obtained from various types of computational summaries (e.g., tallies and more complex statistical analyses) that are derived during the search and provide an insight into the number and characteristics of items satisfying the query.

4. Query enhancement: Various methods exist to improve the user's original query. These techniques involve intermediate output, as described above, and successive searches with no user intervention, as noted in the Retrieval section, while the retrieval operation is in progress. Also, the query may be automatically modified prior to any search using, for example, a thesaurus.

Data Extracting and Reporting

After satisfying the original query, the pertinent information must be extracted from the selected material and reported to the user. In some IS&R systems these functions are accomplished using report formats specified by the user.

During this process, some manipulation of the information may be required in order to group the data for subsequent output. For example, a file could be interrogated to discover all documents on space flight that were written prior to 1958. After selecting the documents involving space flight, their citations would be searched. Those that satisfy the query would be extracted, sorted into a contiguous list based upon date, and reported.

The reports, over which the user exercises varying degrees of control, can contain isolated facts (primarily in data retrieval systems), textual information, bibliographic citations, and information locatives.

Data Base Characteristics

Information is stored in the data base and preserved there pending subsequent retirement or modification. The data base is often divided into files whose contents have similar characteristics. The most general criteria for determining similarity are based upon whether the files contain indexes, documents, or surrogates. Files can be physically combined or separated in storage.

Additional levels are normally defined within the data base by dividing files into various types of lower-level structures. The division of a file will be called a record, which can be further subdivided until a field, the lowest-level data element, is obtained.

The logical and physical arrangement of files, records, and their substructures constitutes the data base organization. The location of these organizational entities can be expressed in terms of their actual (physical) and apparent (logical) positions in the system storage devices. For example, consider the records R_1 and R_2, that are not physically located together but are to be always processed in the sequence indicated by their subscripts. Then R_1 and R_2 are logically contiguous although they are physically separated.

Data Base Organization

The primary means of defining data base organization is by specifying the arrangement of records in a file. Certain key concepts are presented below. The basic types of record organization are:

1. Sequential (or serial): The records are stored in positions relative to one another based upon a specified sequence. This sequence is ordered according to a particular explicit attribute, normally called a key, or implicit characteristic, such as arrival into the system (i. e. , accession number).

2. Linked list: In the list organization, each record is directed to its successor by a pointer. In this type of organization, the logical and physical structures are seldom identical. Typical of the various kinds of list organizations are the simple and ring structures.

The simple list structure employs a record relationship in which each list contains exactly one record that is not a successor to any record in the list and exactly one record that is not a predecessor to any record in the list. These records are, respectively, the first and last records of the list.

The simple list in Fig. 3 contains data records corresponding to the northwestern states. Although the physical storage sequence of these records is indicated by the record number, the logical accessing sequence is as shown in the figure.

In the ring structure the last record of the group points back to the first record as depicted in Fig. 4.

When it is convenient to branch from a particular list, consider a sublist of records, and return to the original list, a ring structure with

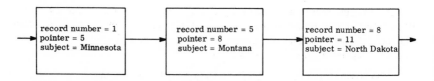

FIG. 3. Simple list structure.

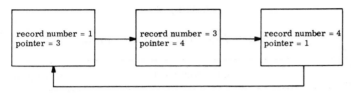

FIG. 4. Ring structure.

"down" (to sublist) and "up" (to original list) pointers is appropriate. For example, expanding upon the simple list shown in Fig. 3, if data records concerning the three largest cities within each of the northwestern states are also involved, the structure depicted in Fig. 5 could be used.

In all of these list structures, any given record can be a member of more than one list at the same or different hierarchical levels. The case illustrated in Fig. 5 shows records 1, 5, and 8 as members of both the primary list and one sublist.

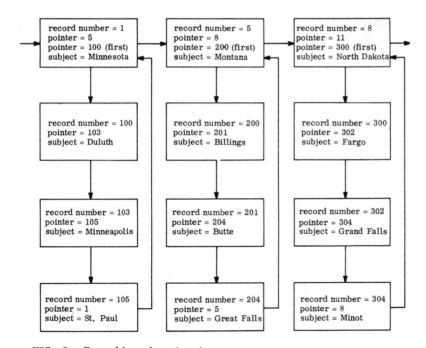

FIG. 5. Branching ring structure.

TABLE 1

Publication Index Term Set and Storage

Publication	Index term set	Storage location
A	In-orbit flight, re-entry, recovery	X
B	In-orbit flight, orbit transfer	Y
C	Launch, in-orbit flight, recovery	Z

Random: The records are stored in random fashion relative to their logical and physical storage locations. The storage location of these records is either directly available or can be obtained by computational or tabular methods.

Inverted: The inverted structure is a special type of data organization which is grouped relative to the index terms that describe the information. Associated with each index term is a reference (usually a storage location) to all of the records to which the term applies. For example, suppose the source material includes three space flight publications having keyword indexes and surrogates that are incorporated as separate records into a single file. Table 1 presents the relationship between each publication, its index term set, and the system storage location of its surrogate.

TABLE 2

Inverted Index

Index term	Storage location(s)
In-orbit flight	X, Y, Z
Launch	Z
Orbit transfer	Y
Recovery	X, Z
Re-entry	X

Data Base Operations

A limited set of ancillary operations may be performed upon the data base. Such functions, normally described within the context of operations upon data files, include:

1. File maintenance: These operations involve updating the data files (or the records and their substructures that comprise these files) by adding, deleting, and modifying information.
2. File creation: This operation involves providing a previously structured file with data. This is frequently accomplished by updating an empty or obsolete file.

In performing both of these operations, various fundamental functions, are necessary to manipulate the data. These include sorting, as described in the paragraph on Data Extracting and Reporting, and merging, in which two or more files are combined into a single file.

Data Processing Concepts

In addition to the topics that are directly related to IS&R, certain other automated data processing concepts are pertinent and should be considered. These primarily involve the methods available to the user for interface with the computer system. They are as follows:

1. Local/remote processing: Data can be submitted for processing jobs either at the computer site (local) or at a location that is physically removed from the computer site (remote).
2. Batch/in-line: Individual data processing jobs can be submitted to the computer in a group (batch) or separately (in-line).
3. On-line/off-line: Data can be processed with the user in either direct (on-line) or indirect (off-line) communication to the computer.
4. Real time/nonreal time: The time required to accomplish processing tasks in real time must adhere to timing standards that are determined by factors external to the computer system. For example, an IS&R data system that provides immediate airline reservation information is a real-time system. Normally, unless otherwise specified, an IS&R system is assumed to be nonreal time.
5. Conversational/nonconversational: Conversational, or interactive, computer operations are those which involve dialogue between computer and user. Most IS&R systems are nonconversational.

SUMMARY

IS&R systems and their applications are characterized by the basic functions they perform, the manner in which these tasks are accomplished, and the nature of the data involved. All of these factors have been discussed in considerable detail above. However, in order to understand any IS&R system fully, it is necessary to determine the relationship between these basic functions. This can be accomplished by establishing the data flow between these tasks and the general sequence in which they are performed.

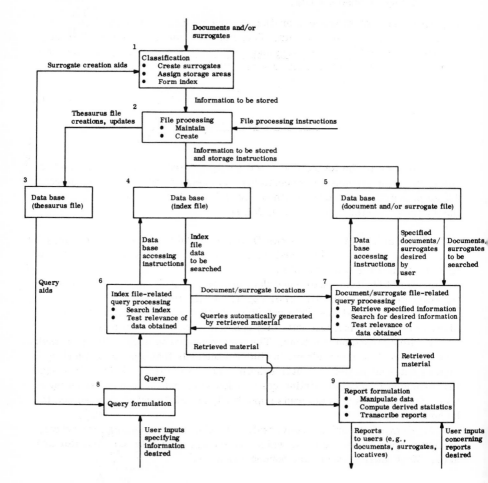

FIG. 6. Functional diagram and data flow.

Figure 6 depicts such a relationship involving the major IS&R functions. Various subsets of the total set of tasks shown in this figure exist in the different IS&R applications. The following paragraphs contain discussions of the basic application types.

Index Only

IS&R applications of this type use the contents of the index file to provide the user with document storage locations. Relative to Fig. 6, such a system normally can be portrayed by blocks 1, 2, 3, 4, 6, 8, and 9 as well as the attendant data flow.

General Document Retrieval

These applications use the contents of the document/surrogate file and, in most cases, the index file to provide the user with documents or their surrogates. The entire figure represents general document retrieval applications that include indexing operations. Applications that do not involve indexing can be depicted by blocks 1 (except form index subtask), 2, 3, 5, 7, 8, and 9 as well as the attendant data flow.

COMPARISON CHARTS

Information Storage/Retrieval

General

The following charts present the technical and administrative characteristics of existing information storage and retrieval packages. Comparison of features among these packages is facilitated by the format of the charts. Note that the terminology is uniform even though it may differ from that used by the vendor.

Chart Contents

All of the charts are divided into four major sections:

1. Cost.
2. System Requirements.
3. Miscellaneous Service Data.
4. Characteristics.

Cost. Both the rent and purchase prices for the basic package are presented, with any additional pricing information noted in the Comments portion of the chart.

System Requirements. In this chart category, both the hardware and software system requirements of the packages are noted so that the user can determine which package will run on his system or which special features he will have to add in order to run a specific package.

Miscellaneous Service Data. Support facilities provided by the supplier, e.g., installation, training, documentation, and maintenance guarantees, are presented in this section.

Characteristics. Under this heading, the operational characteristics of the packages are presented. This information will help the user determine the information storage and retrieval functions performed by each package by indicating its indexing, querying, and reporting capabilities as well as the file structures that can be handled. The file management and maintenance aspects of the package are also considered. Items in this section are introduced in the Information Storage and Retrieval Definitional Report.

Summary

These charts are intended as guidance for the user who wants to compare available information storage and retrieval packages. By reviewing the chart material he can quickly determine which packages fall within his price range, have the support facilities that he requires, will run on his present equipment, and offer the necessary operational characteristics. Once the acceptable packages have been identified, they may be further investigated using the more comprehensive Information Storage and Retrieval Package Reports.

All packages are included in the charts. However, only those packages for which sufficient information is available are described in the Information Storage and Retrieval Package Reports. Charts presenting these packages are grouped together on the pages which immediately follow. The second group of charts present packages that are not described in full reports. Members of this group are denoted by an asterisk adjacent to the company name.

FEATURE	PACKAGE	Computer Resources QUERY	Information Science General Retrieval System	Infodata Systems INQUIRE
		Report Number 61,110	Report Number 61,120	Report Number 986, 4081,020
COST	Purchase	$2,500 plus travel	$4,000 (basic); $10,000 (expanded)	$28,500
	Rental	$300/mo	$400/mo; $4,800/yr	$1,500/mo
HARDWARE / SYSTEM REQUIREMENTS	System	IBM 360; Spectra 70; Honeywell 1200	Many third-generation systems	IBM 360/40 and up
	Main Storage	32K bytes	65K bytes or 40K-byte partition	90–100K byte partition
	Auxiliary Storage	3 units (tape, disc)	4 mag tape and/or 2 disc units	Disc unit
	Input/Output	Card reader; printer	Card reader; printer; tape; disc	Card reader; printer; tape; terminal
	Communications	None	None	Accompanies TTY-compatible terminals
SOFTWARE	Operating System	OS; DOS; TOS; TDOS; Honeywell 1200	OS; DOS	OS
	Source Language	ALC	Cobol	PL/1
SERVICE DATA	Availability	30 days	30 days	30 days
	Installation	Vendor on-site for 1 man-day	Vendor on-site for 3 man-days	Vendor on-site as necessary
	Training	Conducted during installation	System concepts, operation; file definition assistance	Conducted during installation period
	Documentation	User's (functions, programming), operator's manuals	System flowcharts; program listings; block diagrams; operational instructions; control card usage instructions	3 manuals describe system functions, installation, operations
	Maintenance	2 days after installation; optional updates at extra cost	3-year guarantee; updates provided during warranty	Free for 1 yr (includes quarterly updates); thereafter on fee basis
MISCELLANEOUS	Package Type	Search, retrieve information (document, data) from predefined (i.e., not defined by QUERY) file	Interpretive; data oriented; IS&R	IS&R (data, document) using sophisticated file structure
	Surrogates	—	—	Set of keywords represents each data base item

CHARACTERISTICS

Indexes	—	—	Creates keyword index file from user's description; index used to access search file, which has all item locations associated with given keyword
File Organization and Content	Can operate on any sequential file stored on tape, disc; card inputs describe files, records, organization of fields in records	Directory (containing file, record, field structure) entered by card; data base stored on tape, disc; records sequentially stored	Card inputs describe data file provided by user; search file used to access data file; direct access search, data files
Queries	Include logical operators/comparators, relative position, context of query words in file	Formulated using English-word dictionary names; 10 test statements offered; logical operators/comparators, arithmetic operators	Include logical operators/comparators; can control files searched (index, search, data files or only data file), limit number of matches
Reports	First, intermediate; report formats specified by user	User specified, sort key used	User can format reports; summary calculations available
Data Management	None	None	Maintains individual items in files; performs major data base modifications (build additions, reload, etc.)
Man-Machine Interface	Input, output via card, printer, respectively	Card input; hard copy (printed), tape, disc output	Input, output via card, printer, respectively; tape, terminal can also be used; batch, remote terminal processing
Input Checks	None indicated	Search names compared with dictionary names, field lengths	Inputs validated; file of rejected data created
Other Package Uses	None	None	None
Comments	Approximately 10 packages installed Computer Resources Corporation 6825 Redmond Drive McLean VA 22101 (703) 356-5100	Over 100 packages installed; discounts offered Information Science Incorporated 18 New Hempstead Road New City NY 10956 (914) 634-8877	Between 20–25 packages installed Infodata Systems, Inc. 1901 North Ft. Myer Drive Arlington VA 22209 (703) 524-6700

FEATURE \ PACKAGE	Response Technology AKSESS — Report Number 61,190	Computer Audit EASYTRIEVE/300 — Report Number 61,150	Advanced Computer Systems TICON — Report Number 61,160
COST — Purchase	$12,500	$4,800 plus $300 for installation	Negotiable
COST — Rental	—	$240/mo plus installation	Negotiable
HARDWARE — System	Burroughs 5500, 6500	IBM 360/30; Spectra 70/35	IBM 360
HARDWARE — Main Storage	32K words	32K bytes (for 30); 65K bytes (for 35)	Min: 32K-byte partition
HARDWARE — Auxiliary Storage	At least 1 disc unit	1 tape, disc drive	Any random access device; tape
HARDWARE — Input/Output	Terminal, card, tape, disc, I/O	Card reader; tape; disc; printer	Card rdr; prntr; tape; disc; terminal
HARDWARE — Communications	Voiceband telephone line	None	Compatible with 360, terminals
SOFTWARE — Operating System	—	OS; DOS; TOS	OS (can convert to DOS)
SOFTWARE — Source Language	Cobol	BAL	BAL
SERVICE DATA — Availability	Immediate (5500); 30 days (6500)	Immediate	30–90 days
SERVICE DATA — Installation	Vendor on-site less than 1 man-day	Vendor on-site 1 man-day	Not part of basic price; vendor on-site to install system, 1 data file
SERVICE DATA — Training	Vendor provides 15 man-days in system concepts and operation	System concepts, operation; performed during installation	Conducted during installation
SERVICE DATA — Documentation	User's manual; system description; implementation guide; object code	Program user's guide, handbook; object deck (or tape)	System introduction, user's manuals describe package functions, files, use
SERVICE DATA — Maintenance	3-year guarantee	Free updates for 1 yr; all bugs fixed free for life of package	Free debugging; modifications (may be small fee) can include on-site help
MISCELLANEOUS — Package Type	IS&R and data management system for interactive use; extracts data items	Data oriented; IS&R	Timeshared information (data, document) storage, retrieval system
MISCELLANEOUS — Surrogates	—	—	A set of keywords represents each data base item

CHARACTERISTICS			
Indexes	System directory locates data attributes	—	Creates inverted keyword index file; linked list record structure relates each keyword to its associated data file items; 1 record per item
File Organization and Content	Network-like structure links related fields; 2 dictionaries contain data attributes and commands	User-defined directory containing file, record, field names, data structure; data files are user defined	Index file has keywords, pertinent data on each item; data file is direct access with fixed-/variable-length data, is described by separate file
Queries	Formed in plain English statements; using data base vocabulary; logical operators, comparators, and simple arithmetic operators permitted	Formulated using Boolean-like statements containing field names, relational operators, and logical comparators; query enhancements entered separately	Include logical operators/comparators, word ordering/proximity, word root only terms, special char to denote any char; automatic thesaurus use
Reports	User specified; may be conversational replies or standard report form	User specifies format, content; data sorted by keyword; data suppression permitted	User selects 1 of prestored formats; supplies headings; requests preliminary sorts, calculations
Data Management	Creates and maintains files, records, and fields	None	Can maintain, expand, rearrange data base, allocate items to high- or low-activity devices
Man-Machine Interface	Teletype terminal input and output; can also be card, tape, or disc input and output	Card, tape, disc input; hard copy, tape, disc output	Mainly conversational on-line using remote terminals (e.g., TTY, CRT); also batch processing with input, output via cards and printer, respectively
Input Checks	Data validity and operations	None	Inputs verified, errors noted
Other Package Uses	None	Prints mailing labels; accounting, statistical reporting	None
Comments	Discounts to educational institutions; less than 5 packages installed Response Technology, Inc. 4064 Southwest Donovan Seattle WA 98116 (206) 937-7845	About 10 packages installed; discounts offered Computer Audit Corporation 1320 Fenwick Lane Silver Spring MD 20910 (301) 587-0881	No packages currently installed Advanced Computer Systems, Inc. 3131 South Dixie Drive Dayton OH 45439 (513) 294-0586

FEATURE	PACKAGE	Consolidated Analysis Centers QWICK QWERY Report Number 986.2918.020	Share Research Selective Dissemination of Information System (2 models: 710 & 810) Report Number 61.180	Pioneer Data Systems File Exec 70 Report Number 61.230
COST	Purchase	$15,000 (std); $19,000 (customized)	$8,333 (710); $25,000 (810)	$3,500 (basic); $10,000 (extended)
	Rental	$700 (std); $900 (customized); monthly	$215-300 (710); $645-900 (810); monthly	$170/mo (basic); $480/mo (extended)
SYSTEM REQUIREMENTS / HARDWARE	System	Various 3rd-gen IBM, Univac, CDC, GE	IBM 360/30, 40	Univac 1108; 360/30; Spectra; H 1200
	Main Storage	64K bytes	64K; 256K bytes	32K or 65K bytes, depending on version
	Auxiliary Storage	Tape, disc, drum units	4 tape, disc units	2 disc units or mag tape drives
	Input/Output	Card reader; printer	Card reader-punch; printer	Card reader; printer, disc, tape
	Communications	None	None	None
SOFTWARE	Operating System	Std OS for each system	DOS	OS; DOS
	Source Language	Fortran IV	Cobol	Cobol
SERVICE DATA	Availability	30 days	Immediate	Immediate
	Installation	Vendor on-site as required; free with purchase; $3,000 with rental	Vendor on-site 5 man-days	Vendor representative on-site 3 man-days
	Training	Included in installation agreement	System concepts, operations; performed during installation	System concepts, operation, and use; performed during installation
	Documentation	User's (programming guide), file definition manuals; programming forms	User's manual; source, object decks	Source code; system description; operating instructions; flowcharts; common error listing; source listing
	Maintenance	Rental: free; purchase: first year free, $4,000/yr thereafter	6-month guarantee; on-going contract available	1-year guarantee includes updates; maintenance contract available
MISCELLANEOUS	Package Type	Data retrieval system with extensive user-programmed computational capabilities	Document-oriented selective dissemination of information that includes user order; feedback forms on Model 810	Data-oriented IS&R
	Surrogates	—	Can include document abstracts, keywords, bibliographic citations, other citations; obtained manually from various sources	—
	Indexes	—	Terms can be any part of surrogates	—

CHARACTERISTICS

File Organization and Content	Sequential data files; other files describe record/field nomenclature, structure of data files; all files provided by user	Descriptor words, word groups giving user profiles contained in sequential, random file; document surrogates contained in inverted file	Single or modified hierarchical files organized sequentially or index sequentially; user defined dictionary contains file, record, field names
Queries	Include logical operators/comparators, arithmetic operators, expression nesting; written in structural language on preprinted forms	Include weighted descriptor words, word groups; are compared with surrogate parts; match occurs when weight total exceeds threshold	Entered on prestructured forms in English syntax; logical operators, comparators, and simple arithmetic operators permitted
Reports	User specifies data, sorts; reports formatted automatically or by user; statistics automatically included	Match notification on form containing document abstract, citation, order card, user feedbacks (model 810 only)	User specified and formatted; edit, suppression facilities; free-form distribution of data in extended version
Data Management	None	Descriptor word profile, document files may be completely modified	Can change data elements temporarily during run; otherwise no capability offered
Man-Machine Interface	Inputs punched onto cards from programmed forms; outputs via printer	Card input; hard-copy output	Inputs via card, tape, or disc; outputs via hard copy, tape, or disc
Input Checks	None indicated	None indicated	Edit; verification
Other Package Uses	Can program computations, queries, report specifications in structured language on preprinted forms	Model 810 has personalized bibliography, index, user feedback to check abstracts, descriptor weights	Prints labels
Comments	Between 30–35 packages installed Consolidated Analysis Centers, Inc. 225 Santa Monica Boulevard Santa Monica CA 90401 (213) 451–5771	Between 5–10 packages installed; volume discounts offered Share Research Corporation 3704 State Street Santa Barbara CA 93105 (805) 687–5553	Number of installations approximately 15; discounts offered; also available for Univac 1106 and H 2400 Pioneer Data Systems, Inc. Merle Hay Tower Suite 606 Des Moines IA 50310 (515) 276–6746

	PACKAGE FEATURE	Informatics Mark IV (Report Number 984.4091.020)	Data Corporation* Data Central	Infometrics* General Information Retrieval System (GIRS)
COST	**HARDWARE** Purchase	$7,500 to $35,000	None indicated	$1,130
	Rental	$380-2,480 (depends on option, lease)	Negotiable	None indicated
SYSTEM REQUIREMENTS	System	Min: IBM 360/25; RCA Spectra 70/35	IBM 360/30 and up	IBM 1130, 1800
	Main Storage	Min: 65K (OS); 32K (DOS); 50K (TDOS)	64K bytes	8K words
	Auxiliary Storage	1 disc, tape unit	Data cells; 1 disc unit	1 disc unit
	Input/Output	Virtually any device	TTY; card reader; CRT; printer; tape	Console typewriter; card; printer
	Communications	As required; based on I/O devices	Voice-grade telephone lines	None
SERVICE DATA	**SOFTWARE** Operating System	OS, DOS (IBM; TDOS (RCA)	DOS, OS	None
	Source Language	BAL	ALC	Fortran IV
	Availability	Immediate	30 days	Immediate
	Installation	Vendor provides 1 day on-site for installation	3-6 months on-site to ensure satisfactory system operation	Vendor on-site 2 man-days
	Training	Free training for 10 people during first year; advanced classes on fee basis	System concepts, operation; performed during installation	System concepts, operations; assist user in establishing files
	Documentation	5 comprehensive manuals describe system, its use, special features	User's guide (4 manuals) describes system, its use	User's manual, source deck, I/O layouts; object deck, user's manual for $1,100 system
	Maintenance	Includes debugging, updates, monthly visits, semiannual user meetings	Free debugging; otherwise on fee basis	All bugs fixed free for life of installation
MISCELLANEOUS	Package Type	Comprehensive data management system using files defined by either Mark IV, other systems	Document-oriented, IS&R system that can be leased, used in time sharing operations	Data oriented; IS&R
	Surrogates	—	Contains keywords; browsing permitted	—
	Indexes	—	Keyword directory structured automatically from input data; index allows generic, semantic, syntactic searches	—

CHARACTERISTICS

File Organization and Content	Data base contains data files, their descriptions; data files contain sequentially or randomly stored records, hierarchical segments, fields	Central file contains keyword directory in inverted structure; serial file in free text form as input by user	15 files (5 tag, 1 data base, 9 label); directory containing file, record, field names; code association file used only for printout; also includes work file for sorting, report description file
Queries	Include logical operators, comparators, arithmetic operators; written in structured language; can select records and/or fields	English-like statements using file or field name, search requests, Boolean operator statements; can include phrases, keywords	Boolean-like statement containing logical IF followed by field name; arithmetic operators entered via separate routine
Reports	User has varying degrees of control over format, title, etc.; 9 sort levels, many calculations available	Entire documents, abstracts, sorted listings by fields; keyword-in-context reports available via separate user program	User-defined form, content; data suppression permitted
Data Management	User defines file structure; system generates file description; then data provided to create, update files	Entire documents may be added, deleted	None
Man-Machine Interface	Inputs punched onto cards from preprinted forms; outputs via printer (normal) or on-line via CRT (optional); jobs batch processed (local, remote)	Inputs via TTY, CRT, cards; outputs via TTY, CRT, printer, mag tape, cards	Console; card input; typewriter, printer output
Input Checks	Extensive source language/data checks, diagnostic/error printouts	Query terms checked against directory	Edit; field names checked against directory
Other Package Uses	Produces mailing labels; processes text; interfaces Mark IV with any DL/1-created file	Can be modified to retrieve only selected data instead of documents; data may be modified to specific degree of relevancy	Label printing
Comments	Special features increase price; equity on leases; multiple-user discount; over 300 packages installed Informatics, Inc. 21050 Vanowen Street Canoga Park CA 91303 (213) 887-9121	Less than 5 packages installed; support programs may be "hooked on" to perform computational routines Data Corporation 7500 Old Xenia Pike Dayton OH 45432 (513) 426-3111	New package; no current installations; volume discounts offered Informetrics, Inc. 100 Bush Street San Francisco CA 94104 (415) 692-1651

* Not described in package reports

FEATURE	PACKAGE	Programming Methods* SCORE III	Advanced Management Systems* SELECT-OR	Information Associates ASAP I Report Number 61,530
COST	Purchase	$12,500	$5,000 plus expenses to install	$4,500–19,650 depending on version
	Rental	Negotiable	$350/mo (purchase option)	$150–655/mo depending on version
HARDWARE / SYSTEM REQUIREMENTS	System	IBM 360/25 and up or comparable	IBM 360/30 and up; Spectra 70	IBM 360/30
	Main Storage	32K bytes	8K bytes	65K bytes (OS), 100K bytes (DOS)
	Auxiliary Storage	Tape, disc (variable number)	None	1 disc drive, 1 mag tape unit
	Input/Output	Card reader; tape, disc; printer	Card reader; tape; disc; printer	Card reader; printer
	Communications	None	None	None
SOFTWARE	Operating System	OS; DOS	OS; DOS	OS, DOS
	Source Language	Cobol	BAL	BAL
	Availability	Immediate	Immediate	Immediate
SERVICE DATA	Installation	Vendor on-site 2 man-days included	Vendor on-site 2–4 man-days	Vendor on-site 1 man-day
	Training	System concepts, operation; performed during installation	System concepts, operations; performed during installation	4 man-days allotted for training in system concepts and use
	Documentation	User's manual; operator's guide; techniques manual; object deck	Object deck; user's manual	User's guide, programmer's guide, sample problems, object code
	Maintenance	Fully warranted for life of package installation	1-year guarantee; enhancements free; on-going contract offered	Guaranteed for life of installation; continued support by vendor visits
MISCELLANEOUS	Package Type	Data oriented; IS&R	Data oriented; IS&R	Data-oriented IS&R with data management capabilities
	Surrogates	—	—	—

CHARACTERISTICS			
Indexes	—	—	—
File Organization and Content	Master file library; user defines file, record, field names; files linked; 8 files handled (sequential, index sequential)	Handles 9 separate sequential files; files composed of records, fields; file nomenclature provided by user	Operates on 1 sequentially organized file at a time; dictionary describes file, record, and field contents
Queries	English-like statements containing file, record, field name; logical operators/ comparators; arithmetic operators	English, Boolean statements comprised of logical operators/comparators, arithmetic operators; only file name must be specified	Free-form English-like statements entered via card; logical operators and comparators as well as arithmetic operations permitted
Reports	User specifies content, form; sort, merge (up to 6 files) may be specified; data suppression permitted	User specifies contents, form; data suppression permitted	User specified; sorted to tape, disc, card and printed output
Data Management	File history; combining, merging of files	Entire data base may be updated	Creates and maintains record and field data
Man-Machine Interface	Inputs via card (usual), tape, disc; outputs via hard copy, tape, disc, card	Card input; hard-copy output	Card input; outputs via printer, card, tape, or disc
Input Checks	Edit, validation checks	None	Data validation checks
Other Package Uses	Cobol generator for source programs, files, test files, reports; may be used as conversion aid; can be used for audit functions	May be used as a file maintenance system	None
Comments	Over 130 packages installed; discounts offered Programming Methods, Inc. 51 Madison Avenue New York NY 10010 (212) 889-4200	Exits allow special processing routines to be inserted; less than 5 packages installed; discounts offered Advanced Management Systems, Inc. 1905 East 17th Street, Suite 101 Santa Ana CA 92701 (714) 542-1613	Offered on a free trial basis; less than 50 packages installed Information Associates, Inc. 20 Union Street, North Rochester NY 14607 (716) 377-6700

* Not described in package reports

FEATURE / PACKAGE	University Computing MARS (Report Number 61,320)	Information Science* General Maintenance System (GMS)	Cambridge Computer Associates PROFILE/360 (Report Number 61,200)
COST — Purchase	Negotiable	$5,000	$17,500 plus $250/yr maint
COST — Rental	Negotiable	$200/mo; $2,400/yr	—
HARDWARE — System	Univac 1108	Most 3rd-generation systems	IBM 360/40
HARDWARE — Main Storage	50K words	40K bytes	65K bytes
HARDWARE — Auxiliary Storage	3 drums and 1 Fastrand drum	Tapes and/or discs	1 mag tape drive
HARDWARE — Input/Output	Card rdr, trmnl, mag tape; ptr, trmnl	Card rdr; punch; printer; tape; disc	Card reader; printer
HARDWARE — Communications	Voiceband telephone line	None	None
SOFTWARE — Operating System	EXEC II	DOS; OS; or equivalent	OS
SOFTWARE — Source Language	Fortran	Cobol	BAL
SERVICE DATA — Availability	Immediate	30 days	Immediate
SERVICE DATA — Installation	Vendor on-site 1 man-week; fee for this service	Up to 2 days included with vendor on-site as required	Vendor on-site 1 man-day; user must pay travel expenses
SERVICE DATA — Training	Two 3-day seminars; fee for this service	Included with installation	System concepts and operation; performed during installation
SERVICE DATA — Documentation	User's guide and source deck	Program reference manual contains system description, user instructions	User's manual and object code
SERVICE DATA — Maintenance	Guaranteed for life; maintenance contract offered	Debugging free for 3 years; system improvements provided free	Guaranteed for life; updates free; maintenance contract offered
MISCELLANEOUS — Package Type	IS&R with data management capabilities; data oriented	File maintenance when used individually; data management when combined with General Retrieval System (GRS)	Data extraction and report generator
MISCELLANEOUS — Surrogates	—	—	—
MISCELLANEOUS — Indexes	—	—	—

(SYSTEM REQUIREMENTS spans HARDWARE and SOFTWARE)

CHARACTERISTICS			
File Organization and Content	Dictionary contains file, record structure, and data base locations; each file in data base is autonomous	Virtually unrestricted (see Data Management below) data files that, along with source maintenance programs, reside on tape, disc	Data base sequentially organized on magnetic tape
Queries	System-supplied commands allow building, modifying, and deleting data base items	None unless used with GRS	Control statements lists files to be searched, arithmetic and logical expressions, rejection criteria
Reports	User specified; graphs and summary calculations can be output	Include file changes, status before and after changes, optional audit-trail	User specified; output on printer or mag tape
Data Management	Defines, creates, updates, and deletes data; updates dictionary	Generates different maintenance program for each user-provided file structure to update, create file	None
Man-Machine Interface	Card or terminal; printer or terminal	Transactions, new file structures input via cards; errors, new maintenance programs output via cards; errors, changes, net totals output via printer	Card input; mag tape or printed output
Input Checks	Data validation and syntax errors	Input format, validity checks; errors, changes, net totals are output	None
Other Package Uses	None	Extensive file edit capability included	None
Comments	Ideal for time sharing service; less than 10 packages installed	Between 10-15 packages installed; discounts for multiple installations	Number of installations not indicated
	University Computing Company 1949 North Stemmons Freeway P. O. Box 6171 Dallas TX 75222 (214) 741-5781	Information Science Inc. 18 New Hempstead Road New City NY 10956 (914) 634-8877	Cambridge Computer Associates, Inc. 220 Alewife Brook Parkway Cambridge MA 02138 (617) 868-1111

* Not described in package reports

FEATURE	PACKAGE	Share Research* Keyword-Out-Of-Context (KWOC) System	ZVR Systems* SELECTION-70	Information Industries* SEARCHER
COST	Purchase	$900	On request	$15,000
	Rental	None indicated	None indicated	$750/mo
HARDWARE (SYSTEM REQUIREMENTS)	System	IBM 360/30	RCA Spectra 70, IBM 360/25 and up	Burroughs 3500 (pkg planned for IBM 360)
	Main Storage	32K bytes	32K bytes	46K bytes
	Auxiliary Storage	2 disc units	1 disc, 4 tapes units	1 tape, disc unit
	Input/Output	Card reader; tape; disc; printer	Card reader; tape; disc; printer	Card reader; tape; disc; printer
	Communications	None	None	None
SOFT-WARE	Operating System	DOS	DOS	OS
	Source Language	Cobol	BAL	Cobol
SERVICE DATA	Availability	Immediate	Immediate	Immediate
	Installation	Vendor on-site 1 man-day	Vendor on-site 2 man-days	Vendor on-site 1 man-day
	Training	System concepts, operations; performed during installation	System concepts, operations; performed during installation	System concepts, operations; performed during installation
	Documentation	Source, object deck; user's manual	User's guide; object deck	Object deck; user's manual
	Maintenance	All bugs fixed free for life of installation	All bugs fixed free for life of installation	1-year guarantee; on-going maintenance contract offered
MISCELLANEOUS	Package Type	Document-oriented automatic indexing system producing author, KWOC indexes as well as bibliographies	Data oriented; IS&R	Data oriented; IS&R
	Surrogates	Include bibliographies, index terms (KWOC, author); indexes automatically formed from input, bibliographic cards	—	—

CHARACTERISTICS			
Indexes	Author, KWOC indexes associate index terms with document ID numbers	—	—
File Organization and Content	Document file contains bibliographic citations, abstracts; resides on cards, tape, disc	Directory containing file, record, field names; data files defined by user	User-defined directory containing file, record, field names; data files defined by user; separate file used for reports
Queries	User cannot get specific data; all documents in file are output	English-like queries containing field name, length, logical comparator, arithmetic operator	English-like statements containing file, record, field names; logical comparators, arithmetic operators; queries can be nested
Reports	Bibliographic citations containing title, author, publisher, document ID number, abstract, keyword index; author index	Form, content specified by user; sort key used; data suppression permitted	Form, content specified by user; unlimited number of subtotals printed; data suppression permitted
Data Management	Complete file updating capability	None	None
Man-Machine Interface	Input via card, tape, disc; output via hard copy, tape, disc	Input via card, tape, disc; output via hard copy, tape	Input via card, tape, disc; output via hard copy, tape, or disc
Input Checks	Extensive checks, edits, error reports	Syntax, audit checks	Checks query names against directory
Other Package Uses	None	None	None
Comments	About 10 packages installed; discounts offered Share Research Corporation 3704 State Street Santa Barbara CA 93105 (805) 687-5553	Less than 10 packages installed ZVR Systems 280 Park Avenue New York NY 10017 (212) 661-3363	Less than 5 packages installed Information Industries, Inc. 400 East Lancaster Avenue Wayne PA 19087 (215) 687-2340

* Not described in package reports

FEATURE	PACKAGE	Cybertech Data Systems* RE-ACT (4 modules: IS&R, File Maint., Matrix, Utility represented by ISR, FM, M, U, respectively)	Bonner & Moore Associates* Mailing Addresser and Reporting System (MARS)	Computer Retrieval Systems* CRS III
COST	Purchase	$20,000 (ISR);10,000 (FM);5,000 ea (M,U)	$1,500	Not established
	Rental	$500 (ISR); 250 (FM); 125 ea (M, U)	$80/mo (6-month min lease)	None indicated
HARDWARE	System	Honeywell 200; IBM 360/30 and up	Any system with Cobol	IBM 360/65
	Main Storage	16K char (Honeywell); 32K bytes (IBM)	24K bytes	52K bytes
	Auxiliary Storage	4 tape units (or disc equivalent)	2 tape, 1 disc unit	4 cylinders of 2314 disc unit
	Input/Output	Card reader; punch; printer	Card reader; printer	Terminal input, output
	Communications	None	None	Voice-grade telephone line
SOFT-WARE	Operating System	Honeywell Mod 1, TOS, DOS, OS (IBM)	Compatible with Cobol	OS
	Source Language	Easycoder (Honeywell), ALC (IBM)	Cobol	Fortran IV; BAL
SERVICE DATA	Availability	15–20 days	Immediate	Immediate
	Installation	Up to 40 hours on-site included; thereafter $25/hr fee, expenses	Complete (written) instructions provided; otherwise fee basis	1 man-week
	Training	Included with installation	Fee basis	System concepts, operation; performed during installation
	Documentation	User's manual (operations, applications); keypunch/coding aids, forms	User's manual describes package functions, operations	Object deck; user's manual
	Maintenance	Minor improvements free; other support (beyond installation) on fee basis	First year free; thereafter on fee basis	Free debugging for life of package installation
MISCELLANEOUS	Package Type	Primarily data retrieval; also includes modular file maintenance, file utility, matrix output capabilities	Retrieves information (data) on clients in specified categories for mailing lists, reference reports	Document oriented; time shared; IS&R
	Surrogates	—	—	Include keyword index terms
	Indexes	—	—	Key words employed

SYSTEM REQUIREMENTS

CHARACTERISTICS			
File Organization and Content	Contains file description (record, field structure), data files (any structure); both provided by user; includes file security	Sequential file; each record contains information on given client; records arranged according to client name or company and then client name	Files contain index terms, thesaurus, documents; all reside on disc
Queries	ISR module only; English-like; includes logical operators/comparators, arithmetic operators; extracts records, uses their fields to form reports	Alphanumeric codes indicate client categories to be retrieved (e.g., codes for client job title, age, company); file is searched against codes	Keyword accesses thesaurus for hierarchical subject listing used to narrow selection; index entered, information retrieved from specified location
Reports	ISR module only; user can format entire reports; can get multiple reports in single pass of file	Outputs gummed mailing labels and/or reference reports containing information on selected clients	Specified by user with aid of thesaurus
Data Management	Can update records (FM module), perform more extensive file manipulation (U module)	Can create records for new clients, update existing records	None
Man-Machine Interface	Inputs via cards; outputs on printer, tape, disc	Input, output via card, printer, respectively	Terminal input, output
Input Checks	Inputs validated	Inputs edited; new, old records output; new client data verified	Audit check on field names
Other Package Uses	M module prints data into specific locations of predefined forms (check, invoice, W-2, others)	None	None
Comments	Between 5 and 10 packages installed; discounts offered Cybertech Data Systems, Inc. 8383 Stemmons Freeway, Suite 201 Dallas TX 75247 (214) 638-6580	No packages currently installed Bonner & Moore Associates, Inc. 500 Jefferson Building Houston TX 77002 (713) CA 8-0871	New package; no installations Computer Retrieval Systems, Inc. 4900 Auburn Avenue Bethesda MD 20014 (301) 654-6679

* Not described in package reports

FEATURE	PACKAGE	Xerox Data Systems MANAGE — Report Number 61.600	Xerox Data Systems DMS — Report Number 61.601	PHI Computer Services COSMOS — Report Number 61.610
COST	Purchase	—	—	Negotiable
	Rental	$400/mo (batch); $417/mo (interactive)	$425/mo	Negotiable
HARDWARE	System	XDS Sigma 5, 6, 7, 9	XDS Sigma 5, 6, 7, 8, 9	IBM 360/50; RCA 70/46
	Main Storage	15K words	32K bytes	200K bytes
	Auxiliary Storage	1 mag tape or disc unit	1 disc drive, 1 mag tape unit	2 disc drives, 2 tape drives
	Input/Output	Card rdr or terminal; terminal or prtr	Card rdr or terminal; prtr	Card reader; printer
	Communications	Voiceband telephone line	Voiceband telephone line	None
SOFTWARE	Operating System	BPM; BTM; UTS	BPM; BTM; UTS	OS/MFT, MVT; TDOS
	Source Language	Assembly	Metasymbol (Assembly)	Fortran and BAL
SYSTEM REQUIREMENTS	Availability	Immediate	Immediate	30 days
SERVICE DATA	Installation	Vendor on-site less than 1 man-day	Vendor on-site less than 1 man-day	Vendor on-site 6 weeks
	Training	Free 2-week training course in system concepts and operation	2-week training course in system concepts and operations; fee charged for this service	System concepts and operation; performed during installation
	Documentation	User's guide; programmer's manual; object code	User's guide, programmer's manual, object code	Translator system, user, programmer, installation manuals, run-time instructions
	Maintenance	Guaranteed for life of installation; enhancement free	Guaranteed for life of installation; enhancements provided free	2-year package warranty; maintenance contract thereafter
MISCELLANEOUS	Package Type	IS&R and data management system for batch or interactive use; extracts data items	Data management system; operates as subroutine call	File management providing framework for system design, data flow, reports, file maintenance
	Surrogates	—	—	—
	Indexes	—	—	—

CHARACTERISTICS			
File Organization and Content	Sequential file structure; primary and supporting files used; dictionary contains file structure, data attributes, punctuation, column headings	Data base organized into 512-word pages on random access device; dictionary describes names and characteristics of items, groups, and chains	1 sequential master file for all applications or a distinct master file for each application
Queries	Batch uses structured forms; Teletype is free form; up to 99 criteria per request; logical operators, comparators, and arithmetic operators permitted	Formed from statements in host application program	Specifications describe master record, transaction format, report parameters, processing instructions, storage elements, application and user names
Reports	User specified; resequencing performed by system	Error messages and transaction log	Audit and billing reports, user specified
Data Management	Creates and maintains files, records, and fields	Store, retrieve, delete, or modify any group within the data base	Updates and deletes data on master file(s)
Man-Machine Interface	Card or Teletype terminal input; terminal and printer output	Card or terminal input; printer or low-speed terminal output	Input from any medium; output on cards, tape, disc, or microfilm
Input Checks	Edit and validation checks	None	Validates for Cobol syntax and user-specified criteria
Other Package Uses	None	None	None
Comments	Approximately 30 packages installed Xerox Data Systems 701 South Aviation Boulevard El Segundo CA 90245 (213) 679-4511	Less than 5 installations Xerox Data Systems 701 South Aviation Boulevard El Segundo CA 90245 (213) 679-4511	Used primarily by service bureaus, banks, and large companies; number of installations not indicated PHI Computer Services, Inc. 800 Massachusetts Avenue Arlington MA 02174 (617) 648-8550

FEATURE		PACKAGE	Aquila BST EXTRACTO Report Number 986.1411.020	PDA Systems* INFO/1	Computer Resources* AUDIT-THRU Reporter
COST		Purchase	$9,500 for basic; $12,500 for full	$6,500	$4,000-8,750
		Rental	—	None	$200-300/mo
SYSTEM REQUIREMENTS	HARDWARE	System	IBM 360/25, Spectra 70/35, H 200/125	IBM 360/25 and up	IBM 360/30, 40, 50 or comparable
		Main Storage	32K bytes	64K bytes	32-65K bytes
		Auxiliary Storage	1 mag tape drive	2 tape units	2 tape, disc units
		Input/Output	Card reader; printer	Card reader; tape; printer; card	Card rdr/pch; paper/mag tape; disc; prtr
		Communications	None	None	None
	SOFT-WARE	Operating System	OS, DOS; TDOS, TSOS; MOD-1, MSR	DOS	OS; DOS
		Source Language	BAL or Easycoder	BAL	Cobol; BAL; machine language (2nd gen)
SERVICE DATA		Availability	30 days	Immediate	2 weeks
		Installation	Vendor on-site less than 1 man-day	Vendor on-site 1 man-day	Vendor on-site 2 man-days
		Training	Vendor on-site 4 man-days; training in system concept and use	System concepts, operation; performed during installation	System concepts, operation; performed during installation
		Documentation	General reference manual, installation manual, object code	Source, object decks; flowcharts; user's manual	Source deck; operator's manual; user's, run, report request manuals
		Maintenance	Guaranteed for 1 year; enhancements free for 1 year; maintenance contract offered	1-year guarantee; on-going maintenance contract available	All bugs fixed free; updates for 1 year free; on-going maintenance available
MISCELLANEOUS		Package Type	IS&R with data management capabilities; extracts record and field data	Data oriented; IS&R	Data oriented; IS&R
		Surrogates	—	—	—
		Indexes	—	—	—

CHARACTERISTICS			
File Organization and Content	Sequential file organization; user-defined dictionary describes field names and attributes, along with position within a record	Directory containing file, record, field names specified by user; data files in any structure	User-specified directory containing file, record, field name; data files provided by user
Queries	Formed using free-form English-like statements; logical operators, comparators, and arithmetic operators permitted	English-like queries; user specifies field name, logical operator/comparator, arithmetic operator	Formulated using numerical statements; user names field to be searched; includes logical comparators, arithmetic operators; all entered via cards
Reports	User specified; may be tabulated or multiline; all reports derived from tapes	User specified; text form can be changed, data suppressed	User defined, sorted by keyword; data suppression permitted
Data Management	Creates files and maintains data base elements	File updating via cards	None
Man-Machine Interface	Card input; mag tape and printer output	Inputs via card reader, tape; outputs via hard copy, tape, card	Inputs via card, tape, disc, console (machine language); outputs via hard copy, card, tape, disc
Input Checks	Data validation checks	None	Query names checked against directory
Other Package Uses	None	Prints labels, index cards; composes letters	Prints labels; accounting features offered
Comments	Available on a trial basis; approximately 80 installations Aquila BST, Ltd. Pl, Victoria Suite 4000 Montreal 115 Pq. Canada (514) 866-5841	About 5 installed; discounts offered PDA Systems, Inc. 12 East 86th Street New York NY 10028 (212) 736-4644	Over 70 packages installed; discounts offered; record search limitation Computer Resources Corporation P. O. Box 431 Wilton CT 06897 (203) 762-8357

* Not described in package reports

	PACKAGE FEATURE	R. Shriver Associates* GIANT	Mathematica* RAMIS IS&R System	Computer Guidance Associates* AUTO-GEN
COST	Purchase	$7,500	$21,000	$4,800
	Rental	None indicated	$500/mo ($3,000 extra for T/S version)	$400/mo (lease-purchase)
HARDWARE	System	IBM 360/40 and up; IBM 1130	IBM 360/40 and up	IBM 360/25
	Main Storage	128K bytes	128K bytes	52K bytes
	Auxiliary Storage	1 tape, disc unit	1 disc unit	1 tape, disc unit
	Input/Output	Disc; card reader; tape	Console; tape; card rdr;prntr; disc	Card reader; tape; disc; printer
	Communications	None	Voice-grade telephone lines	None
SOFTWARE	Operating System	DOS; OS	OS	DOS; OS
	Source Language	Fortran IV	Fortran IV, BAL	Cobol
SYSTEM REQUIREMENTS	Availability	6 weeks	Immediate	Immediate
SERVICE DATA	Installation	Vendor on-site 3 man-weeks	Vendor on-site 10 man-days	Vendor on-site 1 man-day
	Training	System concepts, operation; performed during installation	System concepts, operations; included during installation	System concepts, operations; performed during installation
	Documentation	Source, object deck; system description; user's guide	Operator's manual; user's guide; applications guide	User's guide
	Maintenance	1-year guarantee; all bugs fixed free; on-going contract available	All system bugs fixed free; on-going contract available (see Comments)	Operation guaranteed for life of package installation
MISCELLANEOUS	Package Type	Data oriented; IS&R	Primarily a data-oriented IS&R with some data management capabilities	Data management package; file maintenance primary function
	Surrogates	—	—	—
	Indexes	—	—	—

CHARACTERISTICS

File Organization and Content	User-defined directory containing file, record, field names; data files (any sequence) specified by user	Directory containing file, record, field names; data files (any structure) provided by user	File organized by file, record, field names
Queries	English-like statements using directory terms; only item name need be specified; logical comparators, arithmetic operators specified	English-like statements; multiple files may be used; includes field name, logical operators/comparators, arithmetic operators; query enhancement allowed; hit limitation permitted	Parameter cards identify requested portions of the data base; 6 different parameter cards can be used to form queries
Reports	Form, content specified by user; data suppression available; unlimited subtotals	User-defined reports; sorts done by keyword; data suppression allowed	User-specified format, content; provide results of maintenance operators
Data Management	File maintenance, report writer programs offered	Updating, deleting, changing individual fields; deleting records; new files may be defined	Card to disc for file changes
Man-Machine Interface	Input via card, disc; output via disc, tape	Inputs via console, tape, disc, card; outputs on same devices	Inputs via card, tape, disc; outputs via hard copy, tape, disc
Input Checks	Syntax tests; queries checked against directory for validity	Edit, audit checks on all files; directory name checked against query field names	Syntax checks
Other Package Uses	None	Label printing; accounting functions; produces graphs; links to user supplied routines; separate generator for financial reports	None
Comments	Between 5-10 packages installed R. Shriver Associates Denville Professional Building Denville NJ 07834 (201) 625-1040	All updates free for first year; $2,000/yr for updates, on-going maintenance thereafter; about 40 packages installed; discounts offered Mathematica P. O. Box 92 Princeton NJ 08540 (609) 924-7090	File creation, file maintenance system; user can add report writing package; over 10 packages installed; discounts offered Computer Guidance Associates 8221 Third Street Downey CA 90241 (213) 773-9556

* Not described in package reports

FEATURE / PACKAGE			Publicate* TEXT Manager	Computer Corporation of America* SERIES 100	Meta-Language Products MUSE — Report Number 61.400
COST	HARDWARE	Purchase	$7,900	$48,800	$100,000 (5-yr lease)
		Rental	$0.20/1,000 char of output	$3,300/mo (6 mo); 1,635/mo (36 mo)	$5,000/mo
SYSTEM REQUIREMENTS	HARDWARE	System	IBM 360/30 and up; comparable RCA	IBM 360/30 and up	IBM 360, RCA, XDS, Brghs, Univac
		Main Storage	48K bytes	64K bytes	64K words
		Auxiliary Storage	7 units (5 tape, 2 disc)	Tape, disc units (variable number)	1 drum, 2 mag tape drives
		Input/Output	Card rdr; paper/mag tape; disc; prntr	Card rdr; tape; disc; terminal; prntr	Low-speed terminals for both
		Communications	None	Voice-grade telephone lines	Voiceband telephone line
	SOFTWARE	Operating System	DOS; TDOS	OS; DOS	OS
		Source Language	Cobol	BAL	Assembly
SERVICE DATA		Availability	Immediate	Immediate	Varies with system
		Installation	Vendor on-site 1 man-week	Vendor on-site 10 man-days	Vendor on-site 1 man-day
		Training	System concepts, operation; 1 man-week at installation	System concepts, operations; file definition; performed during installation	Vendor on-site 6 man-months to assist in use and operation
		Documentation	Source, object decks; user guide; flowcharts; record layouts	User language reference manual; technical reference manual	Executives summary, technical summary, and specifications manual
		Maintenance	1-year warranty	6-month guarantee; on-going maintenance contract for leased system	Guaranteed for life of installation; enhancements may be billed
MISCELLANEOUS		Package Type	Text management system (field oriented); file maintenance primary function	Data oriented, document oriented; IS&R	Interpretive, data-oriented IS&R and data management system; extracts data elements
		Surrogates	—	—	—
		Indexes	—	—	Creates dictionary of data indices during data loading

CHARACTERISTICS			
File Organization and Content	Data base contains file, record, field name plus actual data	User-defined directory containing file, record, field name; document-oriented file is inverted version; data files specified by user	Tree structure of partial identifiers; each data element part of an array; all data entered from terminals
Queries	—	English-like statements designating field names, logical operators/comparators, arithmetic operators	Formed using English-like statements; logical operators, comparators, and arithmetic operators permitted
Reports	User defined; provide results of maintenance operations	User specifies content, form; data suppression permitted	User specified; formatting handled by system
Data Management	Card, tape, disc inputs used to change data base contents	Entire records, fields may be changed on each record	Creates and maintains data elements
Man-Machine Interface	Inputs via card, tape, disc; outputs via hard copy, disc, tape	Inputs via console, card, tape, disc; outputs via hard copy, tape, disc	Low-speed terminal input; CRT, Teletype, printer output
Input Checks	Syntax only	None	Typing, syntax, character string, new words, semantic, and logical
Other Package Uses	None	Prints labels	None
Comments	About 5 packages installed; volume discounts offered Publicate Inc. 7758 Wisconsin Avenue Bethesda MD 20014 (301) 657-2333	4 versions (2 batch, 2 conversational) available at different rates; Between 5-10 packages installed; volume discounts offered Computer Corporation of America 565 Technology Square Cambridge MA 02139 (617) 491-3670	Implemented on a time sharing service; less than 5 installations Meta-Language Products, Inc. 4 East 43rd Street New York NY 10017 (212) 869-1160

* Not described in package reports

	PACKAGE / FEATURE	IBM Corporation IMS/360 — Report Number 984.4239.010	IBM Corporation* GIS/1	IBM Corporation DPS — Report Number 986.4239.010
COST	Purchase	—	—	$25.00
	Rental	$600/mo version 1; $550/mo version 2	$450/mo	—
HARDWARE — SYSTEM REQUIREMENTS	System	IBM 360/50 or comparable 370	IBM 360/40 (batch), /50 (interactive)	IBM 360/40
	Main Storage	524K bytes	153K bytes (batch), 524K (interactive)	128K words
	Auxiliary Storage	10 mag tape units, 2 disc drives	3 disc drives	3 disc drives; 2 mag tape units
	Input/Output	Card rdr or terminal; prtr or terminal	Card reader, terminal; prtr, terminal	Card reader; printer
	Communications	Voiceband telephone line	Voiceband telephone line	—
SOFT-WARE	Operating System	OS (MFT or MVT)	OS	OS
	Source Language	BAL	BAL	BAL
SERVICE DATA	Availability	Immediate	Immediate	Immediate
	Installation	Generally, user responsibility; vendor assists for fee	User responsibility; vendor will assist for fee	User responsibility; vendor will assist for fee
	Training	User responsibility	User responsibility	User responsibility
	Documentation	Program description manual, operations manual, source programs	Program description manual; operations manual; source programs	Program description manual; operations manual; source programs
	Maintenance	Guaranteed for life of installation	Guaranteed for life of installation	Guaranteed for life of installation
MISCELLANEOUS	Package Type	Data management system for batch or interactive use; works with user programs	Data-oriented IS&R	Document- and data-oriented IS&R and data management system
	Surrogates	—	—	Bibliographic citations specified by user
	Indexes	—	—	Keyword-in-content index built by system

CHARACTERISTICS			
File Organization and Content	Sequential or index sequential stored on tape or disc; hierarchically structured, data-oriented	Hierarchically structured files composed of data elements; file descriptions contained in data description tables	Unstructured file data; data retrieved via keyword dictionary
Queries	Formed in user application program; accesses data base through system language called DL/1	Formed using system verbs and statements; logical comparisons permitted	English-like statements in labeled or un-labeled Boolean or weighted forms; dictionary and vocabulary data sets used
Reports	User specified only	User specified and formatted; may be printed out or placed on tape or disc	Bibliographic citation and full document; or keyword and frequency list; lists keywords extracted but not stored
Data Management	Creates and maintains data base elements	Can change any data element permanently or temporarily	Adds and deletes keywords
Man-Machine Interface	Input card or low-speed terminal; terminal, printer output	Terminal or card input; terminal or printer output	Card input; printed output
Input Checks	Data validation checks	Edit; verification	Checks keywords for validity and size
Other Package Uses	None	None	None
Comments	Operates as an on-line data controller; number of installations not indicated International Business Machines Corp. Data Processing Division 112 East Post Road White Plains NY 10601 Contact local marketing representative	Number of installations not indicated International Business Machines Corp. Data Processing Division 112 East Post Road White Plains NY 10601 Contact local marketing representative	Free to IBM users; number of installations not indicated International Business Machines Corp. Data Processing Division 112 East Post Road White Plains NY 10601 Contact local marketing representative

* Not described in package reports

FEATURE (Group)	PACKAGE	Cincom Systems TOTAL	Information Systems Management SERIES	Computer Sciences COGENT/8
		Report Number 984.2163.020	Report Number 61.540	Report Number 61.550
COST	Purchase	$24,500 DOS; $26,500 OS	$25,000	$50,000 (Level 1); $70,000 (Level 2)
	Rental	$750/mo DOS; $950/mo OS	$1,000/mo	$1,650/mo (Lev 1); $2,300/mo (Lev 2)
SYSTEM REQUIREMENTS — HARDWARE	System	IBM 360; RCA 2, 3, 6, 7; Honeywell	IBM 360/40 or comparable 370	Univac 1108/1106
	Main Storage	32K bytes IBM; RCA; 64K Honeywell	128K bytes	65K words
	Auxiliary Storage	2 disc units	None	1 Fastrand drum; 1 mag tape drive
	Input/Output	Card reader; printer	Card reader; remote terminals	Card rdr, terminal; prtr, terminal
	Communications	None	Voiceband telephone line	Voiceband telephone line
SOFTWARE	Operating System	DOS; OS; TDOS, MSR 1, 2; OS 200	OS, DOS	EXEC 2 or 8
	Source Language	BAL or Easycoder	Cobol	Cobol
SERVICE DATA	Availability	Immediate	Immediate	Immediate
	Installation	Vendor on-site up to 2 months as required	Vendor on-site 3 man-days	Vendor on-site until package is running satisfactorily
	Training	Performed during installation	Management and technical seminars; performed during installation	5 man-days allotted; formal classes and on-the-job training
	Documentation	User's guide, programmer's manuals, sample problems, object decks	User's guide, reference manual, and object code	User's guide, programmer's manual, and source decks
	Maintenance	Guaranteed for 2 years after purchase, or for life of rental	Guaranteed for life against source bugs; minor enhancements free	Guaranteed for 180 days; on-going maintenance contract offered; minor enhancements
MISCELLANEOUS	Package Type	Search and retrieve data from a network-type data base; operates as a subroutine call	Search and retrieve data from linear, tree, or network data base; operates batch or interactively	Uses prestructured logic to read, write; update hierarchically structured files
	Surrogates	—	—	—

CHARACTERISTICS			
Indexes	Catalog describes files, records, and fields in data base; and application commands in program	Identification index and content index; dictionaries built for each	Cascading indices locate files
File Organization and Content	Network-type data base; data-base items (files, records, fields) described using special language and entered on cards	Linear, tree, or network; forward pointers link physical records; dictionary entered on cards	Hierarchically structured; files, records, and fields established by user program
Queries	Formed using data base commands and call commands; extracted data returned to host program for processing	Formed using English-like statements; logical operators/comparators, arithmetic operators; uses Cobol procedures	Cobol-generated statements perform file maintenance, file handling, and report preparation
Reports	Error messages and transaction log	User specified in both modes; may be displayed or printed	System formatted and user formatted
Data Management	Maintains individual items; builds, modifies, and deletes data	Creates, modifies, and maintains data base	Aids in structuring, modifying, and maintaining the data base
Man-Machine Interface	Input via card, tape, or disc; output is user specified	Input via card or low-speed terminal; output to printer or terminal	Input via card or terminal; output to printer or terminal
Input Checks	Checks data definition and commands	Validity checks	Validity checks
Other Package Uses	None	None	None
Comments	Number of installations not indicated Cincom Systems Inc. 2181 Victory Parkway Cincinnati OH 45206 (513) 961-4110	Number of installations not indicated Information Systems Management 120 Montgomery Street San Francisco CA 94104 (415) 434-0583	Number of installations not indicated Computer Sciences Corporation 6565 Arlington Boulevard Falls Church VA 22180 (703) 533-8877

FEATURE	PACKAGE	Dynamic Computer Systems* Multi-Purpose Information Processor	Sigma Data Computing IRS Report Number 61,220	Economatics Computer Systems* FLIRT
COST	Purchase	$25,000	$20,000	$6,000
	Rental	None	$650/mo	None
HARDWARE / SYSTEM REQUIREMENTS	System	IBM 360/30 and up	IBM 360/25 or Spectra 70/35 and up	Any system with Fortran IV
	Main Storage	65K bytes	32K bytes	Less than 8K bytes
	Auxiliary Storage	2 disc units	1 mag tape unit	1 unit (tape, disc)
	Input/Output	Card reader; tape; printer	Card reader; printer	Card reader; printer
	Communications	None	None	None
SOFTWARE / SERVICE DATA	Operating System	DOS; OS	OS, DOS, TDOS	Must be compatible with Fortran IV
	Source Language	BAL	BAL	Fortran IV
	Availability	Immediate	30 days	30 days
	Installation	Vendor on-site 2 man-days	Vendor on-site less than 1 man-day	Vendor on-site 2 man-days
	Training	System concepts, operations; performed during installation	3 man-days allotted for training in use and concepts	Conducted during installation
	Documentation	Object tape; user's guide; operator's guide	Combination user's guide and programmer's manual; object code	Operator's manual containing functional, operational descriptions
	Maintenance	Free debugging for life of installation	Guaranteed for life of installation; enchancements provided free	Debugging, 1-year's updates guaranteed, other separately contracted
MISCELLANEOUS	Package Type	Data oriented; IS&R	Data-oriented IS&R with data management capabilities	Cross references documents (e.g., letters, memos, notes) stored in file exterior to computer system
	Surrogates	—	—	Document index term sets containing such terms as types (letter, memo, etc.), origin, pertinent dates/persons/companies, external file location

CHARACTERISTICS

Characteristics			
Indexes	—	—	Alphanumeric code preassigned to each index term; set of codes for document entered, index automatically formed; relates documents having same codes
File Organization and Content	Includes user-specified directory (containing file, record, field name), data file (user-specified), work file, table file	Can operate on up to 44 sequential or index sequential files per run; user-defined dictionary optional	Inverted index file based upon alpha-numeric codes; code for each index term associated with all document code sets that contain the code
Queries	Comprised of field name, logical comparators, arithmetic comparators/ operators; nesting permitted	Converted from forms to punched cards; logical operators, comparators, and arithmetic operators permitted	Alphanumeric codes associated with desired index terms entered; index searched; document code sets con-taining desired codes selected
Reports	User specified; can obtain entire files, specific data (data suppression), select layout (allows data to be printed any-where on page)	User specified; up to 36 levels of sorting permitted	Document code sets containing query codes reported with optional printed statements
Data Management	Files of different formats can be incorporated, files can be added, deleted, changed	Creates files and maintains data base elements	None, other than normal updating of index file
Man-Machine Interface	Inputs via card, tape; outputs via hard copy, card, tape	Card input; outputs via printer, card, tape, or disc	Input, output via card and printer, respectively
Input Checks	Match query terms with directory; audit input data, field lockout	Data validation checks	None indicated
Other Package Uses	Prints labels	None	None
Comments	Produces histograms, time plots; about 5 packages installed Dynamic Computer Systems, Inc. 730 North Post Oak Road Houston TX 77024 (713) 681-3591	Less than 35 packages installed Sigma Data Computing Corporation 4720 Montgomery Lane, Suite 506 Bethesda MD 20014 (301) 657-4455	Less than 5 packages installed Economatics Computer Systems, Inc. 10601 Olson Memorial Highway Minneapolis MN 55427 (612) 544-6919

* Not described in package reports

		PACKAGE FEATURE	Programming Methods, Inc.*	Advanced Management Systems, Inc.*	Information Associates, Inc.*
			SCORE III	SELECT-OR	ASAP (5 packages denoted by A, B, IR, BIR, MIN)
COST		Purchase	$12,500	$5,000 plus expenses to install	$19,650; 16,500; 13,500; 9,000; 4,500
		Rental	Negotiable	$350/mo (purchase option)	$655, 550, 450, 300, 150/mo
SYSTEM REQUIREMENTS	HARDWARE	System	IBM 360/25 and up or comparable	IBM 360/30 and up; Spectra 70	IBM 360
		Main Storage	32K bytes	8K bytes	52K bytes
		Auxiliary Storage	Tape, disc (variable number)	None	1 unit (normally tape, disc)
		Input/Output	Card reader; tape, disc; printer	Card reader; tape; disc; printer	Card reader; tape; disc; printer
		Communications	None	None	As necessary based on remote operations
	SOFT-WARE	Operating System	OS; DOS	OS; DOS	DOS; OS
		Source Language	Cobol	BAL	BAL
		Availability	Immediate	Immediate	Immediate
SERVICE DATA		Installation	Vendor on-site 2 man-days included	Vendor on-site 2–4 man-days	Vendor on-site up to 3 man-days
		Training	System concepts, operation; performed during installation	System concepts, operations; performed during installation	Conducted during installation
		Documentation	User's manual; operator's guide; techniques manual; object deck	Object deck; user's manual	Primer, reference manuals give functional, operational description
		Maintenance	Fully warranted for life of package installation	1-year guarantee; enhancements free; on-going contract offered	2-year guaranteed maintenance; updates for life of package
MISCELLANEOUS		Package Type	Data oriented; IS&R	Data oriented; IS&R	5 packages: A, B (full, basic data management); IR, BIR (full, basic IS&R); MIN (basis for other versions)
		Surrogates	Not applicable	Not applicable	Not applicable
		Indexes	Not applicable	Not applicable	Not applicable

CHARACTERISTICS			
File Organization and Content	Master file library; user defines file, record, field names; files linked; 8 files handled (sequential), index	Handles 9 separate sequential files; files composed of records, fields; file nomenclature provided by user	Sequential file with records containing formatted data, directory giving record structure (all packages); security features included (A, IR only)
Queries	English-like statements containing file, record, field name; logical operators/ comparators; arithmetic operators	English, Boolean statements comprised of logical operators/comparators, arithmetic operators; only file name must be specified	English language using logical operators/ comparators; word orderings to search file, select matching data (all packages)
Reports	User specifies content, form; sort, merge (up to 6 files) may be specified; data suppression permitted	User specifies content, form; data suppression permitted	User can format entire reports (not in MIN package); summary calculations available (A, IR only)
Data Management	File history; combining, merging of files	Entire data base may be updated	Defines, creates, updates, deletes data base records; links user programs with data base (A, B only)
Man-Machine Interface	Inputs via card (usual), tape, disc; outputs via hard copy, tape, disc, card	Card input; hard-copy output	Normally input, output via cards, printer, respectively; modifiable for other devices (e.g., those used in remote, on-line operations)
Input Checks	Edit, validation checks	None	Comprehensive input editing
Other Package Uses	Cobol generator for source programs, files, test files, reports; may be used as conversion aid; can be used for audit functions	May be used as a file maintenance system	Full ASAP capability sold at greatly reduced rates with proviso that it be used for instructional uses only
Comments	Over 130 packages installed; discounts offered; for further information contact: Programming Methods, Inc. 51 Madison Avenue New York, New York 10010 (212) 889-4200	Exits allow special processing routines to be inserted; less than 5 packages installed; discounts offered; for further information contact: Advanced Management Systems, Inc. 1905 East 17th Street, Suite 101 Santa Ana, California 92701 (714) 542-1613	About 15 packages installed; for further information contact: Information Associates, Inc. 6780 Pittsford-Palmyra Road Fairport, New York 14450 (716) 377-6700

* Not described in package reports

FEATURE		D. R. McCord & Associates, Inc.* — Multiple Access Retrieval and Information System	Information Science Inc.* — General Maintenance System (GMS)	Response Technology, Inc.* — Algorithmic Key Selection, Entry and Summarization System (AKSESS)
COST	Purchase	$75,000 (360); $125,000 (1108)	$5,000	$25,000
	Rental	10% of purchase price (annual)	$200/mo; $2,400/yr	Negotiable
SYSTEM REQUIREMENTS	System	IBM 360; Univac 1108; or equivalent	Most 3rd-generation systems	Burroughs 5500
	Main Storage	50K bytes	40K bytes	6K words
	Auxiliary Storage	Depends on system size (drum, tape)	Tapes and/or discs	Disc
	Input/Output	Prntr; card rdr; mag tape; keyset; TTY	Card rdr; punch; printer; tape; disc	Remote terminals; printer; disc
	Communications	None	None	Any network compatible with B 5500
SOFTWARE	Operating System	OS; EXEC II; or equivalent	DOS; OS; or equivalent	Std Burroughs time sharing
	Source Language	Fortran IV	Cobol	Cobol
SERVICE DATA	Availability	90 days (360); 30 days (1108)	30 days	Immediate
	Installation	Available at $28-35/hr	Up to 2 days included with vendor on-site as required	Up to 25 days included
	Training	Available at $28-35/hr	Included with installation	Included with installation
	Documentation	Complete program, system, operator manuals	Program reference manual contains system description, user instructions	Manuals give system operations, technical details, applications, programs
	Maintenance	Annual updates at 10% of purchase price; other support at $28-35 per hour	Debugging free for 3 years; system improvements provided free	Free for 1st year; thereafter negotiable
MISCELLANEOUS	Package Type	Data management package that provides data base and links it to various user programs	File maintenance when used individually; data management when combined with General Retrieval System (GRS)	Information (data) retrieval, file maintenance; primarily for time sharing applications
	Surrogates	Not applicable	Not applicable	Not applicable
	Indexes	Not applicable	Not applicable	Directory links records with similar groups of characteristics in a semi-inverted file

CHARACTERISTICS			
File Organization and Content	Directory contains file, record structure, actual data base locations; data base contains data, program files	Virtually unrestricted (see Data Management below) data files that, along with source maintenance programs, reside on tape, disc	Contains directory, data files; can access records in (random) data files directly (via algorithms), indirectly (via directory); has file security
Queries	Primarily to obtain specific data files for programs; also can obtain programs stored in data base	None unless used with GRS	Include logical operators/comparators, designated character to denote any arbitrary character, max number of matches, level of detail desired
Reports	User can format entire reports; graphs, summary calculations can be obtained	Include file changes, status before and after changes, optional audit-trail	User can format reports, set criteria for sorting, set calculations (e.g., avg, percentage, totals) desired
Data Management	Defines, creates, updates, deletes data base files; updates directory files; links user programs with data base	Generates different maintenance program for each user-provided file structure to update, create file	Can update records
Man-Machine Interface	Input via cards, keyset; output via printer, TTY; conversational and/or remote operations available	Transactions, new file structures input via cards; errors, new maintenance programs output via cards; errors, changes, net totals output via printer	Conversational operations using primarily remote terminals
Input Checks	Extensive input limit checks	Input format, validity checks; errors, changes, net totals are output	Word check; unrecognizable words ignored
Other Package Uses	None	Extensive file edit capability included	Can associate numerical codes with report headings/categories, store for later use
Comments	Less than 5 packages installed; for further information contact: D. R. McCord & Associates, Inc. 1949 North Stemmons Freeway Dallas, Texas 75207 (214) 741-5781	Between 10-15 packages installed; discounts for multiple installations; for further information contact: Information Science Inc. 18 New Hempstead Road New City, New York 10956 (914) 634-8877	Less than 5 packages installed; for further information contact: Response Technology, Inc. 103 East Lynn Seattle, Washington 98102 (206) EA 5-5959

* Not described in package reports

	PACKAGE FEATURE	Pioneer Data Systems, Inc.* FILE EXEC 70	National Computing Industries* WORK TEN	Economatics Computer Systems, Inc.* FLIRT
COST	Purchase	$3,000–7,500	$25,500	$6,000
	Rental	$250–500/mo	$1,500/mo (80% option to purchase)	None
HARDWARE	System	IBM 360/30 or comparable	IBM 360/30 and up	Any system with Fortran IV
	Main Storage	32K bytes	64K bytes	Less than 8K bytes
	Auxiliary Storage	Disc; tape (variable number)	1 disc	1 unit (tape, disc)
	Input/Output	Card reader; tape; disc; printer	Card reader; disc; tape; printer	Card reader; printer
	Communications	None	None	None
SOFTWARE	Operating System	OS; DOS	DOS; OS	Must be compatible with Fortran IV
	Source Language	Cobol	Coboi	Fortran IV
SYSTEM REQUIREMENTS	Availability	Immediate	Immediate	30 days
	Installation	Vendor on-site 2 man-days	Vendor on-site 1 man-day	Vendor on-site 2 man-days
SERVICE DATA	Training	System concepts, operations; performed during installation	System concepts, operations; training at NCI, or on-site	Conducted during installation
	Documentation	Source deck (or tape), systems manual, flowcharts	General information manual; programmer's guide; system design manual	Operator's manual containing functional, operational descriptions
	Maintenance	Free debugging for life of package installation	1-year guarantee; optional on-going maintenance for $1,200/yr	Debugging, 1-year's updates guaranteed; other separately contracted
MISCELLANEOUS	Package Type	Data oriented; IS&R	Data management system; primary function is file maintenance	Cross references documents (e.g., letters, memos, notes) stored in file exterior to computer system
	Surrogates	Not applicable	Not applicable	Document index term sets containing such terms as types (letter, memo, etc.), origin, pertinent dates/persons/ companies, external file location
	Indexes	Not applicable	Not applicable	Alphanumeric code preassigned to each index term; set of codes for document entered, index automatically formed; relates documents having same codes

CHARACTERISTICS			
File Organization and Content	User-defined directory contains file, record, field names; data files (any structure) defined by user; multiple physical records, record lengths on advanced version	Data organized by file, record, field names	Inverted index file based upon alphanumeric codes; code for each index term associated with all document code sets that contain the code
Queries	Syntax-oriented statement includes arithmetic operators, logical comparators/operators; user may specify field name, field address	Not applicable	Alphanumeric codes associated with desired index terms entered; index searched; document code sets containing desired codes selected
Reports	User specified; edit, suppression facilities provided; free-form distribution of data (on advanced system only)	Report writing by stream data; user specifies format; provide results of maintenance operations	Document code sets containing query codes reported with optional printed statements
Data Management	None	Direct card, card to tape/disc for file changes; library maintenance program changes appropriate field	None, other than normal updating of index file
Man-Machine Interface	Inputs via card, tape, disc; outputs via hard copy, tape, disc	Inputs via card, disc, tape; outputs via printer, tape, disc	Input, output via card and printer, respectively
Input Checks	Edit, data validation (advanced system only)	Syntax checks; field validity edited	None indicated
Other Package Uses	Prints labels; performs audit trail accounting	None	None
Comments	Over 10 packages installed; volume discounts offered; for further information contact: Pioneer Data Systems, Inc. 606 Merle Hay Tower Des Moines, Iowa 50310 (515) 276-6746	Over 50 packages installed; volume discounts; can be sold to federal accounts (on GSA schedule); for further information contact: National Computing Industries 3003 North Central Phoenix, Arizona 85012 (602) 264-1394	Less than 5 packages installed; for further information contact: Economatics Computer Systems, Inc. 10601 Olson Memorial Highway Minneapolis, Minnesota 55427 (612) 544-6919

* Not described in package reports

	PACKAGE / FEATURE	National Computing Industries* RSVP	PDA Systems, Inc.* INFO/1	Computer Resources Corporation* AUDIT-THRU Reporter
COST (HARDWARE)	Purchase	$8,500	$6,500	$4,000–8,750
	Rental	$500/mo (90-day min lease)	None	$200–300/mo
SYSTEM REQUIREMENTS (HARDWARE)	System	IBM 360/25 and up; Honeywell; RCA	IBM 360/25 and up	IBM 360/30, 40, 50 or comparable
	Main Storage	32K bytes	64K bytes	32–65K bytes
	Auxiliary Storage	1 disc unit	2 tape units	2 tape, disc units
	Input/Output	Card reader; tape; disc; printer	Card reader; tape; printer; card	Card rdr/pch; paper/mag tape; disc; prtr
	Communications	None	None	None
(SOFTWARE)	Operating System	OS; DOS	DOS	OS; DOS
	Source Language	Cobol	BAL	Cobol; BAL; machine language (2nd gen)
SERVICE DATA	Availability	Immediate	Immediate	2 weeks
	Installation	Vendor on-site 1 man-week	Vendor on-site 1 man-day	Vendor on-site 2 man-days
	Training	System concepts, operation; vendor on-site for 1 man-week	System concepts, operation; performed during installation	System concepts, operation; performed during installation
	Documentation	General instruction manual; user's guide; object tape	Source, object decks; flowcharts; user's manual	Source deck; operator's manual; user's, run, report request manuals
	Maintenance	1-year guarantee; opt on-going maintenance for $1,000/yr	1-year guarantee; on-going maintenance contract available	All bugs fixed free; updates for 1 year free; on-going maintenance available
MISCELLANEOUS	Package Type	Data oriented; IS&R	Data oriented; IS&R	Data oriented; IS&R
	Surrogates	Not applicable	Not applicable	Not applicable
	Indexes	Not applicable	Not applicable	Not applicable

CHARACTERISTICS

File Organization and Content	User-defined directory containing file, record, field names; data files may have any structure	Directory containing file, record, field names specified by user; data files in any structure	User-specified directory containing file, record, field name; data files provided by user
Queries	Entered via card; contains arithmetic operators, logical operators/ comparators	English-like queries; user specifies field name, logical operator/ comparator, arithmetic operator	Formulated using numerical statements; user names field to be searched; includes logical comparators, arithmetic operators; all entered via cards
Reports	User-specified form, content; data may be suppressed	User specified; text form can be changed, data suppressed	User defined, sorted by keyword; data suppression permitted
Data Management*	None	File updating via cards	None
Man-Machine Interface	Inputs via card, tape, disc; outputs via hard copy, tape, disc	Inputs via card reader, tape; outputs via hard copy, tape, card	Inputs via card, tape, disc, console (machine language); outputs via hard copy, card, tape, disc
Input Checks	Syntax checking	None	Query names checked against directory
Other Package Uses	Selects names from mailing list	Prints labels, index cards; composes letters	Prints labels; accounting features offered
Comments	Over 30 systems installed; discounts offered; for further information contact: National Computing Industries 3003 North Central Phoenix, Arizona 85012 (602) 264-1394	About 5 installed; discounts offered; for further information contact: PDA Systems, Inc. 12 East 86th Street New York, New York 10028 (212) 736-4644	Over 70 packages installed; discounts offered; record search limitation; for further information contact: Computer Resources Corporation P. O. Box 431 Wilton, Connecticut 06897 (203) 762-8357

* Not described in package reports

		PACKAGE / FEATURE	Publicate Inc.*	Computer Corporation of America*	Compuvisor, Inc.*
			TEXT Manager	SERIES 100	ASAP
COST	HARDWARE	Purchase	$7,900	$48,800	$4,500–19,000
		Rental	$0.20/1,000 char of output	$3,300/mo (6 mo); 1,635/mo (36 mo)	$225–675/mo
SYSTEM REQUIREMENTS		System	IBM 360/30 and up; comparable RCA	IBM 360/30 and up	IBM 360/30 and up
		Main Storage	48K bytes	64K bytes	64K bytes
		Auxiliary Storage	7 units (5 tape, 2 disc)	Tape; disc units (variable number)	1 disc unit
		Input/Output	Card rdr; paper/mag tape; disc; prntr	Card rdr; tape; disc; terminal; prntr	Card reader; tape; disc; printer
		Communications	None	Voice-grade telephone lines	None
	SOFT-WARE	Operating System	DOS; TDOS	OS; DOS	OS; DOS
		Source Language	Cobol	BAL	BAL
	SERVICE DATA	Availability	Immediate	Immediate	Immediate
		Installation	Vendor on-site 1 man-week	Vendor on-site 10 man-days	Vendor on-site 3 man-days
		Training	System concepts, operation; 1 man-week at installation	System concepts, operations; file definition; performed during installation	System concepts, operations; performed during installation
		Documentation	Source, object decks; user guide; flowcharts; record layouts	User language reference manual; technical reference manual	Object deck; user manual; reference manual
		Maintenance	1-year warranty	6-month guarantee; on-going maintenance contract for leased system	2-year guarantee
MISCELLANEOUS		Package Type	Text management system (field oriented); file maintenance primary function	Data oriented, document oriented; IS&R	Data oriented; IS&R
		Surrogates	Not applicable	Not applicable	Not applicable
		Indexes	Not applicable	Not applicable	Not applicable

CHARACTERISTICS			
File Organization and Content	Data base contains file, record, field name plus actual data	User-defined directory containing file, record, field name; document-oriented file is inverted version; data files specified by user	User-defined directory containing file, record, field names; data files user defined
Queries	Not applicable	English-like statements designating field names, logical operators/comparators, arithmetic operators	English-like statements composed of record type, field names, logical operators/comparators, arithmetic operators; 20 levels of query nesting
Reports	User defined; provide results of maintenance operations	User specifies content, form; data suppression permitted	Form, content specified by user; data suppression permitted
Data Management	Card, tape, disc inputs used to change data base contents	Entire records, fields may be changed on each record	Complete file updating
Man-Machine Interface	Inputs via card, tape, disc; outputs via hard copy, disc, tape	Inputs via console, card, tape, disc; outputs via hard copy, tape, disc	Inputs via card, tape, disc; output via hard copy, disc
Input Checks	Syntax only	None	Audit, user password, syntax, file name, field name, record name, validity check
Other Package Uses	None	Prints labels	Prints labels
Comments	About 5 packages installed; volume discounts offered; for further information contact: Publicate Inc. 7758 Wisconsin Avenue Bethesda, Maryland 20014 (301) 657-2333	4 versions (2 batch, 2 conversational) available at different rates; Between 5-10 packages installed; volume discounts offered; for further information contact: Computer Corporation of America 565 Technology Square Cambridge, Massachusetts 02139 (617) 491-3670	About 10 packages installed; volume discounts offered; for further information contact: Compuvisor, Inc. P. O. Box 381 Ithaca, New York 14850 (607) 272-3269

* Not described in package reports

FEATURE	Dynamic Computer Systems, Inc.* Multi-Purpose Information Processor	Sequoia Electronics* Economy Information Retrieval System
COST — Purchase	$25,000	$25
COST — Rental	None	None
HARDWARE / SYSTEM REQUIREMENTS — System	IBM 360/30 and up	Any system with Fortran III, IV
HARDWARE — Main Storage	65K bytes	Negligible
HARDWARE — Auxiliary Storage	2 disc units	None
HARDWARE — Input/Output	Card reader; tape; printer	Card reader; printer
HARDWARE — Communications	None	None
SOFTWARE — Operating System	DOS; OS	Compatible with Fortran III or IV
SOFTWARE — Source Language	BAL	Fortran
SOFTWARE — Availability	Immediate	Immediate
SERVICE DATA — Installation	Vendor on-site 2 man-days	No assistance provided
SERVICE DATA — Training	System concepts, operations; performed during installation	None
SERVICE DATA — Documentation	Object tape; user's guide; operator's guide	General description; example of operation, flowchart, listing
SERVICE DATA — Maintenance	Free debugging for life of installation	None, other than debugging assistance by mail
MISCELLANEOUS — Package Type	Data oriented; IS&R	Searches card files for certain words, phrases, other character sets; matches are output
MISCELLANEOUS — Surrogates	Not applicable	Not applicable
MISCELLANEOUS — Indexes	Not applicable	Not applicable

CHARACTERISTICS		
File Organization and Content	Includes user-specified directory (containing file, record, field name), data file (user-specified), work file, table file	Sequential card file; records contain titles, abstracts, etc.
Queries	Comprised of field name, logical comparators, arithmetic comparators/ operators; nesting permitted	Consist of unlinked (i.e., by logical operators, etc.) words, phrases, etc.; entire file searched; records containing matches selected
Reports	User specified; can obtain entire files, specific data (data suppression), select layout (allows data to be printed anywhere on page)	Selected records are output
Data Management	Files of different formats can be incorporated; files can be added, deleted, changed	None
Man-Machine Interface	Inputs via card, tape; outputs via hard copy, card, tape	Input, output via cards, printer, respectively; modifiable for other devices (e.g., those used in time sharing operations)
Input Checks	Match query terms with directory; audit input data, field lockout	None indicated
Other Package Uses	Prints labels	None
Comments	Produces histograms, time plots; about 5 packages installed; for further information contact: Dynamic Computer Systems, Inc. 730 North Post Oak Road Houston, Texas 77024 (713) 681-3591	Modifiable for logical operations, various file, input types; less than 5 packages installed; for further information contact: Sequoia Electronics 2109 Cheryl Way San Jose, California 95125

* Not described in package reports

APPENDIX B: Applications of Network
Technology in Pennsylvania

This survey is based primarily upon information provided by Mr. John
A. McCrossan, Coordinator of Library Cooperation, Bureau of Library
Development, State Library of Pennsylvania:

1. N. Wiest, L. Laurea, and B. L. Kenney, Inventory of Pennsylvania
   Interlibrary Cooperatives and Information Networks. Philadelphia,
   Pennsylvania, Drexel University Graduate School of Library Science,
   May 1972.
2. J. A. McCrossan, Statewide and Regional Interlibrary Cooperation,
   Harrisburg, Pennsylvania, State Library of Pennsylvania, June 1972.
3. M. M. Mounce, Library Development in Pennsylvania: A Review.
   Harrisburg, Pennsylvania, State Library of Pennsylvania, January
   1972.

These materials were supplemented by information gathered from press
releases, conversations with area librarians and professional meetings (such
as the February 2, 1973 Conference on Remote Terminal Access to Computer
Data Bases held at the College of Physicians of Philadelphia).

Readers interested in learning of activities in other states should consult
the following two references:

1. E. Olson, R. Shank and H. A. Olson, "Library and Information
   Networks" in Annual Review of Information Science and Technology,
   (C. A. Cuadra, ed.), Vol. 7, 1972, pp. 279-321.
2. D. D. Delaney and C. A. Cuadra, Directory of Academic Library
   Consortia, Santa Monica, California, System Development Corpora-
   tion, 1972.

The following list contains examples of library network technology
applications in Pennsylvania. It is interesting to note that the two most
advanced applications of library technology in Pennsylvania (i. e. , OCLC and
MEDLINE) are both based on systems operated outside of the state.

UTILIZATION OF THE OHIO COLLEGE LIBRARY
CENTER (OCLC) DATA BASE

During 1972 several Philadelphia and Pittsburgh area academic libraries began to utilize the Ohio College Library Center (OCLC) on a remote on-line basis. The Pittsburgh Regional Library Center (PRLC) had laid the foundation for use of the OCLC data base by establishing a communications link between it and OCLC. The Philadelphia area OCLC users also employ the PRLC link.

The OCLC has offered remote on-line access to a data base of cataloging information since August 1971 (OCLC has existed since 1967). The OCLC, serving 50 nonprofit libraries located primarily in the state of Ohio, is a nonprofit corporation located at the Ohio State University in Columbus, Ohio. It is partially subsidized by the State of Ohio, the Council on Library Resources, and the United States Office of Education, and relies upon user charges for the remainder of its funding. The OCLC budget for 1972-1973 was $842,000 including $121,000 in salaries for 14 full-time and 3 part-time personnel.

At present, OCLC on-line data base services are offered via an XDS Sigma 5 computer employing internally generated software written in machine language to emphasize operational efficiency. The system will support either typewriter or CRT terminals and it is reported that OCLC is now negotiating with the Beehive Company for the production of CRT terminal costing about $3500 which will be designed to OCLC's specifications.

The OCLC cataloging data base consists of over 500,000 records. These include 300,000 catalog card records from English language monographs supplied by the Library of Congress MARC (Machine-Readable Catalog) and RECON (Retrospective Conversion) projects. These records go back to 1968. The remainder of the data base consists of catalog card records donated by OCLC member libraries. In utilizing the OCLC data base, member libraries perform on line searches for catalog entries by L.C. card number, ISBN, author or title. If catalog data for the particular work in question is in the data base, this is displayed at the user's terminal. The user can accept the data or modify it if he desires. The user then may order, via his terminal, catalog card sets for the book, in the format he chooses. These card sets are produced offline by OCLC and shipped to the member libraries within a week. OCLC distributed about 450,000 cards per month in this way.

The experience of the Philadelphia area users of OCLC (as reported by Richard L. Snyder, Director of Libraries, Drexel University, in a talk presented on February 2, 1973 at the College of Physicians of Philadelphia) has been favorable. The OCLC Cooperative Cataloging Project (originally conceived under the informal Philadelphia Area Library Automation Conference) was begun in 1972 as a joint effort by the libraries of Drexel, Temple and the University of Pennsylvania. The purpose of the project was to reduce cataloging costs via use of systems technology. The libraries employed Ira-scope CRT terminals connected with the Pittsburgh Regional Library Center via leased Bell System Lines (Full Duplex, C2 Conditioning, 2500 bits per second data rate). PRLC WATS transmission lines are employed from Pittsburgh to Ohio. Average reported transmission time was about 33 min-utes to transmit 1000 titles with an average response time of 2 to 5 seconds.

During 1972, the three Philadelphia libraries ordered about 45,000 cards per month from OCLC, for an average cost of $2.14 per title, all costs included. Drexel's reported costs were about $16,000 for 10,000 titles. This cost, was however, almost completely offset by savings in the area of catalog card typing, card reproduction, and card filing. Snyder of Drexel considers his experience with OCLC an "overwhelming success" financially and techni-cally. He has stated that any library now receiving more than 5000 new titles per year should consider the benefits offered by OCLC participation.

Because of the success of this project, several other libraries in the Philadelphia area have expressed their intent to participate in the OCLC project. By December 1972 (as reported in the Union Library Catalogue of Pennsylvania Newsletter, No. 119, January 1973) Bryn Mawr College, The Union Library Catalogue of Pennsylvania, and the University of Delaware have joined the growing network which is negotiating with OCLC for a new three year contract. It is interesting to note that through the membership of the Union Library Catalogue (ULC) all ULC subscribers also now have access to the OCLC automated system.

At the end of the three year OCLC contract, it is reported that this local network (tentatively named "MALINET" for Mid Atlantic Library Network) will investigate the possibilities of switching its operations to a proposed library center being contemplated by Educational Testing Service — EDUCOM at Princeton, N.J. or possibly establishing its own automated facilities.

UTILIZATION OF THE MEDLINE DATA BASE

In October 1971, the National Library of Medicine initiated a new service known as MEDLINE for MEDLARS On-Line. This service is to provide remote on-line bibliographic search capability for libraries at medical schools, hospitals and research institutions throughout the United States. Several Pennsylvania academic and research libraries are now active members of this network, and as a result, can offer various automated services to users.

The MEDLINE data base located at the NLM in Bethesda, Maryland, contains over 400,000 citations to articles from more than 1,000 leading medical journals indexed for <u>Index Medicus</u> since January 1, 1970. The system allows on-line searching via terminal and provides for either on-line or off-line output. Telecommunications links are either via the TWX dial up network or by private leased line (Tymshare network). It has been reported (talk presented by Davis B. McCarn of the NLM on February 2, 1973 at the College of Physicians of Philadelphia) that use of the Tymshare communications network (with local numbers in 40 cities) allows communications costs to be reduced by up to 75% and should therefore encourage increased MED MEDLINE Usage. Current data rate of the MEDLINE leased lines are 30 characters per second. Current charges for automated searching of the MEDLINE data base at the College of Physicians of Philadelphia is $15 per search.

Current active Members of the MEDLINE network in active Pennsylvania include the following instructions:

1. College of Physicians of Philadelphia Library
2. Hahnemann Medical College (Philadelphia)
   Medical College Library
3. Hershey Medical Center Library, Pennsylvania State University
4. Thomas Jefferson University (Philadelphia)
   Scoll Memorial Library
5. Temple University (Philadelphia)
   Health Sciences Center Library
6. University of Pennsylvania (Philadelphia)
   Medical School Library
7. University of Pittsburgh
   Falk Library

OTHER COOPERATIVE PROJECTS UTILIZING MACHINE READABLE DATA BASES

Bryn Mawr/Haverford College Cooperation Project

The purpose of this informal project is to experiment with combined processing, acquisitions and cataloging. A machine readable data base containing serial holdings data was produced and a computer-produced list of periodicals currently received was produced. Future plans include the expansion of membership to include Swarthmore College.

Lehigh Valley Association of Independent Colleges

The purpose of this formal cooperative is to promote and facilitate interinstitutional cooperation among independent colleges and universities in Eastern Pennsylvania. Three machine readable data bases, CA Condensates, COMPENDEX, and MARC II are maintained at Lehigh University. Telecommunication is maintained via the TWX dial-up network. Membership consists of

1. Allentown College of St. Francis deSales (Center Valley, Pennsylvania)
2. Ceder Crest College (Allentown)
3. Lafayette College (Easton)
4. Lehigh University (Bethlehem)
5. Moravian College (Bethlehem)
6. Muhlenberg College (Allentown)

Northern Pennsylvania Bibliographic Center

The purpose of this informal cooperative, headquartered at King's College, Wilkes-Barre, is to maintain a union catalog and produce a union list of serials for Northeastern Pennsylvania. Machine readable records consist of a union list of periodicals on magnetic tape which is published annually. Telecommunication is maintained via private teletype network and the TWX dial-up network.

Area College Library Cooperative of Central Pennsylvania

This formal cooperative includes undergraduate and two year colleges, plus the State Library. Its machine readable records consist of a magnetic tape of Bucknell's shelf list. Telecommunication is accomplished via the TWX dial-up network and telefacsimile link at Penn State University.

West Chester District Center

The purpose of this center, located at the Chester County Library in West Chester, is to provide central library services and direction uncer the Pennsylvania Library Code. Machine readable data activities include a biannual computer produced Union list of serials (since 1972) and a machine readable Union book catalog (since 1967). Telecommunications employ the TWX dial-up network. The communication pattern is hierarchical with the switching center located in the District Center, allowing 75% of communications to be channeled through the switching Center. Voice grade telephone lines are used.

Pittsburgh Regional Library Center (PRLC)

In addition to the OCLC access described above, the PRLC has also maintained a Pittsburgh Regional Union List of Periodicals in machine readable format since 1967. PRLC member institutions include:

1. Carlow College
2. Carnegie Library of Pittsburgh
3. Carnegie-Mellon University
4. Chatham College
5. Point Park College
6. Robert Morris College
7. University of Pittsburgh

There are also twelve other academic libraries who are associate members.

PENN STATE FACSIMILE NETWORK

Since 1966, a telefacsimile network has linked the Commonwealth Camp Campus Libraries with the main library at University Park. The network employs Magnafax telecopiers which transmit over leased voice grade telephone WATS lines (see W. C. Jackson, "Telefacsimile at Penn State University: A Report on Operations during 1968-1969" Library Resources and Technical Services, 15(2), 223-28 [Spring 1971]).

APPENDIX C
Classified Bibliography

I. Information Storage Technology

1. Application of Associative Array Processor to Data Base Management
   (GER-15260), Goodyear Aerospace Corp., June 9, 1971.
2. A. H. Bobeck and H. E. D. Scobil, "Magnetic Bubbles," Scientific
   American, pp. 78-90, June 1971.
3. H. Byrn, "Automation in University Libraries — The State of the Art,"
   Library Resources and Technical Services, 13, 520-528, 1969.
4. M. Camras, "Information Storage Density," IEEE Spectrum, 2(7), 98-
   105, 1965.
5. M. H. Cannell et al., Concepts and Applications of Computerized
   Associated Processing, Including Bibliography, Washington, D.C.,
   MITRE Corp. (ESD-TR-70-379) (AD879-281).

6. "Coming through Your Front Door: Prerecorded Video Cassettes,"
   American Libraries, 1(11), 1069-1073, 1970.
7. Computer Output Microfilm, Auerbach Publishers, Inc., Philadelphia,
   1970.
8. "Document vs. Digital Storage of Textual Materials for Network Operations," EDUCOM, 2, 1-5, 1967.
9. "It's the Real Thing: 10-Trillion Bit Optical Memory," Electro-Optical
   Systems Design, 4(11), 5-6, 8, 1972.
10. M. V. Mathews and W. S. Brown, "Research Libraries and the New
    Technology," in Libraries at Large, (D. M. Knight and E. S. Nourse,
    eds.), Bowker, New York, 1969, pp. 265-81.
11. R. A. Miner, "Digital/Graphic Record Access," Modern Data, 3(1),
    66-70, 1970.
12. J. A. Murphy, "Microfilm Retrieval Systems," Modern Data, 5(12),
    46-51, 1972.
13. C. E. Price, "Representing Characters to Computers," American
    Documentation, 20(1), 50-60, Jan. 1969.
14. R. L. Shannon, "Atom Agency's Information Falls Out Via Microfiche,"
    Data System News, 9(7), 8-10, 1968.
15. W. Sullivan, "625 Page Book Reduced to Sheet of Microfilm," The
    Sunday Bulletin (Phila.), Sec. 1, p. 8, Nov. 26, 1972.

16. System Development Corporation. "Library Technology," in Libraries at Large, (D. M. Knight and E. S. Nourse, eds.), Bowker, New York, 1969, pp. 600-643.

17. J. W. Weil, "An Introduction to Massive Stores," Honeywell Computer Journal, 5(2), 89-92, 1971.

II. Information Processing and Control Technology

1. I. L. Auerbach, "Computer Technology Forecast — 1971," Presented to IFIP Congress 1971, Ljubljana, Yugoslavia, August 1971.

2. Auerbach Terminal Equipment Digest, Auerbach Publishing, Inc., Philadelphia, 1970.

3. H. B. Becker, "Information Network Design Can be Simplified Step-by-step," Computer Decisions, 4(10), 14-17, 1972.

4. L. H. Berul, "Document Retrieval'," in Annual Review of Information Science and Technology, Vol. 4 (C. Cuadra, ed.), Britanica, Chicago, 1969, pp. 203-228.

5. L. H. Berul, Information Storage and Retrieval: A State-of-the-Art Report (AD630089), 1964.

6. L. H. Berul, "Survey of Equipment Developments in the Information Storage and Retrieval Field," Presented to FID/IFIP Conference, June 14-17, 1967.

7. W. T. Brandhorst and P. F. Eckert, "Document Retrieval and Dissemination Systems," in Annual Review of Information Science and Technology, (C. Cuadra, ed.), Vol. 7, Britanica, Chicago, 1972, pp. 379-437.

8. G. Cadwallader, Format Compatibility and Conversion Among Bibliographic Data Bases, Auerbach Corporation, Philadelphia, June 25, 1969. (Technical Report 1582-100-TR-7) 16p (PB184758).

9. G. Cadwallader, Functional and Software Considerations for Bibliographic Data Base Interaction, Auerbach Corporation, Philadelphia, 1969. Technical Reports 1582-100-TR-4 and PB183816, 44 pp.

10. G. Cadwallader, Query Language and Search Strategy for Bibliographic Data Base Utilization, Auerbach Corporation, Philadelphia, 1969. Technical Reports 1582-100-TR-6 and PB183345, 34 pp.

11. Computer Software (Technology Evaluation Service EDP Series No. 7), Auerbach Publishing, Inc., Philadelphia, 1971.

12. D. D. Cowan and L. Waverman, "The Interdependence of Communications and Data Processing: Issues in Economies of Integration and Public Policy," Bell Journal of Economics and Management Science, 2(2), 657-677, 1971.

13. G. G. Dodd, "Elements of Data Management Systems," Computing Surveys, 1(2), 117-133, 1969.

14. E. Fong, A Survey of Selected Document Processing Systems (National Bureau of Standards Technical Note 599), U.S. Government Printing Office, Washington, D.C., 1971.

15. J. P. Fry et al., Data Management Systems Survey, Mitre Corp.,
    Washington, D.C., 1969 (AD 684707).
16. I. L. Goldhirsh, Common Data Base Computer Center (5029-RP-1),
    Auerbach Corporation, Philadelphia, 1964, 81 pp.
17. M. M. Henderson et al., Cooperation, Convertibility and Compatibility
    Among Information Systems: A Literature Review, Washington, D.C.,
    U.S. Government Printing Office, 1966 (NBS Miscellaneous Publication
    276), 140 pp.
18. H. B. Landau, Classified Bibliography on Bibliographic Data Base
    Interaction, Compatibility and Standardization (1582-100-TR-3),
    Auerbach Corporation, Philadelphia, 70. pp.
19. H. B. Landau, Modes of Data Base Interaction and Initial Screening of
    Alternate Modes (1582-100-TR-2), Auerbach Corporation, Philadelphia,
    1969 21 pp.
20. J. Martin, Introduction to Teleprocessing, Prentic Hall, Englewood
    Cliffs, N.J., 1972.
21. M. E. Stevens, Standardization, Compatibility and/or Convertibility
    Requirements in Network Planning, National Bureau of Standards,
    United States Government Printing Office, Washington, D.C., 1970,
    369 pp. (PB194179).
22. A Survey of Generalized Data Management Systems, Association for
    Computing Machinery, New York, 1969.
23. E. Wall and J. M. Barnes, Intersystem Compatibility and Convertibility
    of Subject Vocabularies (1582-100-TR-5), Auerbach Corporation, Phila-
    delphia, 1969, 130 pp.
24. I. A. Warheit, "Design of Library Systems for Implementation with
    Interactive Computers," Journal of Library Automation, 3(1), 65–78,
    1970.

III. Information Transfer Technology

1. Auerbach Data Communications Equipment Digest, Auerbach Publishers,
   Inc., Philadelphia, 1972.
2. Auerbach Guide to Data Communications, Auerbach Publishers, Inc.,
   Philadelphia, 1970.
3. J. Becker, "Telecommunications Primer," Journal of Library Automation, 2(3), 148–156, 1967.
4. Computer Output Microfilm, Auerbach Publishers, Inc., Philadelphia,
   1970.
5. Data Communications, Auerbach Publishers, Inc., Philadelphia, 1971,
   118 pp.
6. D. L. Dittberner, "Telecommunications Costs," in Proceedings of the
   Conference on Interlibrary Communications and Information Networks
   (J. Becker, ed.), American Library Association, Chicago, 1971, pp.
   160–162.

7. D. A. Dunn, "Principles of Telecommunications Planning" in Proceedings of the Conference on Interlibrary Communications and Information Networks (J. Becker, ed.), American Library Association, Chicago, 1971, pp. 163-169.

8. J. W. Emling, J. R. Harris, and H. J. McMains, "Library Communications," in Libraries and Automation, Library of Congress, Washington, D.C., 1964, pp. 203-219.

9. E. Gentle, ed., Data Communications in Business, American Telephone and Telegraph Company, New York, 1967.

10. W. C. Jackson, "Telefacsimile at Penn State University: A Report on Operations 1968-69," Library Resources and Technical Services, 15(2), 223-228, 1971.

11. W. J. Kessler and Wilhelm, M. J., "Narrow Bandwidth Telecommunications," in Proceedings of the Conference on Interlibrary Communication and Information Networks (J. Decker, ed.), American Library Association, Chicago, 1971, pp. 170-181.

12. K. G. McKay, "Digital Communications — A Tutorial," Bell Telephone Record, 1971.

13. J. Martin, Future Developments in Telecommunications, Prentice Hall, Englewood Cliffs, N.J., 1971.

14. J. A. Murphy, "Microfilm Retrieval Systems," Modern Data, 5(12), 46-52, 1972.

15. S. Schatz, "Facsimile Transmission in Libraries: A State of the Art Survey," Library Resources and Technical Services, 12(1), 5-15, 1968.

16. A. B. Shafritz, "The Use of Computers in Message Switching Systems," presented to the Nineteenth National Conference of the Association for Computing Machinery, 1964.

17. F. F. Spreitzer, "Developments in Copying, Micrographics and Graphic Communications, 1971," Library Resources and Technical Services, 16(2), 135-154, 1972.

18. B. W. Stutzman, "Data Communication Control Procedures," ACM Computing Surveys, 4(4), 197-220, 1972.

19. "Working Group Summary on Network Technology," in Proceedings of the Conference on Interlibrary Communications and Information Networks (J. Becker, ed.), American Library Association, Chicago, 1971, pp. 149-152.

IV. Distribution of Bibliographic
Data on Magnetic Tape

1. H. D. Avram, The MARC Pilot Project Final Report, U.S. Government Printing Office, Washington, D.C., 1968, 183 pp.

2. J. M. Barnes and H. B. Landay, Comparative Description of Bibliographic Data Bases of Interest to the National Agricultural Library (1582-100-TR-1), Auerbach Corporation, Philadelphia, February 15, 1969, 200 pp.

3. J. Egeland, "User Interaction in the State University of New York (SUNY) Biomedical Communication Network," in Interactive Bibliographic Search: The User/Computer Interface (D. E. Walker, ed.), AFIPS Press, Montvale, N.J., 1971, pp. 323-378.

4. M. C. Gechman, "Machine-Readable Bibliographic Data Bases," in Annual Review of Information Science and Technology, Vol. 7 (C. Cuadra, ed.), 1972, pp. 323-378.

5. H. B. Landau, Research Study into the Effective Utilization of Machine-Readable Bibliographic Data Bases, Auerbach Corporation, Philadelphia, 1969 (PB184616).

6. Mechanized Information Services in the University Library. Phase I: Planning, 2 Vols., University of California, Los Angeles, Institute of Library Research, Los Angeles, 1967 (PB178444; PB178442).

7. J. H. Schneider, M. Gechman, and S. Furth, Survey of Commercially Available Computer-Readable Bibliographic Data Bases, American Society for Information Science, Washington, D.C., January, 1973.

V. Existing Networks

1. W. J. Barr, Cost Effective Analysis of Network Computers, University of Illinois, Dept. of Computer Science, Urbana, Ill., August 1972 (Master's thesis).

2. T. H. Bonn, "Standards for Computer Networks," Computer, 4(3), 10-14, 1971.

3. R. M. Braude, "Cost-performance Analysis of TWX-mediated Interlibrary Loans in a Medium-sized Medical Center Library," Bulletin of the Medical Library Association, 59(1), 65-70, 1971.

4. G. W. Brown, J. G. Miller, and T. A. Keenan, EDUNET: Report of the Summer Study on Information Networks, Wiley and Sons, New York, 1967.

5. W. S. Budington, "Network Alternatives and Solutions for Storage," Library Trends, 19(3), 329-340, 1971.

6. J. H. Byrn, "Automation in University Libraries — The State of the Art," Library Resources and Technical Services, 13(4), 520-528, 1969.

7. R. G. Canning, ed., "The Emerging Computer Networks," EDP Analyzer, 11(1), 1-14, 1973.

8. C. A. Cuadra, "Keynote: Library Automation and Networks," in Networks Concepts: Four Points of View, (R. A. Matzek, ed.), Catholic Library Association, Haverford, Pennsylvania, pp. 4-18.

9. D. D. Delaney and C. A. Cuadra, Directory of Academic Library Consortia, Systems Development Corporation, Santa Monica, Calif., 1972; ibid., Suppl. 1.

10. M. Duggan, "Library Network Analysis and Planning (LIB-NAT)," Journal of Library Automation, 2(3), 157-175, 1969.

11. D. J. Farber, "Networks: An Introduction," Datamation, 18(4), 36-39, April 1972.
12. R. V. Katter and D. B. McCarn, "AIM-TWX — An Experimental On-Line Bibliographic Retrieval System," in Interactive Bibliographic Search: The User/Computer Interface (D. E. Walker, ed.), AFIPS Press, Montvale, N.J., 1971, pp. 121-141.
13. R. A. Kennedy, "Bell Laboratories' Library Real-Time Loan System (BELLREL)," Journal of Library Automation, 1(2), 128-146, 1968.
14. F. G. Kilgour, "A Regional Network — Ohio College Library Center," Datamation, 16(2), 87-89, 1970.
15. J. C. LeGates, The ARPA Network Technical Aspects in Nontechnical Language, Interuniversity-Communications Council (EDUCOM), Princeton, N.J., 1971.
16. W. K. Lowry, "Use of Computers in Information Systems," Science, 175, 841-846, 1972.
17. E. Olson, R. Shank, and H. A. Olson, "Library and Information Networks," in Annual Review of Information Science and Technology, (C. A. Cuadra, ed.), Britanica, Chicago, 1972, pp. 279-321.
18. Our Colleges and Universities Today, 8(4), 1970-1971.
19. R. J. Patrick, Guidelines for Library Cooperation — Development of Academic Library Consortia, System Development Corporation, Santa Monica, Calif., 1972, 200 pp.
20. M. E. Stevens, Standardization, Compatibility, and/or Convertibility Requirements in Network Planning, National Bureau of Standards, Washington, D.C., 1970 (PB194179).
21. Federal Information Processing Standards Index, U.S. National Bureau of Standards, U.S. Government Printing Office, Washington, D.C., 1971, 134 pp.

VI. General

1. Auerbach Corporation/DOD User Needs Study: Phase 1. Washington, D.C., Department of Defense, AD 615 501 and AD 615 502, 1965; Auerbach Rept. 1151-TR-3.
2. I. L. Auerbach, "Need for an Information Systems Theory," an address before the International Federation for Information Processing, 10th anniversary celebration, Amsterdam, Netherlands.
3. Proceedings of the Conference on Interlibrary Communications and Information Networks (J. Becker, ed.), American Library Association, Chicago, 1971.
4. W. S. Dix, "Cause and Effect on University Libraries: Two Decisive Decades," American Libraries, 3(7), 725-731, 1972.
5. H. B. Landau, "Can the Librarian Become a Data Base Manager?" Special Libraries, 62(3), 1-8, 1971.

6. Libraries and Information Technology — A National System Challenge, A report to the Council on Library Resources, Inc. by the Information Systems Panel, Computer Science and Engineering Board, Washington, D.C., National Academy of Sciences, 1972, 84 pp.

7. B. E. Markuson, ed., Libraries and Automation: Proceedings of the Conference on Libraries and Automation held at Airlie Foundation, Warrenton, Virginia, May 26-30, 1963, Library of Congress, Washington, D.C., 1964.

8. M. V. Mathews and W. S. Brown, "Research Libraries and the New Technology," in Libraries at Large, (D. M. Knight and E. S. Nourse, eds.), Bowker, New York, 1969.

9. D. S. Price, Collecting and Reporting Real Costs of Information Systems, American Society for Information Science, Special Interest Group on Costs, Budgeting and Economies, Washington, D.C., 1971.

10. D. P. Waite, Library Networks, Book 1, Information Dynamics Corporation, Reading, Mass., 1972.

Chapter 12

RESTORING THE LIBRARY ECOLOGY THROUGH NETWORKS

Melvin S. Day

Deputy Director
National Library of Medicine

The current evolution of electronic interconnected yet independent networks of information systems may seem slow to many of us; however,
interestingly enough, it follows the evolutionary nature of the changes taking
place in man's social world today. This should not be surprising since
today's communications revolution is largely responsive to current economic,
technological, political, and sociological pressures.

Progress has been slow, spotty, and not coordinated on an overall
national systems level. Computerized information systems are being built,
many are operating, many are being linked, but in terms of the total
information process, we have concentrated on sophisticated automated systems and even networks for only part of the total information process.

Our new computerized systems have been successful as far as they go.
In some cases they have added a new dimension to our communications
capability, but we can no longer close our eyes to the fact that this increased
capability at one point in the information cycle is not matched throughout
the cycle. The resulting imbalance is upsetting the operating ecology of
many information service operations. In simple terms, we have stimulated
with our information services more demand for documents than our delivery
systems can supply.

As one who is involved from an operating standpoint with the balanced ecology of a biomedical information network, I am very seriously concerned. On the other hand, I am still confident that the present anomalies in our capabilities will be adjusted by upgrading the total network capability, beginning with the use of our latest technological advances to strengthen the subsystems and systems making up the network. I plan to expand on this thesis shortly, but before I do, let me provide my simple answer to the question of <u>when</u> to share resources. The answer is <u>now</u>.

Complete self-sufficiency in the library world is no longer either possible or desirable. Sharply rising costs coupled with tight budgets are compelling forces none of us can ignore, and the concept of sharing is generally accepted today as fundamental to our continuing capacity to provide economically the type, quality, and volume of information service required by our customers. We all seem to agree on the "why" and I suspect on the "when." The major difficulty, of course, comes in the "how," and my concern about the present imbalance in the total information process cuts across both the "when" and the "how" of resource sharing.

Let me expand briefly on this concern of mine. In the last 20 years, information science has concentrated on information retrieval methods for pulling from a large information base the subset of specific documents that are revelent to a particular information need. Our so-called retrieval systems are being computerized. Information about documents, not the documents themselves, is stored and manipulated in the computer. Some of our systems depend on detailed indexing using controlled vocabularies. Others have computerized full text SCAN capabilities. In fact, our ability to make users aware of documents they may need has expanded greatly. The knowledge of what materials exist stimulates requests for more information among library users, and indeed has overloaded the capacity of many libraries to deliver the documents so effectively advertised by information retrieval systems.

Information technology has enabled us to produce sophisticated bibliographic services like <u>Index Medicus</u>, <u>Current Contents</u>, <u>Science Citation Index</u>, <u>Engineering Index</u> and <u>Nuclear Science Abstracts</u>, to name but a few — all of which give the user information about more documents in his field than almost any library can afford to have in its holdings for his examination.

But all of the information <u>about</u> documents which indexing and current awareness tools present to our library users is of no consequence if the user cannot have access to the documents themselves. "No matter how elegant our network of our retrieval systems for medical (or any other kind of) information become, the nub of the matter remains getting the information to the users. In the library vernacular — 'document delivery'" [1]. In the <u>7th Annual Review of Information Science and Technology</u> we are told that document delivery and the problems of accomplishing it receive precious little attention in the open literature [2]. Weil makes the point that

"...new information systems for alerting and for storage and retrieval have recently monopolized the limelight. Only a few information managers and projects such as MIT's Intrex have clearly pointed out that providing pertinent documents is also vital" [3]. We might restate this by saying that it is crucial that libraries provide requested documents promptly and economically, that is a library's job.

And yet, as surprising as it may seem, I know of a number of cases not in the medical area where access to and use of the computerized information retrieval systems is being sharply curtailed by the librarians simply because of the inability of the librarians to deliver the requested material on any kind of reasonable schedule. This is almost analogous to having a heavily traveled eight-lane super highway feed into a two-lane road, resulting in huge traffic problems. To me, such a situation is deplorable. When one considers the human factors — namely, the overworked library staffs — it is understandable, but nevertheless, it is still deplorable. Fortunately this situation is not yet typical of all our libraries, but it is worsening, and as we now start interconnecting and networking the systems, the severity of the problem is rising exponentially. The growing demand for the librarian to borrow more and more source materials using our current outdated methods is creating burdensome workloads which have to be attended to at the expense of other pressing library duties. If the deterioration continues it will soon reach the critical stage.

Interlibrary loans, including the provision of photocopies in lieu of papers, is an old and established practice. Many libraries have joined in listing their holdings in Union lists of serials and Union catalogs on a local, national, or even discipline basis. These Union lists and agreements to share the holdings they cover in effect constitute library networks. In Libraries and Information Technology: A National System Challenge, the Information Systems Panel of the Computer Science and Engineering Board of the National Academy of Sciences stated that:

> ...the library function contains the "memory" of national information systems. The current embodiment of this memory is in the wide range of the large national libraries, major academic and research libraries, public libraries, school libraries and so on, and various information collections used in support of industry, government and education. [4]

There is at present no national planning for the development of this 'memory' to best advantage. Nevertheless, networks like FAUL, NYSILL, NERMLS, OCLC, SUNY, and others, are springing up, and in some cases establishing network-to-network links. At the Conference on Interlibrary Communications and Information Networks, held in 1970 at Airlie House,

the participants recommended that the National Commission on Libraries
and Information Science be the coordinating agency for planning a national
network of libraries and other information resources.

The National Commission and the National Science Foundation are both
concerned with this resource sharing problem and have commissioned
studies with the Association of Research Libraries which may lead to a
network of comprehensive national, regional, or even disciplinary depository
literature collections to be shared by participating libraries. Perhaps this
type of network of major lending libraries will prove to be more effective
than the status quo, even using today's not too efficient United States Mail
Service for the transmission and delivery of documents.

There are a number of major resource sharing efforts under way. Let
us look at one with which I am most familiar. At the National Library of
Medicine we have established a national resource sharing network of medical
libraries. This network, of course, deals with a limited area of knowledge,
concentrating on biomedicine.

Perhaps a brief word about this network, which admittedly is in its
early stages of development, will provide some insight into a "real-life"
effort currently underway. It is a network with many of the strengths and
weaknesses which have been highlighted in preceding chapters but at the
same time it is one organization's attempt to do something about resource
sharing now.

The Library, which was established in 1836, now houses the largest
and finest collection of health sciences literature in the world — 1,300,000
volumes and 20,000 serials. Into our computerized bibliographic control
system we will add this year approximately a quarter of a million citations
from the workd's medical literature. Photocomposing equipment will
produce from the resultant machine-readable data base Index Medicus,
Current Catalog, and a number of recurring bibliographies.

In this biomedicine area, the overwhelming demand is for information
published in the journal literature. The articles are indexed by a controlled
vocabulary — MESH (Medical Subject Headings). The data base can be searched for combinations of subject headings in conjunction with selected other
information, such as year of publication, language of publication, author,
article title, and journal title.

The backbone of the medical library network is MEDLINE, an on-line,
real time bibliographic searching system, the MEDLINE data base contains
400,000 citations to articles from the most important 1200 of the 2400
journals indexed in Index Medicus since January 1970. It is in effect a core
data base and one which we have found to be most effective as well as
economical to operate.

MEDLINE is queried by remote access terminals via a commercial communications network operated by the Tymshare Corporation with nodes in 40 cities. The MEDLINE terminal operator dials the nearest node city and is automatically connected to the NLM data-base and computer in Bethesda, Maryland. An on-line news file alerts all users to MEDLINE systems developments, changes in the data bases, and scheduling information. The commercial communications network makes effective national coverage possible and economical, and at the same time provides the connection to the data bases of other organizations commercially available on the Tymshare network. For example, anyone with a MEDLINE terminal may also, for a fee, have access to the ERIC data base developed by the Office of Education. Data bases produced by the Chemical Abstract Service are also accessible on Tymshare. NLM itself provides six more data bases to MEDLINE users:

1. SDILINE functions as MEDLINE's current awareness service
2. COMPFILE, available at selected hours, makes it possible to search citations from the remaining 1200 journals covered in Index Medicus but not in MEDLINE
3. BACKFILE furnishes access to citations older than the MEDLINE data base
4. CATLINE carries monographic cataloging information produced by NLM and NLM's cooperative cataloging partners
5. SERLINE, a data base of approximately 6500 substantial serial titles in the field of biomedicine, presents cataloging information and locator codes to aid all participating medical libraries in finding the nearest source of procurement for a periodical available on interlibrary loan.

Currently 160 organizations have access to the MEDLINE network by remote terminal. During the month of March, 17,000 literature searches were performed on the system.

The MEDLINE network with its multiple data bases is the fundamental tool in the Regional Medical Library Program, which is a hierarchical network of libraries that supplies document delivery in the form of interlibrary loan of monographs and photocopy of journal articles. The Regional Medical Library program divides the country geographically into eleven regions, each serviced by a Regional Medical Library (RML). The basic units, or bottom layer of the pyramid, are the libraries in community hospitals, clinics, colleges with health science education programs, and other health related agencies such as research organizations or governmental agencies. The second layer is composed of the resource libraries, which are generally the well-stocked libraries of major medical schools. Each region is headed by its RML. The RML's are also responsible for coordinating MEDLINE service in the regions. MEDLINE service began with the RML's and resource libraries and is being extended to larger hospitals and other institutions.

Requests for documents move upward through the network. All interlibrary loan requests are sent in standard format via TWX or mail. Requests
which resource libraries cannot fill are referred to the RML, which fills
all requests it can from within the region, using whatever locator tools it
has at its disposal. The RML's and a selected group of other libraries are
authorized to refer requests directly to NLM. Generally, most requests
are referred upward, to larger and larger resources.

The hierarchical structure of the network and upward routing pattern
for requests means that the collections of the participating institutions
serve as a unified, decentralized depository collection of biomedical
literature. A user who enters the network at the smallest local hospital
library can successfully tap greater and greater resources to fulfill his
information needs.

The document delivery system of the Regional Medical Library Program
is, in its day to day functioning, a relatively unsophisticated operation
compared with the computerized MEDLINE services for information retrieval. However, totally without automation, this method of document delivery
does work. Last year, the National Library of Medicine alone filled over
150,000 interlibrary loan requests. The RML's and resource libraries
filled many, many more. All of this activity was accomplished manually.
It is still necessary for human beings to go into the stacks, pull volumes,
mail out monographs, make and mail out photocopies, and keep records.

One measure of good document delivery service is speed, that is,
minimum turnaround time for filling requests. I just stated that the NLM
system does work and has been effective, but I do not believe that I will be
giving away any secrets if I say that both we and some of our users would
not object if the turnaround time were shorter. I can assure you I spend a
great deal of my time being personally involved in the continuing effort to
make this process faster, more efficient, and more economical.

The establishment of a national network of lending library depository
collections, such as the Association of Research Libraries is considering,
may be in order; however, unless we can accomplish major technological
improvements in our delivery systems the improvement in the effectiveness
of such systems can only be incremental.

I regret that none of us has a ready-made solution. Work is continuing
on telefacsimile transmission and on the use of cable television where it
exists. Without minimizing the major legal and technical problems inherent
in implementing this new technology, our communications experts tell us
that high cost is still the major obstacle to overcome. Even so, there have
to be more effective methods for obtaining and placing into the hands of a
requester those documents he desires. In a real time mode and in response
to user's questions, our computerized bibliographic retrieval systems
identify for him the articles or books pertinent to his need. But in all too
many cases there are lengthy delays before we can deliver the materials to

him. In the army, a number of years ago, we used to refer jokingly to a "rush and wait" process. I fear that our information retrieval networks today provide the "rush" factor while our document delivery networks unfortunately provide the "wait" factor.

We must give priority attention to the area of document delivery. A major imbalance in the information transfer process does exist, and in some areas has reached the critical state where breakdowns threaten the total process.

The time for resource sharing in libraries is definitely now. However, in some areas such as interlibrary loan and document delivery we need major technology improvements. Technological progress usually comes about in response to a need — an urgent need. I believe that we have an urgent need — an urgent need to restore balance in the library and information transfer process. However, to attract the attention of those who may be able to develop the necessary technology we all must speak with one voice. We must speak with one voice not necessarily to the "how" of solving this problem but rather to the "when" — now.

REFERENCES

1. D. Bishop, "Control and Dissemination of Information in Medicine," in Advances in Librarianship, (Melvin Voigt, ed.), vol. 2, 1971, p. 61.
2. N. Lin and W. D. Garvey, "Information Needs and Uses," in Annual Review of Information Science and Technology (Carlos Cuadra, ed.), vol. 7, 1972, p. 10.
3. B. H. Weil, "Document Access," Journal of Chemical Documentation 11, 179 (August 1971).
4. Libraries and Information Technology: A National System Challenge, National Academy of Sciences, Washington, D.C., 1972, p. 18.

Chapter 13

REGIONAL AND NATIONAL COMPUTER NETWORKS
FOR RESOURCE SHARING BY COLLEGES AND UNIVERSITIES

Henry Chauncey

President
Interuniversity Communications Council, Inc.   (EDUCOM)

The question before us — when to share library resources — has a very
simple answer. The answer is — now. But this simple answer begs the
question in several important ways.

If actually sharing library resources were as simple as saying "do it
now" there would be no need for further discussion. I could terminate this
Chapter at this point, you could stop reading, and resource sharing could
begin tomorrow. Unfortunately, the problem is not that simple and conferences are badly needed to reach a consensus on when and how libraries can
most effectively accomplish the sharing of resources.

As already discussed, a basic problem facing libraries today is the
tremendous increase in available information — not only the absolute quantity
of that information, but the rate at which new information is being produced.
In addition, library patrons are becoming increasingly interested in being
provided with better tools for accessing this information.

Traditional library methods have barely been able to cope with these
increased requirements, and library budgets have had difficulty keeping up
with the ever-increasing spiral of library costs. The Purdue study refer-
enced earlier points out that for the past several decades, the average
academic research library collection has been doubling in size every 16 to

17 years and its total expenditures have been doubling about every 7 years. And yet, despite increasing expenditures and acquisitions, the number of volumes per student in American college and university libraries actually declined from 52.4 to 43.5 volumes over the 12-year period from 1960 to 1972 [1].* Clearly the continuing effectiveness and even the survival of libraries will depend in large measure upon their ability simultaneously to combat rising costs and to provide the increased services which are desired. This will make resource sharing essential.

What do I mean by resource sharing? First, the sharing of library materials and of the professional talent which organizes and maintains those materials. Second, sharing in the setting of priorities and the determination of policies under which this will be done. Third, sharing in the planning, conduct and support of research and development for ways of handling resource-sharing better. Further, I mean resource sharing in completely new ways now made possible by advances in computer and communications technology.

The amazing capabilities of the computer are well known and have been used in a variety of library applications. But significant cost saving from resource sharing requires also the communication between libraries that computer networks provide. This newly available networking technology has the potential of offering the breakthrough in the library and information science field that is needed to lower unit costs and strengthen services, because it offers a way in which technology can be combined with the cooperative efforts of a group of libraries.

Some savings have been effected in the past through libraries agreeing to work together and make reciprocal use of their resources. Savings have also resulted from the introduction of technology into individual libraries. However, it is only when cooperation is combined with technology as in the case of computer networks, that the total savings will be really significant.

Since the technology and art of networking are recent developments, I should like to devote most of my discussion to this facet of resource sharing.

By happy coincidence, Educom just conducted for the National Science Foundation three seminars on computer networking which brought together over 150 people with a variety of backgrounds and expertise. Their competence and wisdom far exceed my own and I am therefore going to make extensive use of the draft of their report.

"The most basic conclusion [of these seminars] became apparent by midway through the first seminar. It took on such force and clarity by the second seminar that it became a main theme in the faculty's summary remarks on that occasion. It received still greater emphasis in the third seminar. The conclusion is here following:

---

*The low point was 41.8 volumes per student in 1968-69. The last three years have shown a slight reversal in the downward trend.

computer networking must be acknowledged as an important new mode for obtaining information and computation. It is a real alternative that needs to be given serious attention in current planning and decision making" [2].

"Articulation of the possibilities of computer networks is not what is new. That goes back to the early 1960's and before. Nor is the implementation and operation of networks new. Many working networks have been in evidence for several years now, both commercially and in universities. What is new is the unmistakable recognition, bordering on a sense of the inevitable, that networks are now practical and are here to stay.... It is time to sit up, take notice, and do some hard-nosed comparative analysis" [2, pp. 21, 22].

"The coming of age of networks takes on special significance in light of the dissatisfaction that participants expressed repeatedly throughout the seminar discussions with the present computing situation. There was a strong feeling that

the current mode of autonomous, self-sufficient operation in the provision of computing and information services is frequently wasteful, deficient, and unresponsive to users' needs.

"The waste was said to come about because of duplication, redundancy of effort from one installation to another, incompatibilities, other impediments to the sharing of resources, and underutilization of installed equipment. Yet, simultaneously, there was thought to be much unsatisfied pent-up demand for computer and information services, as well as widespread unhappiness with the general level of documentation, program support, and user assistance. Complaints were voiced about the relative lack of uniform standards and the paucity of information on what programs and data are available and how to get and use them.

"The human tendency, when beset by problems such as these, is to seek a savior in the next new technology — networks in this case. But the seminar participants were not so ready to delude themselves. The general feeling is expressed in the following conclusion:

Networking does not in and of itself offer a solution to current deficiencies. What it does offer is a promising vehicle with which to bring about important changes in user practices, institutional procedures, and government policy that can lead to effective solutions.

"Thus, more critical than <u>whether</u> networking is developed and applied is <u>how</u> it is developed and applied. For example networking emphasizes the need for standards and good documentation. Unless effective mechanisms are developed and strong measures taken in networking to ensure that suitable standards and documentation are developed, present inadequacies could get worse, not better" [2, pp. 22, 23].

"Participants considered this to be the right time for top level decision makers at different institutions to meet and begin thinking about how large-scale networks might look and work. Officials must question seriously and honestly how well computing and information services are currently supplied, how well users are served, the historical reasons for the present mode of operation, how networks and other fast-advancing technologies might improve the operation, and what changes in government policy and institutional attitudes would be required or helpful in bringing about this improvement. With this in mind, it is recommended that

> Institutions of research and education should commit themselves to a comprehensive reexamination of how they supply and receive computing and information services and they should think imaginatively about future possibilities for networking that could help correct the problems and deficiencies that exist today" [2, pp. 24, 25].

The conclusion of the Seminar participants that the technology for computer networking is available here and now should perhaps have some supporting evidence. It is being used in more than 20 regional networks whose development has been supported by the National Science Foundation. There are operating networks centered at Dartmouth College, the University of Iowa, Illinois Institute of Technology, the University of Texas and the Washington State University. The Triangle Universities Computation Center in North Carolina provides computer services to the North Carolina State University, University of North Carolina and Duke University. The North Carolina Educational Computing Service also provides a mechanism through which computer programs developed at one school can be shared with the others. "The MERIT Network is an arrangement through which the University of Michigan, Michigan State, and Wayne State University can share resources. UNI-COLL is an effort by the University City Science Center of Philadelphia to operate a combined computation center for some twenty-seven colleges and universities in the Delaware Valley." The University of Pennsylvania has turned over its large IBM computer to UNI-COLL and the other colleges in the consortium have access to it through a network.

Several states either already have or are developing statewide computer networks (California, Illinois, New Jersey, New York, Minnesota, Oregon, and Florida). A current EDUCOM study, sponsored by the Exxon Education

Foundation, will examine the extent to which state agencies have been assuming responsibility for coordinating the acquisition of computing resources for state colleges and universities. It will also facilitate and encourage the sharing of information among the states and permit an evaluation to be made of the impact of these developments on computing in higher education and on the relationship between educational and governmental agencies.

The Advanced Research Projects Agency of the Department of Defense has developed the ARPANET, a national network of computers at leading universities and research organizations, which permits heterogeneous computers to communicate with one another in a technologically effective and economical manner using a technology referred to by its developers as "packet switching." The use of high speed (50 kilobit per second) communications lines, and the efficient utilization of those lines, makes the transfer of textual materials both practical and economical. The end-to-end delay in transferring a full screen of information over the ARPANET is less than half a second and this has exciting possibilities for library use.

Originally the exclusive province of researchers in computer science, the ARPANET is being used more and more as a vehicle for sharing computer resources. The IBM 360/91 computer at UCLA receives 25% of its total revenue from network customers within the first year of accepting and the Burroughs 6700 at the University of California at San Diego receives 20%. The University of Illinois gave up its Burroughs 6700 computer and now uses the one at the University of California at San Diego. The cost for getting through the network the same amount of computing formerly provided by that Burroughs computer is reported to be one-third of the amount it cost Illinois to have its own machine.

Harvard has returned its large IBM computer to the manufacturer and greatly reduced its central computing facility. Harvard originally planned to develop a joint computer center with MIT, but this was replaced by an arrangement through which Harvard essentially became a customer of MIT. Most recently Harvard has set out to shop nationally for the best service available for each application which can then be secured through ARPANET or other network facilities directly from the computer center which developed the service.

There are also a growing number of commercial systems which can qualify as national networks. Over twenty companies including TYMSHARE Inc., Control Data Corporation, General Electric Company, Computer Sciences Corporation and University Computing Company now offer national and international network services.

The National Library of Medicine has established a service called MEDLINE (Chapter 12). It uses TYMNET facilities and permits medical researchers throughout the country to have on-line access to over 400,000 citations to articles from about 1200 major journals indexed for Index Medicus. This is almost 60% of the citations printed since January 1, 1970.

The Ohio College Library Center is demonstrating the specific advantages of networking for academic libraries. The heart of this system is a computer based, on-line shared catalog which uses MARC II tapes supplied by the library of Congress and cataloging data input by member libraries. This system produces library catalog cards at a cost considerably below that required by most existing manual methods and has been on-line since October 1971. By allowing each member library to specify its own card format, the system is one of the few applications which use the computer as an instrument for facilitating a healthy diversity rather than as a club to enforce rigid conformity.

OCLC's existing system permits member libraries to share not only the physical facilities of the computer, but also the intellectual efforts involved in cataloging, since cataloging information entered into the system by one library is available to all other member libraries. The system has the potential for providing a complete range of library services, and research work is now under way to develop additional modules which will allow serials control, complete technological processing, interlibrary loan message switching, and bibliographic search and retrieval services.

There are some seven regions which are actively considering replication of the OCLC System. However, the problem of how a system which was set up in a single state can become a national federation of regional systems each of which will have a voice in determining policy has not yet been addressed, let alone solved — and this leads into the critical question.

If networking technology is not only available but is being used and the advantages of resource sharing through computer networks are even being demonstrated in particular library applications, why then is this technology not being applied more generally to solving the problems of the library?

The published report of the study of libraries and information technology which was sponsored by the National Academy of Sciences speaks to this question:

> "The primary bar to development of national computer-based library and information systems is no longer basically a technology-feasibility problem. Rather, it is the combination of complex institutional and organizational human-related problems and the inadequate economic/value system associated with these activities" [3].

In thinking about this problem I have found it useful to classify these inhibiting factors under three broad headings — organizational, psychological and economic.

The National Academy of Sciences report also observed that ".. . science policy must assume a much more effective role in stimulating public and private actions to weld the present localized and fragmentary efforts into nationally coherent programs" [3, p. 5]. In short, what is needed is organization.

The feeling on the part of the participants in the Networking Seminars that "now is the time for institutions of research and education to commit themselves to reexamine, compare, analyze, plan, and begin to organize and coordinate their actions with respect to computing and information services" [2, pp. 25, 26], led to the most action directed and most encompassing recommendation of their report.

> "A planning and organizing council on computing and information services in research and education should be formed to provide educational and research institutions with an organizational locus for continuing the study of networking possibilities, identifying and discussing current problems dealing with funding sources, handling internal relations, and negotiating with one another.

"The Council should be a working group rather than an associational organization of representatives. Its membership should include people from institutions of higher education, research centers, information service groups, libraries, and laboratories (including those of profit-making corporations), selected on the basis of their experience, expertise, and ability to contribute not only to the deliberations and mission of the Council, but also to the national networking arrangements to which the activities of the Council might lead. ... The Council might be set up for a five-year term to

> Commission studies, tests, and experiments exploring the problems and prospects for national networking;

> Draft a plan for the formation of subnets and appoint panels to identify resources;

> Stimulate planning and organizational activities that will provide orderly transition to a large-scale facilitating network operation if one is deemed desirable;

> Recruit entrepreneurial activists knowledgeable about networking to go out, answer questions, determine interest, and enlist support for the work of the Council;

> Inform institutions about plans and future possibilities to help them prepare, adjust, and avoid disruption and surprise;

> Recommend an organizational structure for national networking in the period beyond the life of the council.

"The members of the Council might be organizations and institutions, each served by two officials: Normally one would be the president, chancellor, provost, senior vice president, or director at the topmost level of organizational authority at a point where the financial, operating, and planning responsibilities of the organization meet. The second would be someone in a position that brings him in contact with a broad cross-section of the users of information and computing services; for example, the director of research, the coordinator of computing resources, or the director of computing activities. With the proviso that the Council be a working group, its organizational membership should be as broadly based as possible. It should be supported by a substantial financial contribution from each member that expresses the member's commitment and gives the Council the financial base it must have to commence its activities.

"The expression of commitment and state of solvency thus obtained would help the Council attract the important additional funds from other sources needed to carry forward its activities on a scale commensurate with the magnitude of the endeavor. State legislatures, federal agencies, and private foundations are keenly aware today of the financial problems of educational institutions. They are looking for ways to improve educational efficiency. The work of the Council is certain to be of special interest to them" [2, pp. 26, 27].

Another factor inhibiting the use of technology in the library area is the psychological one. We are all more or less creatures of habit and much prefer to stick with the known rather than venture too far into uncharted waters. We are also somewhat reluctant to exchange procedures which have worked and are still working for new procedures of uncertain merit and even more uncertain expense.

But there are some indications that the fundamental psychological inhibitions to resource sharing are being overcome. As the librarian at a leading academic research library has written to me:

"At long last, I think it safe to say that there is general recognition, at least on the part of librarians, that any attempt at local self-sufficiency in library collections is simply unrealistic. Increasingly over recent decades, no libraries, not even the very largest, have been able to provide in themselves all the resources required by their scholarly clienteles" [4].

Finally, there are some formidable economic inhibitions which must be overcome if there is to be sharing of library resources through a computer network. Developing such a network takes a period of years and during the transitional period, the existing system must still be maintained. This requires a double expenditure of funds, maintaining the old while at the same time inaugurating the new. In addition, for many state systems, there are prohibitions against spending money outside the borders of the state which will somehow have to be overcome if a truly national network is to emerge.

The financial stringencies under which most colleges and universities are operating today make the decision to cooperate and share resources a very difficult one, even though in the long run this will result in economies. It takes a farsighted stance and real courage in these times of financial shortages to divert money from satisfying pressing current needs to research on sharing resources — since the short-term consequences frequently loom larger than the long-range benefits.

To sum up, now is the time to extend resource sharing among libraries. What is needed is a commitment on the part of librarians and top university administrators who recognize the opportunities for resource sharing inherent in computer networking and have the courage to invest in long-range efforts that will benefit not only individual libraries, but ultimately all of higher education.

The technology which will permit greatly increased sharing of library resources by means of computer networks is here, but is only beginning to be applied to the solution of the problems facing academic libraries.

If this technology is to be applied successfully, it will require an organization that represents broadly the library community in the determination of policies and in planning, research, and development; an organization that will minimize wasteful duplication of effort and assure compatibility.

Traditional library methods will have to be modified to include the new technology of computer networking. Even the largest libraries will no longer be able to amass collections which are completely self-sufficient. The rising volume of information and rising level of costs are so great that only through cooperation and the sharing of resources will libraries be able to cope.

And let me repeat, neither the application of technology to library problems by itself, nor cooperative effort by itself will be fully effective. It is rather the combination of technology with cooperative effort which will produce results far greater than either alone could achieve and will enable libraries to reach the seemingly irreconcilable goals of reduced unit costs and increased service to the academic community.

REFERENCES

1. The Bowker Annual, R. R. Bowker Co., New York, 1969, p. 42; 1972, p. 146.

2. Martin Greenberger, Julius Aronofsky, William Massy, and James McKenney, Networks for Research and Education: Sharing Computers and Information, MIT Press, Cambridge, Massachusetts, 1973, p. 21.

3. Libraries and Information Technology: A National System Challenge, Washington, D.C., 1972, p. 10.

4. Letter of Douglas W. Bryant to Henry Chauncey, September 15, 1972.

Chapter 14

LOCAL COOPERATIVES WITH NATIONAL IMPLICATIONS:
THE PLANNED METROPOLITAN PITTSBURGH
SCIENCE AND TECHNOLOGY LIBRARY

Herman H. Henkle

Library Planning Consultant
Chapel Hill, North Carolina
Executive Director (Retired)
The John Crerar Library (Chicago)

In this paper, I wish to touch on three facets of the complex of problems discussed above:

1. Brief observations on the general idea of networks, with notes on three local networks, two of which have attained national importance
2. Description of the proposed Metropolitan Pittsburgh Science and Technology Library
3. Some comments on priorities and actions that can make such a facility possible

I hope that my emphasis will be on the essence of each of these facets.

National networks of libraries have been a dream of librarians for a long time. The increasing intensity of our interest during the past decade has been reflected by a growing emphasis on networks in the literature. Among many useful papers was one by Maryann Duggan on "Library Network Analysis and Planning," which appeared in the Journal of Library Automation for September 1969. Her opening sentence was, "To be a librarian in 1969 is to stand at the crossroads of change." The very need for such a book as this is an indication that we are still pondering which of the roads to take.

It has seemed to me that we have been somewhat preoccupied with the hope that the initiative would be taken by our national libraries. To a limited degree this has been realized. Major contributions to the paraphernalia necessary to the development of networks have come out of the Library of Congress, principally through its system of catalogs from the early printed catalog cards through the publication of the national union catalog in book form, and more recently through the production of the product of its cataloging for distribution in digital form. But the Library of Congress (LC) has not evinced any interest in becoming the coordinating head of a national network. The National Library of Medicine, on the other hand, assumed leadership in this field by initiating a system of regional medical libraries, originally planned to reach all parts of the country. It was my good fortune to work with NLM in helping to establish one of these centers at Crerar Library to serve a five-state area including Illinois, Iowa, Indiana, Minnesota and Wisconsin. The system was conceived at a high level of service objectives and impressed me as being one of the most significant library developments within my professional lifetime.

Recently, however, the system seems to be faltering, due apparently to the depression in federal spending. We are finding much to our confusion, that federal funding can be a highly erratic source of support. If this is to continue for a time, and it seems probable, it seems clear that our dependence for network development should be shifted to emphasis on more limited networks having centers in local institutions, either in existing libraries or new agencies designed for the purpose. A number of notable examples have been developing across the country, some with a very encouraging degree of success. I would like to mention three which are very different in their objectives and operation and may well represent great promise for systems development in the future.

The first is a consortium of seven liberal arts college libraries in the Twin Cities in Minnesota, with the headquarters of the consortium located in an eighth library, nonacademic, the James Jerome Hill Reference Library in St. Paul. The antecedents of this consortium date back to 1952 when Dr. Frederick Kuhlman made a study of several of the college libraries and recommended that they form such a consortium with a formal organization and a director. Cooperation between the libraries gradually increased, but fifteen years went by before they took Dr. Kuhlman's advice to create a formal organization with a director. Shortly after this action was taken, the Trustees of the Hill Library, which was a member of the consortium, offered to fund the cost of implementing a service program. The program was initiated by the generation of a union card catalog of the eight libraries. This catalog was housed in the Hill Library in a large, rotary powered file. Each of the college libraries was tied to the union catalog with direct ringing, dedicated telephone lines. Coupled with this facility for locating materials was a delivery system that touches each library twice a day and — in routine — picks up books for delivery to any of the other libraries and

returns books by the same channel. The books are then available for normal circulation to students and faculty.

The effect of this consortium was striking. In the year preceding the
functioning network, the total inter-library loans by conventional means
among the eight libraries was approximately 1200 volumes. In the first
year of the network this interlibrary flow was 16,000 volumes, and at last
report the rate of lending was still increasing. The smallest of the eight
libraries had 50,000 volumes, the largest about 200,000 volumes. Working
together, the students and faculty of each college had made available to
them a library resourse of a million volumes. It is important to note that
this service is for undergraduates, in a library climate that normally
restricts interlibrary loans to faculty and graduate students. The consortium
has now published a computer produced union list of serials and also an
excellent directory of the library resources throughout the Twin Cities area,
in the hope that the program can now be developed to include direct and
referral reference and information services. It is quite probable that this
network of libraries will continue to operate in a relatively limited area,
but this in no way reduces the impact of the network on the academic
communities which it serves.

The other two examples have both been referred to in this conference;
they are included here for the purpose of characterizing their programs as
prototypes of library networks. They are the Center for Research Libraries
headquartered in Chicago and the Ohio College Library Center. CLR is
devoted primarily to cooperative acquisition and distribution of materials;
OCLC is devoted to cooperative development and distribution of bibliographic
information.

The Center for Research Libraries was established about a quarter of
a century ago as the Midwest Inter-Library Center with ten institutional
members. Although some of its founders conceived of the Center as an
organization to contribute dynamically to the development of library
resources through acquisitions, the Center functioned largely during the
first several years as a library for the deposit of little used books. It
became increasingly clear that this was a much too passive role, and
emphasis gradually shifted to acquisitions. The number of midwest members
increased with the broadening program, and soon came the realization that
the kinds of resources being developed there have national interest.
Accordingly the membership was ultimately opened nationally, and there are
now some ninety library members of the Center. Mr. Evans told us
yesterday of the recent action extending the services of the Center to all
academic libraries in New York at an annual fee of $40,000. There now
seems to be no reason not to view CRL as one of the major networks of
libraries, not only national, but international.

The Ohio College Library Center came into being when it was incorporated on July 6, 1967, as a not-for-profit corporation "to establish, maintain and operate a computerized, regional library center to serve the

academic libraries of Ohio (both state and private) and designed so as to become a part of any national electronic network for bibliographic information." It has accomplished its objective so quickly that it is fully cost effective; it is extending its area of service into neighboring states. I can hardly exaggerate my excitement when I first watched one of its bibliographic entries appear on a console in the Carnegie Library of Pittsburgh, followed by a line of symbols indicating the several libraries already holding that title in their collections. The power of the system struck me with far greater force than it did by just reading about it. To young librarians, it may be easy to be blasé about such a development; but to an old warhorse like me, it is the miracle for which I have waited all my professional life. A notable quality of OCLC is the speed with which it has developed its resource and service. I heard Fred Kilgour speak about the Center at the University of North Carolina recently. He stated that as of a few weeks earlier the OCLC system included 850,000 titles and that by summer the number would reach one million.

In discussing local cooperatives with national implications my primary assignment is to describe another networking development, in this instance the development of a new library agency in Pittsburgh which could become a major node in a national network of libraries for science and technology. This is the proposal to establish a Metropolitan Pittsburgh Science and Technology Library. In the process of becoming such a node it would have the potential of adding great strength to the organization and utilization of "sci-tech" library and information resources of Pittsburgh, the metropolitan area surrounding the city, and the whole state of Pennsylvania.

Although the idea is a reincarnation of a proposal that has been in and out of local attention for many years, its most recent rebirth occurred on November 17, 1970, when the librarians of the Carnegie Library of Pittsburgh, Carnegie-Mellon University and University of Pittsburgh agreed that something should be done to prevent another demise.

As first proposed, the Metro-Sci-Tech Library would be created as a new agency in Pittsburgh, created by amalgamating all of the science and technology library resources of the three cooperating institutions. Early in the discussion of the proposal, it was agreed that complete centralization would be unrealistic, because of the generally felt need for local access in academic departments of the universities. Paralleling this agreement, however, was the conviction that there is more duplication between libraries than is required or justifiable. Working closely with the committee of librarians, Joseph Shipman and I, as consultants, have formulated a set of recommendations for the full Planning Committee of the three institutions.

The nature of the proposal and its implications for library development in the metropolitan area and the state can be accomplished by my quoting or paraphrasing the principal recommendations with some explanatory comment, followed by a brief discussion of priorities and actions to be taken. The basic recommendation is that the Metropolitan Pittsburgh Science-Technology Library be established as a division of the Carnegie Library of Pittsburgh as an extension of the present Science and Technology Department.

It is recognized that there is some possibility of this recommendation being interpreted as simply one to beef up the Science and Technology Department of CLP. To the extent the other recommendations fail to make clear that this is a new agency being recommended, I hope the lack will be supplied by my discussion at the end of this Chapter on interpretation of the proposed functional organization of the Metro-Sci-Tech Library.

It will be recognized that the purposes in designating CLP as the administrative home of the Metro-Sci-Tech Library are to preserve the already well-established sources of municipal and county, as well as state, support, and to provide the possibility for close integration of many of the housekeeping operations with comparable operations for other departments of CLP. But it will be equally obvious that if the Metro-Sci-Tech Library is to have interinstitutional support, there will need to be specifications covering this objective. It therefore follows that our second recommendation is that a multi-agency agreement to be drafted and formally confirmed by the Carnegie Library of Pittsburgh, Carnegie-Mellon University, and University of Pittsburgh, and such other agencies as may subsequently be drawn into the agreement. There follow half-a-dozen specifications that should be included in the agreement.

Why, it may be asked, is reference made in this recommendation to "such other agencies as may be drawn into this agreement." Perhaps the question answers itself. There are many libraries in metropolitan Pittsburgh — academic, industrial and governmental — that have equal need for better resources. The proposal has assumed from its first discussion that many of these libraries will wish to participate. Because of this expectation, and because the proposed library is conceived of as user oriented, a third recommendation is that an Advisory Council be provided for in the contract to serve in reviewing and making formal recommendations on collection and service policies for Metro-Sci-Tech.

There follows in our report to the Planning Committee an extended discussion of the service program — naturally the heart of the proposal — involving many specific recommendations. An effort has been made to touch base on every reasonable suggestion for library and information services, which need not be detailed to a group of academic librarians and administrators.

One recommendation which might be singled out for special attention here is that planning be initiated for a new building to house the Metro-Sci-Tech Library. In the present economic bind, this may appear to some to be an unrealistic recommendation. We think it is not unrealistic for two reasons. The first is that CLP has been feeling the pinch for space for some time and will be faced sooner rather than later with necessity to press for city and county support of new construction. The second is that the concept of a sci-tech library to carry out the service program proposed for it will require not only more, but also more functional space. A construction proposal could serve both purposes and deserves full community support.

Before discussing the functional organization of the Metro-Sci-Tech Library within the administrative organization of CLP, I would like to describe why Mr. Shipman and I have been drawn enthusiastically into study of this proposal.

Our reactions have been conditioned by personal experiences in two of the major science-technology libraries in the United States — the Linda Hall Library in Kansas City and the John Crerar Library in Chicago. The concept of a Metropolitan Science-Technology Library appeals to us for several reasons:

1. We are both intensely aware of the impossibility of any one institution encompassing the full range of library resources and services in the fields of the basic and applied sciences.

2. The interdisciplinary relations between the various sciences and technologies provide strong rationale for coordinated resources and services in all related subjects and for all of the varied communities of users.

3. Such a library can make very significant contributions to the educational resources and the sci-tech information services of a metropolitan community consisting of educational institutions, industrial organizations and the general public.

Examples (educational): Linda Hall Library is surrounded by the campus of the University of Missouri at Kansas City and serves numerous other colleges and universities within a range of 100 miles or more of Kansas City. The John Crerar Library is located on the campus of Illinois Institute of Technology and is heavily used by students from other educational institutions in the area.

Examples (industrial): Not only are both Linda Hall and John Crerar libraries heavily used by industrial researchers, but both have been the determining factor in industrial research laboratories being located in their respective cities. Spencer Chemical Company centered its research activities in Kansas City because of the Linda Hall Library. The scientists of Chem-Agro-Research voted to locate in Kansas City because of the Linda Hall Library, and management acted favorably on their advice. The Quaker Oats Company established research laboratories in Chicago, instead of another city under consideration, because of the availability of Crerar Library. Many other companies are able to limit their own libraries to the most intensively used sci-tech literature because of these two major libraries in their respective cities. Similar conditions can already be cited for Pittsburgh and would certainly be augmented with development of the proposed Metro-Sci-Tech Library.

4. In both academic and industrial research, the base of scientific and technical information is international, calling for a range of foreign language publications much too extensive for duplication in several libraries in a community.

5. Development of such a library will provide an agency for regional cooperation between research libraries. In this connection, Crerar and Linda Hall are already feeling the pressure to coordinate their collections and services. For example, Crerar has arrangements for receiving satellite communications from Buenos Aires for photocopy service and draws on the resources of Linda Hall in filling requests as a supplement to its own collections. In this connection, we are recommending specifically, that the contract give recognition to the role of Metro-Sci-Tech as the center of a regional and state-wide network and as a node in a national network.

Underlying all of these reasons for our interest are developments in the growth of scientific literature and research libraries which Mr. Shipman discussed in Chapter 7. Naturally, we are concerned with seeing conditions established which will assure maximum utility of existing collections and the augmenting of collections where this may be needed. These concerns can be met by two conditions proposed.

A major condition is that the two cooperating universities commit their total science and technology library resources — wherever they may be located — to a common pool of library collections and services available for service not only throughout the area of Metropolitan Pittsburgh but also throughout the state of Pennsylvania, and elsewhere, as programs of regional cooperation are developed for mutual resources and reciprocal access to them. Another condition is that the subject base of the library resources to be broadened to give greater emphasis to certain areas which are less well represented than we believe they should be. Examples are: the biological sciences including such subjects as physical anthropology and phsychopharmacology; oceanography and ecology especially as related to such matters as environment and food supply; mission oriented indexes and the literature indexed by them; better coverage of the publications of experiment stations and such literature formats as reviews and conference proceedings; and interdisciplinary materials bearing on the history of science, technology and medicine.

Let me turn now to some general comments on the proposed Metro-Sci-Tech Library and how the proposal affects priorities in planning. Perhaps this can be done most effectively by constructing a functional organization chart within an administrative organization chart of CLP.

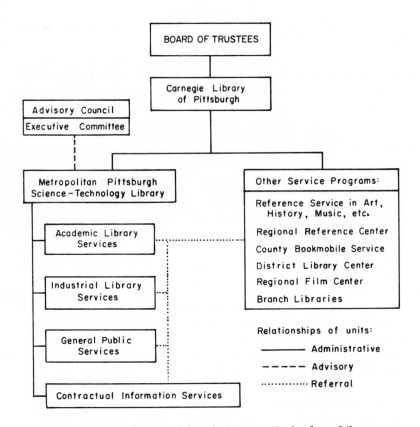

FIG. 1. Metropolitan Pittsburgh Science-Technology Library.

Figure 1 indicates the general administrative position of the Metro-
Sci-Tech Library in the organization of CLP. Not made clear by Fig. 1
is a recommendation in the proposal that the Metro-Sci-Tech Library be
given the status of a division in the CLP organization rather than that of a
department, and that it function largely as a separate library.

Four items in the chart should be given special emphasis:

1. the role of the Advisory Council
2. the establishment of special personnel to serve the three major user
   communities
3. the introduction of contractual services as a normal part of the
   service program
4. the special attention given to the principle of referral throughout the
   service system.

First, the high degree of importance given to the Advisory Council is indicated by the recommendation, already quoted, that provision for such a council be made in the formal contract between the cooperating institutions. If the Metro-Sci-Tech library is to be truly a metropolitan and regional library, its governing service policies should be subject to review by representative users. It may be anticipated that the formulation of some policy statements will be initiated by the Advisory Council. The implement- ation of each service objective will normally depend on the resources available to the cooperating institutions and in turn to the management of the library. But the availability of the resources may well be influenced to an important degree by the existence of a functioning group of representatives from all user groups.

Second, the need for service personnel having special knowledge of the service requirements of each principal user group — academic, industrial, and general public — may seem to be self-evident. However, this kind of specialization is not characteristic of public library staff. With respect to the Metro-Sci-Tech Library, it is deemed to be of overriding importance. It is anticipated that intially one well-qualified librarian with appropriate experience will be added to the staff to serve primarily as a staff officer in his or her respective area, and as a line officer as may seem advisable by the management of the library, each of the three user groups being repre- sented.

The third point emphasized is the proposal that contractual services be introduced as a normal part of the service program of the Metro-Sci-Tech Library. The concept of nonprofit fee services, i.e., services for which a library may be reimbursed for costs, has been recognized for at least a quarter of a century as a means by which a public library can extend its services. The fact that the concept has been applied in only a few libraries (except for charges for photocopy service) may be due to the deeply ingrained ethic of the _free_ public library. But the public library is free only in the sense that the immediate user is not charged for the services received. For the most part everyone pays for the service, whether or not it is used, through payment of taxes. It seems to have been generally accepted that reference and information service should be _free_ to the immediate user as part of the tax supported services. But largely ignored is the potential of both intensive and extensive information services that could be made avail- able, largely to the industrial and professional communities, beyond the limits of tax supported personnel. The issue is made especially important by the development of computer stores of information that in cost are clearly beyond the capacity of present public library budgets.

The final item to which special attention is directed is provision in the organization chart for referrals. The Metro-Sci-Tech Library is conceived as a service agency which will never limit its services to just those which can be provided "in house." The premise that decentralization of library

resources will continue to a substantial degree imposes on the Metro-Sci-
Tech Library a major obligation to develop means for full utilization of
library and information resources for science and technology wherever they
may be located — within the Carnegie Library of Pittsburgh, the libraries
of neighboring academic institutions, the libraries of industrial and governmental agencies in the metropolitan region, and all other libraries throughout the state and nation. The role of the Metro-Sci-Tech Library as a
major node in a national network will make referrals and receipt of referrals
a way of life. As an integral part of the CLP system, it will be using as
effectively as possible all channels for seeking and communicating the
services it will be designed to offer.

In conclusion, it may be appropriate to refer to remarks which have
been made to Trustees and others with whom we have discussed the proposal.
This is the reminder that conversations about library cooperation have been
going on between these three major institutions for some twenty-five years
with negligible results. It is our considered view that the curves of growth
of scientific literature and the cost of maintaining scientific and technical
libraries are rising so rapidly that research librarians, faculties and
administrators will not have another quarter century to deliberate over
ways to pool their library resources. And further, we believe,that, by
seizing now the opportunity which exists to pioneer an exciting concept of
library cooperation, Pittsburgh will make a significant contribution to
solving a set of problems that are of national import.

Part Four

HOW TO PROCEED?

Many institutions feel overwhelmed by growth and inflation and knew that they must take steps to apply available ideas and technology to solve their problems.

Chapters 15 through 17 examine the criteria for successful systems that provide the basis for better service at lower cost, leading to an identification of the next steps that must be taken.

Chapter 15

RESOURCE SHARING IN LIBRARIES – THE NEXT STEP

K. Leon Montgomery

Interdisciplinary Doctoral Program in Information Science
University of Pittsburgh
Pittsburgh, Pennsylvania

INTRODUCTION

As we have seen in chapter 1 on why we should opt for resource sharing, interlibrary cooperation is not a new phenomenon. An appreciation of the growing world literature and of the concept of service to faculty, students, and staff has led academic libraries to explore many interlibrary cooperative arrangements. A recent study by the System Development Corporation [1] shows that 90% of the currently existing academic library consortia have been established since 1960 and over 75% since 1965. These data seem to reflect an increasing realization among academic librarians and institutions that resource sharing or interdependence is at least a partial solution to some of their problems.

Chapter 6 on how libraries share resources, has examined the basic library operations in terms of acquisitions, technical processing, storage, and delivery of services. It has demonstrated that librarians have identified certain focal points for the sharing of resources and established mechanisms for the accomplishment of their goals. Chapter 6 has also identified the basic problem of cooperation as the willingness of libraries and their parent institutions to cooperate even if local independence is weakened or lost. In addition, it has also shown the benefits and improved services that have been achieved as a result of cooperation.

Chapter 11, on <u>when</u> to share library resources, has demonstrated that there is a wide variety of technological options for implementing library networks. A similar conference held ten years ago would have had to confront innovative and untried technological developments for establishing these networks. Today, we are able to focus on cost benefit tradeoffs. Today, considerable experience has been garnered from pioneer library networks. In essence, the problems today tend to be human, institutional, and administrative.

As used in this discussion, the word "academic" means institutions of higher education. The phrase "library consortia" is used for cooperative efforts among libraries which meet the following criteria:

1. Participating institutions are autonomous in the sense that they report to separate Boards of Trustees or Regents.
2. At least two libraries are involved. At least one of these is an academic institution.
3. Members are pursuing activities that provide increased access to materials and/or services of the other libraries.
4. Exploratory, developmental, or operational status has been achieved.

Private, state-related, and state-supported colleges and universities alike seem to share the problem of limited fiscal resources and increased need for services among their faculty, students, and staff. The purposes of this chapter are: to review several major library cooperative efforts on the national scene, to review the current cooperative efforts involving academic libraries in Pennsylvania, and to suggest several alternatives for further library resource sharing among Pennsylvania institutions of higher learning.

The methodology utilized is first to examine several library consortia on the national scene and the current academic Pennsylvania library consortia in terms of a parametric library consortia model. Then several alternatives for expanded cooperative activities among Pennsylvania institutions of higher learning are developed. Finally, some criteria are developed for choosing among these alternatives.

PARAMETERS OF LIBRARY CONSORTIA

In the Guidelines for Library Cooperation, [1, p. 14] a parametric model of current library consortia is established in terms of fourteen major parameters. These have been adapted for use as follows:

1. Type
   a. Member of higher level educational consortium
   b. Independent entity

2. Area Served
   a. City
   b. Region
   c. State
   d. Interstate

3. Headquarters
   a. Centralized
   b. Not centralized

4. Objectives
   a. Design objectives or goals

5. Stages of Development
   a. Planning stage
   b. Development stage
   c. Operational stage

6. Funding Sources
   a. Dues or fees
   b. Grants
   c. Contributed resources

7. Funding Level (Annual)
   Usually funds for material or services beyond staff time

8. Type of Agreement
   a. Legal
   b. Informal

9. Rules for Participation
   a. Specified
   b. Unspecified

10. Computer Usage
    a. Has computer
    b. Uses university computer
    c. Uses service bureau
    d. Does not use computer

11. Membership Count
    Simple numeric count of participating members

12. Activities
    List of operational cooperative activities

13. Direct Services from Headquarters
     List of services if different from activities

14. Leadership
     a. Director or Coordinator
     b. Advisory Board

It seems to be a common experience for a library which has chosen to participate in cooperative efforts to be involved in more than one library consortium.

EXAMPLES OF LIBRARY CONSORTIA ON THE NATIONAL SCENE

Five major cooperative efforts on the national scene are reviewed to provide a sense of the state-of-art and to provide a comparison for Pennsylvania library consortia.   The five consortia reviewed are:

1. Colorado Academic Libraries Book Processing Center — 1969
2. Five Associated University Libraries (FAUL) — 1967
3. New England Library Information Network (NELINET) — 1966
4. North Dakota Network for Knowledge — 1967
5. Ohio College Library Center (OCLC) — 1967

Much of the data used in this review have been taken from the Directory of Academic Library Consortia [2].   These five cooperative efforts are analyzed in terms of the parametric model previously introduced (see Appendix A).

In summary this national survey [1, p. 71] indicated that the cooperative activities among the one-hundred twenty-five library consortia reviewed include:

1.	Reciprocal borrowing privileges	78%
2.	Expanded interlibrary loan service	64%
3.	Union catalogs or lists	62%
4.	Photocopying services	58%
5.	Reference services	40%
6.	Delivery Services	35%
7.	Mutual notification of purchase	32%
8.	Special communication services	28%
9.	Publication program	27%
10.	Catalog card production	27%

11. Cataloging support   26%
12. Joint purchasing of materials   24%
13. Assigned subject specialization in acquisitions 22%
14. Other acquisition activities   18%
15. Microfilming   17%
16. Central resource or storage center   17%
17. Bibliographic center   14%
18. Joint research projects   14%
19. Clearinghouse   12%

CURRENT RESOURCE SHARING AMONG ACADEMIC LIBRARIES IN PENNSYLVANIA

Moving from library cooperation on a national scene, this section focuses on activity in Pennsylvania academic institutions. The purpose is to understand the present scope of cooperation so that subsequent plans can include and expand upon these efforts.

There are two significant surveys from which the data in this section are taken. The first is the Directory of Academic Library Consortia [2]. This directory and its soon to be published supplement will identify and describe all library consortia and cooperatives in the continental United States which include at least one academic member. This survey was taken by the System Development Corporation and was sponsored by HEW, Office of Education. The second is an Inventory of Pennsylvania Interlibrary Cooperatives and Information Networks [3]. This survey was done under the direction of Brigitte Kenney of the Drexel Library School and was sponsored by the State Library of Pennsylvania. Sixty-five interlibrary cooperatives and information networks are identified and described in this survey. Twenty-seven of these involve at least one academic library. Each of the academic library consortia is described in terms of the parametric model previously introduced (see Appendix B).

Five significant spheres of library cooperation in Pennsylvania academic institutions emerge from these data. These are:

1. Area College Library Cooperative of Central Pennsylvania (ACLP), which involves seventeen members, with delivery service to sixty college and university libraries. It was founded in 1965.
2. Lehigh Valley Association of Independent College Libraries, which was founded in 1969 and involves six members.
3. Northeastern Pennsylvania Bibliographic Center (NEPBC), which was founded in 1956, and involves twelve members.

4. Pittsburgh Regional Library Center, which was founded in 1967 and involves nineteen members.
5. Tri-state College Library Cooperative (TCLC), which was founded in 1967 and involves twenty members.

Several important charts emerge from an analysis of these data presented in Appendix B. Chart 1 provides an overview of the <u>services</u> that the academic library consortia are now engaged in. Chart 2 provides an overview of the delivery of services. Charts 3 and 4 show the <u>telecommunications</u> and <u>machine-readable data bases</u> now being utilized by the consortia. These charts are subsets of those found in the <u>Inventory of Pennsylvania Interlibrary Cooperatives and Information Networks</u> [3]. These charts are presented in Appendix C.

A PRESCRIPTIVE MODEL FOR DEVELOPING ACADEMIC
LIBRARY CONSORTIA

Now that the present cooperative efforts have been reviewed, this section attempts to suggest further means of cooperative activity. First, a prescriptive model is presented for use in considering other alternatives. Then, a number of proposals are presented. Finally, some criteria for choosing among these alternatives are delineated.

A general prescriptive model that might be used follows:

1. Planning phase
2. Design phase
3. Implementation phase
4. Operation and Evaluation phase

At present we are obviously in the early planning phase. Our purposes here as I see them are:

1. To review existing library consortia in Pennsylvania
2. To discuss the desirability and feasibility of establishing one or several library consortia
3. To identify potential objectives of several library consortia
4. To suggest the next step(s) in the planning and design of such consortia

In their study [1] System Development Cooperation identified four general types of consortia. A brief review of these follows:

1. "Large" consortia, which are concerned primarily with computerized, large-scale technical processing. A "large" consortium may comprise a few large scale libraries or a larger number of small libraries often geographically distributed over a state. "Large" consortia seem to be required for long range, large scale projects. The new England Library Information Network (NELINET) and the Ohio College Library Center (OCLC) are examples.

2. Small consortia which are concerned primarily with user services and everyday problems. A characteristic of this type of consortium is geographical proximity which facilitates telephone and face-to-face communication. Smaller consortia provide an opportunity for individual involvement. Projects such as reciprocal borrowing privileges, workshops, specialization of acquisitions, storage, small-scale automation projects, and multimedia projects. An example of this type of consortium is Tri-State College Library Cooperative (TCLC).

3. Limited-purpose, cooperating with respect to limited special subject areas. Activities here include building special collections, providing reciprocal borrowing privileges, and maintaining union lists. The Consortium of Western Colleges and Universities, headquartered in California, is an example of this type of consortium.

4. Limited-purpose consortia, concerned primarily with interlibrary loan or reference network operations. A state-wide network which facilitates interlibrary loan is an example.

It should be noted that college and university libraries often belong to several consortia. That is, there seems to be little reason to believe that a single consortium can provide all cooperative needs.

Some of the issues that must be considered in the planning and design of Pennsylvania's library consortia are:

1. Objectives or goals of each consortium.
2. Identification of potential members.
3. Relationships with nonacademic libraries.
4. Geographical distribution of each consortium, i.e., local, regional or state-wide.
5. Size of the libraries of potential members. The major problem seems to be that the large libraries are utilized disproportionately by the smaller libraries.

With this background, then, several consortia for Pennsylvania are proposed. These are by no means the only consortia that might be proposed. The purpose of suggesting specific consortia is to stimulate the discussion process. Each consortium is presented in terms of selected parameters from the parametric model that has been used throughout.

PROPOSAL 1

Series of Coordinated Regional Consortia

Objectives

1. To provide Pennsylvania with a series of integrated and coordinated regional library consortia
2. To work with the State Library to coordinate the state's library resources

Funding source(s):

Combination of grants, dues, fees, and contributed resources

Funding level (annual):

$50,000-$100,000

Membership count:

Three to seven regional consortia

Activities:

1. Reciprocal borrowing privileges
2. Expanded interlibrary loan service
3. Union catalog and/or serials list
4. Photocopying services
5. Reference services
6. Delivery services
7. Mutual notification of purchase or intent to purchase
8. Joint research projects
9. Central storage center

Leadership:

Regional Director. Statewide Coordinator. Advisory Board of Regional Directors

PROPOSAL 2

Statewide Information Network for Access to Machine-Readable Data Bases

Objectives:

To provide access to machine-readable data bases of interest to the consortia

Funding source(s):

Combination of grants, dues, fees, and contributed resources

Funding level (annual):

$100,000-$200,000

Activities:

Access by mail, telephone, TWX or eventually computer terminal to machine-readable data bases such as:
1. Library of Congress Machine-Readable Catalog tapes
2. Regional or statewide lists of serials

PROPOSAL 2

Statewide Information Network for Access to Machine-Readable
Data Bases (continued)

Activities (cont'd):	3. Regional or statewide union catalog
	4. Professional society data bases such as Chemical Abstracts Services Condensates tape or Engineering Index's Compendex tape
	5. Government produced data bases such as NASA and AEC tapes
	6. Commercially produced data bases such as those by Institute for Scientific Information
Leadership:	Director. Advisory Board of Representatives of Consortia Members.

PROPOSAL 3

Statewide Processing Center

Objectives:	1. Operate computerized systems to assist Pennsylvania's colleges and universities in providing a fast, efficient search and retrieval system for library books and journals, and research development, and implementation of such systems
	2. Make the library resources of each member library available to the faculty and students of each participating institution
	3. Provide for the cooperative acquisition, joint ownership, and joint use of specialized and less frequently used library materials
	4. Carry out joint research projects which might provide the consortia with improved techniques for dealing with the library problem.
Funding source(s):	Combination of grants, dues, fees, and contributed resources

PROPOSAL 3

Statewide Processing Center (continued)

Funding level (annual): $1,000,000-$1,250,000

Activities: 1. Computerized on-line shared catalog-
                                    ing
                                 2. Card catalog production and other
                                    bibliographic support
                                 3. Production and maintenance of an on-
                                    line union catalog
                                 4. Joint purchasing of little used materials
                                 5. Joint research projects
                                 6. Reciprocal borrowing privileges

Leadership: Director. Advisory Board of Represent-
                                 atives of Consortia Members

Criteria for evaluating these or any alternative proposals can be
generalized into the following areas:

1. Can the proposed consortia be implemented to achieve the stated
   objectives?
2. Does the technology permit the solution proposed?
3. Can a suitable organization or mechanism be established to implement
   the proposed consortia?
4. Is it possible to locate the necessary funding for the proposed consortia?

THE NEXT STEP(S)

The next few steps will, of course, be administrative in nature. The
next steps must:

1. Identify those who may be willing to participate in library consortia
2. Identify the needs of these participants in terms of services and
   delivery of services
3. Formulate these needs into specific objectives
4. Identify the characteristics of specific consortia that can be
   developed to satisfy these needs
5. Determine specific institutions willing to participate in each
   consortium
6. Proceed with the planning phase

This conference has reviewed the necessity for library consortia. Indeed, this necessity has been clearly recognized in the twenty-seven current library consortia in Pennsylvania. The real question is whether we can continue to take local or regional points of view in assessing the library resource problem. The answer to this question seems obvious. There must be an integrated plan that permits the academic community in Pennsylvania to better utilize their library resources in the service of faculty, staff, and students.

In pursuit of this goal a questionnaire will be sent to all the academic institutions in Pennsylvania. This questionnaire will attempt to identify those institutions that may wish to begin or enlarge upon their commitment to library resource sharing. Objectives of the questionnaire will be to:

1. Identify those willing to participate in the proposed consortia
2. Identify consortia other than those proposed that are of interest
3. Identify resources that potential members may be willing to share
4. Identify realistic next steps toward achieving the proposed library consortia

Specific questions concerning the resources, services, and funding that each member can contribute will be asked. Those who respond will be interviewed and the results will be analyzed and presented in the near future.

We have been able to benefit from the foresight of others who have done the pioneering work. Fortunately, they shared the results of these labors with us. The next step toward more cooperation is really up to us.

REFERENCES

1. Ruth J. Patrick, Guidelines for Library Cooperation: Development of Academic Library Consortia, System Development Corporation, Santa Monica, California, 1972.
2. Diana D. Delaney and Carlos A. Cuadra, Directory of Academic Library Consortia, System Development Corporation, Santa Monica, California, 1972.
3. Natalie Wiest, Lea Lourea and Brigitte L. Kenney, Inventory of Pennsylvania Interlibrary Cooperatives and Information Networks, Drexel University Graduate School of Library Science, Philadelphia, Pennsylvania, 1972.

APPENDIX A
Examples of Library Consortia on the National Scene

COLORADO ACADEMIC LIBRARIES BOOK PROCESSING CENTER — 1969

Type:	Independent entity
Area served:	State of Colorado
Headquarters:	Norlin Library, University of Colorado
Objectives:	To perform centralized processing services for member libraries, including ordering of materials, cataloging, card production, and labelling of books
Stage of development:	Operational: See Activities
Funding sources:	Service fees from member libraries and government appropriations
Funding level (annual):	$90,000
Type of agreement:	Formal
Rules for participation:	Informal agreement
Computer usage:	Nonstated
Membership count:	Twelve college and university libraries
Activities:	1. Acquisitions activities 2. Catalog card production and other cataloging support 3. Bindery services
Direct services from Head-quarters:	All services seem to be from headquarters
Leadership:	Coordinator. Board of Directors meet quarterly. Executive Committee of the Board of Directors meets as necessary.

Membership list:

Adams State College	Lorreto Heights College
Colorado Mountain College	Metropolitan State College
Colorado School of Mines	Temple Buell College
Colorado State University	University of Colorado
Community College of Denver	University of Northern Colorado
Fort Lewis College	Western State College

FIVE ASSOCIATED UNIVERSITY LIBRARIES (FAUL) — 1967

Type:	Includes both independent institutions and members of a higher level educational consortium
Area served:	Serves the central and western New York State region
Headquarters:	Centralized
Objectives:	1. Improve and develop library cooperation among the Five Associated University Libraries
	2. Work towards a coordinated policy for long-range library growth and development with coordinated acquisition policies, shared resources, and development of compatible machine systems, provision of easy and rapid communications systems among the membership, the provision of shared storage facilities, and exploration of other areas of cooperation
	3. Cooperate with other educational, library, and research institutions and organizations inside and outside the geographical area to further the purposes of this association
State of development:	Planning, development and operational (see Activities)
Funding source:	Dues and contributed resources
Funding level (annual):	$65,00

Type of agreement:	Informal
Rules for participation:	Specified rules
Computer usage:	Service bureau and subcontract
Membership count:	Five

Activities:

1. To develop coordinate acquisitions policies
2. To develop means for sharing resources including people's ideas, the work they do, materials, and facilities
3. To develop shared storage facilities
4. To develop easy and rapid communication systems among membership
5. To develop compatible machine systems
6. To explore and develop other areas of cooperation
7. To develop a coordinated policy for long range growth

Direct services from Headquarters:	Some
Leadership:	Full-time director
Membership list:	SUNY — Binghamton SUNY — Buffalo Cornell University Syracuse University University of Rochester

NEW ENGLAND LIBRARY INFORMATION NETWORK (NELINET) — 1966

Type:	Member of higher level consortium, New England Board of Higher Education
Area served:	States of Connecticut, Maine, Massachusetts, Rhode Island, New Hampshire and Vermont, with affiliate arrangements with library consortia outside of the New England area
Headquarters:	New England Board of Higher Education

Objectives:	1. Make the library resources of each member library available to the students and faculty of the participating institutions
	2. Provide for the cooperative acquisition, joint ownership, and joint use of specialized and less frequently used library materials
	3. Strengthen existing interlibrary channels of communication and mutual aid
	4. Promote, develop, and support the creation and establishment of a regional computer-operated center for providing cataloging, acquisitions, serials, circulations, reference and management services to each member library
	5. The intention is to reduce the incidence of redundant costs associated with library operations, including Research and Development and implementation; to reduce the rate of unit costs increases where possible; and to provide services economically impractical for libraries operating alone
Stage of development:	Planning: Additional acquisition activities; reference services; personnel training or upgrading; user orientation programs
	Operational: See Activities
Funding sources:	Dues from member institutions and government appropriations
Funding level (annual):	$60,000
Type of agreement:	Written one-year agreement with each member
Rules for participation:	Formal set of rules outlining conditions of participation
Computer usage:	None stated
Membership count:	Twenty college and university libraries
Activities:	1. Joint purchasing of materials
	2. Assigned subject specialization in acquisitions

Activities (continued):

3. Mutual notification of purchase or
    intent to purchase
4. Catalog card production and other
    cataloging support
5. Production and/or maintenance of
    union catalogs, lists, and directories
6. Operation of a bibliographic center
7. Joint research projects
8. Publication program

Direct services from Headquarters:

Most services seem to come from
headquarters

Leadership:

Director, Assistant Director, Assistant
Director for Systems Design, full-time
and part-time secretaries; Executive
Committee, composed of directors of
member libraries, with meetings as
necessary; National Advisory Committee
Membership Council with meetings as
necessary

Membership list:

Boston University	Rhode Island College
Brown University	Rhode Island Junior College
Colby College	Tufts University
Connecticut College	University of Connecticut
Curry College	University of Maine
Dartsmouth College	University of New Hampshire
Hampshire College	University of Rhode Island
Massachusetts Institute of	University of Vermont
Technology	Wesleyan University
Naval War College	Worcester Polytech
Northeastern University	

NORTH DAKOTA NETWORK FOR KNOWLEDGE — 1967

Type: Independent entity

Area served: State of North Dakota

Headquarters: State Librarian's Office

Objectives:	Ensure that all library resources with the state are interrelated to the end that all kinds of libraries are fully utilized to make it possible for all North Dakota residents to have an opportunity to obtain the services and materials needed
Stage of development:	Planning: Joint purchasing of materials; assigned subject specialization in acquisitions; catalog card production and other cataloging support; joint research projects Operational: See Activities
Funding source:	Government appropriations
Funding level (annual):	$30,000
Type of agreement:	Informal
Rules for participation:	Informal
Computer usage:	None indicated
Membership count:	Thirteen Public Libraries Seventeen College and University Libraries
Activities:	1. Reference services 2. Operation of a bibliographic center 3. Photocopying services 4. Expanded interlibrary loan service 5. Delivery services 6. Production and/or maintenance of union catalogs, lists, and directories 7. Reciprocal borrowing privileges 8. Special communication services
Direct services from Headquarters:	Most services seem to originate at headquarters
Leadership:	Director, two Library Technical Staff, clerk typist

Membership list:

Bismarck Junion College	University of North Dakota,
Dickinson State College	Bureau of Mines Library
Jamestown College	University of North Dakota,
Lake Region Junior College	Geological Library
Mary College	University of North Dakota,
Mayville State College	Grand Forks

Membership list (continued):

Minot State College	University of North Dakota,
North Dakota State University,	Law Library
Bottineau Center	University of North Dakota,
North Dakota State University,	Medical Library
Fargo	University of North Dakota
State School of Science Library	Williston Center
	Valley City State College

OHIO COLLEGE LIBRARY CENTER (OCLC) — 1967

Type: Independent entity

Area served: Interstate

Headquarters: Columbus, Ohio

Objectives:
1. Operate computerized systems to assist member Ohio colleges and universities in providing a faster, more efficient search and retrieval system for library books and journals, and research, development, and implementation of such systems
2. Increase availability of library for use in educational and research programs of member libraries
3. Lower the rate of rise of per student library cost while increasing the availability of library resources

Stage of development:
Planning: (All on-line processes.) Circulation control; remote catalog access, serials control, technical processing system; access by title and subject indexing

Operational: See Activities

Funding sources:
Dues from member institutions, government appropriations, and Council on Library resources

Funding level (annual): $733,332

Type of agreement:	Payment of membership fee
Rules for participation:	Formal set of rules
Computer usage:	Uses computer

Membership count:
1. Within Ohio: 48 college and university libraries
2. Outside Ohio: Not specifically stated

Activities:
1. Computerized on-line shared cataloging
2. Catalog card production and other bibliographic support
3. Production and maintenance of an on-line union catalog
4. Reciprocal borrowing privileges
5. Expanded interlibrary loan service
6. Research projects

Direct service from Head-
quarters: Computer-related activities

Leadership: Director, four system analyists, programmer, part-time library technician,
secretary, computer operations technician,
part-time keypunch operator; Board of
Trustees, with bimonthly meetings

Membership list:

Antioch College	Miami University
Ashland College	Mount Union College
Athenaeum of Ohio	Muskingum College
Bluffton College	Oberlin College
Bowling Green State Univ.	Ohio Dominican College
Capital University	Ohio Northern University
Case Western Reserve Univ.	Ohio State University
Cedarville College	Ohio University
Central State University	Ohio Wesleyan University
Cleveland State University	Otterbein College
College of Mt. St. Joseph	Pontifical College Josephinum
on the Ohio	Rio Grande College
College of Steubenville	Sinclair Community College
College of Wooster	University of Akron
Defiance College	University of Cincinnati
Denison University	University of Dayton
Findlay College	University of Toledo
Hebrew Union College	Urbana College
Hiram College	Walsh College
John Carroll University	Western College for Women

Membership list (continued):

Kent State University
Kenyon College
Lake Erie College
Malone College
Marietta College

Wittenberg University
Wright State University
Xavier University
Youngstown State University

APPENDIX B
Current Resource Sharing Among Academic Libraries in Pennsylvania

ALIQUIPPA DISTRICT CENTER

Type:	Member of higher level library consortia
Area served:	Beaver County, Pennsylvania
Headquarters:	B. F. Jones Memorial Library, Alquippa
Objectives:	1. To make resources and services available without charge whether directly or through the libraries in the District Center system to all residents of the district
	2. To provide supplementary library services to the local (mostly public) libraries within the district
	3. To coordinate library services and to exchange, contract, or provide other library services with some of the nearby District Center Libraries
Stage of development:	1. Planning: Closer interchange with other districts in Western Penna. for 1972/73, especially a cooperative purchasing association
	2. Operational: See Activities
Funding sources:	28.2% from Federal grants
	71.8% from State funds
Funding level:	$71,000 for fiscal year 1971-1972
Type of agreement:	Formal, by contract and State law.
Rules for participation:	College and university patrons have limited use unless a member of a public library
Computer usage:	Do not use computer
Membership count:	Public Libraries — 9
	College and University Libraries — 3

Activities: 1. Interlibrary loan
                                     2. Reference assistance
                                     3. Bibliographic verification
                                     4. Photoduplication
                                     5. Loan of film and/or filmstrips
                                     6. Some cooperative cataloging
                                     7. Cooperative acquisitions
                                     8. Union List of Serials
                                     9. Union List of Monographs
                                    10. Administrative and advisory services

District services from Head-
quarters: 1. To public library patrons
                                     2. To college and university libraries

Leadership: Part-time director

Membership list:

                                     Community College of Beaver County
                                     Geneva College
                                     The Pennsylvania State University,
                                       Beaver Campus

AREA COLLEGE LIBRARY COOPERATIVE OF CENTRAL
PENNSYLVANIA (ACLP) — 1965

Type: Independent entity

Area served: Central Pennsylvania

Headquarters: None

Objectives: Strengthen library resources and services
                             in the area through a program of mutually
                             supporting acquisitions, greater communi-
                             cations, and increased service

State of development: Plans: Incorporation; expansion of
                             programs through Union Catalogs; more
                             sophisticated communication for more
                             members; expansion to eventual network
                             of total library service in Pennsylvania

                             Developmental and Operational: See
                             Activities

Funding source: Dues from member institutions

Funding level: $1,275

Type of agreement: Written agreement

Rules for participation: Formal set of rules outlining conditions

Computer usage: Union List of Serials only

Membership: State Library and sixteen college and
                                   university libraries

Membership list:

Bucknell University	Messiah College
Dickinson College	Millersville State College
Elizabethtown College	Pennsylvania State University
Franklin and Marshall College	Pennsylvania State University,
Gettysburg College	Capitol Campus
Harrisburg Area Community	Shippensburg State College
College	Susquehanna University
Lebanon Valley College	Wilson College
Juanita College	York College of Pennsylvania

Activities:

1. Interlibrary loan	8. Loan of films and/or filmstrips
2. Reference assistance	9. Loan of microforms
3. Bibliographic verification	10. Facsimile transmission
4. Literature searches	11. Cooperative acquisitions
5. Photoduplication	12. Some cooperative cataloging
6. Loan of audiotapes	13. Union List of Serials
7. Loan of videotapes	14. Union List of some monographs

Direct services from Head-
quarters: To libraries

Leadership: Executive Rotating Steering Committee

AREA COLLEGE LIBRARY COOPERATIVE PROGRAM
DELIVERY SERVICE (ACLP DELIVERY SERVICE)

Type: Independent entity

Area served: Southeastern quarter of Pennsylvania

Headquarters: Centralized

Objectives: To provide speedy transportation of
                                   materials — primarily those which are
                                   library oriented — between member insti-
                                   tutions. This is done through the use of
                                   two delivery vehicles operating on regular
                                   schedules.

Stage of development: Plans: Possible expansion to include a
                                   statewide network

                                   Operational: See Activities

Funding sources: One-third from state funds
                                   Two-thirds from members

Funding level (annual):   Not stated

Type of agreement: Formal

Rules for participation: By contract

Computer usage: Does not use computer

Membership count: 14 public and private libraries
                                   51 college and university libraries
                                   State library

Activities: Delivery of library oriented materials
                                   among member institutions

Direct services from head-
quarters: Library-to-library

Leadership: Part-time director

Membership list:
        Beaver College   PMC Colleges
        Bryn Mawr College   Penn State University, Pattee
        Bucknell University   Penn State University, A-V Service
        Cabrini College   Penn State University,
        Chestnut Hill College   Capitol Campus
        Cheyney State College   Philadelphia College of Art
        College of Physicians   Philadelphia College of Pharmacy
        Community College of   and Science
           Pennsylvania   Philadelphia Divinity School
        Delaware County Community   Rosemont College
           College   St. Charles Seminary
        Dickinson College   St. Joseph's College
        Drexel University   Shippensburg State College
        Eastern Baptist College   Susquehanna University
        Elizabethtown College   Swarthmore College

Franklin and Marshall
 College
Gettysburg College
Hahnemann Medical College
Harrisburg Area Community
 College
Haverford College
Holy Family College
Immaculata College
Juniata College
La Salle College
Lebanon Valley College
Lincoln University
Messiah College
Millersville State College
Moore College of Art
Our Lady of Angels College

Temple University,
 Health Sciences Center
Temple University, Paley
Thomas Jefferson University
 Medical
University of Pennsylvania,
 Medical School
University of Pennsylvania
 Van Pelt
Ursinus College
Villanova University
West Chester State College
Wilson College
York College of Pennsylvania

BRYN MAWR/HAVERFORD COLLEGE LIBRARY
COOPERATION PROJECT

Type:	Independent entity
Area served:	Region
Headquarters:	No centralized headquarters
Objectives:	1. To experiment in combined processings, acquisitions, and cataloging
	2. To facilitate communications between the two libraries by a direct phone line
	3. To prepare and circulate a computerized list of periodicals and continuations (serial publications)
Stage of development:	Plans: To include Swarthmore College
	Operational: See Activities
Funding source:	75% foundation grants
	25% shared by members
Funding level (annual):	Not stated
Type of agreement:	Informal

Rules for participation: By custom

Computer usage: Uses college computer

Membership count: Two

Activities:
1. Interlibrary loan   8. Loan of films and/or filmstrips
2. Reference assistance   9. Loan of microforms
3. Bibliographic verification   10. Cooperative acquisitions
4. Literature searches   11. Cooperative cataloging
5. Photoduplication   12. Cooperative processing
6. Loan of audiotapes   13. Union List of Serials
7. Loan of videotapes   14. Union Catalog

Direct services from head-
quarters: Library-to-library

Leadership: Governed by informal committee

Membership list: Bryn Mawr College
                                Haverford College

CABRINI COLLEGE/EASTERN COLLEGE INTERLIBRARY COOPERATION

Type: Independent entity

Area served: Region of Pennsylvania

Headquarters: No centralized headquarters

Objectives: To increase mutual holdings by sharing
                                resources

Stage of development: Plans: To construct walkway between
                                the two libraries to facilitate access.

                                Operational: See Activities

Funding source: Member institutions

Funding level (annual):   Not stated; involves staff time only

Type of agreement: Informal

Rules for participation: Oral agreement

Computer usage: Does not use computer

Membership count: Two

Activities:
1. Interlibrary loan   6. Loan of microforms
2. Reference assistance   7. Cooperative acquisitions
3. Bibliographic verification   8. Union List of Serials
4. Photoduplication   9. Union List of Monographs
5. Loan of Audiotapes   10. Union Catalog

Direct services from head-
quarters: Library-to-library services

Leadership: Respective librarians

Membership list: Cabrini College
                             Eastern College

CAMBRIA-SOMERSET LIBRARY DISTRICT —JOHNSTOWN

Type: Member of Higher Level Library
                             Consortium

Area served: Region of Pennsylvania, Cambria and
                             Somerset Counties

Headquarters: Centralized headquarters

Objectives: 1. To provide direct library service to
                                persons residing within the district
                             2. To provide supplementary library
                                services to all local libraries within
                                the district
                             3. To exchange or provide services with
                                other District Library Centers
                             4. To contract for the provision of library
                                services with other District Library
                                Centers
                             5. To improve library services throughout
                                Cambria and Somerset Counties
                             6. To deliver books and library materials
                                to all public, college, and specialized
                                libraries in Cambria and Somerset
                                counties that desire such service

Stage of development:

Plans: Van delivery service

Operational: See Activities

Funding sources:

60% Federal grants
40% State funds

Funding level (annual):

Not stated

Type of agreement:

Formal; Informal for college and non-public libraries

Rules for participation:

Oral agreement

Computer usage:

Does not use computer

Membership count:

3 college and university libraries
20 public and private libraries

Activities:

1. Interlibrary loan
2. Reference assistance
3. Bibliographic verification
4. Photoduplication
5. Loan of Film and/or Filmstrips
6. Cooperative Acquisitions[7]
7. Cooperative Cataloging[8]
8. Cooperative Processing[9]

Direct services from head-quarters:

Library-to-library

Membership list:

Cambria Rowe Business College
Mt. Aloysius Junion College
St. Francis College

CENTRAL PENNSYLVANIA CONSORTIUM

Type:

Independent entity

Area served:

Central Region of Pennsylvania

Headquarters:

Gettysburg College

Objectives:

To strengthen total college programs through shared faculty, student exchange, course offerings, and facilities, including library resources

Stage of development: <u>Development and operational</u>:   See
                               Activities

Funding source: 100% from members

Funding level (annual):   Unstated

Type of agreement: Informal

Rules for participation: By oral agreement

Computer usage: Do not use computer

Membership count: Four colleges

Activities:
1. Interlibrary loan   7. Reference assistance
2. Bibliographic verification   8. Photoduplication
   and literature searches   9. Loan of audiotapes
3. Loan of films and/or film-   10. Loan of videotapes
   strips   11. Loan of microforms
4. Facsimile transmission   12. Cooperative acquisitions
5. Some cooperative cataloging   13. Union List of some monographs
6. Union List of Serials

Direct services from head-
quarters: Library-to-library

Leadership: Full time director for total college
                               programs

Membership list: Dickinson College
                               Franklin and Marshall College
                               Gettysburg College
                               Wilson College

COMMITTEE ON LIBRARY COOPERATION OF THE UNION
LIBRARY CATALOG OF PENNSYLVANIA

Type: Independent entity

Area served: Region of Pennsylvania

Headquarters: No centralized headquarters

Objectives: To explore feasible areas of cooperation
                               among member institutions in the
                               immediate geographical area

Stage of development: Planning: Attempt to discover areas for
                               cooperation among area libraries

Funding source: None established

Funding level (annual):   No costs yet incurred

Type of agreement: Informal

Rules for participation: Oral agreement

Computer usage: Do not use computer

Membership count: Six college and university libraries
                               Eight public and private libraries

Activities: None stated

Direct services from head-
quarters: None stated

Leadership: Committee with a rotating chairman

Membership list:
     Bryn Mawr College   La Salle College
     College of Physicians Library   Tempel University Libraries
     Drexel University   University of Pennsylvania

DISTRICT CENTER — INDIANA

Type: Member of Higher Level Library Consortium

Area served: Region of Pennsylvania

Headquarters: Centralized headquarters, Indiana
                               University of Pennsylvania

Objectives: 1. To provide direct library service to
                                  persons residing within the district
                               2. To provide supplementary library
                                  services to all local libraries within
                                  the district
                               3. To exchange or provide services with
                                  other District Library Centers
                               4. To contract for the provision of library
                                  services with other District Library
                                  Centers
                               5. To connect the public libraries together

Objectives (continued):	with the University Library in a service unit to increase the quantity and quality of public service, especially in areas presently without service
Stage of development:	Plans: Pursue the possibility of establishing a cooperative of District Library Centers with Johnstown, Aliquippa, New Castle, Altoona, and as many of the private colleges as are interested. A network could be established and could extend to the secondary schools.
	Operational: See Activities
Funding sources:	91.5% from funds made available for operation of the University library 6% from local government contribution 2.5% from state funds
Funding level:	Not stated
Type of agreement:	Formal, by state law
Rules for participation:	Formal
Computer usage:	Does not use computer
Membership count:	1 college and university library 9 public libraries
Activities:	1. Interlibrary loan 2. Reference assistance 3. Bibliographic verification 4. Literature searches 5. Photoduplication 6. Records 7. Loan of films and/or filmstrips 8. Loan of microforms 9. District Center List of Serials 10. District Center List of Monographs 11. Union Catalog
Direct services from headquarters:	Library-to-library
Leadership:	Part-time director plus Advisory Board
Membership list:	Indiana University of Pennsylvania

EAST CENTRAL PENNSYLVANIA INTERLIBRARY
COOPERATION COUNCIL (EPIC COUNCIL)

Type:	Independent entity
Area served:	East central region of Pennsylvania
Headquarters:	No centralized headquarters
Objectives:	The East central Council will meet regularly to discuss and act on cooperative possibilities, and it will work with state library agency staff in planning cooperative activities
Stage of development:	Planning stage
Funding source:	Not yet established
Funding level (annual):	Not yet established
Type of agreement:	Informal
Rules for participation:	By oral agreement
Computer usage:	Does not use computer
Membership count:	Membership being currently explored

Activities:
1. Interlibrary loan
2. Bibliographic verification
3. Reference assistance
4. Union List of Periodicals

Direct services from headquarters:	Library-to-library
Leadership:	Rotating chairmanship

FREE LIBRARY OF PHILADELPHIA

Cooperative Acquisitions Program for Purchase of Microfilm Copy
of United States House and Senate Bills and Resolutions

Type:	Independent entity
Area served:	State of Pennsylvania

Headquarters: Acquisitions Department, Free Library
                                 of Philadelphia

Objectives: A cooperative purchasing program to
                                 enable members to have access to an
                                 expensive set of materials beyond the
                                 financial means of individual member

Stage of development: See Activities

Funding source: Costs absorbed by each institution

Funding level (annual):   None stated

Type of agreement: Informal

Rules for participation: Oral agreement

Computer usage: Does not use computer

Membership count: 5 college and university libraries
                                 1 professional society

Activities: Interlibrary loan and cooperative acqui-
                                 sitions

Direct services from head-
quarters: Mechanisms for cooperative purchase

Leadership: Acquisitions librarian, Free Library of
                                 Philadelphia, part-time

Membership list: Penn State University, Pattee
                                 Temple University Libraries
                                 University of Pennsylvania, Biddle Law
                                   Library
                                 University of Pennsylvania, Van Pelt
                                 Villanova University

THE LEHIGH VALLEY ASSOCIATION OF
INDEPENDENT COLLEGES, INC. (LVAIC)

Lehigh Valley Association of Independent College Libraries (1969)

Type: Member of Higher Level Educational
                                 Consortium

Area served:	Region of Pennsylvania, Eastern Pennsylvania
Headquarters:	Centralized headquarters
Objectives:	To promote and facilitate interinstitutional cooperation among independent college and university libraries in Eastern Pennsylvania to improve and strengthen library services, resources and facilities supporting the educational programs of the LVAIC member colleges
Stage of development:	Plans: Joint purchasing of materials; assigned subject specialization in acquisition
	Operational: See Activities
Funding source:	Service fees from member institutions
Funding level (annual):	$8036
Type of agreement:	Formal, written agreement
Rules for participation:	Formal set of rules
Computer usage:	Uses Lehigh University's computer
Membership count:	6 colleges and universities
Activities:	1. Mutual notification of purchase or intent to purchase 2. Photocopying 3. Production and/or maintenance of Union Catalogs, lists and directories 4. Reciprocal borrowing privileges 5. Reference assistance 6. Bibliographic verification
Direct services from headquarters:	Delivery service to member libraries
Leadership:	Part-time coordinator
Membership list:	Allentown College of St. Francis de Sales Cedar Crest College Lafayette College Lehigh University Moravian College Muhlenberg College

MEDLINE (MEDLARS-ON-LINE)

Type:	Independent entity
Area served:	Interstate
Headquarters:	National Library of Medicine (NLM), Bethesda, Maryland
Objectives:	To help medical practitioners in isolated areas, to assist in undergraduate, graduate, and continuing medical education, and to provide information rapidly for medical research and health care
Stage of development:	Operational: See Activities
Funding source:	1. NLM finances compilation and maintenance of the machine-readable data base and network loan charges 2. Local costs are absorbed by each institution, with no formal financing provided
Funding level (annual):	None stated
Type of agreement:	Formal, by agreement with NLM
Rules for participation:	Formal. Limited to libraries at medical schools, hospitals, research institutions, and regional medical libraries throughout the country
Computer usage:	Uses own computer
Membership count:	3 active, 3 applications pending
Activities:	1. Bibliographic verification 2. Comprehensive literature searches
Direct services from headquarters:	Most services seem to emanate from headquarters
Leadership:	NLM

Membership list:	Active Members
	    Pennsylvania State University, Hershey
	        Medical Center Library
	    College of Physicians Library
	    University of Pittsburgh, Falk Library

Membership list (continued):   Applications pending
    University of Pennsylvania, Medical
      Library
    Temple University, Medical Library
    Thomas Jefferson University, Scott
      Library

MIDDLE ATLANTIC RESEARCH LIBRARIES
INFORMATION NETWORK (MARLIN) — 1968

Type: Independent entity

Area served: Interstate: Delaware, Maryland, Pennsylvania, and New Jersey

Headquarters: None

Objectives:

1. To develop and improve cooperation among the member libraries
2. To work towards a coordinated policy for long-range library growth and development with provision for:
   a. efficient systems
   b. rapid communication among the membership
   c. shared resources
   d. cooperative and coordinated purchasing
   e. exploration of other areas of cooperation
3. To cooperate with the other educational, library, and research institutions and organizations within and without the geographical area so as to further the purposes of the network

In pursuit of its purposes, this organization initiates, promotes and supports research studies, projects and operational systems which may lead to a knowledge of available resources and services, and which provide the means for increased interlibrary cooperative plans and services among the member institutions.

Stage of development: Plans: Other acquisition activities;
                                   reference services

                                   Operational: See Activities

Funding source: 1. Costs absorbed by each institution, no
                                       formal financing provided
                                   2. Council on Library Resources grant
                                       for preparation of Resource Guide

Funding level (annual):   None

Type of agreement: Formal, written agreement

Rules of participation: Formal

Computer usage: None indicated

Membership count: 12 colleges and universities

Activities:
 Services:
   1. Interlibrary loan   7. Loan of films and/or filmstrips
   2. Reference assistance   8. Loan of Microforms
   3. Bibliographic verification   9. Informing members of major
   4. Photoduplication   new acquisition
   5. Loan of audiotapes   10. Exchange of publications and
   6. Appraisal of equipment   lists

 Delivery of services:
   1. First class mail for photocopy of article, interlibrary loan request,
       verification, reference question, microforms and maps
   2. Bulk rate mail for monograph or other volumes, tapes, films
   3. TWX for interlibrary loan requests, photocopy of articles, reference
       question, and verification

Direct services from headquarters: None

Leadership: Governed by the chief librarians or their
                                   designates from each member institution

Membership list: University of Pennsylvania, Van Pelt
                                   Pennsylvania State University, Pattee

MID-EASTERN REGIONAL MEDICAL LIBRARY SERVICE (MERML)

Type:	Member of higher level consortium
Area served:	Interstate: Pennsylvania, Delaware, Southern New Jersey
Headquarters:	College of Physicians Library
Objectives:	To provide interlibrary loan, reference, and consultation services to the medical libraries of the Mid-Eastern Area of the United States as a part of the Regional Medical Network under the National Library of Medicine
Stage of development:	Operational: See Activities
Funding sources:	Federal grants and contracts
Funding level (annual):	$200,000
Type of agreement:	Formal, agreement with the National Library of Medicine
Rules for participation:	Formal
Computer usage:	Uses computer
Membership count:	Not specifically stated; includes all institutions (or unaffiliated individuals) in the MERML area having health science needs

Activities:
Services:
1. Interlibrary loan
2. Photoduplication
3. Loan of 8mm. cartridge films
4. Location of other audiovisual materials
5. Reference assistance
6. Library training programs
7. Hospital library consultation
8. Literature searches, including MEDLINE and MEDLARS

Delivery of services:
1. Book rate mail is used for monographic and first class mail for photocopies
2. Document delivery service is also expedited by truck delivery from the College of Physicians Library to other member subscribers of the ACLCP delivery service
3. Telephone is used for reference questions

Direct services from head-
quarters: As indicated

Leadership: Director

Membership list: All institutions (or unaffiliated individuals)
                                   in the MERML area having health science
                                   needs

NORTHEASTERN PENNSYLVANIA BIBLIOGRAPHIC CENTER (NEPBC) — 1956

Type: Independent entity

Area served: Region of Pennsylvania, Northeastern
                                   Pennsylvania

Headquarters: King's College, Wilkes-Barre,
                                   Pennsylvania

Objectives: To maintain a Union Catalog and produce
                                   a Union List of Serials, so that holdings
                                   may be shared throughout Northeastern
                                   Pennsylvania

Stage of development: Plans: Expansion of Bibliographic Center

                                   Operational: See Activities

Funding source: None

Funding level (annual):   No formal budget

Type of agreement: Informal

Rules of participation: By vote of membership

Computer usage: Uses computer at King's College

Membership count: 13 colleges and universities

Activities:
  Services:
    1. Interlibrary loan   6. Union Catalog
    2. Reference assistance   7. Loan of audiotapes (Reciprocal)
    3. Bibliographic verification   8. Loan of videotapes (Reciprocal)
    4. Photoduplication   9. Loan of film and/or filmstrips
    5. Union list of serials   10. Loan of microforms
                                      11. TWX

Delivery of services:

1. First class mail for photocopy of articles and interlibrary loan requests
2. Bulk rate mail for monograph or other volumes, tapes, films and microforms
3. Telephone for verification
4. Osterhaut Library truck service (Wilkes-Barre) is available, free of charge, to all libraries in the area

Direct services from headquarters:

1. Union List of Periodicals stored on magnetic tape; published annually
2. Union Catalog

Leadership

Governed by committee of head librarians of all participating libraries

Membership list:

College Misericordia Library, Dallas, Pennsylvania
Hazleton Public Library, Hazleton, Pennsylvania
Hoyt Library, Kingston, Pennsylvania
King's College Library, Wilkes-Barre, Pennsylvania
Keystone Junior College Library, LaPlume, Pennsylvania
Luzerne County Community College Library, Wilkes-Barre, Pennsylvania
Luzerne County Medical Society Library, Wilkes-Barre, Pennsylvania

Marywood College Library, Scranton, Pennsylvania
Osterhout Free Library, Wilkes-Barre, Pennsylvania
Scranton Public Library, Scranton, Pennsylvania
Scranton University Library, Scranton, Pennsylvania
Veteran's Administration Hospital Library, Wilkes-Barre, Pennsylvania
Wilkes College Library, Wilkes-Barre, Pennsylvania

OHIO COLLEGE LIBRARY CENTER (OCLC)

Type: Independent entity

Area served: Interstate

Headquarters: Columbus, Ohio

Objectives: 1. Operate computerized systems to assist member Ohio colleges and universities in providing a faster, more efficient

search and retrieval system for library
books and journals, and research,
development, and implementation of such
systems

2. Increase availability of library for use in
educational and research programs of
member libraries

3. Lower the rate of rise of per student
library cost while increasing the availability of library resources

Stage of development:	Planning: Cooperative processing and Union List of Serials (1972). While primarily an Ohio operation, OCLC has terminals in Pittsburgh, Philadelphia, and New England (NELINET). The assumption is that other areas, such as Philadelphia, will experiment via OCLC; if their experience warrants it, they will set up similar operations for their own area later. Operational: See Activities
Funding sources:	Dues from member institutions, government appropriations, and Council on Library Resources
Funding level (annual):	$733,332
Type of agreement:	Payment of membership fee
Rules for participation:	Formal set of rules
Computer usage:	Uses computer
Membership count:	Within Ohio: 48 college and university libraries In Pennsylvania: 4
Activities:	1. Computerized on-line shared cataloging 2. Catalog card production and other bibliographic support 3. Production and maintenance of an on-line union catalog 4. Reciprocal borrowing privileges 5. Expanded interlibrary loan service 6. Research projects
Direct service from headquarters:	Computer-related activities

Leadership: Director, four system analysts, program-
                               mer, part-time library technician, secret-
                               ary, computer operations technicians,
                               part-time keypunch operator; Board of
                               Trustees, with bimonthly meetings

Membership list: Members in Pennsylvania:
                                 Pittsburgh Regional Library Center
                               Experimental members in Philadelphia:
                                 Drexel University
                                 Temple University
                                 University of Pennsylvania

PENNSYLVANIA STATE UNIVERSITY LIBRARIES
COMMONWEALTH CAMPUS LIBRARIES SYSTEM

Type: Member of higher level educational con-
                               sortium

Area served: State

Headquarters: Pennsylvania State University, University
                               Park

Objectives: To provide library services necessary to
                               support the branch campus program

Stage of development: Operational: See Activities

Funding sources: Pennsylvania State University Libraries
                               budget

Funding level (annual)   Not stated

Type of agreement: Formal, by the organizational structure of
                               the University Libraries

Rules for participation: Formal, by the organizational structure of
                               the University Libraries

Computer usage: None indicated

Membership count: 20

Activities:
 Services:
  1. Interlibrary loan   4. Loan of films and/or filmstrips
  2. Bibliographic verification   5. Facsimile transmission
  3. Photoduplication   6. Cooperative cataloging

   7. Union List of Serials   11. Loan of audiotapes
   8. Union Catalog   12. Loan of microforms
   9. Reference assistance   13. Cooperative acquisition
 10. Literature searches (compre-   14. Cooperative processing
      hensive)   15. Union List of Monographs

Delivery of services:
   1. First class mail for monograph or other volume, photography of article, interlibrary loan request, verification, reference question, literature searches, tapes, films, microforms, and maps
   2. Via bulk rate mail for monograph or other volume, tapes, films, microforms, and maps
   3. By telephone for interlibrary loan request, verification, reference question, and literature searches
   4. Also by facsimile transmission for photocopy of article, interlibrary loan request, verification, reference question, literature searches, and maps

Direct services from head-quarters:	As indicated in Activities
Leadership:	Coordinator
Membership list:	Pennsylvania State University, Allentown
	Pennsylvania State University, Altoona
	Pennsylvania State University, Beaver (Monaca)
	Pennsylvania State University, Ogontz (Abington)
	Pennsylvania State University, Behrend (Erie)
	Pennsylvania State University, Berks (Wyomissing)
	Pennsylvania State University, Delaware (Media)
	Pennsylvania State University, Dubois
	Pennsylvania State University, Fayette (Uniontown)
	Pennsylvania State University, Hazleton
	Pennsylvania State University, King of Prussia
	Pennsylvania State University, McKeesport
	Pennsylvania State University, Mont Alto
	Pennsylvania State University, New Kensington
	Pennsylvania State University, Schuylkill (Schuylkill Haven)
	Pennsylvania State University, Scranton

Pennsylvania State University, Shenango
Valley (Sharon)
Pennsylvania State University, University
Park
Pennsylvania State University, Wilkes-Barre
Pennsylvania State University, York

PHILADELPHIA AREA LIBRARY AUTOMATION
CONFERENCE (PALAC)

Type:	Independent entity
Area served:	Interstate Philadelphia area
Headquarters:	None indicated
Objectives:	To consult together on area library automation requirements
Stage of development:	Planning: 1. All activities are in planning stage 2. Contemplate the "transplanting" of the Ohio College Library Center (OCLC) under the Union Library Catalog of Pennsylvania
Funding source:	None indicated
Funding level (annual):	None indicated
Type of agreement:	Informal, by oral agreement
Rules for participation:	Informal, by oral agreement
Computer usage:	None indicated
Membership count:	13 college and university libraries (12 are in Pennsylvania)
Activities:	Systems level librarians and member librarians meet twice yearly
Direct services from headquarters:	None indicated
Leadership:	Chairman

Membership list:
Drexel University   Swarthmore College
Haverford College   Temple University

Lincoln University   University of Pennsylvania
PMC Colleges   Ursinus College
Rosemont College   Villanova University
St. Joseph's College   West Chester State College

PHILADELPHIA COLLEGE OF ART/PHILADELPHIA MUSIC ACADEMY

Type: Independent entity

Area served: City

Headquarters: None indicated

Objectives: To divide acquisition by subject and share all library resources

Stage of development: Planning: Expand membership to include adjacent educational institutions

                             Operational: See Activities

Funding sources: Costs are absorbed by each institution

Funding level (annual):   No formal budget

Type of agreement: Informal, oral agreement

Rules for participation: Informal, oral agreement

Computer usage: None indicated

Membership count: 2

Activities: Services:
                               1. Monograph or other volume
                               2. Photocopy of articles
                               3. Interlibrary loan request
                               4. Bibliographic verification
                               5. Reference assistance
                               6. Literature searches
                               7. Loan of microforms
                               8. Loan of audiotapes
                               9. Maps

                             Delivery of services:
                               Walking distance

Direct services from headquarters: None

Leadership: Coordinators

Membership list: Philadelphia College of Art Library
                                     Philadelphia Music Academy Library

PITTSBURGH REGIONAL LIBRARY CENTER, INC.
(PRLC) — 1967

Type: Independent entity

Area served: Interstate, Pittsburgh Area

Headquarters: Centralized headquarters

Objectives: The Center is formed exclusively for the
                             charitable, scientific, literary and educa-
                             tional purposes of advancing library science,
                             for the promotion of library services, and
                             for the promotion of interlibrary cooperation
                             among the public and private libraries in the
                             City of Pittsburgh, Pennsylvania and sur-
                             rounding areas to a distance of 200 miles
                             from said city

Stage of development: Planning:
                             1. Union List of Periodicals, 2nd edition
                                (1973), Newspaper list (1973)
                             2. Assigned subject specialization in
                                acquisitions
                             3. Clearinghouse

                             Operational: See Activities

Funding sources: Membership—84%
                             Library Services and Construction Act,
                               Title III funds — 16%

Funding level (annual):   Budget for fiscal 1971-1972 was $54,892

Type of agreement: Formal, by incorporation

Rules for participation: Formal

Computer usage: Uses university computer

Membership count: 20 academic institutions
                             1 public library

Activities:

Services:
1. Mutual notification of purchase or
   intent to purchase
2. Catalog card production and other
   cataloging support
3. Production and/or maintenance of
   Union catalogs, lists, and directories
4. Reciprocal borrowing privileges
5. Expanded interlibrary loan service
6. Joint research projects
7. Publication program
8. Special communication services

Delivery of services:
Delivery service for monograph or other
volumes, interlibrary loan requests.
Available only in Pittsburgh, through
arrangement with the University of
Pittsburgh.

Direct services from headquarters:

1. Editing of Union List of Periodicals
2. Coordination of all consortium programs,
   projects, and services
3. PRLC Newsletter (bimonthly)
4. Directory of member libraries

Leadership:

Executive Director, Board of Trustees,
Executive Council

Membership list:

Voting Members
Carnegie Library of Pittsburgh
Carnegie-Mellon University
Chatham College
Point Park College
Robert Morris College
University of Pittsburgh

Associate Members
Bethany College
California State College
Clarion State College
Community College of Allegheny County,
    Boyce Campus
Community College of Allegheny County,
    South Campus
Community College of Allegheny County,
    Allegheny Campus
Pittsburgh Theological Seminary

St. Francis College
Slippery Rock State College
Westminster College
Duquesne University
Carlow College
Indiana University of Pennsylvania
Westmorland County Community College
Wheeling College

REGIONAL RESOURCE LIBRARY — CARNEGIE LIBRARY OF PITTSBURGH

Type:	Member of higher level consortium
Area served:	State
Headquarters:	State Librarian, Harrisburg
Objectives:	The Center shall have the responsibility and power to acquire major research collections and, under rules and regulations promulgated by a Board consisting of the head librarians of all Regional Library Resource Centers and under the chairmanship of the State Librarian, to make them available to the residents of the Commonwealth on a statewide basis. Subjects for which this Resource Library is responsible are: astronomy, physics, chemistry, earth sciences, biology, and botanical sciences, technology, engineering, business, manufacturers, building construction, and anthropology
Stage of development:	Operational: See Activities
Funding sources:	1. Library materials budget $100,000 per year, approximately 20-25% of total 2. Materials budget from city and county funds, approximately 75% of total 3. Materials budget from Endowment Fund, approximately 4-5% of total
Funding level (annual):	As indicated in Funding sources
Type of agreement:	Formal, by state law

Rules of participation: Formal, by state law

Computer usage: None indicated

Membership count: All libraries in Pennsylvania

Activities: Services:
                             1. Interlibrary loan
                             2. Reference assistance
                             3. Bibliographic verification
                             4. Photoduplication
                             5. Loan of microforms
                             6. Cooperative acquisition
                             7. Union Catalog

                             Delivery of services:
                             1. First class mail for monographs,
                                photocopy, interlibrary loan request,
                                verification, reference question, and
                                microforms
                             2. Bulk rate mail for monographs
                             3. TWX for interlibrary loan requests,
                                verification, and reference questions

Direct services from head-
quarters: None indicated

Leadership: Director; Board consisting of head librar-
                             ians of all Regional Library Resource
                             Centers under the chairmanship of the
                             State Librarian

Membership list: All libraries in Pennsylvania; access also
                             provided for citizens of the Commonwealth

REGIONAL RESOURCE CENTER — FREE LIBRARY
OF PHILADELPHIA

Type: Member of higher level consortium

Area served: State

Headquarters: State Librarian, Harrisburg

Objectives: The Center shall have the responsibility and
                             power to acquire major research collec-
                             tions, and, under rules and regulations

promulgated by a Board consisting of the
head librarians of all Regional Library
Resource Centers and under the chairman-
ship of the State Librarian, to make them
available to the residents of the commonwealth on a state-wide basis. Subjects for
which this Resource Library is responsible
are: religion and philosophy, costume,
theatre, folklore, modern literature, fic-
tion, geography and travels, insurance,
fine arts, music, sports, criminology,
anthropology, ancient and modern history

Stage of development: Operational: See Activities

Funding source: State funds

Funding level (annual): $100,000

Type of agreement: Formal, by state law

Rules for participation: Formal, by state law

Computer usage: None indicated

Membership count: All libraries in Pennsylvania

Activities: Services:
                              1. Interlibrary loan
                              2. Reference assistance
                              3. Bibliographic verification
                              4. Photoduplication
                              5. Loan of films and/or filmstrips

                             Delivery of services:
                              1. First class mail for photocopy of
                                 article
                              2. Bulk rate mail for monographs or
                                 other volumes, interlibrary loans
                                 requests, and films
                              3. Telephone and TWX for verification
                                 and reference questions

Direct services from head-
quarters: None indicated

Leadership: Director; Board consisting of head librar-
                             ians of all Regional Library Resource
                             Centers under the chairmanship of the State
                             Librarian

Membership list: All libraries in Pennsylvania; access also
                             provided to citizens of the Commonwealth

REGIONAL RESOURCE LIBRARY — PENNSYLVANIA
STATE LIBRARY

Type: Member of higher level consortium

Area served: State of Pennsylvania

Headquarters: State Librarian, Harrisburg

Objectives: The Center shall have the responsibility and
                             power to acquire major research collections,
                             and, under rules and regulations promul-
                             gated by a Board consisting of the head
                             librarians of all Regional Library Resource
                             Centers and under the chairmanship of the
                             State Librarian, to make them available to
                             the residents of the Commonwealth on a
                             statewide basis. Subjects for which this
                             Resource Library is responsible: psych-
                             ology, military science, languages,
                             mathematics, zoological sciences, home
                             economics, labor economics, agriculture,
                             Latin and Greek literature, Russian and
                             other Slavic literature and history, pre-
                             historic archaeology

Stage of development: Planning: Expanded truck delivery service

                             Operational: See Activities

Funding source: State funds

Funding level (annual): $400,000

Type of agreement: Formal, by State Law

Rules for participation: Formal, by State Law

Computer usage: None indicated

Membership count: All libraries in Pennsylvania

Activities:
 Services:
    1. Interlibrary loan   6. Loan of videotapes
    2. Reference assistance   7. Loan of films and/or filmstrips
    3. Bibliographic verification   8. Loan of microforms
    4. Photoduplication   9. Union Catalog
    5. Loan of audiotapes

Delivery of services:
1. First class mail for photocopy of article, interlibrary loan request, verification, reference question, microforms, and maps
2. Bulk rate for monograph or other volume, tapes, and films
3. Own delivery service for monograph or other volume and photocopy of article
4. TWX for interlibrary loan requests, verification, and reference question
5. Truck delivery (twice-a-week) is available to three of the libraries

Direct services from head-quarters:	None indicated
Leadership:	Coordinator; Board of head librarians of all Regional Library Resource Centers under chairmanship of the State Librarian
Membership list:	All libraries in Pennsylvania; access also provided to citizens of the Commonwealth

REGIONAL RESOURCE LIBRARY — STATE LIBRARY OF PENNSYLVANIA

Type:	Member of higher level consortium
Area served:	State
Headquarters:	State Librarian, Harrisburg
Objectives:	The Center shall have the responsibility and power to acquire major research collections and, under rules and regulations promulgated by a Board consisting of the head librarians of all Regional Library Resource Centers and under the chairmanship of the State Librarian, to make them available to the residents of the Commonwealth on a statewide basis. Subjects for which this Resource Library is responsible are: library science, sociology, law, public administration, political science, statistics (theory and methods), social welfare, education, public service and utilities, genealogy including heraldry, journalism, printing and publishing, Pennsylvania history, economics

Stage of development:	Operational: See Activities
Funding sources:	State funds — 17% Local tax funds — 67% Other local funds (endowment, etc.) — 16%
Funding level (annual):	Total expenditures for all public libraries was $30,268,175
Type of agreement:	Formal, by State Law
Rules for participation:	Formal, by State Law
Computer usage:	None indicated
Membership count:	All libraries in Pennsylvania
Activities:	Services: 1. Interlibrary loan 2. Reference assistance 3. Photoduplication 4. Loan of films and/or filmstrips 5. Loan of microforms 6. Cooperative acquisitions 7. Union Catalog

Delivery of services:
1. First class mail for interlibrary loan requests and reference questions
2. Bulk rate mail for monograph or other volume, films, microforms, and maps
3. Telephone for interlibrary loan requests and reference questions
4. TWX for interlibrary requests and reference questions

Direct services from head-quarters:	None indicated
Leadership-Director:	Board consisting of head librarians of all Regional Resource Centers under the chairmanship of the State Librarian
Membership list:	All libraries in Pennsylvania; also provides access for citizens of the Commonwealth

THEOLOGICAL LIBRARIANS OF SOUTHEASTERN PENNSYLVANIA
(TSSP) — 1961

Type:	Independent entity
Area served:	Southeastern Pennsylvania
Headquarters:	None
Objectives:	1. Seek to improve total library resources for scholarships in the area, particularly in theological research
	2. Avoid unnecessary duplication of materials
	3. Provide a locus for meeting, sharing of ideas and expertise in order to serve individual institutions more adequately
	4. Foster library cooperation and provide coordination for the theological institutions with all other area libraries
Stage of development:	Planning:
	1. Membership for theological libraries in New Jersey
	2. Membership for religion departments of universities
	Operational: See Activities
Funding sources:	Costs are absorbed by each institution
Funding level (annual):	No formal budget
Type of agreement:	Informal
Rules for participation:	Informal
Computer usage:	None indicated
Membership count:	9 seminaries
	1 historical society
Activities:	Services:
	1. Interlibrary loan
	2. Reference assistance
	3. Bibliographic verification
	4. Photoduplication
	5. Loan of audiotapes
	6. Loan of microforms
	7. Cooperative acquisitions

8. Cooperative cataloging
9. Union list of serials and monographs

Delivery of services:
1. First class mail for interlibrary loan requests, literature searches, tapes, films, microforms, and maps
2. Bulk rate mail for monographs and other volumes, and photocopies of articles
3. Telephone for verification and reference programs
4. ACLCP delivery service is also used

Direct services from head-
quarters: None

Leadership: Governed by a committee composed of representatives from member institutions; Chairman rotates; biannual meetings

Membership list: Eastern Baptist Seminary, Lancaster Theological Seminary, Lutheran Theological Seminary at Gettysburg, Lutheran Theologic al Seminary at Philadelphia, Mary Immaculate, Moravian Seminary, Philadelphia Divinity School, St. Charles Seminary, Westminster Theological Seminary

TRI-STATE COLLEGE LIBRARY COOPERATIVE (TCLA) — 1967

Type: Independent entity

Area served: Interstate

Headquarters: Holy Family College

Objectives: 1. Exchange information and share existing resources to greater advantage
2. Strengthen existing resources and library services through joint application for private and government funds
3. Increase research potential through a mutually supported acquisition program

Stage of development: Planning:
1. Cooperative cataloging and processing
2. Union Serials catalog and central serials bank

3. TWX and possibly WATS
4. Universal identification for students of
   member colleges
5. Joint fund raising and more extensive
   cooperation in acquisitions, especially
   of specialized and costly reference and
   research materials
6. Cooperative planning and consultation
   services
7. Cooperative data processing
8. Negro Affairs research collection to be
   housed at Lincoln University and a
   supplementary basic collection for each
   member library
9. Annotated film brochure (1972)
10. Workshops in the areas of technical
    processing (1972), acquisition (1972) and
    reader services (1972)

Operational: See Activities

Funding sources:

1. Contributions from members
2. Federal grants
3. Fee structure
4. Membership

Funding level (annual):   Not specified

Type of agreement: Formal, by service agreement

Rules for participation: Formal, by service agreement

Computer usage: None indicated

Membership count: 21 college and university libraries

Activities: Services:
1. Interlibrary loan
2. Loan of films and/or filmstrips
3. Cooperative acquisitions
4. Reference assistance
5. Bibliographic verification
6. Photoduplication
7. Loan of audiotapes and disk recordings
8. Loan of videotapes
9. Loan of microforms
10. Cooperative film library
11. Advisory services roster: reference
    cataloging, subject specialists, data
    processing and automation

Delivery of services:
1. First class mail for photocopy of articles, interlibrary loan requests, verification
2. Bulk rate mail for monograph or other volumes, tapes, films
3. Telephone for interlibrary loan requests, verification, reference questions
4. Cooperative Interlibrary Truck Delivery Service (17 members subscribe to this service, which was sponsored originally by the ACLCP and is partially funded by a State grant; this service delivers monographs or other volumes, photocopies of articles, interlibrary loan requests, tapes, films, microfilms, and maps)

Direct services from head-
quarters: None indicated

Leadership: Board of Directors, composed of official representatives of member libraries with meetings as necessary

Membership list:

Beaver College	Moore College of Art
Cabrini College	Our Lady of Angels
Chestnut Hill College	Philadelphia College of Pharmacy
Eastern Baptist College	and Science
Gwynedd-Mercy College	Philadelphia College of Textiles
Holy Family College	and Science
Immaculata College	PMC Colleges
La Salle College	Rosemont College
Lincoln University	St. Charles Seminary
	Ursinus College
	West Chester State College

UNION LIBRARY CATALOG OF PENNSYLVANIA, INC.

Type: Independent entity

Area served: State

Headquarters: Centralized headquarters

Objectives:

The Union Library Catalog of Pennsylvania consists of a card file of 3.75 million main entries on 3 × 5 cards describing and locating about 8 million volumes in 207 libraries (including 127 active libraries) in Pennsylvania

Stage of development:

Planning
1. To phase out the card catalog file and develop a computer based cooperative cataloging service and union catalog locations service via computer among Pennsylvania libraries
2. To experiment with the Ohio College Library Center

Operational: See Activities

Funding source:

Annual service subscriptions

Funding level (annual):

$72,000

Type of agreement:

Nonprofit corporation

Rules for participation:

Formal

Computer usage:

None indicated

Membership count:

8 public and private libraries
6 college and university libraries

Activities:

Services:
1. Bibliographic verification
2. Union catalog
3. Location service

Delivery of services: First class mail, telephone, and TWX

Direct service from headquarters:

See Activities

Leadership:

Director

Membership list of Pennsylvania College and University Libraries:

LaSalle College
Bryn Mawr College

Drexel University
College of Physicians Library
Temple University Libraries
University of Pennsylvania

UNION OF INDEPENDENT COLLEGES OF ART/LEARNING RESOURCES EXCHANGE PROGRAM (UICA/LREP)

Type: Member of higher level consortium

Area served: Interstate

Headquarters: Kansas City, Missouri

Objectives: To share library and audio visual resources of special importance to art colleges (LREP is only one part of the consortium UICA whose objectives are broader, e.g., institution-wide cooperation)

Stage of development: Planning:
1. Transmission via satellite or cable or programs, images on microfiche, tapes, etc. to all member colleges from computerized center at Minneapolis Institute of Art and Design (target date — 1975)
2. Transmission also to be received by terminals in public schools and libraries in Minneapolis; tie-ins possible to all who wish to subscribe

Operational: See Activities

Funding sources: Federal grants

Funding level (annual):   Not specified

Type of agreement: Formal

Rules for participation: Formal

Computer usage: None indicated

Membership count: 8 colleges and institutes of art

Activities: Services
1. Loan of audiotapes
2. Loan of videotapes
3. Loan of films and/or filmstrips
4. Loan of microforms
5. Cooperative acquisition

Instructional units are generated by UICA grants filling specific art college needs. Loans and help are given when local sources cannot supply

Delivery of service:
First class mail for tapes, films, library
originated programs

Direct services from head-
quarters: None indicated

Leadership: Executive Director

Membership list of Pennsylvania College and University
Libraries: Philadelphia College of Art

APPENDIX C: Summary Charts for Cooperation
Among Academic Libraries in Pennsylvania*

Four important charts emerge from an analysis of these data. Chart 1
provides an overview of the services that the academic library consortia are
now engaged in. Chart 2 provides an overview of the delivery of services.
Charts 3 and 4 show the telecommunications and machine-readable data bases
now being utilized by the consortia.

---

*Excerpted from the Inventory of Pennsylvania Interlibrary Cooperatives and
Information Networks by Natalie Wiest, Lea Laurea, and Brigitt L. Kenney
(Project Director).

CHART 1 Notes

Services

Other

1.   Delivery service.

1a.   Mutual notification of purchase of items to $100 and over on date of order.

2.   Records.

3.   Resource guide, MARLINE Notes, exchange of publications and lists, appraisal of equipment.

4.   Location of AV materials, library training programs, hospital library consultation, newsletter.

5.   In planning stage.

6.   Free access to the libraries' holdings.

7.   Directory of newspapers, list of major microforms in Pittsburgh area, file of expensive items ($100 and over), undergraduate ILL borrowing privileges, delivery service for voting members.

8.   Cooperative film library, advisory services roster: cataloging, reference, subject specialists, data processing and automation.

9.   Instructional units are generated by UICA grants fortifying specific art college needs.

Program	Interlibrary Loan	Reference Assistance	Bibliographic Verification	Literature Searches (Comprehensive)	Photoduplication	Loan of Audiotapes	Loan of Videotapes	Loan of Films and/or Filmstrips	Loan of Microforms	Facsimile Transmission	Cooperative Acquisition	Cooperative Cataloging	Cooperative Processing	Union List of Serials	Union List of Monographs	Union Catalog	Instructional TV	ETV Broadcasts	Other
District Center — Aliquippa	×	×	×	O	×	O	O	×	O	O	×	×	O	×	×	O	O	O	
Area College Library Cooperative Program (ACLCP)	×	×	×	×	×	×	×	×	×	×	×	×	O	×	×	O	O	O	*1a
ACLCP — Delivery Service	O	O	O	O	O	O	O	O	O	O	O	O	O	O	O	O	O	O	*1
Bryn Mawr/Haverford College Library Cooperative Project	×	×	×	×	×	×	×	×	×	O	×	×	×	×	O	×	O	O	
Cabrini College/Eastern College Interlibrary Cooperative	×	×	×	O	×	×	O	O	×	O	×	O	O	×	×	×	O	O	
Central Pennsylvania Consortium	×	×	O	×	×	×	×	×	×	×	×	×	O	×	×	O	O	O	
Committee on Library Cooperation of the Union Library Catalog of Penna.	O	O	O	O	O	O	O	O	O	O	O	O	O	O	O	O	O	O	
Eastcentral Penna. Interlibrary Cooperation Council (EPIC Council)	×	×	×	O	O	O	O	O	O	O	O	O	O	×	O	O	O	O	
Free Library of Philadelphia Cooperative Acquisitions Program for Purchase of Microfilm Copy of U.S. House and Senate Bills and Resolutions	×	O	O	O	O	O	O	O	O	O	×	O	O	O	O	O	O	O	
District Center — Indiana	×	×	×	×	×	O	O	×	×	O	O	O	O	×	×	×	O	O	*2
District Center — Johnstown	×	×	×	O	×	O	O	×	O	O	×	×	×	O	O	O	O	O	

Legend of organizations (columns):

1. Lehigh Valley Association of Independent Colleges, Inc.
2. MEDLINE
3. Middle Atlantic Research Libraries Information Network (MARLIN)
4. Mideastern Regional Medical Library Service
5. Northeastern Pennsylvania Bibliographic Center (NEPBC)
6. Ohio College Library Center (OCLC)
7. Penna. State University Libraries — Commonwealth Campus Libraries System
8. Regional Resource Library — Penna. State University Library
9. Regional Resource Center — Philadelphia
10. Philadelphia Area Library Automation Conference (PALAC)
11. Philadelphia College of Art/ Philadelphia Music Academy (PCA/PMA)

Activity	1	2	3	4	5	6	7	8	9	10	11
Interlibrary Loan	x	o	x	x	x	o	x	x	x	o	x
Reference Assistance	x	o	x	x	x	o	x	x	x	o	x
Bibliographic Verification	x	x	x	o	x	x	x	x	x	o	x
Literature Searches (Comprehensive)	o	x	o	x	o	o	x	o	o	o	o
Photoduplication	x	o	x	x	x	o	x	x	x	o	x
Loan of Audiotapes	o	o	x	o	x	o	x	x	o	o	o
Loan of Videotapes	o	o	o	o	x	o	o	x	o	o	o
Loan of Films and/or Filmstrips	o	o	x	x	x	o	x	x	x	o	x
Loan of Microforms	x	o	x	o	o	o	x	x	o	o	o
Facsimile Transmission	o	o	o	o	o	o	x	o	o	o	o
Cooperative Acquisition	x	o	o	o	o	o	x	o	o	o	o
Cooperative Cataloging	o	o	o	o	o	x	x	o	o	o	o
Cooperative Processing	o	o	o	o	o	o	x	o	o	o	o
Union List of Serials	x	o	o	o	x	o	x	o	o	o	o
Union List of Monographs	o	o	o	o	o	o	x	o	o	o	o
Union Catalog	o	o	o	o	x	x	x	x	o	o	o
Instructional TV	o	o	o	o	o	o	o	o	o	o	o
ETV Broadcasts	o	o	o	o	o	o	o	o	o	o	o
Other			*3	*4						*5	*6

Service	Regional Resource Library — Pittsburgh	Pittsburgh Regional Library Center, Inc. (PRLC)	Regional Resource Center — State Library of Pennsylvania	Theological Seminaries of Southeastern Penna. (TSSP)	Tri-State College Library Cooperative Program (TCLC)	Union Library Catalog of Pennsylvania, Inc.	Union of Independent Colleges of Art/Learning Resources Exchange Program (LICA/LREP)
Other		*7			*8	*9	
ETV Broadcasts	O	O	O	O	O	O	O
Instructional TV	O	O	O	O	O	O	O
Union Catalog	X	O	X	O	O	X	O
Union List of Monographs	O	O	O	X	O	O	O
Union List of Serials	O	X	O	X	O	O	O
Cooperative Processing	O	O	O	O	O	O	O
Cooperative Cataloging	O	X	O	X	O	O	O
Cooperative Acquisition	X	O	X	X	X	O	X
Facsimile Transmission	O	X	O	O	O	O	O
Loan of Microforms	X	O	X	X	X	O	X
Loan of Films and/or Filmstrips	O	X	X	O	X	O	X
Loan of Videotapes	O	O	O	O	X	O	X
Loan of Audiotapes	O	O	O	X	X	O	X
Photoduplication	X	X	X	X	X	O	O
Literature Searches (Comprehensive)	O	O	O	O	O	O	O
Bibliographic Verification	X	O	O	X	X	X	O
Reference Assistance	X	O	X	X	X	O	O
Interlibrary Loan	X	X	X	X	X	O	O

CHART 2 Notes

Delivery of Service

Other

1.   ACLCP delivery service.

2.   CRT terminals in member libraries.

3.   ACLCP delivery service.

4.   Teletype.

5.   Free mail for ILL requests, literature searches, tapes.

	First Class Mail	Bulk Rate Mail	Bus	Own Delivery Service	Telephone	Fax	TWX	Other
District Center — Aliquippa	X	X	O	X	X	O	X	
Area College Library Cooperative Program (ACLCP)	O	O	O	X	X	O	X	
ACLCP — Delivery Service	O	O	O	X	O	O	O	
Bryn Mawr/Haverford College Library Cooperative Project	O	O	O	X	O	O	O	
Cabrini College/Eastern College Interlibrary Cooperative	O	O	O	O	X	O	O	
Central Penna. Consortium	O	O	O	X	X	O	X	
Committee on Library Cooperation of the Union Library Catalog of Penna.	O		O	O	O	O	O	*1
Eastcentral Penna. Interlibrary Cooperation Council (EPIC Council)	O	O	O	X	O	O	O	
Free Library of Philadelphia Cooperative Acquisitions Program for Purchase of Microfilm Copy of U.S. House and Senate Bills and Resolutions	X	O	O	O	O	O	X	
District Center — Indiana	O	X	O	O	X	O	O	
District Center — Johnstown	O	O	O	X	X	O	O	

	First Class Mail	Bulk Rate Mail	Bus	Own Delivery Service	Telephone	Fax	TWX	Other
Lehigh Valley Association of Independent Colleges, Inc.	O	O	O	X	O	O	X	
MEDLINE	O	O	O	O	O	O	O	
Middle Atlantic Research Libraries Information Network (MARLIN)	X	X	O	O	O	O	X	
Mideastern Regional Medical Library Service	X	X	O	X	X	O	X	
Northeastern Penna. Bibliographic Center (NEPBC)	X	X	O	X	X	O	O	
Ohio College Library Center (OCLC)	O	O	O	O	O	O	O	*2
Penna. State University Libraries — Commonwealth Campus Libraries System	X	X	O	O	X	X	X	
Regional Resource Library — Penna. State University Library	X	X	O	X	O	O	X	
Regional Resource Center — Philadelphia	X	X	O	O	X	O	X	
Philadelphia Area Library Automation Conference (PALAC)	O	O	O	O	O	O	O	
Philadelphia College of Art/ Philadelphia Music Academy (PCA/PMA)	O	O	O	O	O	O	O	

	First Class Mail	Bulk Rate Mail	Bus	Own Delivery Service	Telephone	Fax	TWX	Other
Regional Resource Library — Pittsburgh	X	X	O	O	O	O	X	
Pittsburgh Regional Library Center, Inc. (PRLC)	X	O	O	X	X	O	O	
Regional Resource Center — State Library of Pennsylvania	X	X	O	O	X	O	X	
Theological Seminaries of Southeastern Penna. (TSSP)	X	X	O	O	X	O	O	*3
Tri-State College Library Cooperative Program (TCLC)	X	X	O	X	X	O	O	
Union Library Catalog of Pennsylvania, Inc.	X	O	O	O	X	O	X	
Union of Independent Colleges of Art/Learning Resources Exchange Program (LICA/LREP)	X	O	O	O	O	O	O	

CHART 3 Notes

Telecommunications

<u>Other</u>

1.   Telefacsimile at PSU only.

2.   TWX at Bucks County Free Library only.

3.   TWX through the District Center.

4.   TWX at Kings College only.

5.   CRT terminals in member libraries hooked to Columbus center.

6.   TWX only at University Park.

7.   CRT computer console connected by telephone lines to OCLC in Columbus.

	Private, Leased Telephone Line	IN-WATS	OUT-WATS	Private Teletype Network	TWX	Video Transmission (Type)	Computer—to—Computer	Telefacsimile	Other
District Center — Aliquippa	o	o	o	o	x	o	o	o	
Area College Library Cooperative Program (ACLCP)	o	o	o	o	x	o	o	x	*1
ACLCP — Delivery Service	o	o	o	o	o	o	o	o	
Bryn Mawr/Haverford College Library Cooperative Project	x	o	o	o	o	o	o	o	
Cabrini College/Eastern College Interlibrary Cooperative	o	o	o	o	x	o	o	o	
Central Penna. Consortium	o	o	o	o	x	o	o	o	
Committee on Library Cooperation of the Union Library Catalog of Penna.	x	o	o	o	o	o	o	o	
Eastcentral Penna. Interlibrary Cooperation Council (EPIC Council)	o	o	o	o	o	o	o	o	
Free Library of Philadelphia Cooperative Acquisitions Program for Purchase of Microfilm Copy of U.S. House and Senate Bills and Resolutions	o	o	o	o	x	o	o	o	
District Center — Indiana	o	x	x	o	x	o	o	o	
District Center — Johnstown	x	o	o	o	o	o	o	o	

	Private, Leased Telephone Line	IN-WATS	OUT-WATS	Private Teletype Network	TWX	Video Transmission (Type)	Computer-to-Computer	Telefacsimile	Other
Lehigh Valley Association of Independent Colleges, Inc.	O	O	O	O	X	O	O	O	*3
MEDLINE	O	X	X	O	X	O	O	O	
Middle Atlantic Research Libraries Information Network (MARLIN)	O	O	O	O	X	O	O	O	
Mideastern Regional Medical Library Service	X	O	O	O	X	O	O	O	
Northeastern Penna. Bibliographic Center (NEPBC)	O	O	O	X	X	O	O	O	*4
Ohio College Library Center (OCLC)	X	O	O	O	O	O	O	O	*5
Penna. State University Libraries — Commonwealth Campus Libraries System	X	X	X	O	X	O	O	X	*6
Regional Resource Library — Penna. State University Library	O	O	O	O	X	O	O	O	
Regional Resource Center — Philadelphia	X	O	O	O	X	O	O	O	
Philadelphia Area Library Automation Conference (PALAC)	O	O	O	O	O	O	O	O	
Philadelphia College of Art/ Philadelphia Music Academy (PCA/PMA)	O	O	O	O	O	O	O	O	

	Private, Leased Telephone Line	IN-WATS	OUT-WATS	Private Teletype Network	TWX	Video Transmission (Type)	Computer-to-Computer	Telefacsimile	Other
Regional Resource Library – Pittsburgh	o	o	o	o	X	o	o	o	
Pittsburgh Regional Library Center, Inc. (PRLC)	o	o	o	o	X	o	o	o	*7
Regional Resource Center – State Library of Pennsylvania	o	o	X	o	X	o	o	o	
Theological Seminaries of Southeastern Penna. (TSSP)	o	o	o	o	o	o	o	o	
Tri-State College Library Cooperative Program (TCLC)	o	o	o	o	o	o	o	o	
Union Library Catalog of Pennsylvania, Inc.	o	o	o	o	X	o	o	o	
Union of Independent Colleges of Art/Learning Resources Exchange Program (LICA/LREP)	o	o	o	o	o	o	o	o	

CHART 4 Notes

Machine-Readable Data Bases

Other

1.   Magnetic tape shelf list of Bucknell's holdings.

2.   Data base of currently received periodicals is in preparation.

3.   COMPENDEX.

4.   There is also a Union List in Ohio. Original cataloging is available in addition to MARC tapes.

	Union List of Serials	Union Catalog	Chemical Abstracts	MARC	MEDLINE	Other
District Center — Aliquippa	o	o	o	o	o	
Area College Library Cooperative Program	o	o	o	o	o	*1
ACLCP — Delivery Service	o	o	o	o	o	
Bryn Mawr/Haverford College Library Cooperative Project	o	o	o	o	o	*2
Cabrini College/Eastern College Interlibrary Cooperative	o	o	o	o	o	
Central Penna. Consortium	o	o	o	o	o	
Committee on Library Cooperation of the Union Library Catalog of Penna.	o	o	o	o	o	
Eastcentral Penna. Interlibrary Cooperation Council (EPIC Council)	o	o	o	o	o	
Free Library of Philadelphia Cooperative Acquisitions Program for Purchase of Microfilm Copy of U.S. House and Senate Bills and Resolutions	o	o	o	o	o	
District Center — Indiana	o	o	o	o	o	
District Center — Johnstown	o	o	o	o	o	

	Union List of Serials	Union Catalog	Chemical Abstracts	MARC	MEDLINE	Other
Lehigh Valley Association of Independent Colleges, Inc.	O	O	X	X	O	*3
MEDLINE	O	O	O	O	X	
Middle Atlantic Research Libraries Information Network (MARLIN)	O	O	O	O	O	
Mideastern Regional Medical Library Service	O	O	O	O	X	
Northeastern Penna. Bibliographic Center (NEPBC)	X	O	O	O	O	
Ohio College Library Center (OCLC)	O	O	O	X	O	*4
Penna. State University Libraries — Commonwealth Campus Libraries System	O	O	O	O	O	
Regional Resource Library — Penna. State University Library	O	O	O	O	O	
Regional Resource Center — Philadelphia	O	O	O	O	O	
Philadelphia Area Library Automation Conference (PALAC)	O	O	O	O	O	
Philadelphia College of Art/ Philadelphia Music Academy (PCA/PMA)	O	O	O	O	O	

	Union List of Serials	Union Catalog	Chemical Abstracts	MARC	MEDLINE	Other
Regional Resource Library — Pittsburgh	o	o	o	o	o	
Pittsburgh Regional Library Center, Inc. (PRLC)	x	o	o	x	x	
Regional Resource Center — State Library of Pennsylvania	o	o	o	o	o	
Theological Seminaries of Southeastern Penna. (TSSP)	o	o	o	o	o	
Tri-State College Library Cooperative Program (TCLC)	o	o	o	o	o	
Union Library Catalog of Pennsylvania, Inc.	o	o	o	o	o	
Union of Independent Colleges of Art/Learning Resources Exchange Program (LICA/LREP)	o	o	o			

Chapter 16

A VIEW FROM THE PITTSBURGH REGIONAL LIBRARY CENTER

Virginia Sternberg

Pittsburgh Regional Library Center
Pittsburgh, Pennsylvania

INTRODUCTION

We have heard in the preceding chapters from distinguished colleagues about resource sharing in libraries. I want to point out in the beginning that many libraries in Pennsylvania have been sharing resources and are already members of library consortia. Some of these consortia are leaders in the field and have undertaken many types of resource sharing activities.

My role is to talk about our own regional library consortium. I would like to review briefly its history, tell you about its current activities and its plans for the future, and finally talk about the next action step.

HISTORY

The Pittsburgh Regional Library Center (PRLC) has a long history of promoting and participating in resource sharing, beginning in 1947. At that time the Director of the Carnegie Library of Pittsburgh, the Chancellor of the University of Pittsburgh, the President of Carnegie

367

Institute of Technology, and the Director of the Mellon Institute asked their librarians to study possible ways to cooperate. Basically, the purpose of the study was to find ways to avoid unnecessary duplication and to continue to provide effective library service. One and a half years later these institutions issued a news release announcing the development of a cooperative program which included exchange of catalog cards on books purchased in specialized fields, a division of purchasing in various subject fields, plans to develop a union catalog, reciprocal borrowing privileges for faculty, and a system of interlibrary loans with regular book deliveries between the institutions. This was the first step in resource sharing which eventually led to PRLC.

June 15, 1973 will be the 25th anniversary of that announcement. We all know "there's nothing new under the sun." The concepts advocated 25 years ago added up to resource sharing and were similar to those now being promoted.

The pioneers who provided the impetus for the coordination of library services, Ralph Munn of Carnegie Library and Drs. Fitzgerald, Doherty and Weidlein of Pitt, Carnegie Tech and the Mellon Institute, respectively, retired from the scene, and the Committee on Library Coordination met occasionally for several years.

Then, in 1962, new faces appeared on the scene and the concept of resource sharing was revitalized. Under the aegis of the Director of the Carnegie Library of Pittsburgh regular meetings of the Librarians of the academic institutions in this area with the public library director were reinstated. Once again these librarians attempted to find ways to cooperate. Although they met informally they called themselves the Pittsburgh Library Cooperation Group. (I understand that Sister Jane Scully, President of Carlow College, coined a term for the group while she was a member. In her own inimitable style she referred to it as the "Coop Group.") Other prominent members were Eleanor McCann, Duquesne University Librarian; Keith Doms, Carnegie Library Director; C. Walter Stone, University of Pittsburgh Library Director; and Kenneth Fagerhaugh, the head of the Carnegie-Mellon University libraries. This was the second step in PRLC's history of resource sharing activities.

This group worked diligently, identified their most pressing needs, and justified to the A. W. Mellon Foundation and to the Pennsylvania State Library the need for funds to establish a formal organization for library cooperation. It took five years, but finally, in 1967, the Pittsburgh Regional Library Center was incorporated. The Charter Members of PRLC were the farsighted administrations of Carnegie Library, Carnegie-Mellon University, Chatham College, Duquesne University, Mellon Institute, Carlow College, Point Park College, Robert Morris College, and the University of Pittsburgh. Their librarians, as well as one other member of their respective administrations, represent their institutions on the PRLC

Board of Trustees. This was the third step in the history of PRLC, the result of twenty years of effort and cooperative resource sharing.

CURRENT ACTIVITIES

Since 1967, PRLC has grown from nine members to twenty-one. There are again new faces on the scene and the advantages of consortia and resource sharing are apparent to all of them. The Center continues to attract new members. We expect to include some company and association libraries soon, along with additional college, university, and public libraries.

In the past six years the Center has developed several ongoing cooperative, resource-sharing projects. A list of the programs, services, and publications of PRLC is given in appendix A. Let me review them briefly. I would like to point out that all of these PRLC activities are in the "top six" as analyzed by Dr. Montgomery in Chapter 15. None of these are new ideas, but they are actually in operation.

1. Reciprocal borrowing privileges for students and faculty permit more efficient use of collections. The books are being used, not just being "collected. "

2. Computerized cataloging provided by the Ohio College Library Center network. This on-line computer system for obtaining catalog cards from Library of Congress computer tapes is helping to get books on the shelf faster, and eliminate the backlogs in cataloging. Thus, we have shared cataloging.

3. The "File of Expensive Items" and the "File of Periodicals on Order" are consulted when member libraries are considering purchases. Confirmation of the fact that another member library already has an expensive book or periodical may result in substantial savings.

4. The Truck Delivery Service provides for fast service to deliver books or journals on interlibrary loan.

5. The Union List of Periodicals of course can be used (a) to determine what other libraries have the journal; thus a decision can be reached whether to retain it; (b) to find out where to borrow or obtain photocopy of specific journal articles requested by patrons. PRLC received two grants from the Pennsylvania State Library for this Union List. PRLC acknowledges this financial assistance. At this time I think it is also appropriate to acknowledge the time and effort of librarians from 70 libraries whose holdings are listed in this Union List, thus sharing their resources.

6. The Directory of Member Libraries shows special collections or strengths in the libraries so they can be utilized by others in the area.

7. The list of Newspaper Holdings shows who has what newspaper and how many years it has been held. This aids another library in making a decision about whether to retain in full size or microfilm, or to retain at all.

8. The List of Major Microforms in Eight Pittsburgh Regional Library Center Libraries is handy to consult when a decision has to be reached concerning "buy" or "no buy" for an expensive set.

9. The checklist of holdings of certain works listed in Constance Winchell's Guide to Reference Books not only establishes locations of reference books in member libraries but points up areas of duplication. Once these are established, decisions can be made on where to stop the duplication.

Now that these cooperative projects are under way, others are being considered. PRLC now serves as the Council for Commonwealth of Pennsylvania Interlibrary Cooperation Region II, which consists of 11 counties in Southwestern Pennsylvania. The Council's purpose is to foster cooperation among all types of libraries in the region, including school libraries, small public libraries, special company libraries, as well as the large public and university libraries.

FUTURE PLANS

As to PRLC's plans for the future, many steps have been taken in developing resource sharing. These steps have taken time, are arduous, and require staff and money. And these are only the beginning of phasing into statewide and nationwide networks. PRLC wants to plan for the future, wants to project a model for 1973, and get it moving in 1973. Briefly, the model consists of the following steps:

1. Find out what resources are available throughout the state
2. Develop a step by step plan for the future and publish it so that everyone is on the same track
3. Integrate with state and national networks
4. Share resources for better utilization of money
5. Sell reference services to offset some costs
6. Computerize systems so others can dial up and get information. (we need a Pennsylvania computerized cataloging system similar to the Ohio system)

7. Follow up on holography — it may be the answer to library storage problems
8. Force the issue of publishers providing the book ready for the shelf when it arrives in a library
9. Find space for consolidating holdings
   That is our plan. But PRLC cannot do it alone.

Library budgets are being cut, government funding for libraries seems to be drying up, but the publications proliferate, the public clamors for more services, everything costs more (including space, equipment, people, and books).

This consortium has been fostered by tough thinking administrators and librarians who have recognized that they cannot continue to build their own little empires. They must share their resources, and they have taken the first steps. Now additional help is needed. Where is it going to come from?

Dr. Montgomery (Chapter 15) suggests a triumvirate of consortia. We know that the state is working on a Master Plan, which Mr. Doerschuk discusses in Chapter 17. PRLC members would like to have something concrete. Just one accomplishment. Just one ACTION step or objective that all can work toward.

WHAT IS THE NEXT ACTION STEP?

In considering this question, one realizes that there are so many steps to take that it is difficult to settle on just one. Therefore, I have categorized them into these five groups of Action Steps:

1. Action steps for librarians
2. Action steps for college and university administrators
3. Action steps for industry
4. Action steps for users
5. Action steps for the state

Following are brief resumés of page-long lists of action steps. Most of these have already been mentioned by other speakers yesterday and today.

Action Steps for Librarians

1. Resolve to continue to share resources.
2. Demand action from consortia, administrators, legislators, and the state to assist in finding avenues for library support.
3. Be creative and innovative in finding new methods for library operation.

Action Steps for Administrators

1. Back the librarians in resource sharing; for example, enlist the faculty's assistance in investigating their actual need for on-campus access to little-used materials.
2. Support the consortia financially. Some one or some group has to be at the control panel to keep things moving.

Action Steps for Industry

1. Be willing to pay for the library services obtained from the public and college libraries.
2. Support the libraries in the area financially to the same extent that support is given to other cultural activities.

Action Steps for Users

1. Think ecology: library materials have to be handled effectively just like energy.
2. Be willing to use new formats such as microfilm and cable television.
3. Remember: there is no free lunch; there is no free library. A library must be paid for by somebody. Make sure:
   a. Your legislators know that you want to support the library
   b. Your administrators know that you need the library

Action Steps for the State

1. Promote networks.

2. Support resource sharing consortia financially, by giving them seed money, and by encouraging them to continue.

3. Obtain money for library support from the legislature and the federal government.

PRLC members are hopeful that the pooling of imaginations will result in at least one practical recommendation for the next step in resource sharing.

APPENDIX:
PITTSBURGH REGIONAL LIBRARY CENTER*

Programs and Services

1. Interlibrary borrowing for faculty, graduate students, and undergraduate students of member institutions. Available to associate as well
as voting members, except that the University of Pittsburgh's Hillman
Library restricts its lending to faculty and graduate students of associate
member institutions.
2. Opportunity to participate in computerized cataloging provided by
the Ohio College Library Center network. Restricted to voting members.
3. Conferences, seminars and "open houses," for membership staffs.
4. File of Expensive Items in PRLC Libraries, maintained at PRLC
Office. Includes information on books and nonbook material, except
periodicals and newspapers, which cost over $100.
5. File of Periodicals on Order, maintained at PRLC Office. May be
consulted when considering acquisition of expensive periodical, or for
location purposes.
6. Truck delivery service for charter member libraries in Pittsburgh.

PRLC also serves as the Council for Commonwealth of Pennsylvania
Interlibrary Cooperation Region II, which consists of eleven counties in
Southwestern Pennsylvania. The Council activities are directed by a
special committee of PRLC, composed of representatives of public,
academic, school, and special libraries; trustees, and library patrons.
Their purpose is to foster cooperation among all types of libraries in the
region.

Publications

1. Pittsburgh Regional Union List of Periodicals. First edition of
February 1970 and its three supplements contain periodical holdings
information for about 19,700 titles in more than fifty libraries in the
Pittsburgh District. A second revised and expanded edition, in two volumes,
is scheduled for publication in the summer of 1973.
2. Directory of PRLC Member Libraries. Looseleaf compilation

---

*Beatty Hall, Chatham College, Pittsburgh, Pennsylvania, 15232

which indicates locations, personnel, lending regulations, and special collections or other unique strengths of each member library.

3. Newspaper holdings in PRLC Member Libraries. Computer produced list now in process. Publication expected in summer of 1973.

4. Major microform holdings of eight PRLC Member Libraries. December 1972 revision of earlier list, which will be considered for expansion to include holdings of all member libraries.

5. Checklist of Winchell Holdings of eight PRLC Member Libraries. Indicates holdings of reference works listed in seven sections of Constance Winchell's Guide to Reference Books, and Supplements 1 and 2. Distributed in the spring of 1973.

6. PRLC Newsletter. Issued bimonthly.

Chapter 17

A VIEW FROM THE STATE LIBRARY

Ernest E. Doerschuk, Jr.

State Librarian
State Library of Pennsylvania

We have heard above excellent position papers about the varied activities
in resource sharing now in progress, and of some possibilities for the
future. What is needed now, I think, is a pulling together of the various
strands into a whole piece of cloth.

These strands include at least the following:

1. Interlibrary cooperation councils are already organized on a
regional basis. One council is preparing a directory of library resources
in its area. Another is conducting a user survey of the different types of
libraries in the council's area.

2. An ad hoc committee has been appointed by the state librarian to
work up a plan for, or at least determine the feasibility of, a series of
interconnecting delivery systems to cover the state. Already one such
system is moving materials quickly and efficiently among libraries from
Philadelphia to Altoona.

3. Eight libraries clustered around Philadelphia, the State Library
among them, are hooking up with the Ohio College Library Center in
Columbus through a consortium sponsored by the Union Library Catalogue
of Pennsylvania, and a group of libraries in Western Pennsylvania is doing
the same thing under the sponsorship of the Pittsburgh Regional Library

Center. Each group has its own planning committees at work. The Union
Library Catalogue of Pennsylvania has of course been a very important
tool for resource sharing ever since the New Deal days.

4. As you may be aware, Senator Bell has introduced Senate Bill 294
which would provide $360,000 to the Department of Property and Supplies
to expand the Pennsylvania State University Library's proposed computerized catalog and inventory function to accomodate all state-owned libraries.
This bill was referred to the Education Committee on Valentine's Day, and
I do not know of any plan to move it, especially since Penn State's plans
are in abeyance for the time being. I mention the bill to illustrate the
variety of planning under way.

5. Charles Nelson has nearly completed a study of the Northeast
Pennsylvania Regional interlibrary cooperative that will recommend a
model for other such cooperatives in Pennsylvania.

6. Several academic library consortia are actively planning and
carrying out cooperative programs and services: ACLCP, TCLC, and
Lehigh Valley are examples.

7. A "Master Plan Committee" is working toward an overall plan for
the development and coordination of all types of libraries in the Commonwealth. A progress report of the committee's work has just been mailed
to Pennsylvania libraries and will appear in the next issue of the Pennsylvania Library Association Bulletin; I urge all to read it carefully and to
send comments and criticisms to Richard Thomson, the Committee
chairman, in care of the State Library.

8. The Governor's Advisory Council on Library Development is
charged by statute with recommending general policy for the Commonwealth's
library program. The Council itself feels that its role should be stronger.

9. The Pennsylvania Library Association has an active library
development committee.

10. State College librarians meet together on a regular basis, along
with the Director of the library of Indiana University of Pennsylvania to
discuss mutual problems and plans.

11. Drexel University recently conducted a three-day workshop on
interlibrary loan networks.

12. We have conducted a statewide conference on library resource
sharing.

All this is to the good, since the creative talents of diverse librarians
and planners are being brought into play. It is participatory planning, not
imposed from above.

There is some risk, however, that the diverse planning elements might
not be brought together into a coherent and effective statewide program.

What is needed is leadership. Not dictatorship, but leadership.

The State Library should provide such leadership and it does provide
it to the limit of our ability.

The State Library has a statewide library coordinating role based on statute. While the statute relates this role to the system of local, district, and regional resource center libraries — almost all of them public libraries — we have, through the application of federal funds under the Library Services and Construction Act, assumed responsibility for assisting hospital and prison libraries, academic libraries and special libraries, and for encouraging the development of cooperative programs among different types of libraries. Many of the activities alluded to in preceding Chapters have had their origin in the federally (though meagerly) funded Title III program ably directed by Dr. John McCrossan of our Library Development Bureau. *

But now, just as we are beginning to see the emergence of various kinds of networks, federal funding of interlibrary cooperation is to be cut off. The sparse staff we have assembled at the State Library may have to be decimated. At the same time, state funding of library programs is at a standstill, and in times of inflation, that is the same as going backward. You will see the magnitude of the difficulty we face in operating the State Library next year when I tell you that $800,000 in federal money that was anticipated for 1973-1974 to help operate the library will not be there if the President's budget prevails; this represents over 40% of our present State Library operating budget.

An essential step toward more effective sharing of resources is therefore in my judgement the strengthening of the State Library's leadership capability. This should include:

1. Clear statutory authority for the state library to coordinate inter-type of library activity
2. Budgetary provision for state library staff to carry out the planning and coordinating role effectively
3. Provision of state funds to facilitate such cooperative activities as delivery systems, shared catalog and inventory, centralized purchase and processing of materials, central warehousing of little used materials, union catalogs and union lists of serials, communications networks, and the like.

It seems to me that college administrators, librarians of all kinds, public library trustees, and the library user whose name is legion ought to be demanding this of state government and of the State Library. As Secretary Pittenger has indicated, unlimited funding of academic and public libraries is not in sight. An alternative is more finely targeted funding for library resource sharing.

Here I would like to insert a few interesting statistics:

1. The annual dollar investment in Pennsylvania's academic libraries is in the neighborhood of $41.5 million, while the investment in public libraries is about $30.5 million annually

---

*Dr. McCrossan is now State Librarian of Vermont-Au.

2. Academic libraries are spending about $14 million for materials
a year as against $5 million by the public libraries

3. Ranked with other states in public library expenditure and performance, Pennsylvania ranks eighth in amount of state aid per capita that goes
to public libraries, twenty-fourth in per capita total income; thirty-sixth
in volumes per capita held by public libraries, and fortieth in number of
books per capita borrowed from public libraries. This could be the subject
of another chapter in this book! For the state of Benjamin Franklin and the
Benjamin Franklin Open University, this is not good enough.

To return to my theme: a second essential step is to coordinate the
planning now being done. This has to take place whether or not the state
library has a coordinating staff or takes on the assignment. It has to take
place, or Pennsylvania's libraries will fall still deeper into the doldrums.
I suggest that the State Library is a logical and obvious agent for such
coordination; but no matter what agency assumes the role — The University
of Pittsburgh and the PRLC have clearly assumed such a role with the
planning of the recent conference — there must be another ingredient.

The third ingredient is an advisory and consultative body that is
representative of the varied library interests and activities, that is of a
reasonably permanent nature, that has a clearly defined and widely recognized mission, that can meet regularly and have access to staff supportive
services, and that can afford the time and expense involved in planning.
Again this clearly calls for state money and staff. Lacking that, it calls
for a greater degree of voluntary action than has heretofore been prevalent.
The present Advisory Council on Library Development partially fulfills the
role described. The Master Plan Committee in its preliminary report
recommends that the Advisory Council be replaced with a commission or
board with duties toward libraries analogous to those of the State Board of
Education toward schools.

A fourth step, one that is taking place continuously and at various
levels, is the consideration of actual modes of organizing for cooperation
and the act of cooperation itself. This step will become a stride when a
responsible, widely representative and high level council, board, task
force, commission or similar body has the facts, is recognized by libraries
and their sponsoring agencies, and gives sanction to a particular set of
plans and alternatives, preferably accompanied by some secure, recurring
funds to support them.

I think the following persons in state government should be apprised of
the need and should be urged to take action:

1. The Governor
2. The Secretary of Education
3. The Commissioner of Higher Education

4. The Commissioner of Basic Education
5. The State **Board** of Education
6. The Advisory Council on Library Development
7. The State Librarian
8. The Legislature

Thus, a final step is to keep clamoring   Libraries <u>must</u> be heard.

INDEX*

Academic library consortia,
  services, 341
Accreditation and resource sharing,
  51-53
Acquisitions,
  basic operations, 59
  definition, 106
  and resource sharing, 62-75, 99-
    108
Advanced Computer Systems Ticon,
  IS & R software, 206
Advanced Management Systems
  Select-or, IS & R software, 212,
  234
Aliquippa District Center, 310
Allentown Public Library, 29
American Book Center for Water-
  devastated Libraries, 73
American Library Association, 5, 15
American National Standards
  Institute (ANSI) Committee Z39
  on library work, documentation
  and related publishing practices,
  177
Ampex Terabit Memory, 149
Anglo-American Cataloging Rules, 82
Aperture cards, 151
Approval plans, 71
Aquila BST EXTRACTO, IS & R
  software, 222
Area College Library Cooperative of
  Central Pennsylvania (ACLP),
  28, 250, 293, 311

delivery service, 312
Aronofsky, W. M., 269(1), 270[2],
  273[2], 274[2], 276
ARPANET, 271
Associations of College and
  Research Libraries, 5
Associative memories, 149
Atomic Energy Commission, 3, 12
Auerbach, Isaac L., 139, 156[20],
  160, 181, 253, 257
Avram, Henriette, D., 78[17],
  83[17], 97, 116, 255

Babcock, Judith, 59[4], 96
BACKFILE, 263
Baker, L.R., 116
Baker, W.O., 4[4], 31
Baker Panel, 4
Balmforth, C.K., 116
Barnes, J.M., 254, 255
Barr, W.J., 256
Barriers to resource sharing, 13
Baumol, William, 37[4], 43
Becker, H.B., 253
Becker, Joseph, 26[32], 33, 59[1],
  96, 172[35], 182, 254
Berul, L.H., 157[23], 181, 253
Bibliographic citations and delivery
  of services, 130
Bibliographic data on magnetic tapes,
  distribution, 172
  roster of organizations, 174

---

*Within the body of the index, numerals in square brackets indicate that the
author cited is referred to by reference number on the page involved. An
underlined page number indicates that a full citation is to be found at that
location.